NEW GOVERNMENTS
IN EUROPE

NEW GOVERNMENTS IN EUROPE

The Trend Toward Dictatorship

By

Vera Micheles Dean
Bailey W. Diffie
Malbone W. Graham
Mildred S. Wertheimer

With an Introduction by

Raymond Leslie Buell

*A Publication of
the Foreign Policy Association
Incorporated*

THOMAS NELSON AND SONS

NEW YORK   1935

PRINTED IN THE UNITED STATES OF AMERICA

PREFACE

UNTIL recently, it has been customary for students of government to devote the greater part of their attention to the study of parliamentary institutions. It was assumed that with the spread of popular education the principles and methods of democracy would eventually prevail among all enlightened peoples.

The events of the post-war period have seriously shaken these assumptions. Today three leading countries in Europe are under the rule of authoritarian dictatorships, which have come into existence because of the failure of previous systems of government to settle pressing domestic and international problems. The world today is witnessing what Spengler calls the return of the Cæsars.

Although authoritarian rule has dominated the world during the greater part of its history, present-day dictatorships differ widely from the arbitrary régimes which prevailed in many countries before the World War. In the first place, the three leading dictatorships of the present day rest on a system of ideas which gives a sense of direction to the state and restrains dictators from indulging in purely whimsical rule. In the second place, dictatorship in Russia, Italy, and Germany relies upon public opinion to a much greater degree than is supposed. Although political officials in each of these countries

iii

ruthlessly suppress opposition to the existing system, they recognize that their position depends on their success in enlisting the active support, if not the enthusiasm, of a large element in the public. Soviet leaders are constantly resorting to propaganda devices to make the principles of Communism popular among the people. In Italy Mussolini frequently makes dramatic appeals from the balcony of Palazzo Venezia and organizes vast parades and other spectacles. In Germany Hitler did not seize power by means of a military *coup d'état,* but by the pressure of a vast propaganda system which he had patiently organized and directed for years. From the constitutional point of view, present-day dictatorships may be largely irresponsible, but all of them realize the importance of winning the support of public opinion. It is not too much to say that the majority of the people in Russia, Italy, and Germany support their present leaders in the belief, which may or may not be well founded, that these men are moved by more disinterested devotion to the national good than is demonstrated by political leaders in supposedly democratic countries.

When Russia adopted Communism in November 1917, and when Italy turned to Fascism after the famous march on Rome in 1922, defenders of democracy remained undisturbed. They explained that party government had never taken root either in Italy or in Russia, and that these countries had merely turned from one form of dictatorship to another. Their optimism was severely shaken, however, when the German Republic was overthrown by Hitler in 1933. The Weimar Constitution, drawn up in 1919, has been hailed by publicists as the most democratic in the world—a model which all other states should adopt. Yet in 1933 the Weimar system succumbed to a Nazi dictatorship.

Among the Great Powers the three remaining exponents of democracy are France, England and the United States. While these countries have experienced democratic rule during a much longer period than Germany, it is by no means certain that they will not adopt some form of dictatorship. In all three countries growing discontent has been expressed with the pettiness of parliaments, the irresoluteness of administrations fearful of overthrow at the next elections, and the dominance of local and group interests at the expense of the general good. If democracy cannot develop a type of leader and political organization which will consider the interests of the forgotten man—if democracy cannot cope with the problems created by the defects of capitalism—then peoples in despair will turn to more authoritarian rule.

In France growing discontent with the Republic —provoked by constant changes in ministries, a financial policy that increased the cost of living in a period of dwindling employment and trade—came to a head after the Stavisky affair of January 1934. Alexandre Stavisky, a notorious swindler and gambler, managed to gain control of the municipal pawnshop in Bayonne, with the complicity of government officials. Through issuing bonds upon the supposed security of pawnshop pledges, he defrauded insurance companies and private individuals to the amount of two hundred million francs. Not only were the Mayor of Bayonne, a deputy, and several journalists implicated in this swindle, but a member of the Cabinet, who had written letters calling the attention of insurance companies to the possibility of investing in these bonds, was compelled to resign. The Stavisky scandal, which in many respects is similar to a dozen scandals recently revealed in the United States, was the match that touched off the growing indignation of many Frenchmen with the parliamentary régime. For two days in February mobs in Paris actually fought the police, the troops, and the mobile guards. Quiet was restored only after the formation of a non-partisan cabinet headed by Gaston Doumergue, the seventy-one-year-old ex-president. The Paris riots did not represent the work of a patiently organized and well-disciplined movement against the Republic. They were merely the spontaneous outbursts of various sections of opinion against the six hundred "dictators" who occupy the Palais Bourbon. It is also significant that, although the Chautemps and Daladier cabinets which preceded the Doumergue ministry managed to secure votes of confidence from parliament, they both resigned office because of the fury of the mob. If public opinion cannot properly vent itself through constitutional methods, it will make itself heard through extra-legal channels.

The Doumergue government, composed largely of old men, constitutes a truce between the Right and the Left. Unless this government carries out radical reforms and adopts a constructive foreign policy, Fascist sentiment in France, already pronounced among several organizations of young men, may continue to grow.

In Great Britain many voices also declare that the traditional forms of parliamentary government cannot cope with the problems created by technology. In August 1931 the party system was virtually abandoned when Prime Minister MacDonald forced the resignation of the Labor Cabinet and established a National government composed of four Conservatives, three former Laborites, and two Liberals. This action only served to increase underlying dissatisfaction with the existing methods. The Fascist League organized by Sir Oswald Mosley won the support of the Rothermere papers in the winter of 1933–34. Certain leading personalities, such as Sir Stafford Cripps, also attempted to commit the Labor party in favor of government by means of emergency powers—a movement which was defeated when the party executive on January 25, 1934 adopted a strong resolution adhering to the principles of parliamentary government.

Discontent with existing forms of governmental procedure also arose in the United States at the end of the Hoover Administration. Here a widespread revulsion set in against the policy of using government machinery to increase the profits of private business, while doing little to combat unemployment. Universal disgust was also felt at the revelation of corruption in municipal government. Fortunately a presidential election in November 1932 gave the American public a constitutional outlet for their discontent. The result was an overwhelming victory for the opposition candidate, Franklin D. Roosevelt.

Although ostensibly a party Democrat, President Roosevelt developed an administration which constitutes a radical departure from any previous form of government the American people has experienced. He did not abolish the Constitution, nor did he assume any illegal powers; he did, however, induce Congress to vest in him far-reaching control over the economic life of the country. This control was delegated not to the ordinary Cabinet departments but to a series of new agencies, chief of which were the National Recovery Administration, the Reconstruction Finance Corporation, and the Agricultural Adjustment Administration. Under this system the powers of Congress, of the Cabinet, and of the States were vastly reduced.

That the American government had not become a dictatorship similar to those existing in Soviet Russia, Fascist Italy, or Hitlerized Germany was indicated by the fact that Congress remained the ultimate source of authority; that fair elections were held; that universal suffrage continued in effect; that it was still possible to appeal to the courts against the acts of public officials; and that freedom of the press, speech and radio were not curtailed. The Roosevelt Administration, moreover, did not ferret out opposition by a system of espionage and secret police. Nor did it attempt to suppress the Labor Unions.

The underlying purpose of this new system of administration was to bring about economic recovery and at the same time reform our economic and social system. While the methods employed by President Roosevelt involve many unique departures, they respect the underlying principles of democracy. If the Roosevelt system succeeds in meeting the economic and social crisis, democracy will be vindicated in the United States. Should the Roosevelt Administration fail, it is not improbable that Fascism and Communism will continue their march across the world.

In view of recent developments, the Foreign Policy Association believes that the publication of this book describing the principles and methods of the new governments of Europe is of timely importance. Since its establishment in 1925, the Research Department of the Foreign Policy Association has closely followed political developments in every part of the world. The results of its studies, which have been based not only on a careful examination of documents, both official and unofficial, but also on widespread travel and first-hand contacts, have been presented in fortnightly publications, now called *Foreign Policy Reports*. The present volume is based largely on a collection of the reports devoted to the new governments of Europe, but revised so as to bring them up to date.

The introductory chapter on the theories of Democracy, Fascism and Communism, and the sections on Fascist Italy and Communist Russia have been written by Dr. Vera Micheles Dean, the section on Germany by Dr. Mildred S. Wertheimer, both members of the Foreign Policy Association staff. The section on Spain, which portrays the effort of a country to realize Socialism by parliamentary means, has been written by Bailey W. Diffie, instructor at the College of the City of New York. The final chapters on the new Baltic republics, where Fascist sentiment seems to be growing, are the work of Malbone W. Graham, professor of political science at the University in California at Los Angeles.

RAYMOND LESLIE BUELL
President, Foreign Policy Association

CONTENTS

xi

CONTENTS

THE
ATTACK ON DEMOCRACY

WE are living in a period when the most coura-
geous face moments of profound discouragement,
when the hopes for social and international appease-
ment salvaged from the wreckage of the World War
seem sadly illusory. It is natural that in such a period we should seize on every creed which contains
a promise, no matter how vague, of new relations
between men and states. The more chaotic the world
around him, the more distraught his mind and soul,
the more urgent is man's desire to believe in something outside himself, to surrender to the tide of
a mass movement, little as he knows where this
movement may lead him. It is only too easy, in
an age of recurring crises, to be stampeded into acceptance of authority, no matter what its source, and
to demand that the Western heritage of political and
economic traditions be jettisoned in favor of a new
system, be it Fascism or Communism. Yet the very
prevalence of mass hysteria makes it supremely important to assay, with as much detachment as one
can summon, both that which it is proposed to surrender and that which it is hoped to achieve.

Loss of faith in traditional institutions and traditional patterns of life—intellectual skepticism and
emotional instability—have marked not only political and economic speculation, but art and litera-

15

ture since the World War. To the generation nurtured on Victorian faith in human progress and the ultimate goodness of mankind the war was a catastrophe, shattering a world of unrealized ideals. The war severed a historical nerve connection which no amount of political surgery has succeeded in restoring. Confronted by the unprecedented strain of a world conflict, countries which had appeared dedicated to democracy resorted to the methods of dictatorship, and drastically curtailed, or altogether suspended, individual liberty for the sake of the common cause. The liberal state, once committed to the policy of *laissez faire,* assumed control of economic activities to a degree unprecedented in modern history. The unlimited powers which individuals had been willing to grant the state for the duration of the emergency could not be laid aside overnight. War had exalted the state and diminished the individual. Peace, with its manifold problems and its heritage of economic disorganization culminating in world-wide depression, only emphasized the helplessness of the individual and his need for an authoritarian state. In this sense, 1914 marked the end of an era which had made a cult of democracy, individual liberty and economic *laissez faire.*

From the Renaissance and the Reformation the Western world has inherited a conception of the dignity and worth of the individual which even now it finds it difficult to discard. The French Revolution, defying the tyranny of monarchs and the glaring inequalities of a society built on privilege of birth, asserted the right of all individuals within the state to political liberty and equality. The driving force of this revolution came from the middle class, which desired to exercise political powers commensurate with its economic achievements. This class regarded the state as a necessary evil, whose functions should be strictly limited by a written constitution, and never allowed to interfere with individual liberty. It demanded that the business of government be transacted not by a few irresponsible ministers closeted with the king or the king's mistress, but in the full light of day, through elected assemblies representing the will of the people. To assure its control of political power, it demanded the extension of suffrage, liberty of association and the press, free access to the courts and educational facilities. To assure its control of economic power, it demanded that the state adopt a policy of *laissez faire,* abstain from interfering with trade and industry, and give full scope to individual initiative in the acquisition of property. The political theories of the French Revolution closely paralleled the economic practices sponsored by the Industrial Revolution. Historically the birth of democracy coincided with that of capitalism. The nineteenth century may thus be described as a period of capitalist democracy.

That century opened on a world which seemed to hold unlimited possibilities of progress. There were still frontiers to conquer, hinterlands to explore, markets and raw materials to develop. Man felt that his vigor had not yet been tested, and was ready to challenge nature in laboratory, field and factory. The increase in production made possible by the machine seemed to hold out a promise of indefinite improvement in the standard of living. Armed with the twin weapons of industry and science, man thought he could fearlessly confront the future, rising from one peak of progress to the next. The full-blooded optimism of that period was both ruthless and sentimental.

This optimism, this faith in material progress, had a far-reaching influence on political and economic institutions. The middle class, entrenched in parliament, could afford to be relatively generous. It resisted the introduction of universal suffrage and improvement in the living conditions of the rising industrial proletariat, but seldom resorted to violence. Meanwhile the workers were confident that, with strong trade-union organization, with able and honest leadership, they too would soon reach the level of economic prosperity achieved by the middle class. Not that this period was free of strikes and lockouts, of conflicts between capital and labor. These clashes, however, were not yet fought out as ultimate issues, to be solved only by resort to violence and thoroughgoing revolution. Common agreement still existed regarding the basic conceptions of the political and economic system, and the conflicting groups were not only able, but willing, to air their differences in parliament and the press.

These two factors—common agreement regarding basic concepts and willingness to discuss existing problems—facilitated the successful operation of democracy in the nineteenth century. Democracy prospers in societies with a fairly simple political and economic organization, in which the issues at stake are not complex, are easily understood by the average man, and lend themselves to clear-cut and dramatic discussion in representative assemblies. Democracy presupposes readiness on the part of the majority, in parliament or outside, to give the minority a hearing, and willingness on the part of the minority to accept, even if it attacks, the policies of the majority as long as the latter holds power. Democracy has functioned most successfully in countries like Great Britain and France, where a homogeneous population, no matter how divided by individual and party differences, is closely bound by similar traditions, and usually refuses to sacrifice the welfare of the nation as a whole to party or local interests. It has also functioned most successfully in periods when economic conditions have been sufficiently sound and elastic to prevent sharp class differentiation and conflicts between various classes over control of property. Where the disposition to rational discussion of fundamental problems is lacking, where differences between political or economic groups appear irreconcilable, where these groups prefer to fight out the ultimate issues involved rather than effect a compromise, where a continuing state of crisis, of emergency, exists—democracy no longer functions with success, and must sooner or later yield to some other form of government.

It is to the presence of these factors that the current reaction against democracy may be traced. The increasing complexity of modern life has created a multiplicity of technical problems which cannot be properly understood by the electorate or efficiently solved by discussion in popular assemblies. The intricacies of currency stabilization, the manifold difficulties raised by adjustment of wages and prices, are beyond the scope of both the voters and their representatives, who prefer to leave them in the hands of a strong executive. The prolonged economic crisis has only increased the individual's desire to throw the burden of his personal problems on the shoulders of the state. Finding himself unable to cope with the economic anxieties which assail him on all sides, the individual is ready to surrender a large portion of his liberty in return for economic security, which he believes it the task of the state to assure. The state is alternately implored and bullied by various groups of the population—industrialists, farmers, taxpayers, war veterans, unemployed—to assume ever growing powers and to enter spheres of activity from which it had previously been barred in the name of individual liberty and private initiative.

At the same time the economic crisis tends to sharpen political conflicts, and reduces the willingness of various classes to settle these conflicts by peaceful means. Emergencies demand rapid and decisive action, for which democratic institutions are essentially unsuited. Parliamentary debates, absorbing and important in normal times, become dangerous obstacles to effective action in moments of crisis. The population begins to demand that authority be concentrated in the hands of a few leaders. These leaders, in turn, insist that they can act decisively only if not hampered by the necessity of constantly consulting the electorate or its representatives.

Democracy is attacked not only on the ground that its political institutions are ill devised to cope with modern problems, but because it is identified with capitalism, which has failed to assure the perpetuation of material prosperity. It is contended that political equality, as guaranteed by written constitutions, has become illusory—that it is drastically curtailed, if not altogether nullified, by glaring economic inequalities which capitalism has failed to correct. Nor do critics of democracy believe that the economic inequalities which have developed under capitalism can be corrected by democratic methods.

The attack on capitalist democracy has been particularly violent in countries like Germany and Italy, which lack democratic traditions. In both countries the reaction against democracy, while differing in some of its manifestations, has taken the form of Fascism. This tendency toward Fascism springs, in the first place, from disillusionment with the outcome of the World War and the events of the post-war period. Italy, it is true, was among the victors, and satisfied its principal territorial ambitions in Europe. It failed, however, to obtain colonies in Africa, which it regards essential as an outlet for its rapidly growing population. If Italy was embittered by what it described as a Pyrrhic victory, Germany was overwhelmed with a sense of humiliation and despair. A nation which had been inordinately proud of its military prowess and technical achievements had been forced to yield to the superior numbers of the Allies and accept a Draconian peace. Millions of Germans believed that defeat had been brought about by the treachery of liberals, socialists and pacifists, who had given the army a "stab in the back," and had blindly subscribed to President Wilson's Fourteen Points, few of which had found place in the peace treaties. Nor did the events of the post-war period serve to assuage Germany's moral wounds. Severe inflation ruined a large section of the middle class and fanned the discontent of industrial workers. The failure of the League of Nations to correct the inequities of the Versailles treaty and the reluctance of the Allies to meet Germany's demands with regard to reparation and arms equality, perpetuated the Germans' sense of injury and humiliation. The Weimar republic had little opportunity to strike roots in German soil.

Both in Germany and Italy democratic institutions were charged with incompetence, indecisiveness, inability to meet the problems of the post-war period. The necessity for a strong government, for centralized and unlimited authority, was stressed on every hand. At the same time the trend toward Socialism and Communism, encouraged by the success of the Bolshevik revolution in Russia in 1917, alarmed the industrialists and the middle class, who feared destruction of private property and resulting economic chaos. The appearance of Fascism in Germany and Italy constituted, on the one hand, a revolution against democracy and liberalism and, on the other, a reaction against Communism and all forms of left extremism.

That discontent with existing institutions should have taken the form of Fascism, rather than Communism, was due primarily to the presence in both Germany and Italy of a strong middle class, which had been lacking in Russia, and whose political importance has been underestimated by Marxist philosophy. The Marxist assumption that, with the progress of industrialization, society inevitably divides into two irreconcilable groups—a small handful of capitalists, and masses of industrial proletariat—is not supported by the experience of Western states. Nor does the middle class, as argued by Marxists, tend to join Communist ranks when it becomes impoverished and proletarianized. The middle class is a broad term, which covers several social and economic groups—professional men, technical experts, small merchants and shopkeepers, clerks and skilled workers. The average member of the middle class may have risen from humble beginnings, from the ranks of peasants or industrial workers. In the course of his career, however, he cultivates a standard of living patterned on that of the wealthy, acquires some property, perhaps a house of his own, and develops ambitions for the future of his children. The middle class usually lacks the class consciousness of industrial workers, as well as their organization. It can seldom act coherently or harmoniously on political and economic issues. It is knit together, however, by a sense of professional dignity, by attachment to personal property and domestic privacy. To this class Communism, with its demand for state control of property, with its emphasis on the dictatorship of the proletariat, which presupposes destruction of the middle class, is distinctly repugnant as a solution of its problems. Even when the white collar worker is reduced to the lowest level of subsistence, when he is forced to tramp the streets in search of employment, when he has lost the white collar, symbol of his class, he is not yet ready to throw in his fate with Communism. *Little Man, what now?* asks the German writer Hans Fallada in his poignant novel depicting the plight of a humble member of the middle class, and his answer is that the little man, even on the verge of starvation, will turn Nazi rather than Communist. This attitude of the middle class has been cleverly utilized by Nazi propaganda in Germany to assure the triumph of Fascism against both liberalism and Communism.

The middle class seeks in Fascism not only protection against revolution from the left, not only economic security, but a new faith in life, a new assurance and inspiration which would contrast, on the one hand, with the agnosticism of the liberal state and, on the other, with the materialism of the Communist philosophy. After years of disillusionment with political and economic institutions, the traditional conceptions of home, love and religion, of frantic search for new values, mankind inevitably experiences a period of reaction, and passionately, even hysterically, seeks new gods to worship. Fascism attempts to fill this need by its emphasis on the conception of the state as a mystic entity, representing the continuance of a nation's spirit through the ages; by its demand that the individual surrender his will to supreme and unquestioned authority; by its support of religion, its demand for purification of morals, its championship of the home and family, and the glamour it confers on the military virtues of men and the housekeeping skill of women.

The mystic aspects of Fascism make an especially powerful appeal to the young generation, adrift in a crumbling world without star or compass. It is consequently not surprising to find a predominance of youth in Fascist ranks. The generation born just before or during the war knows little of democratic institutions or the spirit of liberalism. Its conscious years have been spent in an atmosphere of hopelessness and instability. This situation has been particularly acute in Germany, which has suffered severely from intellectual unemployment. Students leaving the universities had no outlook except further study, since all professions were overcrowded and vacancies were at a premium. Lack of opportunity for work fostered a dangerous spirit of resentment against existing governments, which had failed to assure the possibility of employment, and created a whole group of *déracinés*, restless and ready for any adventure. Enforced idleness stirred the desire for direct action, for channels which could use up the excess energy of youth. Fascism offers such a channel. It accepts youth with all the defects of its virtues—its intransigeance and violence, its arrogance and enthusiasm, its disregard of tradition and precedent, and its readiness to undergo supreme sacrifices for a cause which has fired its imagination. Fascism stresses the advantages of physical vigor, athletic prowess, youthful leadership, and gives the young generation an opportunity to exercise its lungs and muscles, if not its intellect, on the parade ground and in training camps. Fascism takes complete charge of the education of the young, insulates them against all contacts with the outside world, and inoculates them with its doctrines. A generation trained under such conditions would furnish excellent cannon-fodder should the Fascist state embark on a policy of territorial expansion. In fact, it is difficult to see how youth could long be restrained from demanding to be transferred from the parade-ground to the battlefield. The dangers of this situation are particularly acute because this young generation knows nothing of the horrors of modern warfare, has been taught to scorn the searing portrayals of Remarque and Barbusse, and considers the dangers of war far preferable to the stagnant atmosphere of peace without employment.

Another cause which has contributed to the rise of Fascism is the despair of the average individual, his desire to find warmth and security in contact with masses of his fellow beings. Individualism has flourished in periods relatively free of economic pressure, where opportunity still waited around the corner, and the individual was able to shape his own destiny. When the possibilities for individual development disappear, when economic difficulties apply a brake to individual initiative, the average man is less ready to challenge the world, and more willing to submit to authority as long as that authority undertakes to clothe and feed him. This tendency of the individual to become merged in a group, a collectivity, which offers him a modicum of protection against economic insecurity is not without danger. The individual who is normally kind, generous and tolerant may, when absorbed in a group, be easily swayed by mob emotion, and may condone, or even participate in, acts of violence which his better judgment would ordinarily condemn. No matter what his integrity and force of character, he may yield to mass pressure to preserve his job, his life, the security of his family, and in so doing may commit acts which his conscience repudiates. A mass movement seeks and finds its lowest level. The actions of a crowd may achieve supreme heroism. More often they result in shocking injustice or brutality.

The masses, however, do not act long without guidance—they crave leadership. Their selection is based on no process of rationalization. Most frequently it is determined by emotional factors. Not that the masses necessarily follow a worthless or inept figure—neither Hitler nor Mussolini could be described in these terms—but they demand from their leaders personal magnetism, glowing oratory, rather than demonstrated ability. This emotionalism of the masses, their desire to identify themselves with a man whom they can regard as a superior being, a symbol of their confused desires, has been capitalized by Mussolini and Hitler with striking success.

The political system of Fascism faithfully mirrors the various trends which go to make up the Fascist state of mind. Fascist philosophy conceives the state as a "totalitarian" entity, which absorbs the individual as well as all groups—the church, the school, the trade union—and in which alone the individual can fulfill his destiny. This concept is expressed in Mussolini's famous phrase: "Everything within the state; nothing outside the state." Within the framework of the Fascist state all human activities and interests must be coördinated under government control. Individual liberty is entirely subordinated to the interests of the state, which are paramount. If it threatens to conflict with the aims of the state, it must be curtailed or destroyed.

The Nazi program in Germany declares that "common welfare comes before individual welfare." By its exaltation of the authoritarian state, Fascist philosophy challenges both liberal agnosticism and Marxist materialism. To the individual weary of skepticism and emphasis on material ends, Fascism offers a philosophy which prescribes discipline and acquiescence in authority, and at the same time glorifies the romantic elements of national tradition. Thus Fascist Italy exalts the glamourous memories of imperial Rome, while Nazi Germany glorifies the simple virtues of the German race.

Fascism rejects the conception of popular sovereignty and the traditional institutions of democracy. Parliaments are regarded not only as obsolete and useless, but as a grave obstacle to efficient administration. According to the Fascists democracy, which may have had a *raison d'être* in the nineteenth century, is today an anachronism. Sovereignty resides not in the people, but in society organized as a state. The great mass of citizens, argues Fascism, is too ignorant or too concerned with narrow private and local interests to undertake the complicated task of government. This task must devolve on a chosen few, a governing élite, selected not by popular suffrage, which is a blundering method, but from the ranks of the Fascist party, on the basis of merit.

This governing class, in turn, must be led and animated by a man who can give expression to its ideals—*Il Duce* in Italy, *Der Führer* in Germany. This leader, once he has seized power, becomes the object of a sentiment closely akin to divinization. Mussolini has frequently expressed the conviction that he is a man of destiny, fated to guide Italy to a brilliant future. Hitler, when he addresses the throngs of his adherents, becomes mystically exalted, and speaks in terms of almost sensuous delight of his spiritual communion with the masses.

The supremacy of the state—which in practice means the dominance of the Fascist party—requires ruthless suppression of all opposition by word or deed. The introduction of Fascism in Italy and Germany has been accompanied by the exile, imprisonment or murder of political opponents, even when these offered no resistance to the new régime; suspension of civil liberties; suppression of all organs of public opinion and substitution of a colorless official press; and strict regulation of economic activities.

Fascism recognizes the importance of private initiative in industry, trade and agriculture. This is one of the important factors of its appeal to the middle class and the conservative peasantry, who fear that Communism would suppress private property. At the same time Fascism contends that private initiative should serve the interests of the state, and never interfere with them. Fascism recognizes the existence of the class struggle, of conflicts between workers and employers, but demands that such conflicts be adjusted by peaceful means, and should never be allowed to disturb public order. For the network of scattered and conflicting economic interests characteristic of the capitalist system, Fascism would eventually substitute a coordinated "corporative" state in which workers, employers and consumers would harmoniously cooperate under the ægis of the government, and where a council representing professional and economic interests would replace outworn parliaments selected on political lines.

In a period of political and economic disruption, Fascism exercises a strong fascination over the minds of men in all countries. Not only has it triumphed in Italy and Germany, but it has won adherents in traditionally democratic states like Great Britain and France. Fear of Fascism, moreover, has served as an excuse for the introduction of authoritarian government in Czechoslovakia and Austria, which believe that the menace of Germany, coordinated under Nazi rule, cannot be successfully met by democratic régimes. The German Social

Democrats, considered the strongest and best organized Socialist party in Europe, yielded to Fascism without a struggle because they stubbornly refused to resort to violence, and insisted on dealing with the Nazi movement by constitutional methods. Yet Fascism has not swept Europe unchecked. When in February 1934 Gaston Doumergue organized a cabinet of strong men following a series of anti-parliamentary riots, the French Socialist Confederation of Labor staged a general strike, warning the government that it would not tolerate adoption of Fascist measures. In Austria the Social Democrats, who had ruled Vienna since 1918, put up a desperate fight in February 1934 against the attempt of Chancellor Dollfuss to establish a Fascist system modeled on that of Italy. The ruins of Vienna's municipal apartment houses serve as a silent monument to the heroic decision of workers led by a handful of intellectuals to die rather than accept suppression of liberty and democracy as they conceived them.

Should Fascism finally triumph over liberalism and Socialism in Europe, will the workers submit to Fascist rule, as they have in Germany and Italy, or will they turn to Communism as a last resort? The middle class prefers Fascism, under which, for the time being, it retains control of private property. Have the European workers, in Marx's phrase, "nothing to lose but their chains," or will they, too, shun the thought of a Communist system modeled on that of the Soviet Union? Thus far Communism appears to have made little headway outside of Russia, where it has achieved a lasting victory. The workers have been less successful than the mid-

dle class in producing strong and daring leaders; no Communist Hitler or Mussolini has yet
appeared on the European scene. Nor does the
technique of government championed by Fascism and Communism offer much choice to workers nurtured in Social Democratic traditions. Both
Fascism and Communism denounce parliamentary methods and economic *laissez faire.* Both
advocate dictatorship and suppression of individual
liberties. Neither hesitates to employ violence
against its opponents. Both envisage an ultimate
stage at which all citizens, usefully employed for
collective ends—whether in field or factory, whether
with hand or brain—will peacefully coöperate under the benevolent supervision of the state. But if,
in the Fascist state, political power and control of
economic resources are vested in representatives of
the middle class, in the Communist state they are
wielded by representatives of the workers. Is there
as sharp a cleavage between workers and other social
groups in leading European states as there was in
Russia in 1917? Are the workers ready to destroy
the middle class? Or will they prefer to accept its
rule, as long as it maintains order and a modicum
of material well-being? It is possible that Communism may spread in backward agrarian countries
whose economic system resembles that of Russia on
the eve of the Bolshevik revolution, like Bulgaria
and Yugoslavia, but it seems doubtful today that it
will triumph in industrialized countries as long as
the middle class continues to be replenished from the
ranks of the workers.

Even should Communism sweep Europe in the
wake of Fascism, it is by no means certain that it

would everywhere assume the same form as in the Soviet Union. Fascism and Communism may be articles of export, as claimed by both their protagonists and their opponents. No political or economic system, however, can be made to fit all countries like a standardized garment. Racial characteristics, national traditions, divergences in economic development could not fail to influence the form which Fascism or Communism might assume in different countries. Fascist Italy and Nazi Germany, starting from similar points of philosophical departure, are already following divergent roads, and might even be found arrayed against each other in a European conflict. It is consequently idle to hope that, should all Europe turn Fascist, international conflicts would be eliminated and peace immediately restored. Fascism has proved a disruptive force in international relations. Abroad as at home Fascism repudiates democratic concepts and parliamentary methods. It ridicules the deliberative procedure of the League of Nations; it demands settlement of international conflicts at small conferences of great powers, free from responsibility to public opinion; it glorifies war. By exalting the national state, Fascism perpetuates and embitters existing international differences. Communism, unlike Fascism, preaches international peace—but peace only between workers of all nations, who are simultaneously urged to suppress other social classes. The Communists argue that wars are provoked by the unbridled greeds and hatreds of capitalists and imperialists; that, once all states have adopted Communism, they will unite in an international proletarian community, and war will become obsolete. It remains to be seen, however, whether the interests of workers throughout the world, in countries so different in economic development as Great Britain and Yugoslavia, are any less conflicting than those of the middle class. If democracy, as contended by those who deride it, has failed to assure international peace and economic co-operation, Fascism and Communism have yet to demonstrate their ability to achieve these ends.

While dictatorship of the Right or Left temporarily has a powerful appeal for the masses, everywhere distracted by the economic crisis, it is fraught, in the long run, with the gravest dangers. By suppressing individual responsibility and initiative, it may simplify the daily life of the average man, but it stultifies him, and robs him of all power to formulate opinions on political and economic questions. Dictatorship creates a society where unquestioning obedience, secured and maintained by force, is substituted for intelligent and often fruitful dissension, where thought on all subjects is strictly regimented, and opposition is driven underground. By abolishing parliamentary procedure and muzzling public opinion, dictatorship leaves no alternative except civil war. The very violence of the methods which a dictatorship must necessarily employ to maintain itself in power is bound to provoke, sooner or later, an equally violent reaction which, with the passing of years, may bring about another swing toward democracy.

For with all its faults, democracy offers the individual a way of life superior to that prescribed by dictatorship. Where democracy functions most successfully, as in the Scandinavian countries, society finds it possible to achieve a balance of economic interests without repression of any social group, and permits each individual to develop to his full spiritual stature in an atmosphere of peace which fosters the finest flowering of civilization. Democracy is a far more difficult method of government than dictatorship. It makes much greater demands on the intelligence and unselfishness of the individual, and confronts him with more arduous tasks. Yet democracy does not force the individual to accept a rigid political or economic system. Its very lack of cohesion, often ridiculed by Fascists, renders it more elastic than dictatorship, more adaptable to changing conditions, and permits a wider range of peaceful political and economic experimentation. The breakdown of democracy in countries like Germany and Italy need not be interpreted as the death verdict of democracy elsewhere. If, as President Roosevelt has stated, "the machinery of democracy has failed to function" in recent years, this is due not only to defects in democratic institutions, but to "inertia on the part of leaders and on the part of the people themselves," who have permitted "the operations of government" to fall into the hands of special groups and, in a sense, have allowed democracy to go by default. The present crisis challenges the people of traditionally democratic countries like France, Great Britain and the United States to organize the state in such a way that it can cope effectively with the social problems created by the machine age without sacrificing the political and economic liberty of the individual. The success of democracy in meeting this challenge depends, in the last resort, on the willingness of each citizen to look beyond the immediate preoccupations of his daily life and develop a long-range view of the needs of society as a whole.[1]

[1] For further discussion of this subject, *cf.* G. D. H. Cole, *A Guide Through World Chaos* (New York, Knopf, 1932); Harold J. Laski, *Democracy in Crisis* (Chapel Hill, University of North Carolina Press, 1933); José Ortega y Gasset, *The Revolt of the Masses* (New York, Norton, 1932); John L. Strachey, *The Coming Struggle for Power* (New York, Covici-Friede, 1933).

FASCIST RULE IN ITALY

NOWHERE in Europe, perhaps, were the doubts
and disillusions engendered by the World War so
sharply crystallized as in Italy. Nominally a victor,
Italy regarded its share of the Versailles settlement
far from commensurate with its sacrifices in wealth
and manpower. War-weariness and discontent facilitated the rise of the Fascist party, which undertook to terminate the parliamentary system and to
reorganize Italy's economic life along corporative
lines. Fascism, essentially opposed to capitalist democracy, encountered little opposition in a country
which had had little experience with parliamentary
institutions, and had remained relatively unaffected
by modern capitalism.

The unification of Italy, begun with the revolutions of 1821 and 1848, has been effected under conditions of considerable difficulty. The Italian *Risorgimento,* which had rallied all liberal and patriotic
elements under the leadership of Mazzini and
Cavour, and had given intellectual impetus to the
process of unification, was essentially the movement
of an *élite.* The Italian people as a whole, divided
for centuries into semi-feudal principalities, oppressed by foreign rulers and absorbed in matters
of local concern, had no sense of national unity,
no knowledge of freedom and no experience with par-

liamentary institutions. "We have made Italy," said
the statesman D'Azeglio in 1861, "now we must
make Italians."

The country, poor in natural resources, was further weakened by a conflict of economic interests
between the North, which had begun to develop its
industries, and the agrarian South, whose progress
was hampered, first by absentee landlordism, and
later by the indifference of the central government.
Italy, like Germany, discovered that it had emerged
on the international scene too late to profit by
colonial expansion, which seemed to offer the only
outlet for a rapidly growing population. Conscious
of a brilliant past, Italy found it difficult to accept
a position which it regarded as that of a proletarian
among nations.

The form of government adopted by the Kingdom of Italy in 1861 was the product not so much
of Italy's political experience as of the cult for
liberalism and democracy which then reigned in
Western Europe. The *Statuto* granted by Charles
Albert to Piedmont in 1848 became the constitution
of the new kingdom. It provided for a monarch,
and a Parliament consisting of a Chamber of Deputies elected on a narrow franchise and a Senate, the
members of which were appointed by the King for
life from among twenty-one specified categories.
Legislative power was to be exercised jointly by the
King and the two chambers.

Parliamentary government, imposed from above
at a time when a large minority of the population
were illiterate, never became thoroughly acclimated
in Italy's political life. The deputies, as in other
countries, represented local rather than national
interests, and were frequently out of touch with the

broad masses of the population. The political leaders who succeeded Cavour—Minghetti, Depretis,
Crispi, Giolitti—enjoyed a personal, more than a
party following, and the formation of each new
cabinet involved a considerable amount of intrigue
and compromise. Elections, especially during Giolitti's several terms as Prime Minister, were accompanied by fraud and violence. The absence of political tradition and the diversity of the country's
interests prevented the emergence of a single group
which could be regarded as the ruling class.

ITALY'S POLITICAL LIFE, 1861–1914

During the fifty-three years which elapsed between the establishment of the kingdom and the
outbreak of the World War, Italy was continuously
governed by liberals, first of the Right and, after
1876, of the Left. The liberals achieved a considerable measure of success in creating national unity
and in solving Italy's most pressing economic problems. The Socialist party, organized in the early
nineties, began to participate in parliamentary work
at the beginning of the present century, and obtained a series of important social reforms, including
the electoral law of 1912, which increased the number of voters from over three million to more than
eight and a half million. Socialism, which drew its
chief support from the small bourgeoisie (*piccola
borghesía*) and the intellectuals, was weakened in
1912 by a cleavage between its moderate and radical
elements. The former seceded under the reformist
Bissolati, while the latter remained within the party,
and attempted to find a remedy for the growing
social unrest in the ranks of the proletariat. Meanwhile the Nationalist party, formed in 1910, advo-

cated a policy of expansion and imperialism.[1] The country's renewed interest in colonial questions found practical expression in the Italo-Turkish war of 1911–1912, as a result of which Italy obtained Tripoli and Cyrenaica.[2]

ITALY AND THE WORLD WAR

At the outbreak of the World War, the Italian government decided that it was not bound by the Triple Alliance to join the Central Powers in a war which it regarded as one of offense, and made a declaration of neutrality. Public opinion, however, was divided. The Nationalists demanded, while the Socialists opposed, Italy's entrance into the war. The Prime Minister, Salandra, stated that the country's policy would be dictated by "sacred egoism." After some hesitation Benito Mussolini, an extreme Socialist and the editor of the party organ, *Avanti*, suddenly pronounced himself in favor of intervention on the side of the Allies.[3] Expelled from the party, he founded his own newspaper, *Il Popolo d'Italia*, in Milan, where he was followed by the more revolutionary Socialist elements. Mussolini welcomed the war as a prelude to revolution. In 1915 he organized his followers in *Fasci d'Azione Rivoluzionaria*, and instructed them to be ready for everything—"for the trenches as well as for the

[1] The leaders of the Nationalist party—Enrico Corradini, Luigi Federzoni, Roberto Forges-Davanzati—became prominent in Fascist circles.

[2] For the history of Italy, 1859–1915, *cf.* Benedetto Croce, *A History of Italy, 1871–1915* (Oxford, Clarendon Press, 1929); F. Quintavalle, *Storia dell' Unità Italiana* (Milan, Hoepli, 1926); Luigi Villari, *Italy* (London, Benn, 1929); G. Volpe, *L'Italia in Cammino* (Milan, Treves, 1927).

[3] For Mussolini's earlier years, *cf. Benito Mussolini*, *My Autobiography* (New York, Scribner's, 1928); Margherita Sarfatti, *Dux* (Milan, Mondadori, 1926).

barricades."[4] When Italy finally entered the war in May 1915, he greeted the event as a definite triumph of popular sentiment over a cautious government.[5]

During the war, in which he participated as a private, Mussolini denounced the defeatism of the Socialists and advocated the use of force for its suppression. He favored centralization of power in the hands of the government, as well as restrictions on the freedom of speech and of the press. The defeat which the Italian army suffered at Caporetto in October 1917 aroused both the government and the country, and a fresh drive against the enemy resulted in 1918 in the victory of Vittorio Veneto. Mussolini exulted at the breakdown of the Central Powers: Italy, he said, would now enjoy a new springtime, a new *risorgimento,* and would at last obtain its appointed place in the sun.

The hopes of Mussolini and his followers were dealt a severe blow by the wave of war-weariness which swept over the country in 1919, and by the results of the Paris Peace Conference which, in their opinion, left Italy with a "mutilated victory." The army, returning from the front to reap the reward of its sacrifices, found that the more profitable posts had meanwhile been occupied by those who had stayed safely at home. The cost of living had risen considerably, with no corresponding adjustment of salaries. The lower bourgeoisie, the civil employees and the intellectuals, many of whom were faced by unemployment, were in a worse economic plight than the peasants and industrial workers. The country was seething with disillusion and discontent.

---

[4] Mussolini, *Diuturna* (Milan, Imperia, 1924), p. 15.
[5] *Ibid.,* p. 52.

GROWTH OF SOCIALISM AFTER THE WAR

The Socialists, who had bitterly opposed Italy's participation in the war, now openly assailed the government for its failure to keep the country out of the conflict, and attacked officers and soldiers who ventured to appear publicly in uniform. Impressed with the success of the Soviet government, the Socialists advocated revolution by violent means as the only solution of Italy's problems. In the elections of 1919, held on the basis of proportional representation, the Socialists won an outstanding victory, returning 157 candidates to the Chamber of Deputies, and capturing the government in over two thousand municipalities. This success, however, marked the high tide of Italian Socialism. Strikes and disorders inspired by Socialists reached a climax in September 1920, when workers occupied the metallurgical factories of Lombardy and Piedmont. Neither the government nor the industrialists offered any resistance, and the workers, finding that they could not operate the factories without capital or technical experts, evacuated them after a few days. The revolutionary leaders suffered a loss of prestige. The Socialist party was further weakened in 1921 by the secession of its Left wing elements, which formed the Maximalist Communist party.[6]

ORGANIZATION OF FASCIST GROUPS

Meanwhile, two new political groups were attracting those opposed to the Socialist program. The *non-expedit,* by which the Church in 1857 had advised Catholics to abstain from political activities,

[6] Ivanoe Bonomi, *Dal Socialismo al Fascismo* (Rome, Formiggini, 1924).

was permitted to lapse in 1919 when a priest, Don Luigi Sturzo, organized the Popular party, with a democratic program "inspired by Christian ethics." [7] On March 23, 1919, Mussolini formed the first *Fascio di Combattimento,* modeled on the earlier *Fasci d'Azione Rivoluzionaria.*[8] These *fasci* were to devote their efforts to the restoration of public order and the suppression of Socialism. Fascism recruited its early adherents from the Nationalist party and from the ranks of the bourgeoisie, especially among World War veterans. Its program at that time was "a little of everything," combining democratic, republican, nationalist, monarchist and anarchist ideas,[9] tinged with a romantic idealization of Italy's destiny. The Fascists were entirely ineffective in the elections of 1919, when Mussolini himself was defeated at the polls.

In the autumn of 1920, however, Mussolini and other local leaders formed armed bands of Fascists (*squadre*), which carried on a vigorous campaign against Socialists and Communists. The propertied classes—landowners and industrialists—irritated and alarmed by constant disturbances of public order, gradually turned to Fascism. In the elections of 1921, thirty-five Fascist candidates, including Mussolini, were elected to the Chamber of Deputies, chiefly on the Nationalist ticket. Once in Parliament, Mussolini broke with the Nationalists, declared himself to be anti-monarchical and republican,

[7] Luigi Sturzo, *Italy and Fascismo* (London, Faber and Gwyer, 1926).

[8] Dino Grandi, *Il Fascismo* (Rome, Licinio Capelli, 1922), p. 52. The name *fascio* is taken from the word *fasces*—the Roman symbol of the lictor's power, which consisted of rods bound about an ax; it was borne in public processions before consuls and magistrates, and signified the union of all powers in one.

[9] *Ibid.,* p. 61.

and in August 1921 concluded a "pact of pacification" with the Socialists. Neither of the two groups, however, succeeded in persuading the rank and file of its followers to abstain from acts of violence. The Fascists outside Parliament finally prevailed upon Mussolini to abandon his program of co-operation with other parliamentary groups.

Thereafter, the National Fascist party, formed on November 6, 1921, engaged in a bitter struggle with both Socialists and Popularists. On both sides hostilities were marked by extreme violence. The government was not sufficiently strong to restore order and, with the backing of industrialists, gave the Fascists a free hand, hoping to find in them an ally against Socialism. "Such conduct on the part of the government," says the Fascist historian Villari, "would have been wholly reprehensible in an orderly society, but Italy in 1919–1922 was nothing of the kind." [10]

THE "MARCH ON ROME"

A number of observers believe that by 1921 Socialism was in retreat, and that the threat of a Bolshevik revolution had practically disappeared.[11] The economic crisis had passed. The parliamentary crisis, however, showed no signs of improvement. Successive Prime Ministers, summoned from the ranks of Liberals, Socialists and Popularists, failed to rally the Parliament and the country to a national program directed at the solution of the country's pressing economic problems. In the summer of 1922 the

[10] Luigi Villari, *The Fascist Experiment* (London, Faber and Gwyer, 1928), p. 39.

[11] Bonomi, *Dal Socialismo al Fascismo,* cited, p. 147; Villari, *The Fascist Experiment,* cited, p. 38; Gaetano Salvemini, *The Fascist Dictatorship in Italy* (New York, Holt, 1927).

Fascists were offered subordinate positions in the cabinet. Mussolini refused, saying that he would not "reach power through the service entrance," or sacrifice his ideals "for a miserable dish of ministerial lentils." [12] At the party congress held in Naples on October 24, 1922, Mussolini made a *volte face,* and declared his allegiance to the King. This declaration won him the sympathies of many sections of the population, notably the army, which had previously been repelled by his republican principles. The Fascists, efficiently organized as a militia, and armed with the connivance of the government, were ready and eager for action. In October they occupied the large cities, taking possession of city halls, railway stations and postoffices. On October 27 the Fascist militia assembled at Civitavecchia, north of Rome, under the leadership of a "quadrumvirate"— General De Bono, De Vecchi, Michele Bianchi and Italo Balbo—and began the famous "March on Rome." The following day the militia entered the capital, where it met with no resistance.[13] On October 29 the King summoned Mussolini, who had remained in Milan, to form a cabinet, which he did on October 30. The Fascist revolution had taken place.

Opinion differs widely regarding the necessity of a revolution in 1922. Opponents of Fascism claim that the country had entered on a period of convalescence in 1921, and that the number of strikes

---

[12] Mussolini, *Discorsi della Rivoluzione* (Milan, Imperia, 1923), p. 77.

[13] On October 28 the cabinet, headed by Prime Minister Facta, decided to proclaim martial law and to oppose the March on Rome. On the advice of army leaders the King refused to sign the decree proclaiming martial law. *Cf.* Count Carlo Sforza, *Makers of Modern Europe* (Bobbs Merrill Company, 1930), Chapter XXXI, "Facta, or the Immediate Origins of Fascism."

had decreased in spite of a reduction in salaries.[14]
They believe, moreover, that the post-war parliamentary crisis was not indicative of the decadence
of democracy in Italy, and that it could have been
overcome by peaceful means if both Fascism and
Socialism had transferred their struggle to the constitutional sphere.[15] Mussolini, however, asserts that
the legal transformation of the state by means of
elections under a new electoral law, which he had
suggested before the March on Rome, had been
blocked by the government on the ground that it
would disturb public order; the problem had become, therefore, "one of force."[16] Parliamentary government, in his opinion, had been reduced to impotence after the war. He declared that the Fascist
revolution was directed not against the constitutional organization of the state, but against the
political group which for four years had failed to
give a government to the country.

The policies and acts of the Fascist government
have also given rise to diverse interpretations. The
Fascist revolution, effected by a former Socialist who
had held anti-bourgeois, anti-clerical and anti-
royalist views, has been denounced as the triumph
of a "White Guard" of industrial and agrarian
capitalists,[17] later supported by the Catholic Church.
The Fascist government has been attacked at one

---

[14] Bonomi, *Dal Socialismo al Fascismo,* cited, p. 89 *et seq.*
Bonomi estimates that 79,296 agricultural workers went on strike
in 1921, as compared with 1,045,732 in 1920, and 644,564 industrial
workers, as compared with 1,267,667 in 1920.

[15] *Ibid.; cf.* also Guglielmo Ferrero, *Four Years of Fascism*
(London, King & Son, 1924).

[16] *Cf.* Mussolini's speech at the Fascist party congress in
Naples, October 24, 1922. Mussolini, *Discorsi della Rivoluzione,*
cited, p. 78.

[17] Francesco Nitti, *Bolchévisme, Fascisme et Démocratie*
(Paris, "Progrès Civique," 1926).

and the same time for reaction in politics and radicalism in the economic field. The Fascists, meanwhile, claim that they have created the only political and economic structure which can assure Italy's orderly development, as well as its progress in world affairs. No general conclusions regarding the character of the Fascist state can be reached until the theory of Fascism has been examined, and its practical application analyzed.

CHAPTER I

THE THEORY OF FASCISM

FASCISM traces its intellectual origins to Machiavelli's *The Prince*, through Georges Sorel, Hegel, Nietzsche and Vico. From Machiavelli it has learned that the preservation of the state justifies recourse to force, and that politics are distinct from ethics. In the syndicalism of Sorel it finds intuition and passion exalted above reason, and direct action advocated even when it involves violence. To Hegel it owes the conception of the state as a mystical entity, superior to individuals, who find realization only in acceptance of the law. Vico's theory that political institutions are not immutable, but undergo transformation in accordance with time and place, has proved of practical value in Fascist politics. The thinker who has been acclaimed as the prophet of Fascism, however, is the Italian economist Vilfredo Pareto,[1] whose lectures at the Univer-

[1] Vilfredo Pareto (1848–1923), *Traité de Sociologie Générale* (Paris, Payot, 1921, 2 vols.); *Trasformazione della Democrazià* (Milan, "Corbaccio," 1921). *Cf.* G. H. Bousquet, *Vilfredo Pareto: Sa Vie et son Œuvre* (Paris, Payot, 1928). "Fascism may to a

sity of Lausanne Mussolini attended during his so-
journ in Switzerland in 1902. Pareto believes that
no social cycle can last indefinitely, and that the
cycle of "demagogic plutocracy," which he identifies with the nineteenth century, may disappear
when new elements arise, armed with knowledge,
force and will-power. No form of government, in his
opinion, is superior to any other in an abstract sense;
the test of a "good" government is whether or not it
is adapted to the society in which it is established.
The governing class—the *élite*—must rely on both
force and consent if it is to remain in power. Pareto
lived to see the advent of Fascism, some aspects of
which, notably its restrictions on the freedom of the
press, he subjected to searching criticism.

LACK OF PROGRAM

Fascism takes pride in the fact that it has no
program. To those who accused him of vagueness,
Mussolini replied in 1922 that Italy lacked, not
programs, but men and will-power.[2] Fascist writers
declare that Fascism is, above all, action and sentiment.[3] "Fascism as an idea is indefinable. It is a
fact which is taking place." [4] In its emphasis on
facts rather than theory, Fascism represents a revolt
against positivism, which permeated Italian education before the war, and against all social philoso-

large extent be regarded as an experimental proof of the doctrine
[of Pareto]." Sergio Panunzio, *Che Cos'è il Fascismo* (Milan,
Alpes, 1924), p. 77. For Pareto's influence on Mussolini, *cf.*
Sarfatti, *Dux*, cited, p. 69. The futurist poet, Marinetti, is also
regarded as a precursor of Fascism.

   [2] Mussolini, *Discorsi della Rivoluzione*, cited, p. 27.

   [3] Alfredo Rocco, *The Political Doctrine of Fascism*, Address
delivered at Perugia, August 30, 1925, published in Carnegie En-
dowment for International Peace, *International Conciliation*,
October 1926, No. 223, p. 394.

   [4] Panunzio, *Che Cos'è il Fascismo*, cited, p. 75.

phy based solely on speculation. Fascist leaders, the greater part of whose life has been spent in conflict, either at the front or in the field of politics, place more reliance on action than on intellect. "Every time we have taken up a volume," says Turati, former Secretary-General of the party, "there has resounded in our ears the cry of alarm, the sound of the trumpet, and we have had to fling away our book and take hold of the rifle."[5]

Fascism, however, chooses to be symbolized by the book as well as the rifle (*libro e moschetto*). It is not merely action; it has a theory. This theory is essentially in conflict with the historical materialism of Marx, which conceives history as a predetermined class struggle inevitably resulting in the collapse of capitalism. Political and economic factors, according to Fascism, are neither predetermined nor eternal, but mobile and subject to change in different historical environments. Nor are the state or the individual concerned solely with material ends. Society is profoundly influenced by such spiritual factors as culture, religion, custom and tradition, and strives to preserve them for future generations.

FASCIST SLOGANS: AUTHORITY, ORDER, DISCIPLINE

Unlike Marxism, Fascism holds out no promise of a millennium.[6] It offers, however, the prospect of an ordered and disciplined existence within the framework of the state. The Fascist state is conceived not as an aggregate of groups and individuals, but as a spiritual entity which survives and transcends

[5] Augusto Turati, *A Revolution and its Leader* (London, Alexander Ousley, 1930), p. 40.
[6] "We shall promise nothing special. We shall not assume the appearance of missionaries who are the bearers of revealed truth." Mussolini, *Discorsi della Rivoluzione*, cited, p. 61.

successive generations. "For Fascism, society has historical and immanent ends of preservation, expansion, improvement, quite distinct from those of the individuals which at a given moment compose it; so distinct in fact that they may even be in opposition."[7] Individuals are merely the means by which society achieves its ends. When it is objected that such worship of the state is nothing less than a new form of idolatry, Fascist writers reply that it constitutes a "religion of the spirit," which saves the mind from "the abject blindness of materialism."[8]

The individual, according to Fascism, is subordinated to society, but not eliminated. He remains an element of society "however transient and insignificant he may be."[9] The individual, however, cannot lead an existence distinct from that of the state. He owes a duty to the state, and in the exercise of this duty may be called on to sacrifice everything, including life. The preëminence of duty is regarded as the highest ethical value of Fascism. The Fascist state is not merely an administrative organization, concerned with political or economic issues; it is "totalitarian," embraces all interests and activities, whether of groups or individuals, and permeates the spiritual content of life. Nothing can exist outside or above the state. "One cannot be Fascist in politics . . . and non-Fascist in school, non-Fascist in the family circle, non-Fascist in the workshop."[10]

Where Fascism departs most radically from the

[7] Rocco, *The Political Doctrine of Fascism*, cited, p. 402.
[8] Giovanni Gentile, *Che Cos'è il Fascismo* (Florence, Valecchi, 1925), p. 36.
[9] Rocco, *The Political Doctrine of Fascism*, cited, p. 402.
[10] Gentile, *Che Cos'è il Fascismo*, cited, p. 38.

accepted doctrines of liberalism, socialism and democracy is in its conception of the liberty of individuals and groups. Individual rights are recognized by Fascism only in so far as they are implied
in the rights of the state.[11] The conditions that make
for the free development of the individual are to be
safeguarded. Fascism, however, does not accept a
bill of rights "which tends to make the individual
superior to the state" and empowers him "to act
in opposition to society." [12] Freedom, whether political or economic, is a concession on the part of
the state, and can be granted only on condition that
it be exercised in the interest of society as a whole
and within the limits set by social exigencies. Fascism recognizes that individual ambition is "the
most effective means of obtaining the best social
results with the least effort," and regards a degree
of economic liberty compatible with the social good.
This liberty, however, must be severely curbed
whenever it threatens to result in economic conflict
and disturbance of public order. Measures of class
self-defense, such as strikes and lockouts, are therefore prohibited by Fascism. Economic justice is to
be achieved, not in consequence of class struggle, but
by means of Fascist syndicates subject to the authority of the state.[13] It is particularly important,
according to Fascism, that peace should be preserved
in a country like Italy, which is poor in natural
resources.

"Public order must not be disturbed for any motive,
at any cost. Italy must have economic peace in order
to develop its resources. . . . It is necessary for syndical-

---

[11] Rocco, *The Political Doctrine of Fascism,* cited, p. 403.
[12] *Ibid.,* p. 403.
[13] *Ibid.,* p. 406–407.

ism and capitalism to realize the new historical reality: that they must avoid bringing matters to the breaking-point, must avoid war between classes, because when such a war is fought within the nation, it is destructive. . . . The government is at the orders of neither group. The government stands above all groups in that it represents not only the political consciousness of the nation today, but also all that the nation will constitute in the future." [14]

THE INDIVIDUAL AND THE FASCIST STATE

The subordination of classes and individuals to the state creates no ethical problem for Fascism, which believes that "the legitimate will of the citizen is that which coincides with the will of the state." [15] If this be true, opposition is not only unreasonable, but reprehensible. Should opposition nevertheless appear, it must be regarded as a social disease, to be eradicated as promptly as possible from the body politic. The method advocated in such cases is that of violence. "Discipline must be accepted," says Mussolini. "When it is not accepted, it must be imposed." [16] Fascist theory distinguishes between private violence, which is arbitrary and anarchic, and violence directed to social ends. The latter is "willed by God and by all men who believe in God and in the order and laws which God certainly desires for the world. . . ." [17] Such violence is holy and highly moral. [18]

[14] Mussolini, *La Nuova Politica dell' Italia* (Milan, Imperia, 1924), Vol. II, p. 136–139.
[15] Gentile, *Che Cos'è il Fascismo,* cited, p. 34.
[16] Mussolini, *Discorsi della Rivoluzione,* cited, p. 17.
[17] Gentile, *Che Cos'è il Fascismo,* cited, p. 31.
[18] *Ibid.,* p. 31. *Cf.* also Mussolini, *Discorsi della Rivoluzione,* cited, p. 19: "Violence is not immoral. Violence is sometimes moral. . . . When our violence is a solution of a cancerous situation, it is highly moral, sacrosanct and necessary."

The form of government advocated by Fascism differs fundamentally from that sponsored by liberal and democratic thinkers. Fascism rejects the conception of popular sovereignty.[19] Democracy, which may have had meaning in the nineteenth century, has no place in the modern state, with its multiplicity and variety of functions. Sovereignty resides, not in the people, but in society juridically organized as a state. The great mass of citizens is incapable of undertaking the difficult task of government. This task, in Fascist theory, devolves on "the chosen few," an *élite* selected for their peculiar gifts. In practice, this governing class (*classe dirigente*) is recruited from among men noted for their loyalty to the Fascist party. "Fascism and the Fascist governing class are born together." [20] Presumably, until Italy has been thoroughly "fascistized," the range of choice for positions of responsibility will remain comparatively limited.

The governing class, in turn, must be led by a man who can crystalize its ideals. Fascism has found such a leader in Mussolini. His energy, personal magnetism and political success have won admiration even outside the immediate circle of his supporters, with the result that, for many Italians, he has come to personify the spirit of a new Renaissance. Mussolini believes that he has been chosen by fate to create a new and greater Italy.[21]

[19] Mussolini, *Discorsi della Rivoluzione,* cited, p. 21: "You know that I do not adore that new divinity, the masses. It is a creation of democracy and socialism. Only because they are many they must be right. Nothing of the kind. The opposite is true, that numbers are contrary to reason."

[20] Roberto Cantalupo, *La Classe Dirigente* (Milan, Biblioteca di Coltura Politica, 1926).

[21] *Cf.* Mussolini, *Discorsi del 1925* (Milan, Alpes, 1926). "Every great movement must have a representative man who suffers all the passion of that movement and carries its flame

The injection of a new spirit into national life is regarded by Fascism as one of its major accomplishments. "Our battle," says Mussolini, "was directed primarily against a state of mind, a mentality of renunciation, a spirit always more ready to avoid than to accept responsibility." [22] Fascism claims to have replaced the pessimism and discouragement of the post-war years by confidence in Italy's future, and to have substituted direct action for political apathy and confusion. The Fascist conception of the state as a mystical source of authority, and its recognition of religion as a necessary element in modern society, challenge the "agnosticism" of the liberal, anti-clerical state, committed to a policy of *laissez faire*.

FASCISM AND ITALIAN YOUTH

Fascism has found its most ardent adherents among World War veterans, especially those who had entered the war while still in their youth. These soldiers, many of whom had not yet come in contact with democratic institutions, spent their most impressionable years at the front, and there learned the value of direct action, discipline and submission to authority. They became, moreover, imbued with the desire to reap the fruits of victory. Fascism offered an avenue of escape from post-war weariness and disillusionment, as well as an instrument for the realization of nationalist aspirations. They turned to Fascism as to a "springtime of the nation," and from them Fascism acquired both the defects and

within him." *Cf.* Pietro Gorgolini, *La Rivoluzione Fascista* (Turin, Silvestrelli and Cappellato, 1923), who extols Mussolini as the "Man" called on by destiny to rescue Italy from the old political régime.

[22] Mussolini, *La Nuova Politica dell' Italia,* cited, Vol. II, p. 52.

qualities of youth—self-confidence, violence, defiance of opposition, as well as spontaneity, buoyancy and a sense of adventure.[23] The predominance of youth in Fascist ranks explains a number of phenomena, such as hero-worship of Mussolini, glorification of virility, emphasis on sport and physical education, and the juvenile punishments meted out to opponents, notably administrations of castor oil. The Fascist anthem, *Giovinezza*, originally a song of the *Arditi*,[24] extols youth in the same breath with Fascism.

> *Giovinezza, Giovinezza,*
> *Primavera di belleza.*
> *Nel fascismo è la salvezza*
> *Della nostra libertà.*[25]

The youthful energy released by Fascism has been directed not only to the development of Italy's resources, but to expansion of the national boundaries as well. The rapidly growing population cannot be adequately supported within the country's present boundaries, while emigration is regarded as an unsatisfactory solution, since it deprives Italy of both manpower and financial resources. Fascist Italy, therefore, seeks new worlds to conquer, and finds precedent and inspiration in the history of imperial Rome. The glorious past is constantly invoked, and many Fascist customs and institutions are modeled on those of the Roman Empire. The urge to expand, which sprang originally from economic neces-

---

[23] *Cf.* Robert Michel's *Socialismus und Fascismus in Italien* (Munich, Meyer and Jessen, 1925), p. 313; Herbert W. Schneider, *Making the Fascist State* (New York, Oxford University Press, 1928), pp. 350–351.

[24] Italian shock troops during the World War.

[25] "Youth, youth, springtime of beauty, Fascism is the safeguard of our liberty."

sity, has been consecrated by exaltation of the nation's spiritual heritage. This tendency has found literary expression in the work of the poet Gabriele d'Annunzio, who led the Fiume expedition in 1920.

CHAPTER II

THE FASCIST PARTY

THE National Fascist party was officially organized at a congress held in Rome on November 6, 1921. The program adopted at the congress stated that the party was "a voluntary militia placed at the service of the nation," which based its activities on three fundamental principles—"order, discipline, hierarchy." It is estimated that at that time the party numbered 151,644 members, and included merchants, manufacturers, professional men, government employees, teachers, students, landowners and agricultural workers.[1] Many of the members had joined Fascism for personal ends, and were little concerned with its ideals. Mussolini frequently has deplored the original composition of the party. The Fascist revolution, he said in 1924, had been effected by a party hastily formed at a time when rigid selection presented practical difficulties. To his opponents, who accuse Fascism of violence and illegal acts, Mussolini answers that the revolution had thrown together "the good and the bad, the ascetics and the men eager for lucre, idealists and profiteers."[2] "The one weak point about the new

[1] Cf. Odom Por, *Fascism* (London, Labour Publishing Company, 1923), p. 122.
[2] Mussolini, *La Nuova Politica,* cited, Vol. III, p. 180–181.

régime," says the Fascist writer Villari, "was that not all the persons surrounding Mussolini were up to his standard, either intellectually or morally. . . . In the case of Fascism, moreover, as it was a movement essentially of young men, there was also a lack of experience and other faults of youth." [3]

Opponents of Fascism charge members of the party with a series of outrages following the March on Rome, such as floggings, forcible administrations of castor oil, illegal seizure of newspapers, wreckage of private houses and offices, and a number of murders. They claim that these outrages went unpunished, for the most part, due both to the connivance of the police and to the fact that the cases were tried by Fascist judges and juries. Moreover, it is asserted that a number of Fascist offenses were wiped out by the amnesty granted on December 22, 1922, which covered all crimes committed for a "national end," and by subsequent amnesties.[4] The Fascist government denies that members of the party have engaged in illegal activities, except in some isolated instances, and claims that every effort has been made to remove such offenders from the ranks of the party.

FUNCTIONS OF THE PARTY

The functions of the party were defined by its supreme organ, the Grand Council,[5] in a statute adopted in 1926 and amended in 1929.[6] It reaffirms

[3] Villari, *The Fascist Experiment,* cited, p. 63.

[4] *Cf.* Salvemini, *The Fascist Dictatorship in Italy,* cited; Giacomo Matteotti, *The Fascisti Exposed* (London, Independent Labour Party, 1924).

[5] The Grand Council was established in 1923.

[6] The amended statute was published in the official organ of the party, *Foglio d'Ordine; cf. Corriere della Sera,* December 22, 1929.

the principle that the party is a civil militia at the service of the state, whose object is "to achieve the greatness of the Italian people." Fascism, it declares, is not merely a political program; it is, above all, a faith, professed and translated into action by its militant followers, the new Italians. The party is an essential factor in the organization of the state, and is indispensable to the existence of the régime.

The nucleus of the party is the *fascio di combattimento,* the local party organization, which must rally all Italians distinguished for the Fascist virtues of "loyalty, honesty, courage and intellect." The *fasci* are organized in provincial federations, which are subject to the authority of the National Directorate and the Grand Council; the latter determines the program of action which is to be followed by the party in all fields of national life. The members of the party are subject to a hierarchy (*gerarchià*) of local, provincial and national secretaries, acting under the supreme command of the leader—*Il Duce*—the title given to Mussolini. The Secretary-General of the party is appointed for three years by the King on proposal of the head of the government; he acts as secretary of the Grand Council and may be invited to participate in the work of the Council of Ministers. Roberto Farinacci, appointed Secretary-General of the party in December 1925, at the height of anti-Fascist agitation, pursued a policy of violence and intransigeance against those suspected of opposition to the government. He was replaced in 1926 by Augusto Turati, who inaugurated a milder policy. Following Turati's resignation in 1930, Giovanni Giuriati, president of the Chamber of Deputies, was appointed to that office; he was succeeded in 1932 by Achille

Starace, who occupies that office at the present time.

In 1926 the Grand Council decided to admit no one to the party except those who "graduate" from the Advance Guard (*Avanguardisti*), the Fascist organization of young boys. On March 4, 1931 it voted to admit no fresh elements to the party until 1932.[7] In the autumn of 1932 the party inaugurated a "back to the people" policy, and announced that it would receive applications for membership. On July 23, 1933, however, Mussolini ordered that no members should be enrolled in the party after August first except those graduating from Fascist youth organizations, thus barring further enrolment from the ranks of adults. The Fascist badge (*tessera*) is given to new Fascists only after careful scrutiny of their antecedents and qualifications. The party statute, as amended in 1929, provides that persons admitted to the party must take the following oath: "I swear to follow without discussion the orders of *Il Duce,* and to serve the cause of the Fascist revolution with all my strength and, if necessary, with my blood." A disciplinary court under the presidency of the Secretary-General of the party examines all cases in which members fail to exhibit the prescribed Fascist virtues. Offenders may be warned, admonished, suspended and, in the gravest cases, expelled from the party.

COMPOSITION OF THE PARTY

In October 1933 the total membership of the party was estimated at 5,467,560, of whom a million and a half were enrolled in *fasci* (the local party organizations), and three and a half million in the *Opera Nazionale Balilla* (the Fascist organization of chil-

[7] *Corriere della Sera,* October 27, 1933.

dren and youths),[8] while the remainder were registered with Fascist syndicates and associations. The government expects that as Fascism penetrates into national life the basis of selection to the ranks of the party will be correspondingly broadened, and that the party will eventually be fused with the nation. "The Fascist party," says a Fascist publicist, "must not become a closed professional class. Fascists should not represent themselves as the only national element in a population of forty-two million." [9] The party, in turn, is expected to serve as a training school for the ruling class (*classe dirigente*). This class, according to Mussolini, must not withdraw to an ivory tower, remote from the masses. It must, on the contrary, establish direct contact with the needs and aspirations of the people, and thus become a truly "popular régime." [10]

CHAPTER III

THE POLITICAL STRUCTURE OF THE FASCIST STATE

THE extent to which Fascism has transformed the state in accordance with its doctrines may be ascertained only after a study of the political and eco-

[8] The *Opera Nazionale Balilla,* established by a law of April 1926, comprises four organizations: *Balilla* (boys aged 8 to 14); *Avanguardisti* (Advance Guard—boys aged 14 to 18); *Piccole Italiane* (girls aged 8 to 14); and *Giovani Italiane* (girls aged 14 to 18). The *Opera Nazionale Balilla* is placed under the control of the Ministry of National Education. *Cf.* Balbino Giuliano, "L'Opera Nazionale Balilla," *Lo Stato Mussoliniano* (Rome, Rassegna Nazionale, 1930), p. 256.

[9] Virginio Gayda, " I Cicli del Fascismo," *Il Giornale d'Italia,* October 10, 1930.

[10] Mussolini, *Discorsi del 1926,* cited, p. 339.

nomic changes introduced since 1922. Fascist leaders claim that the March on Rome, while it involved no social upheaval and resulted in little bloodshed, was a revolution in the broadest sense of the term. This revolution has left its marks on the political and economic structure of the state. The power of the monarch has been curtailed; government has been entrusted to a single party and primarily to its leader, Mussolini; and the Fascist Grand Council has become a constitutional organ, while the Chamber of Deputies has been reorganized and shorn of many of its previous functions. The maintenance of public order has been confided to a voluntary militia recruited from Fascist ranks, all opposition has been suppressed, and a special tribunal has been established for crimes against the safety of the state. The government has prohibited action by either workers or employers in defense of class interests, and has created a system of Fascist syndicates which alone represent the interests of the two groups, subject to control by the state. Finally, changes have been effected in education which are intended to produce a new spirit in Italian youth, and pave the way for complete "fascistization" of national life.

When the Fascist party came to power, it expressed the intention to preserve the existing political structure, and to govern within the framework of the *Statuto*.[1] Later, however, Mussolini came to the conclusion that Italy could not be "fascistized" without alteration of the constitution. "We must violate the *Statuto*," he declared in 1925.[2]

---

[1] *Cf.* address of Mussolini in the Senate, November 27, 1922, Gorgolini, *La Rivoluzione Fascista*, cited, p. 111.
[2] Mussolini, *Discorsi del 1925*, cited, p. 97.

He defended his position by claiming that the *Statuto* no longer corresponded to the needs of the country and had, in fact, been revoked by the march of events.[3] Fascism, he said, intended to do no more than prune the constitution of the overgrowths which had gradually obscured its original meaning. He denied that any constitution could be regarded as immutable. "Are we dealing with archeology or with politics . . . ? Constitutions are but instruments resulting from given historical conditions, which undergo birth, development and decline."[4] The avowed aim of the government, at that time, was to conserve, not revolutionize, the constitution.

THE EXECUTIVE POWER

Mussolini's first act was to assert the preëminence of the executive over the legislative power. In the past, he claimed, the executive had been merely a puppet of Parliament. This condition could be tolerated no longer. The ultimate source of executive power presented a constitutional problem. In the early days of Fascism, Mussolini had declared himself opposed to the monarchy. In 1922, however, he made a concession to popular sentiment, especially in the ranks of the army. He said: "We shall leave monarchy outside our game, because we think that Italy would look with suspicion on a transformation of the government which would eliminate monarchy."[5] He believed that the King would not find it to his interest to obstruct the Fascist revolution. Should the monarchy attempt to resist, "we would have to abolish it, as it would

[3] Mussolini, *Discorsi del 1928* (Milan, Alpes, 1929), p. **101**.
[4] *Ibid.*
[5] Mussolini, *Discorsi della Rivoluzione*, cited, p. **32**.

be a question of life or death."[6] Still later, he expressed the conviction that "the unitary régime of Italy rests solidly on the House of Savoy," and that the monarchy, by reason of its origins and historical development, could not oppose the new national forces.[7]

Mussolini's expectations were realized. The House of Savoy appears to have accepted Fascism without reservations. Both Victor Emanuel III and Prince Humbert, the heir to the throne, have participated in Fascist functions and, outwardly at least, have sanctioned the acts of the Fascist government. The King's acceptance of Fascism has been denounced by anti-Fascists as treason to the constitution. When a young anti-Fascist, De Rosa, attempted to assassinate Prince Humbert in Brussels in 1929, he defended his act on the ground that the prince had proved unworthy of Italy's faith in the monarchy.[8]

The "Head of the Government"

Constitutionally the executive power is still vested in the King.[9] Actually, however, a significant transformation has been effected by the law of December 24, 1925, concerning "the attributes and prerogatives of the head of the government" (*Il Capo del Governo*).[10] This law is intended to legalize the

[6] *Ibid.*, p. 33.

[7] Speech at Fascist Congress in Naples, October 24, 1922, *ibid.*, p. 80.

[8] *Cf. Le Procés De Rosa* (Paris, Valois, 1930), particularly the testimony of MM. Nitti and Trachiani, pp. 64 and 78. De Rosa was tried in Brussels in 1930 by the Court of Assizes, and condemned to five years' imprisonment. His counsel made a sweeping attack on the Fascist government, and was supported by a number of anti-Fascists called as witnesses.

[9] Article 5 of the *Statuto* provides that the King alone possesses executive power.

[10] *Gazzetta Ufficiale del Regno d'Italia,* No. 301, December 29, 1925, p. 5067.

position and functions of the Prime Minister, who had hitherto been recognized by parliamentary practice but had remained unknown to the constitution. It states that the executive power is to be exercised by the King with the aid of his government. The government is composed of the Prime Minister and other ministers. The Prime Minister is the "head of the government"; he is nominated and recalled by the King alone. He directs and coördinates the work of the government, and is responsible to the King for its general political direction. No question can be included in the agenda of either chamber without the consent of the Prime Minister. He has power to ask that any bill rejected by either chamber be reintroduced when at least three months have elapsed since the first vote. In such a case vote by secret ballot takes place without further discussion. If the government, meanwhile, has proposed amendments to the bill, discussion is limited to these amendments. The Prime Minister may likewise demand that a bill rejected by either chamber be transmitted to the other, there to be examined and voted upon; this provision is intended to reduce to a minimum the delay formerly occasioned by parliamentary procedure. Finally, the law provides various terms of imprisonment for any act directed against the life, liberty or integrity of the Prime Minister. The law of November 25, 1926 on the defense of the state goes further, and prescribes the death penalty for such acts.[11]

When presenting the law concerning the head of the government to the Chamber of Deputies, Alfredo Rocco, Minister of Justice, stressed the fact that the Prime Minister was a true *capo del governo*, not

[11] *Gazzetta Ufficiale*, No. 281, December 6, 1926, p. 5314.

merely *primus inter pares:* on him, and not on the
Council of Ministers, devolves the task of co-
ordinating and directing the work of his colleagues.
"Our Prime Minister," said Rocco, "is the recognized
head of the great political, economic and moral
forces of the country and those represented in Parliament, the evaluation of whose importance is subject to the decision of the sovereign." [12] The government, he explained in the Senate, "can no longer
express conflicting political thoughts; it must be the
expression of a single political thought, of a single
conception of the state; else there would be paralysis,
such as existed during the years which preceded
Fascism." [13] It is significant that the law contains
no reference to parliamentary responsibility on the
part of the Prime Minister.

In practice, Mussolini has undertaken the work
of several ministries in addition to the office of head
of the government. At the present time *Il Duce*
holds six out of thirteen cabinet posts—foreign affairs, interior, corporations, war, marine and aviation. It is expected that the latter three ministries
will soon be combined into a single Ministry of
Defense.[14]

Promulgation of "Decree-Laws" by the Executive

The scope of the Prime Minister's power has been
further broadened by the law of January 31, 1926,
concerning the power of the executive to promulgate
decrees having the force of law.[15] The *Statuto* provides that the legislative power shall be exercised

[12] Alfredo Rocco, *La Trasformazione dello Stato* (Rome, "La
Voce," 1927), pp. 199–202.
[13] *Ibid.,* p. 204.
[14] *Corriere della Sera,* November 7, 1933.
[15] *Gazzetta Ufficiale,* No. 25, February 1, 1926, p. 426.

collectively by the King and the two chambers.[16] The Italian government had frequently invoked this article to adopt legislative measures by means of decree-laws (*decreti-leggi*). This practice became more deeply rooted during the World War and the early years of Fascism. In 1924, when public opinion had been aroused by the Matteotti affair,[17] Mussolini declared that he would no longer resort to such decrees. The law of 1926, however, provides that decrees may be promulgated regarding the execution of the laws, the exercise of the executive power, and the organization of state administration. Decrees having the force of law may also be issued in extraordinary cases where urgent action is required. Such decrees must be published immediately in the the official gazette, and submitted to Parliament without delay; they cease to be in force after two years if they have not meanwhile been adopted by Parliament. The Fascist government defends the law of 1926 on the ground that it regulates and limits a power which otherwise would be subject to abuse. Opponents of Fascism, however, declare that the government has frequently promulgated legislation by decree without giving it publicity, that it has failed to consult Parliament within the prescribed period of time, and that the law of 1926 legalizes a dangerous encroachment of the executive power on the legislature.[18]

Three other legislative measures have served to broaden the scope of the executive power and to consolidate the position of the Fascist government. A law of December 24, 1925, authorized the govern-

[16] Article 2.
[17] *Cf.* p. 73.
[18] *Cf.* Francesco Ferrari, *Le Régime Fasciste Italien* (Paris, Editions Spès, 1928), pp. 114–115.

ment to dismiss civil and military employees who had failed to give a guarantee of their fidelity to duty or had placed themselves in a position incompatible with the general policy of the government.[19] This law, which was first announced as a transitional measure, was prolonged, and extended to local administrative employees, teachers in elementary schools and other grades of public service; its provisions were permanently embodied in a decree of January 3, 1927, regarding the legal status of civil employees. By a law of December 24, 1925, the government was empowered to amend the penal code, to modify the civil code and to reorganize the system of judicial administration.[20] In accordance with this law, the government undertook the re-codification of civil and penal laws, adopted a new penal code in 1931, and in 1926 established the Special Tribunal for the Defense of the State.[21] Finally, a law of December 31, 1925, authorized the government to modify the laws concerning public safety, and to promulgate a single law on the subject.[22] The provisions of this law were given effect by a decree of November 6, 1926, which regulates all questions relating to public safety.[23]

THE GRAND COUNCIL

The consolidation of the Fascist government raised two important issues—the extent to which the Fascist party had become a permanent factor in national life, and the method of assuring its continuance in power. Mussolini's favorite slogan is

[19] *Gazzetta Ufficiale*, No. 2, January 4, 1926, p. 11.
[20] *Ibid.*, No. 301, December 29, 1925, p. 5066.
[21] For discussion of the work of this tribunal, *cf.* p. 94.
[22] *Gazzetta Ufficiale*, No. 4, January 7, 1926, p. 34.
[23] For analysis of the provisions of this decree, *cf.* p. 91.

durare (to last). He recognizes, however, that this aim can be achieved only by means of the "fascistization" of Italy. An attempt to settle both issues simultaneously is made in the law of December 9, 1928, which establishes the Fascist Grand Council as the supreme coördinating organ of the state, and vests it with the power to regulate succession to the government.[24]

Composition of the Council

The Grand Council is charged with the task of coördinating all the activities of the Fascist régime. The head of the government is "by right" president of the Grand Council; he alone can convoke it and determine its procedure. The secretary of the Fascist party serves as secretary of the Grand Council. The membership of the council falls into three categories. The first category is composed of the *quadrumviri* who participated in the March on Rome and who are appointed to the council for an unlimited period of time. The second category includes the presidents of the Senate and Chamber of Deputies; the Ministers of Foreign Affairs, the Interior, Justice, Finance, National Education, Agriculture and Forests, and Corporations; the commander-general of the militia; the secretary and the two vice-secretaries of the Fascist party; the president of the Royal Italian Academy; the president of the Special Tribunal for the Defense of the State; the presidents of the National Fascist Confederations and of the National Confederations of Fascist Syndicates of Industry and Agriculture. Members of this category

[24] *Gazzetta Ufficiale*, No. 287, December 11, 1928, p. 5978; amended by law of December 14, 1929, *ibid.*, No. 292, December 17, 1929.

form part of the Grand Council as long as they hold their respective offices; they are nominated by royal decree on proposal of the head of the government, and may be recalled at any time. Finally, the head of the government may nominate for three years, with the right of reappointment, any persons who have "deserved well of the nation and the cause of the Fascist revolution."

Members of the Grand Council receive no remuneration. No member may be arrested or subjected to police procedure without the authorization of the council. No disciplinary measures may be taken against any member of the council who is at the same time a member of the Fascist party without the approval of the council. The meetings of the council are secret, and are usually held at night. The *communiqués* of the council's proceedings are generally brief, and more concerned with the action adopted than with the discussion which may have preceded it.[25]

Relations of the Council with the State and the Party

The Grand Council is vested with both consultative and advisory functions. It acts as a consultative body in "all cases specified by law." These include the statutes, ordinances and policies of the Fascist party; the nomination and recall of Fascist officials and other members of the party organization; and the selection of candidates for the Chamber of Deputies. The advice of the Grand Council must be sought on all questions of a constitutional

[25] For a record of the early years of the council, *cf.* Partito Nazionale Fascista, *Il Gran Consiglio nei Primi Cinque Anni dell' Era Fascista* (Rome, Libreria del Littorio, 1927), p. 69.

character. These include all bills concerning the following subjects: succession to the throne; the attributes and prerogatives of the Crown; the composition and functions of the Grand Council, the Senate and the Chamber of Deputies; the attributes and prerogatives of the head of the government; the right of the executive to issue decrees having the force of law; the organization of syndicates and corporations; relations with the Holy See; and international agreements involving territorial changes. In addition, the Grand Council acts in an advisory capacity on all political, economic and social questions which the head of the government may submit to it.

The Grand Council, however, is not merely a consultative and advisory body; it is, in a sense, the ultimate source of both executive and legislative power, subject only to the control of the head of the government, and responsible to him alone. On proposal of the head of the government, the Grand Council draws up a list of names which are to be submitted to the Crown in the event of vacancy, and from which the King is to select Mussolini's successor. The Grand Council also prepares the official list of four hundred candidates to the Chamber of Deputies, which is presented to the voters for a plebiscite, and directs the application of the corporative system.

By the law of December 9, 1928 the Grand Council, which was and remains the governing body of the Fascist party, was transformed into a constitutional organ of the state, charged with effecting a synthesis of the country's political, economic and social forces. In a speech to the Senate on November 8, 1928, Mussolini declared that this legalization of the Grand Council would have far-reaching implications. "The National Fascist party has in this manner been incorporated in the state and has become one of its fundamental institutions. . . . Thus is completed the evolution by which the National Fascist party, from a simple private association like the parties of the old régime, has been transformed into a great institution of public law, the fundamental instrument of the régime. . . . Fascism henceforth identifies itself with the nation and with the state. To say Grand Council of Fascism is equivalent to saying Grand Council of the nation and the state." [26] The law was approved by the Chamber of Deputies without discussion. In the Senate, however, it met with considerable opposition. "This bill," said Mussolini, addressing the Senate on November 15, 1928, "has given rise to comprehensible and respectable hesitations, but also to oblique manœuvres and to insulting vociferations." [27] The Senate finally passed the bill by a vote of 181 to 19, with two absentions. [28]

Criticism of the Council

The chief criticism directed against the Grand Council by opponents of Fascism is that it constitutionalizes and perpetuates the rule of a single political party, while materially curtailing the functions of both King and Parliament. Anti-Fascists claim that no reforms of a constitutional character

[26] *Corriere della Sera*, November 9, 1928.
[27] *Ibid.*, November 16, 1928.
[28] The following senators voted against the law: Abbiate, Albertini, Bergamasco, Bergamini, Bollati, Casati, Cornaggia, Croce, Della Torre, Diena, Paterno, Federico Ricci, Ruffini, Stoppato, Valenzami, Vigliani, Volterra, Wollemborg and Zupelli. Senators De Cupis and Nava, who were present, abstained from voting.

can henceforth be initiated by the Chamber of Deputies, and that the Grand Council thus blocks political and economic evolution by peaceful means. Fascist spokesmen assert that the Grand Council does not limit the power of the King, but merely facilitates his selection of a successor to the post of head of the government. In their opinion, the Grand Council does not supplant Parliament, since its functions are largely consultative; its existence simply reaffirms the principle established by the *Statuto,* that the government must enjoy the confidence of the monarch rather than of Parliament. Finally, they believe that the Grand Council fulfills the indispensable function of assuring both unity and continuity in administration.[29]

THE CHAMBER OF DEPUTIES

The Fascist party, as has already been pointed out, rejects the doctrine of popular sovereignty and regards parliamentary institutions as both harmful and obsolete. Nevertheless, Mussolini did not undertake to reform Parliament immediately on his advent to power. In his first speech to the Chamber of Deputies on November 16, 1922, he stated that his appearance there was an act of deference. "I could," he said, "make of this dim gray hall a bivouac of Fascist soldiers. I could close Parliament and constitute an exclusively Fascist government. I could, but do not wish, at least at first, to do this." He warned the Chamber, however, that "it must feel its peculiar position, which makes its dissolution possible within two days or two months." [30] Speaking in

[29] *Cf.* Giovanni Corso, *Lo Stato Fascista* (Rome, Libreria del Littorio, 1929), p. 457.
[30] Mussolini, *Discorsi della Rivoluzione,* cited, p. 104.

the Senate on November 27, 1922, he said: "Who prevents me from closing Parliament? Who prevents me from proclaiming a dictatorship of two, three or five persons . . . ? No one!" He added that he had subordinated egoism to the supreme interests of the country, and had decided to confine the Fascist movement to the limits of the constitution.[31]

The Fascist party, which soon absorbed the Nationalist party, did not at the outset appear intransigeant toward other political groups. The first Fascist cabinet contained two Liberals, two Popularists and two Social-Democrats.[32] Fascist co-operation with these parties, however, was more nominal than real. In 1923 the government broke with the Popular party, and in 1924 with the Social-Democrats. These breaks were the outward sign of a widening rift between the government and the Chamber, which Mussolini described as the last refuge of forces hostile to Fascism.[33] The Chamber was finally dissolved, and new elections were called for April 6, 1924.

The Elections of 1924

These elections were held under the terms of an electoral law by which the country was divided into fifteen large constituencies, in each of which the various parties were to present their respective candidates. The party whose lists secured relatively the largest number of votes was to obtain two-thirds of the 535 seats in the Chamber of Deputies,

---

[31] Gorgolini, *La Rivoluzione Fascista,* cited, p. 111.

[32] The Liberals were Gentile and De Capitani; the Popularists were Tangorra and Cavazzoni; the Social-Democrats were Carnazza and the Duke of Cesarò. Of these Gentile, De Capitani and Carnazza subsequently became Fascists.

[33] Mussolini, *La Nuova Politica,* cited, Vol. II, p. 204.

numbering 356. The remaining 179 seats were to be distributed among other parties on the basis of proportional representation. The chief merit of this system, according to a Fascist writer, was "that the majority was compact and amenable to strict party discipline." [34] The opposition parties were unable to come to an understanding, and each went to the polls with its own list, while Fascist supporters and sympathizers presented a united front. Of the total vote, estimated at over seven and a half million, four and a half million votes were cast for the Fascist party (including the Nationalists), which received 375 seats in the Chamber, and nearly three million for opposition parties, which were assigned 160 seats. [35]

The Matteotti Affair

On May 30, 1924, the Socialist deputy Giacomo Matteotti made a speech in the new Chamber in which he contested the validity of the Fascist majority. He declared that the voters had not been given an opportunity to express their opinion freely, and that the government had prejudged the results of the elections by stating that, whatever the outcome, it would still remain in power. He described and denounced various violations of the electoral law, and closed his speech, which had been con-

[34] Villari, *The Fascist Experiment,* cited, p. 207.

[35] The seats assigned to the Fascist party included those given to so-called "philo-Fascists"—Liberals, Democrats and others who, while not members of the Fascist party, were in sympathy with its policy. The opposition seats were divided as follows: 25 followers of Giolitti and other small independent groups, 40 Popularists, 25 Unitary Socialists, 14 Maximalists, 19 Communists, 8 Republicans and 25 Democrats. For an account of this election from the anti-Fascist point of view, *cf.* Sturzo, *Italy and Fascismo,* cited; Salvemini, *The Fascist Dictatorship in Italy,* cited; Ferrari, *Le Régime Fasciste,* cited, pp. 55–56.

stantly interrupted, by demanding annulment of
of the elections.[36] Commenting on this speech, Mussolini's organ, *Popolo d'Italia,* said on June 1, 1924:
"The honorable Matteotti has made a monstrously
provocative speech which would merit something
more tangible than the epithet 'ruffian' [which had
been applied to him by a Fascist deputy]." Addressing the Chamber of Deputies on June 6, 1924,
Mussolini praised the example of Russia, "where
there are magnificent teachers. . . . We made a
mistake," he declared, "not to imitate them fully,
because at this hour you would no longer be here,
you would be in prison. . . . You would have had
lead in your back. But we have courage, and we
shall prove it to you." [37] On the following day, again
in the Chamber of Deputies, Mussolini declared that
he would make Parliament function, and invited
the opposition to give him "positive or negative
collaboration"; political indifference, he said, would
condemn the opposition to "perpetual exile from
history." [38]

Three days after this speech, on June 10, Matteotti suddenly disappeared. On June 12 Mussolini
attempted to reassure the Chamber of Deputies regarding the fate of Matteotti, and stated that the
police were making every effort to probe the mystery. The disappearance, he said, had taken place
"in circumstances of time and place not yet ascertained but such as to arouse suspicion of a crime
which, if it had been committed, could but arouse
the indignation and emotion of Parliament." The

[36] Italy, *Atti del Parlamento Italiano, Camera dei Deputati,
XXVII Legislatura, Sessione 1924–25, Discussioni* (Rome, Printing Office of the Chamber of Deputies, 1925), Vol. I, p. 57 *et seq.*
[37] *Ibid.,* p. 206.
[38] *Ibid.,* p. 246.

Socialist deputy Gonzales cried: "Then Matteotti is dead!" In the midst of general commotion the Republican deputy Chiesa shouted: "Let the head of the government speak! He is silent! He is an accomplice!" [39] On June 13, when it became apparent that Matteotti had been murdered, Mussolini said in the Chamber of Deputies:

"If there is anyone here who has the right to be grieved and, I may add, exasperated, it is I. Only an enemy of mine, who for many a long night had meditated on some diabolic act against me could have committed this crime which today fills us with horror and draws from us a cry of indignation. The situation . . . is extremely delicate." [40]

On June 24, in the Senate, he quoted Talleyrand, and said of the Matteotti affair: "It is not only a crime but a blunder." Senator Albertini, an opponent of Fascism, made the following statement on that occasion:

"The apparent order which now reigns in Italy is founded not on the restoration of the authority of the Italian state but on the application, by irresponsible powers, of sanctions as humiliating for human dignity as they are terrible in their uncertainty against whoever disapproves too much of what takes place on the periphery or at the centre." [41]

Police investigation revealed that Matteotti had been kidnapped on June 10 by five Fascists, and had subsequently been murdered. The body was not recovered until two months later. The investigation implicated Finzi, Under-Secretary for the Interior,

[39] *Ibid.*, p. 323 *et seq.*

[40] Mussolini, *La Nuova Politica*, cited, Vol. III, pp. 172–173.

[41] Italy, *Atti Parlamentari della Camera dei Senatori, Legislatura XXVII, Discussioni, 1a Sessione 1924* (Rome, Senate Printing Office, 1924), p. 84.

and Cesare Rossi, chief of the Press Department. Fascist writers do not attempt to defend Finzi who, they claim, proved "a broken reed" when Mussolini, burdened by other duties, entrusted him with the bulk of the work in the Ministry of the Interior.[42] Finzi resigned but asked for an official inquiry into his conduct, which was refused. Yielding to public indignation, Mussolini placed Luigi Federzoni, formerly a Nationalist, in charge of the Ministry of the Interior. General De Bono, who had hitherto combined the duties of Director of Public Safety and Commander-General of the militia, was forced to resign the former office; subsequently he was appointed Governor of Tripoli, and is now Minister for the Colonies. Other prominent Fascists were involved in the affair, and it was even rumored that both Finzi and Rossi had implicated Mussolini in their confessions. Following preliminary examination of the case by a parliamentary committee, the five men accused of murdering Matteotti were brought to trial in 1926. The trial was held in the small town of Chieti in the Abruzzes, and Farinacci, Secretary-General of the Fascist party, acted as counsel for the defendants. Two of the defendants were acquitted, and the three others condemned to imprisonment; they were, however, released two months later, under the terms of an amnesty granted in 1925.[43] It is

---

[42] Villari, *The Fascist Experiment,* cited, p. 69.
[43] For details of this trial, *cf.* Salvemini, *The Fascist Dictatorship in Italy,* cited, and Villari, *The Fascist Experiment,* cited. For Matteotti's views on Fascism, *cf.* Matteotti, *The Fascisti Exposed,* cited. In addition to Matteotti, the Fascist government is charged by its opponents with the death of Giovanni Amendola, a Liberal deputy, and Piero Gobetti, a Liberal editor, both of whom died in exile, as a result, it is claimed, of maltreatment at the hands of Fascists.

believed, in Fascist circles, that Matteotti was murdered by extreme Fascists who wished to prevent any possibility of further collaboration between the government and the opposition.

The Opposition Withdraws from Parliament

The Matteotti affair aroused public opinion to an extraordinary pitch. The government was attacked in the Senate, and bitterly denounced by the press. The Italian historian Guglielmo Ferrero described the elections of 1924 as a "strangulation of the country." [44] Mussolini himself, addressing the Grand Council on July 22, 1924, acknowledged that the murder of Matteotti had produced "a profound moral oscillation in the Italian masses." [45] The Opposition parties, as a sign of protest, withdrew from the Chamber of Deputies immediately following the murder of Matteotti, and became known as the *Aventine.*[46] The "elder statesmen"—Giolitti, Orlando and Salandra—who hitherto had sympathized with the Fascist government while maintaining an independent position in Parliament, now joined the ranks of the opposition. It is the opinion of competent observers that at no time in its history was the Fascist government in such grave danger of downfall as in the summer and autumn of 1924.

Mussolini Inaugurates Policy of Intransigeance

The Opposition parties, however, failed to rally the country against Fascism. The government, sup-

[44] Guglielmo Ferrero, *La Democrazia in Italia* (Milan, Edizioni della Rassegna Internazionale, 1925).

[45] Mussolini, *La Nuova Politica*, cited, Vol. III, p. 209.

[46] This name was given the Opposition parties because their secession resembled the withdrawal of the Roman plebs to the Sacred Mount in 494 B.C. as a sign of protest against the exactions of the patricians.

ported by the propertied classes, which desired the maintenance of public order at any cost, and strengthened by sympathizers in the ranks of other parties, known as *fiancheggiatori* (flankers), adopted a policy of repression and intransigeance. On January 3, 1925, in a speech which inaugurated a new era in the history of Fascism, Mussolini denied the existence of a Fascist *Cheka,* and challenged the Chamber of Deputies to impeach him for the murder of Matteotti. He declared that he accepted full responsibility for the Matteotti affair.

"If Fascism has been nothing more than castor oil and cudgels, and not a magnificent passion of the best youth of Italy, the fault is mine. If Fascism has been a criminal association, well, I am its chief, and I am responsible! If all the acts of violence are the result of a certain historical, political and moral atmosphere, the responsibility for this is mine, for this historical, political and moral atmosphere was created by me, by means of propaganda which starts with Italian intervention in the war and comes down to the present day." [47]

Mussolini's watchwords to the Fascists were: "Absolute intransigeance, theoretical and practical," and "All power to all Fascism!" He reaffirmed his conviction that opposition is neither sacred nor untouchable. He denounced the *Aventine* as seditious and unconstitutional. The Opposition parties replied by a manifesto which declared that the *Aventine* was a "resolute and irrepressible protest against the most atrocious crime of the régime."

The government, however, had gained the upper

---

[47] Mussolini, *Discorsi del 1925,* cited, pp. 13–14. Commenting on this speech, Salvemini remarks that Mussolini accepted moral, political and historical, but not penal, responsibility for the Matteotti affair. *Cf.* Salvemini, *The Fascist Dictatorship in Italy,* cited.

hand, and proceeded to strengthen its position in 1925 by a series of legislative measures known as *leggi fascistissime* (most Fascist laws), dealing with the press, secret associations, the civil service and public safety. These measures were adopted with little discussion by the Chamber of Deputies, now composed only of Fascists and Fascist sympathizers. Various acts of violence committed at this time against anti-Fascists were pardoned under the terms of an amnesty granted by the King on the twenty-fifth anniversary of his reign.

Collapse of the Opposition

Meanwhile, the Opposition parties, temporarily united by the Matteotti affair, gradually drifted apart, and after July 1925 the *Aventine* ceased to exist except as a convenient phrase. Continued abstention from parliamentary work robbed the opposition of the last vestiges of power, while the government's legislation concerning the right of association and the press deprived them of all means of action and expression. The government, for its part, had no intention of parleying with the opposition. When members of the Popular party attempted to return to the Chamber of Deputies in January 1926, Mussolini declared that the secessionists would be "tolerated" only if they undertook to accept Fascism unconditionally and to dissociate themselves from anti-Fascist activities at home and abroad.[48] This ultimatum marked the close of parliamentary government in Italy.

The task of examining various problems regarding "the fundamental relations between the state and the forces which it must contain and guarantee" had

[48] Mussolini, *Discorsi del 1926,* cited, pp. 10–11.

been entrusted by the government on January 31, 1925, to a commission of eighteen Senators, deputies and experts, headed by the philosopher Giovanni Gentile, formerly Minister of Education.[49] The Gentile Commission favored modernization of the *Statuto,* and elaborated a reform of the Chamber of Deputies which formed the basis of the law "on political representation of May 17, 1928." [50] This law was passed by the Chamber of Deputies acting, to use Mussolini's phrase, as a constituent assembly.

The Electoral Law of 1928

The law of May 17, 1928 established a single electoral district—the nation. Eight hundred candidates are to be designated by Fascist syndicates, and two hundred by "the legally constituted bodies and by associations, the scope of which is cultural, educational, charitable or propagandist, and which exist owing to the fact that they are of national importance." Candidates are assigned to the various organizations in accordance with the relative weight of the latter in the productive life of the country. The candidates must be men not only of recognized professional ability, but capable as well "of furthering the historical aims of the nation." That none but Fascists may expect to be selected was indicated by Mussolini when he said, in his farewell speech to the old Chamber of Deputies on December 8, 1928: "If the Chamber which is about to conclude its labors today has been, from the point of view of

[49] This commission took the place of a similar body of fifteen men appointed in 1924 by the Fascist party for the same purpose.

[50] *Gazzetta Ufficiale,* No. 118, May 21, 1928, p. 2150. Some of the recommendations of the Gentile commission were not finally embodied in the law of May 17, 1928.

numbers, eighty-five per cent Fascist, the Chamber which will assemble for the first time on Saturday, April 20 of Year VII (1929), will be a one hundred per cent Fascist Chamber." [51]

Preparation of the National List

From the one thousand names presented by the syndicates and other associations, the Grand Council selects a list of four hundred names, which is then submitted to the voters for a "plebiscite." The right to vote is conditioned on active participation in national life, whether as producers or taxpayers. All male Italian citizens who have reached the age of twenty-one (or eighteen, if they are married and have children), may vote if they pay syndicate contributions, or one hundred lire in taxes; if they receive a pension from the state; or if they belong to the clergy. The voters are asked only one question: "Do you approve of the list of deputies designated by the National Grand Council?" and their sole function consists in answering "yes" or "no." In other words, the voters are invited to express their views, not regarding individual candidates, but regarding the program of the government as a whole. In the event the country should reject the list prepared by the Grand Council, lists of deputies shall be drawn up by all the associations, and the voters shall be permitted to make a choice among these lists. All candidates on the list which obtains the greatest number of votes shall then be declared elected and the seats reserved for the minority shall be distributed among the remaining

[51] *Corriere della Sera,* December 9, 1928. The year 1922 is regarded as year I of the Fascist era, and all public documents bear a double date, such as 1929 (A.VII).

lists. This provision, however, is viewed by Fascist spokesmen as of little importance, since rejection of the list prepared by the Grand Council is regarded as impossible.[52] Moreover, Mussolini declared in the Chamber of Deputies on December 8, 1928 that even a vote unfavorable to Fascism would not cause the overthrow of the government. "We are mathematically certain of continuance in power." [53]

The "Plebiscite" of 1929

The new electoral law was first put to the test in the "plebiscite" held on March 24, 1929. The confederations of employees and employers in each branch of national economy were assigned the same number of candidates. This apparent equality resulted actually in considerable inequality between the two groups. Thus the employers' and employees' confederations of industry each presented 80 candidates, although the former consisted of 71,459 and the latter of 1,300,000 members. Similarly, the employers' confederation of agriculture composed of 314,658 members named 96 candidates, the number assigned to the employees' confederation, representing 1,021,461.[54] Critics of this procedure claim further that it fails to give the various economic interests a representation commensurate

[52] "La Elezione dei Deputati," *Corriere della Sera,* February 1, 1929.

[53] *Corriere della Sera,* December 9, 1928. *Cf.* also speech by Achille Starace, vice-secretary of the Fascist party, April 23, 1929: "If the twelve million votes 'yes' should transform themselves into twenty-four million 'noes,' Mussolini would still remain at Palazzo Venezia and the revolution of the Black Shirts would not thereby have suffered any check." *Il Popolo d'Italia,* April 24, 1929, translated by Carmen Haider, *Capital and Labor under Fascism* (New York, Columbia University Press, 1930), p. 257.

[54] The distribution of the eight hundred candidates assigned

with their actual weight in the life of the country. Thus agriculture, which forms the occupation of more than fifty per cent of the population, is accorded less than one-fourth of the total number of candidates.[55]

The list prepared by the Grand Council and published on March 1, 1929, consisted entirely of Fascists selected, according to the official *communiqué*, on the basis of personal qualifications and length of service in the party. Of the 400 candidates, 55 had joined the Fascist organizations in 1919, 54 in 1920, 65 in 1921, 60 in 1922, 59 in 1923, 36 in 1924 and 30 in 1925.[56] The elections were preceded by a week of active propaganda. Deputies and members of the government designated for this purpose by the Grand Council were sent to the more important centres to deliver speeches illustrating the activities of the government in various fields.[57] Individuals and groups opposed to Fascism

to National Confederations of Fascist Syndicates was made as follows:

Agricultural Employers	96	(12%)
" Employees	96	(12%)
Industrial Employers	80	(10%)
" Employees	80	(10%)
Commercial Employers	48	(6%)
" Employees	48	(6%)
Maritime and Air Transportation Employers	40	(5%)
" " " " Employees	40	(5%)
Land Transportation and Inland Navigation Employers	32	(4%)
Land Transportation and Inland Navigation Employees	32	(4%)
Bank Employers	24	(3%)
" Employees	24	(3%)
Professional Men and Artists	160	(20%)
TOTAL	800	

[55] Haider, *Capital and Labor under Fascism*, cited, p. **255**.
[56] *Ibid.*, p. 256.
[57] *Corriere della Sera*, March 14, 1929.

were given no opportunity to advocate their views. The voters were warned by their respective syndicates, and frequently by their employers, that they might be deprived of various privileges, and even of their jobs, if they failed to appear at the polls or cast a negative vote. The president of the National Confederation of Fascist Syndicates of Industry issued a circular stating that "industrial workers must go to the polls perfectly organized, and demonstrate their acceptance of the régime."[58] The Catholic clergy, gratified by the conclusion of the Lateran accord on February 11, 1929,[59] urged their parishioners to vote for the government list.[60] The Federation of Catholic Men advised its members to vote "yes" in a plebiscite "by which the Italian people is called on to express its own thought regarding the government program."[61] Finally, the tenth anniversary of the *Fasci di Combattimento* was celebrated on March 23, the day preceding the elections, and was the occasion for public demonstrations of loyalty to the government.

Fascists Victorious at the Polls

Critics of Fascism assert that the vote was cast under conditions which made the voters' apparent freedom of choice completely illusory. The voting was not secret. The voters were offered the choice of two ballots: one was decorated with the Italian tricolor, which remained visible after the ballot had been folded, and was inscribed: "Do you approve of the list of deputies designated by the national

[58] *Ibid.,* March 23, 1929.
[59] *Cf.* V. M. Dean, "The Lateran Accord," Foreign Policy Association, *Information Service,* Vol. V, No. 9, July 10, 1929.
[60] *Corriere della Sera,* March 9, 1929.
[61] *Ibid.,* March 21, 1929.

Grand Council? Yes." The other was plain, and inscribed with the single word "No." Various subterfuges, it is claimed, were employed to intimidate those voters who attempted to cast a negative ballot.[62] Of the 9,673,049 registered voters, 8,663,412 went to the polls, and 8,519,559 voted "yes," 135,761 voting "no." [63]

The new Chamber of Deputies, whose term expired in March 1934, was solemnly inaugurated by the King on April 20, 1929. On April 9 the Grand Council had declared that the Chamber, "corporative in origin, is political in character and has political functions." The Chamber, according to the Grand Council, has a two-fold task: it is to control all questions pertaining to the administration of the state, especially by means of budgetary discussion; and it is to collaborate in the preparation of bills introduced by the government or by individual deputies.[64] Expulsion or suspension from the Fascist party automatically causes cessation or suspension of the parliamentary mandate. The rules of the Chamber, elaborated by Augusto Turati, then Secretary-General of the Fascist party, state that no questions which are not already on the agenda can be discussed by the Chamber, except on proposal of the head of the government. Furthermore, *a priori* opposition to any proposed legislation is definitely eliminated. In practice, bills are first submitted by the head of the government to the Grand Council,

[62] Haider, *Capital and Labor under Fascism*, cited, pp. 259–260; C. H. Abad, "Fascist Italy's Suppression of Free Thought," *Current History*, January 1931, p. 534.

[63] Official *communiqué, Corriere della Sera*, March 31, 1929. The *communiqué* stated that 8,092 ballots had been nullified or contested.

[64] *Communiqué* of the Press Office of the Fascist party, *Corriere della Sera*, April 9, 1929.

examined by the Council of Ministers, and only then placed before the Chamber of Deputies. The Chamber may at that time "freely discuss the work of the government, not, of course, for the purpose of overthrowing it, but for the purpose of criticism and collaboration." [65]

Senate Opposition to the Electoral Law

The new electoral law met with strong opposition in the Senate. "It means going backward," said Senator Ruffini on May 12, 1928, "to take from the Italian people the right freely to choose their own representatives." [66] Senator Albertini went further and denounced the absolutism of the Fascist government:

"The existence of an elective chamber does not suffice to take the absolute character from a régime, when the country is not allowed openly to fight . . . a régime which defends the captured position by such means as are used by Fascism. . . . The calling of elections has only a relative value when the executive power paralyzes the legislative power and where a situation is created in which but a single opinion is tolerated and regarded as worthy of respect, that of the government, that is, of the head of the government." [67]

A resolution presented by Senator Ruffini and signed by forty-two Senators declared that the electoral law deprived the Italian people of the most essential of its rights, and one guaranteed by the constitution. This resolution was rejected by a vote

[65] Mussolini, speech in the Chamber of Deputies, December 8, 1928, *Corriere della Sera*, December 9, 1928.
[66] Italy, *Atti Parlamentari della Camera dei Senatori, Legislatura XXVII, 1a Sessione 1924–1928, Discussioni* (Rome, Senate Printing Office, 1928), Vol. IX, p. 10244.
[67] *Ibid.*, p. 10246.

of 161 to 46, and the law was finally adopted by the
Senate.

Conflict of Views Regarding the Chamber of Deputies

Opponents of Fascism assert that the Chamber of
Deputies has lost all significance, since it is merely
the creature of the Grand Council, which is, in turn,
a party as well as a government organ, and since any
deputies unfavorable to the régime may be removed
by expulsion from the party. In their opinion, it
would be more logical to abolish the Chamber altogether. The Fascist government has defended the
1928 electoral law on the ground that it eliminates
agitation for personal or local advantages, and that
the Chamber, which represents the "totality of the
country's interests," is more truly "popular" than
one elected by popular suffrage. Mussolini, however,
declared on December 11, 1933 that the Chamber
of Deputies, which had never "pleased" him, is "now
anachronistic in its very name," and it is expected
that it will be replaced in the near future by a body
representing producers grouped in "corporations"
or guilds.[68]

THE SENATE

The Senate, according to the constitution, is composed of princes of the royal house, and an unlimited
number of members nominated by the King from
among twenty-one specified categories.[69] The age

---

[68] Cf. p. 112.

[69] These categories are as follows: (1) Archbishops and
Bishops; (2) President of the Chamber of Deputies; (3) Deputies
having served for six years or in three legislatures; (4) Ministers of State; (5) Ministers Secretaries of State; (6) Ambassa-

and social position of the men appointed to the Senate generally have tended to make this body conservative in character. Despite this fact, the most consistent and determined opposition to the Fascist government has come from a group of some forty liberal Senators. Mussolini has always appealed to the higher wisdom and sense of responsibility of the Senate, emphasizing the danger of public disturbance should Fascism be overthrown. Nevertheless, he has found the liberal Senators arrayed against him on such important measures as the electoral law, the law on the Grand Council and the Lateran accord. This opposition has been materially curtailed by the recent absence from the Senate of outstanding opponents of Fascism such as Senators Luigi Albertini and Benedetto Croce. Various proposals have been made for a reform of the Senate which, without displacing the present members, would transform the Senate into a body based on trade and professional affiliations and elected by corporations. No steps, however, have as yet been taken to effect this reform, and the wisdom of establishing a body which would duplicate the Chamber of Deputies is doubted in some quarters. The opposition encountered by Fascism in the Senate has had little practical effect

dors; (7) Envoys extraordinary having served three years; (8) First presidents and presidents of the Court of Cassation and the Court of Accounts; (9) First presidents of the Courts of Appeals; (10) The Attorney-General and Procurator-General; (11) Presidents of chambers of Courts of Appeals having served three years; (12) Counselors of the Court of Cassation and Court of Accounts; (13) Advocates and officials of public ministries (*fiscali generali*) having served five years; (14) Generals of army and navy; (15) Counselors of State having served five years; (16) Members of provincial councils; (17) Prefects; (18) Members of the Royal Academies; (19) Members of the Supreme Council of Public Instruction; (20) Those who, by their merits or services, have honored the fatherland; (21) Persons who, for three years, have paid three thousand lire in direct taxes.

on legislation. The government is assured of a majority and could, in any case, obtain the necessary number of votes by appointing Fascist sympathizers to the Senate.

LOCAL GOVERNMENT

Centralization of power, which constitutes a basic policy of Fascism, has been applied to local government as well. By a law of April 3, 1926, the powers of the prefect were extended to all state activities within his province, with the exception of justice, war, marine and aëronautics. The prefect is regarded not merely as a civil servant, but as a collaborator of the Fascist government in the province,[70] and is charged with the task of preventing all demonstrations of opposition, especially in the press.[71] In the communes, which were formerly considered the cradle of local autonomy, and where Socialism had been strongly entrenched, the elective *syndic* (mayor) and municipal council have been replaced by a *podestà,* appointed by the government, and a council partly appointed by the prefect and partly elected by syndicates and other organizations. The *podestà* exercises both executive and legislative power, subject to strict control and surveillance on the part of the prefect and the provincial council. The functions of the municipal council are purely consultative.

Fascist spokesmen commend the reforms effected in provincial and municipal government on the ground that local party feuds and maladministration by elective officials have given way to unified, continuous and efficient administration. Opponents

---

[70] Corso, *Lo Stato Fascista,* cited, pp. 432–433.
[71] *Cf.* p. 96.

of Fascism deny that municipal government is either more honest or more efficient than in the past, and deplore the disappearance of autonomous communes which, in their opinion, offered the Italian people an opportunity to acquire experience in self-government.[72]

THE FASCIST STATE AND INDIVIDUAL LIBERTY

It has already been pointed out that Fascism regards individual liberty not as a right, but as a concession on the part of the state; the latter reserves the right to impose what limitations it may see fit whenever the exercise of liberty by individuals or groups appears to threaten public order.[73] In accordance with this conception, the Fascist government has adopted a series of legislative measures dealing with public safety, the right of association, and the press.

The law of January 31, 1926, provides that a citizen who commits abroad an act intended to disturb the public order of Italy, or injurious to Italian interests or prestige, shall lose his citizenship, even if the act in question does not constitute a crime (delitto). Loss of citizenship may be accompanied by sequestration or, in grave cases, confiscation of property.[74] This law was applied in 1926 to seventeen noted Italians then living abroad, including the historian Gaetano Salvemini, the former Fascist deputy Massimo Rocca and the Catholic-Democrat editor Giuseppe Donati.[75] No attempt has been made to apply

[72] Cf. Ferrari, Le Régime Fasciste Italien, cited, p. 299.
[73] Rocco, The Political Doctrine of Fascism, cited; Corso, Lo Stato Fascista, cited, p. 435.
[74] Gazzetta Ufficiale, No. 28, February 4, 1926, p. 462.
[75] Cf. ibid., No. 243, October 19, 1926, p. 4628 et seq., for decrees applying the law in each of these cases.

the law since that time. A law of November 25, 1926, however, punishes by imprisonment of from five to ten years those citizens who spread false rumors abroad concerning the internal situation of Italy, or engage in activities contrary to national interests.[76]

Legislation Regarding Public Safety

The decree of November 6, 1926,[77] which covers all aspects of the question of public safety, provides that every citizen must be in possession of a *carta d'identità*. No person may emigrate without the permission of police authorities, and anyone who attempts to leave the country for political motives without a passport is subject to both fine and imprisonment. Persons accused of crimes against the state, or described as "ill-famed" (*diffamata*),[78] and those regarded as dangerous to public order, may be "admonished" by an administrative commission, from whose verdict there is no appeal. "Admonished" persons must report all their movements to the police. The administrative commission may deport such persons, as well as those who have committed, or have "manifested a serious intention to commit," acts directed against the public order. Deportation for a period of from one to five years may be made to various points in Italy or to the colonies. Political prisoners must perform the tasks assigned to them, and must conduct themselves in a manner such as not "to give grounds for suspicion." [79]

[76] *Ibid.*, No. 281, December 6, 1926, p. 5314, Article 5.
[77] *Gazzetta Ufficiale*, No. 257, November 8, 1926, p. 4822.
[78] This description is also applied to ordinary criminals.
[79] These provisions of the decree of November 6, 1926, apply to ordinary criminals as well.

It is estimated that, by 1927, 1,541 persons had been listed as "ill-famed," 959 had been "admonished" and 698 had been deported, chiefly to the penal colony situated on the Lipari Islands, off the coast of Sicily.[80] The actual number of those affected by the law, however, is not definitely known, and opponents of Fascism claim that the government intentionally maintains uncertainty on this point in order to terrorize the population. On November 6, 1932, between 15,000 and 20,000 prisoners, including some anti-Fascists, were amnestied by the government, and a supplementary decree of November 16 pardoned leading political prisoners and persons in exile for political reasons.

Persons who have spent a term on the islands of Lipari claim that the physical hardships of deportation, considerable in themselves, are greatly increased by the moral ill-effects of imprisonment at the mercy of ignorant and often brutal police officials.[81] Moreover, even when released, the prisoners remain subject to police surveillance, and find it difficult to resume their former occupations. The Fascist government justifies these measures on the ground that they constitute a "prophylactic treatment," necessary to remove diseased elements from the body politic.[82] In presenting the decree on the defense of the state to the Chamber of Deputies, Rocco, Minister of Justice, stated that the enemies of Fascism, defeated on the political field, had sought

[80] Ferrari, *Le Régime Fasciste Italien*, cited, p. 146. These figures were given by Mussolini on May 26, 1927, *Discorsi del 1927*, cited, p. 114.

[81] *Cf.* Francesco F. Nitti, *Escape* (New York, Putnam, 1930); Emilio Lussu, "Flight from Lipari," *Atlantic Monthly*, July 1930, p. 31.

[82] Mussolini, speech in Chamber of Deputies, May 26, 1927, *Discorsi del 1927*, cited, p. 118.

refuge in the sphere of crime, and must be fought in that sphere on their own terms.

The Law on Secret Associations

According to Fascist theory, no groups or organizations, whether political or economic, can exist outside the framework of the state. The law of November 26, 1925,[83] directed primarily against Freemasonry, therefore provides that all associations in Italy and the colonies must communicate to the police their charters, statutes and internal regulations, the list of their members and activities, and any other information which may be requested by the authorities in the interest of order and security. An association which fails to submit such a declaration, or which furnishes false or incomplete data, may be dissolved by the prefect. Civil and military employees are required to declare whether they have ever belonged in the past to associations of any kind. Judges, administrative officials, university professors, teachers in secondary schools and persons employed in the ministries of Foreign Affairs, the Interior and the Colonies cannot become members of professional organizations.[84] Students may not organize associations for the protection of their interests.[85] Finally, the reconstitution of parties or associations dissolved by the government is punishable by imprisonment of from three to ten years. Membership in such associations, and propaganda of their doctrines by any means whatsoever, is punishable as a crime.

The essential features of the law of November 26,

[83] *Gazzetta Ufficiale*, No. 277, November 28, 1925, p. 4714.
[84] Law of April 3, 1926.
[85] Law of July 1, 1926.

1925 on secret associations are reproduced in the penal code adopted by the Fascist government in 1931, which provides various terms of imprisonment for those who form associations prohibited by the government, or attempt to spread their doctrines. In addition, those who form an association "having an international character" without the authorization of the government, or join similar associations abroad, are punishable by a fine or six months' imprisonment.

The law of November 26, 1925 was sharply attacked in the Senate by a minority which claimed that it constituted a violation of the fundamental rights of the Italian people. Several Senators, who approved of the law in general, objected to the provision making it obligatory for civil employees to declare whether they had previously participated in secret societies. This provision, as a matter of fact, was allowed to remain in abeyance after it was discovered that its strict enforcement would implicate a number of Fascists.

THE SPECIAL TRIBUNAL FOR THE DEFENSE
OF THE STATE

By the law of November 25, 1926,[86] certain political crimes, notably the reconstitution of parties and associations dissolved by the government, were removed from the jurisdiction of ordinary courts and submitted to the newly created Special Tribunal for the Defense of the State.[87] This tribunal is composed of a president chosen from among officers of the army, navy, air-force or militia, and five judges

[86] *Gazzetta Ufficiale,* No. 281, December 6, 1926, p. 5314.
[87] This law was supplemented by a decree of December 12, 1926.

selected from officers holding the rank of consul (colonel) in the militia. During the preliminaries of the trial, the president may forbid the inspection of documents, cognizance of which "may be detrimental to the public interest." The president, at the request of the public prosecutor, or if he thinks it necessary "in the public interest," may exclude non-military counsel. At the trial in October 1930 of a group of Slovenes accused of throwing a bomb on the premises of a Fascist newspaper in Trieste, counsel for the defense, who was appointed by the president of the court, declared that his clients "were in a terrible position, and that a death sentence would be the proper thing."[88] At the trial of the group known as *Alleanza Nazionale*[89] on December 22, 1930, the president of the Special Tribunal interrupted the proceedings to denounce the defendants as "liars" and "worms" unworthy of mercy. Foreign correspondents are usually excluded from these trials, while Italian newspapers publish only *communiqués* issued by the government. No appeal can be taken from the verdict of the Special Tribunal, although the sentence may be reviewed if fresh evidence showing the innocence of the condemned has been collected in the meantime. The King, moreover, may exercise his prerogative of reprieve if the commander of the prison consents to forward the petition of the condemned. In the case of the Trieste Slovenes, the commander failed to do this, and the men were executed twenty-four hours following the close of the trial.

The Special Tribunal for the Defense of the State is unreservedly condemned by opponents of Fascism

[88] *Corriere della Sera,* September 6, 1930.
[89] *Cf.* p. 121.

as an organ of party, as contrasted with state, justice.[90] Fascist spokesmen, for their part, defend the
tribunal as an institution essential for the preservation of public order; they claim that "the rapidity
and rigor" of its procedure "give the most certain
guarantee of the equity and, at the same time, rigor
of the decisions." [91]

THE FASCIST GOVERNMENT AND THE PRESS

The sole function of the press in the Fascist state
is that of collaboration with the government. After
the March on Rome the Italian press, which had always served as the principal source of information
on political subjects, was outspokenly critical of
Fascism, and exercised considerable influence, especially in the industrial centres of the North. The
"fourth estate" was denounced by Fascist spokesmen on the ground that it made irresponsible use
of its undisputed powers. The Fascist press, however, lacked journalistic talent, and could not
compete with liberal and socialist organs for the attention of the public.[92] Following the murder of Matteotti, the anti-Fascist press became virulent in its
attacks on the government, and various restrictions
were gradually imposed on it, culminating in the law
of December 31, 1925, which brought the press under
government control.[93] This law, supplemented by the
regulations of March 4, 1926 and the decree of February 28, 1928, provides that a responsible director,
approved by the government, must be in charge of
all periodical publications. Only journalists whose
names appear on a special register kept by regional

[90] Ferrari, *Le Régime Fasciste Italien,* cited, p. **130.**
[91] *Ibid.,* p. 131.
[92] Villari, *The Fascist Experiment,* cited, p. **210.**
[93] *Gazzetta Ufficiale,* No. 3, January 5, 1926, p. **22.**

Fascist syndicates of journalists may contribute to newspapers or periodicals, and no persons who have engaged in "public activity contrary to the interest of the nation" can be so listed. Properly registered publications are thereafter subject to supervision by the prefect, who may sequestrate them at any time. After a certain number of sequestrations, the prefect may issue a "warning" (*diffida*), and two such "warnings" may be followed by suspension or even suppression of the offending newspaper. The law provides that an appeal from the decision of the prefect may be taken to the Ministry of Justice. Measures adopted against opposition newspapers, however, have generally not been followed by court proceedings.

The rigorous application of the press laws dealt a sharp blow to the circulation and, consequently, the finances of independent newspapers, which have been forced or persuaded, one by one, to sell out to Fascist interests. *Il Corriere della Sera* (Milan), formerly directed by Senator Albertini, retains the largest circulation, and is distinguished by the literary quality of its contributions. *Il Popolo d'Italia* (Milan), founded by Mussolini in 1914 as a Socialist organ, is now directed by his nephew, Vito Mussolini, and may be regarded as a mouthpiece of the government. For the most part Fascist editorials are simply variations on the theme of the day, as expressed by Mussolini. Intolerance of all but official opinion has reduced the Italian press to a uniform level of monotony. In view of the strict censorship, greater credence is often given by the population to rumor and gossip than to published news. Foreign correspondents are also subject to censorship. All cables and radio messages pass through the

Ministry of the Interior, and while messages may not always be deleted, their transmission is considerably delayed.[94]

THE FASCIST MILITIA

The maintenance of public order is entrusted by the Fascist government to the Voluntary Militia for National Security (*Milizia Voluntaria per la Sicurezza Nazionale*), organized on January 14, 1923. The militia was originally composed of the squads of Black Shirts which participated in the March on Rome, and one of the *quadrumvirs,* General De Bono, was appointed Commander-General.[95] It was expected that these irregular troops would be disbanded by the Fascist government once it had come to power. Mussolini, however. claimed that the disbandment of the Black Shirts would not only constitute an act of ingratitude to his followers, but might lead to violence and disorder, especially in regions remote from the capital. He decided, therefore, to regularize the status of the Black Shirts by creating the militia.

The "voluntary militia," which now numbers over 300,000 men, constitutes a part of the armed forces of the state, and is directly under the orders of the head of the government, who acts as its Commander-

[94] *Cf.* Ralph W. Barnes, special article on conditions in Italy, *New York Herald Tribune,* March 5, 1931; Herbert L. Matthews. *New York Times,* March 12, 1933.

[95] Estimates of the number of men enrolled in Fascist squads in October 1922 vary considerably. Villari estimates the total number at 300,000 (Villari, *The Fascist Experiment,* cited, p. 163). Mussolini has stated that 52,000 actually participated in the March on Rome, and entered the city. Salvemini questions the latter figure, and asserts that there were only 8,000 Black Shirts in Rome on October 28, 1922. Fascist supporters adopted the · uniform worn by the *Arditi* (shock troops) toward the close of the war, which included a black shirt.

General. Following the excitement created by the Matteotti affair, it was decreed on August 4, 1924, that the militia should take an oath of loyalty to the King, and this was done on the second anniversary of the March on Rome, October 28, 1924. At first no restrictions were placed on the political affiliations of members of the militia. In October 1930, however, the Grand Council adopted a regulation which provided that all members of the militia must be enrolled in the Fascist party.[96] Service in the militia is voluntary; with the exception of the permanent general staff, the officers and men are paid only for days of actual service, and are not required to live in barracks. In case of mobilization, the members of the militia are to be incorporated in units of the armed forces. The organization of the militia is modeled on that of the Roman legions, and consists of legions, cohorts, centuries and maniples.

Functions of the Militia

The object of the militia, as set forth by the Grand Council on January 14, 1923, is "to safeguard the inevitable and inexorable development of the October [1922] revolution." Its duties are those of a political police. The militia is charged with the task of preventing "every disturbance of public order, every gesture or attempt at sedition against the Fascist government," thereby assuring "constant normalcy in the productive and social life of the na-

---

[96] *Corriere della Sera,* October 21, 1930. The regular (conscript) Italian army numbers 491,398 men. The militia is responsible for preparatory military training in accordance with the rules and regulations issued by the Ministry of War under the supervision of the latter and of the territorial military authorities.

tion." [97] Ordinary police activities and the repression of common delinquency are left to the police. The militia is assigned to railways, ports, postal and telegraph offices, and to duty in the colonies, notably in Libya. The cost of the militia, estimated at 40,000,-000 lire in 1929, is defrayed by the Ministry of the Interior. This sum, however, does not include the money expended on the militia of railways and ports, which is charged to the budget of the Ministry of Communications, nor the cost of the Libyan militia, borne by the Ministry for the Colonies.

Opponents of Fascism denounce the militia as a partisan body, designed to enforce Fascist rule by force, and demand either its abolition or its absorption into the regular army. The Fascist government, however, regards the militia as an instrument indispensable to the maintenance of public order.

In addition to the militia, the Fascist government has established a secret police, known as the O.V.R.A. (*Organizzazione Vigilanza Reati Antifascisti*),[98] directly under the orders of the Ministry of the Interior, which is headed by Mussolini. The activities of this police became known to the public for the first time in an official *communiqué* of December 4, 1930, which stated that the O.V.R.A. had disclosed the existence of three anti-Fascist organizations which had for some time been conducting criminal activities against the régime.[99]

[97] Partito Nazionale Fascista, *Il Gran Consiglio nei Primi Cinqui Anni dell' Era Fascista*, cited, p. 69.
[98] Organization for Surveillance of Anti-Fascist Crimes.
[99] *Corriere della Sera*, December 5, 1930. For the activities and trials of members of these organizations, *cf.* section on opposition to Fascism, p. 121.

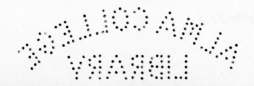

CHAPTER IV

THE CORPORATIVE SYSTEM

THE development of industry in Northern Italy in the first decade of the present century was accompanied by the emergence of a new social class, the industrial proletariat. The Italian workers, employed chiefly in small-scale industries, were for the most part poorly paid and inadequately organized. The Socialist party, which had at first drawn its strength from the small bourgeoisie and the intellectuals, attempted to improve the economic condition of the proletariat by organizing the workers in Socialist labor unions, the most important of which was the General Confederation of Labor. A similar attempt to solve the social and economic problems of industrialization was made by the Catholic labor unions. Meanwhile the syndicalist movement, which had originated in France, and had been elaborated into a philosophic system by Georges Sorel, made considerable headway in Italy. Syndicalism conceives of society as a decentralized union of federated and self-governing industries, the basic unit of which is the syndicate, an organization of producers free to manage its own affairs. The syndicalists oppose existing forms of government which, they claim, merely serve to perpetuate social injustice, and advocate their overthrow by means of the general strike.[1]

[1] Georges Sorel, *Réflexions sur la Violence,* 5th ed. (Paris Rivière, 1921). Sorel himself regarded the general strike as a convenient "myth," not as a practical solution. *Ibid.,* p. 177 *et seq.*

The outcome of the World War and the establishment of the Soviet government strengthened the syndicalist elements in the Socialist party, which demanded the organization of a general strike and the overthrow of the government. It is estimated that in 1920 there were 1,881 industrial strikes, in which 1,267,953 workers were engaged, and 189 agricultural strikes, involving 1,045,732 workers. In 1921 the number of industrial strikes had been reduced to 1,045, and that of agricultural strikes to 522. A further improvement took place in 1922, when 89 industrial strikes, supported by 79,298 workers, and 23 agricultural strikes, involving 25,146 workers, took place.[2] In 1920, when the metallurgical industrialists in Lombardy and Piedmont refused to raise wages and threatened a lockout, the workers first planned to declare a general strike, and then proceeded to occupy the factories. The government, adhering to the liberal policy of *laissez faire,* made no attempt to interfere in these conflicts between workers and industrialists, which served to dislocate the economic life of the country, already greatly impaired by the war.[3]

EARLY HISTORY OF FASCIST SYNDICATES

The program of the Fascist party, adopted in 1922, provided for the establishment of "corporations," [4] which were intended to be an expression of national solidarity as well as a means of developing production. The Fascist congress, held at Bologna on

---

[2] Haider, *Capitalism and Labor under Fascism,* cited, p. 25.

[3] Bonomi, *Dal Socialismo al Fascismo,* cited; Salvemini, *The Fascist Dictatorship in Italy,* cited; Sturzo, *Italy and Fascismo,* cited.

[4] Until 1925 the Fascists used the expression "corporation" to describe a national federation of syndicates.

January 24, 1922, created "national corporations,"
which were defined as "national organizations consisting of combinations of the various provincial
syndicates interested in the same kind of labor and
industry." The supreme organ of this system, the
National Confederation of Syndicate Corporations,
declared that the nation, "considered as a supreme
synthesis of all material and spiritual values of the
race," stands "above individuals, groups and classes,"
and repudiated the idea of the class struggle. It has
been claimed that at that time Fascism favored syndicalism not as a means of improving the economic
position of the workers, but as a method of organizing the labor elements within its own ranks.[5]

On his advent to power, Mussolini declared that
the Fascist government would undertake the "guard-
ianship" of all economic interests of the nation,
would tolerate no conflicts between workers and employers resulting in an interruption of the country's productive life, and would not favor one group
at the expense of the other.[6] The Fascist state, he
said, rejected the *laissez faire* policy of the "ag-
nostic" liberal state, and would henceforth interfere
whenever economic conflicts threatened to impair
national interests.

The Fascist syndicates did not at first attract industrial workers, the majority of whom remained
affiliated with Socialist and Catholic labor unions.
The government, having failed to reach an understanding with the General Confederation of Labor,
proceeded to adopt a series of measures directed at
the elimination of all but Fascist syndicates. The

---

[5] Haider, *Capitalism and Labor under Fascism,* cited, p. 57.
[6] Mussolini, speech in the Chamber of Deputies, November 16,
1922. *Cf. Discorsi della Rivoluzione,* cited, pp. 101–102.

Gentile Commission of Fifteen, appointed in 1925 to study the question of constitutional reform, was unanimously in favor of the legal recognition of syndicates; it declared, however, that the state could not recognize syndicates which, for their part, failed to recognize the state, followed aims contrary to the interests of the nation, or were affiliated with international labor organizations. The latter provision, while permitting the existence of Catholic labor organizations, excluded the possibility of granting recognition to Socialist labor unions. In December 1925 the National Confederation of Fascist Syndicates[7] demanded that Fascist syndicates be recognized as the sole representatives of the workers. At the invitation of Mussolini, a meeting of Fascist workers' organizations and representatives of employers was held at the Palazzo Vidoni on October 25, 1925, when a pact was concluded whereby the employers recognized Fascist syndicates as the workers' sole representatives. The "Pact of Palazzo Vidoni" was denounced by the General Confederation of Labor on the ground that it was contrary to the interests of the workers. It became law, nevertheless, on November 25, 1925, when the employers recognized that Fascist labor organizations had the exclusive right to represent the workers.[8] The Fascist organization of syndicates was finally established by the law of April 3, 1926, supplemented by a decree of July 1, 1926, while the relations of workers and employers with each other and with the state were defined by the Charter of Labor, promulgated on April 21, 1927.

[7] It had replaced the earlier General Confederation of Fascist Syndicates.

[8] For a detailed study of this period, *cf.* Haider, *Capitalism and Labor under Fascism,* cited.

THE CHARTER OF LABOR

The Charter of Labor [9] has been described as the constitution of a new, corporate Italian society.[10] It declares that the nation is an organism having ends, life and means superior to those of the separate individuals or groups which compose it. The nation is a moral, political and economic unity integrally realized in the Fascist state. Labor in all forms, intellectual, technical and manual, is regarded as a social duty and, as such, is to be safeguarded by the state. The process of production is unitary from the national point of view, and its aims are summed up in the welfare of the producers and the growth of the national power.

Professional or syndical organization is free; only those syndicates, however, which are recognized and controlled by the state have the right to represent the category of workers or employers for which they are established. The conflict of interests between workers and employers is recognized, but must be subordinated to the higher interests of production, and regulated by means of collective labor contracts.

The Charter of Labor regards private initiative in the field of production as the most effective and useful instrument for the achievement of national ends. Private organization or production, however, is a national function, and organizers of various enterprises are therefore responsible to the state. The latter intervenes in production only when private

[9] *Gazzetta Ufficiale,* No. 100, April 30, 1927, p. 1794.
[10] *L'Organisation Syndicale et Corporative Italienne,* cited, p. 25. For interpretations of the Charter of Labor, *cf.* Augusto Turati and Giuseppe Bottai, *La Carta del Lavoro* (Rome, Il Diritto del Lavoro, 1929); Giuseppe Bottai, *Esperienza Corporativa* (Rome, Il Diritto del Lavoro, 1929).

initiative is lacking or insufficient, or when its political interests are at stake. Such intervention may assume the form of control, encouragement or direct management.

In addition to this general declaration, the Charter of Labor sets forth the broad principles which are to govern the conclusion of collective labor contracts, the establishment of employment agencies, and various measures for the education and insurance of the workers.

FASCIST SYNDICATES

The basic unit of the Fascist corporate system is the syndicate. The state recognizes only one syndicate for each territorial unit (commune, province, region) and in each professional category of workers or employers. Syndicates of employers and workers must always be separate; mixed syndicates are not accorded recognition. A syndicate is recognized when it contains ten per cent of the workers engaged in a given kind of work or, in the case of employers, when its members give work to at least ten per cent of the workers engaged in that industry; when, in addition to economic activities, it undertakes the assistance, instruction, moral and political education of its members; and when its directors give a guarantee of ability, morality and strong patriotic convictions. The percentage of membership was set at a relatively low figure on the ground that Italian labor is as yet inadequately organized, especially in the agrarian South, and that the adoption of a higher figure would have hampered the establishment of syndicates for certain categories of workers.[11] Membership in syndicates is open to all citi-

[11] *L'Organisation Syndicale et Corporative*, cited, p. 53.

zens who have reached the age of eighteen, and have always given evidence of "good moral and political conduct from the national point of view." [12]

Recognition of a professional association is effected by royal decree, on proposal of the competent minister; the same decree approves the statutes of the association, which must be published at its expense in the *Gazzetta Ufficiale del Regno d'Italia*. Recognition is refused whenever it appears inopportune for reasons of a political, economic or social nature.[13] Under no circumstances can recognition be accorded to associations in any way connected with international organizations.

Functions of the Fascist Syndicates

The recognized syndicate has legal personality, and represents all persons in the category for which it is established, whether members or not. It has the right to conclude collective labor contracts, to charge syndical dues, to discipline its own members, and to appear before labor courts on their behalf. Only regularly enrolled members, however, may participate in the activities of the syndicate.

In addition to the recognized legal syndicates, the law permits the organization of *de facto* associations by various professions; these associations, however, enjoy none of the rights or privileges conferred on recognized syndicates. Associations of civil employees are subject to special regulation, and are directly controlled by the Fascist party.[14]

[12] Law of April 3, 1926, Regarding the Legal Regulation of Collective Relations of Labor, *Gazzetta Ufficiale*, No. 87, April 14, 1926, p. 1590; decree of July 1, 1926, *ibid.*, No. 155, July 7, 1926, p. 2930, Article 1.

[13] Decree of July 1, 1926, Article 13.

[14]*Foglio d'Ordini*, December 1, 1930; *Corriere della Sera*, January 26, 1931.

The organization of professional associations by members of the armed forces, magistrates, university professors, teachers in secondary schools, employees and agents of the Ministries of the Interior, Foreign Affairs and the Colonies, and students, is strictly prohibited.

The syndicates, following recognition, are subject to the control of the prefect, if their activities are restricted to the boundaries of one province, or to that of the Ministry of Corporations, if they cover two or more provinces. Ten per cent of the dues charged by each syndicate is set aside as its contribution to the expenses of the Ministry of Corporations.

The National Confederations of Fascist Syndicates

The various syndicates in each category may be grouped into provincial and regional federations and into national confederations. Until 1934 there were six confederations respectively for employers and workers in the following fields of production: industry, agriculture, maritime and aërial transportation, land transportation and inland navigation, commerce, and banking.[15] In addition to these twelve confederations, provision is made for a national confederation of professional men and artists. The following table shows the number of persons enrolled in and represented by the National Confederations of Fascist Syndicates in 1932.[16]

The law envisaged the eventual establishment of corporations (*corporazioni*), which were to serve as

[15] Royal decree of July 1, 1926, regarding the application of the law of April 3, 1926, Article 41.

[16] *Italy America Society Bulletin* (New York), October 1932, p. 146. These figures, as of June 30, 1932, are the most recent available.

MEMBERSHIP IN FASCIST SYNDICATES [17]

	EMPLOYERS		WORKERS	
	Enrolled	Rep-resented	Enrolled	Rep-resented
National Fascist Con-federation of Italian Industry	66,678*	......**	1,042,796	2,208,550
National Fascist Con-federation of Agri-culture	466,852	2,700,000	870,337	2,815,788
National Fascist Con-federation of Com-merce	380,026	767,610	220,457	811,555
National Fascist Con-federation of Land Transportation and Inland Navigation ..	10,621	27,734	140,414	303,352
National Fascist Con-federation of Banking	3,479	7,588	30,543	50,480
National Fascist Con-federation of Air and Maritime Transporta-tion	1,210	2,440	34,437	124,563
National Fascist Con-federation of Profes-sional Men and Art-ists	103,121	550,000	70,119	120,122
TOTAL	1,031,987	4,055,372	2,409,103	6,434,410

* Firms.
** Whole class of employers.

liaison organs between the employers' and workers' organizations in each professional category.[18] No steps toward the creation of these corporations, however, were taken until July 1, 1933, when Mussolini announced his intention to proceed with their organization. Each corporation will be composed of representatives of employers, workers and technicians in its field of production, will include members

[17] *Ibid.*
[18] Law of April 3, 1926, Article 11; decree of July 1, 1926, Article 94. The Italian term "corporation" can best be translated into English as "guild."

of the Fascist party representing the consumers and will be headed by a Cabinet Minister or an Under-Secretary. The corporations will have three principal functions: they will act as advisory bodies to the government, will conciliate disputes between capital and labor, and will regulate wages and production costs within their respective "categories," as well as relations between the several categories. On May 9, 1934 Premier Mussolini announced the formation of twenty-two corporations grouped according to three main divisions of production—agriculture, industry, and activities productive of services, such as savings, credit, professions and transportation. Syndicate organization was at the same time simplified, the existing thirteen national confederations being reduced to nine. The establishment of corporations, according to Mussolini, does not constitute state socialism. The Fascist state does not intend to monopolize production. "A guild," he said, "is a category in production which controls itself, taking into account general interests, which are already safeguarded through the intervention of the state." [19]

The National Council of Corporations

The corporations, when formed, will be represented on the National Council of Corporations, established in 1930.[20] This council, convoked by the head of the government, who acts as its president, is composed of representatives of syndical and other organizations, as well as members of the cabinet and secretaries of the Fascist party. It is a co-ordinating and consultative body, charged with the task of achieving unity in national production, and

[19] Benito Mussolini, *New York American,* November 4, 1933.
[20] *Cf. Gazzetta Ufficiale,* No. 74, March 28, 1930.

ranks with the Grand Council and the Chamber
of Deputies as a supreme organ of the state.[21] The
council is divided into seven sections, corresponding
to the seven fields of production covered by the national confederations of syndicates (industry, agriculture, commerce, banking, maritime and aërial
transportation, land transportation and inland navigation, liberal professions and arts). By a decree of
February 4, 1931, the functions which will eventually
be entrusted to these corporations were vested in
the seven sections of the National Council of Corporations. The function of conciliation in labor disputes, however, was to be exercised, as in the past,
by the Ministry of Corporations[22] which actually
regulates and coördinates the work of the syndicates
and supervises the development of national production. The expenditures of this ministry are partly
included in the state budget, and partly paid from a
special fund constituted by the contributions of
syndicates.[23]

The Corporative System

On November 13, 1933 Mussolini took an important step toward the realization of the Fascist
concept of a "corporative" state when he introduced
a resolution in the National Council of Corporations
providing for the establishment of "corporations of
category" to be headed by the Council. This Council, which may be regarded as Italy's economic par-

[21] Cf. "Il Consiglio delle Corporazioni," *Corriere della Sera,*
September 25, 1929; Report of Giuseppe Bottai, Minister of
Corporations, regarding the law on the National Council of Cor-
porations. *Ibid.,* November 23, 1929.

[22] *Corriere della Sera,* February 5, 1931.

[23] Haider, *Capital and Labor under Fascism,* cited, p. 147.
The Ministry of Corporations publishes a bulletin, *Bolletino
Ufficiale,* and a monthly review, *Il Diritto del Lavoro.*

liament, will be charged with broad authority, including legislative powers to be taken over from the Chamber of Deputies. The Fascist Grand Council will be entrusted with all decisions as to future developments of a political and constitutional nature which may arise from the practical operation of the corporative system.[24]

The new law, which gives Mussolini, as President of the National Council of Corporations, full and direct control of the corporative system, was approved by the Grand Council on December 10, 1933 by an overwhelming majority in the Senate on January 13, 1934, and by the Chamber of Deputies on January 18.

On November 14 Mussolini amplified his plans regarding the rôle of the National Council of Corporations in the Fascist state when he declared that the Council must supplant the Chamber of Deputies. The new Chamber, to be elected in March 1934, will be called on to "decide its own destiny"—a statement which has been interpreted to mean that the Chamber will be invited to vote itself out of existence. When the Grand Council was created, said Mussolini, "we buried political liberalism. . . . Today we bury economic liberalism." [25]

Many observers believe that, once the corporations of category, which are to link the syndicates to the National Council of Corporations, have been established, Italy will have the framework for a planned economy and that the Council of Corporations will be in a position to guide and control all economic activities in the state. Legislative powers

[24] *Corriere della Sera*, November 14, 1933; Joseph B. Phillips, *New York Herald Tribune*, November 14, 1933.

[25] *Corriere della Sera*, *New York Times* and *New York Herald Tribune*, November 15, 1933.

will then be taken out of the hands of the Chamber of Deputies, which still represents political and mainly local interests, and entrusted to the National Council of Corporations, representing the productive forces of the nation.

THE END OF PRIVATE INITIATIVE?

While the establishment of the corporative system definitely means the end of *laissez faire,* which in Fascist opinion is inseparably associated with decadent capitalism and outworn democracy, the Fascist government denies that it will mark the end of private initiative. The corporations, it is admitted, will function as state organs. The state itself, however, will intervene in economic activities only when the corporations have failed to harmonize conflicting economic interests, and will then act as the representative of the great unorganized mass of consumers—the collectivity of citizens. According to Mussolini, the corporations will function "under the ægis of the state" for "the development of the wealth, political power and welfare of the Italian people.[26]

That the government will not hesitate to intervene whenever it considers it necessary is indicated by the work of the Industrial Reconstruction Institute. This government organization, established in January 1933, is designed to reorganize Italian industries which were overcapitalized in the boom period or are otherwise unsound. It will not only provide for the liquidation of uneconomical concerns by furnishing state aid to their creditors, but

---

[26] Mussolini's speech before the National Council of Corporations, *Corriere della Sera,* November 14, 1933; "Italy Puts a Curb on Individualism," *New York Times,* December 10, 1933.

will finance and improve sound undertakings by issuing long-term loans. Probably the most important task accomplished by the Institute during the first year of its existence was the reorganization of the Piedmont Hydroelectric Company, one of the largest electrical concerns in Italy. The company's capital was reduced from $67,760,000 to $27,120,000, the company itself was split into three separate concerns, and the government guaranteed the principal and a fixed interest on a bond issue floated to finance one of the three companies. Government guarantee of bonds issued by private companies was authorized by a decree of November 9, 1933. According to many observers this measure, as applied in the case of the Piedmont Hydroelectric Company, will eventually give the government control not only of industry, but also of all sources of industrial investment.[27] Another government organization, *Istituto Mobiliare,* has been charged with the task of aiding the banks to unload their industrial securities and thaw out their frozen assets. Some Fascists would go further, and advocate substitution of state control for private initiative in industry and banking.

COLLECTIVE LABOR CONTRACTS

The effect of the corporative system on relations between capital and labor also raises a number of questions. Each corporation, when established, will be expected to make a study of the manufacturing cost of its product. It will then set a "fair price," which must assure a margin of profit for the employer and proper remuneration for the worker without overcharging the consumer. By its par-

[27] *New York Herald Tribune,* November 10, 1933.

ticipation in the work of each corporation, the government will exercise a predominant influence in the regulation of prices, profits and wages.

At the present time relations between capital and labor are regulated by collective labor contracts. The recognized syndicate alone has the right to conclude such contracts, which are applicable to all persons in the category it represents, whether members or not. These contracts are binding in all cases, except when the terms of a contract made by an individual worker with his employer are more favorable than those of a collective contract. The Charter of Labor provides that each collective contract must cover the subjects of labor discipline, period of probation, scale and payment of wages, hours of work, vacations, and conditions of dismissal.[28] No minimum wage is established by the Charter of Labor, which declares that wages in all cases must be determined by collective contracts. The government undertakes to collect and publish statistical data on conditions of work and production, the situation of the financial market and variations in the standard of living of the workers, which may serve as a criterion for the determination of wages.

Collective contracts must be made in writing, approved by the Ministry of Corporations and published. Workers and employers are legally responsible for the fulfillment of the contracts, and may be punished by a fine in case of violation. The respective syndicates likewise are responsible when they have guaranteed the execution of a contract, or have failed to do everything in their power to insure its application.[29] It is estimated at present that

[28] Articles XI–XXI.
[29] Law of April 3, 1926, and decree of July 1, 1926.

some 150 national and inter-provincial contracts have been concluded for such categories as commercial employees, metallurgical workers, chemists, journalists, dramatic and lyric artists, cement workers, bank employees, workers in automobile factories, and others. In addition, over 3,000 contracts of narrower territorial application have been concluded since 1926.[30] The largest number of contracts have been made in industry, which is more highly organized than other branches of production, notably agriculture.[31]

Fascism, as has already been pointed out, repudiates the idea of the class struggle. Measures of class self-defense, such as strikes and lockouts, are therefore strictly prohibited, and are subject to punishment by heavy fines. Should strikes and lockouts involve recourse to force, the participants may be condemned to imprisonment. Organizers of strikes and lockouts are in all cases subject to imprisonment for a period of from one to two years. Suspension of public services is regarded as a crime against the state. In addition to telephone, telegraph, railways, gas, water and other necessities of modern life, public services are made to include the work of physicians, lawyers, engineers, architects, land surveyors and agricultural experts.[32]

LABOR COURTS

Workers and employers are obliged to resort to the procedure of conciliation or to the courts for the settlement of their conflicts. The Ministry of Corporations must always attempt to effect a reconciliation between opposing groups of workers and

[30] *L'Organisation Syndicale et Corporative Italienne,* cited, p. 108.
[31] Bottai, *Esperienza Corporativa,* cited, p. 210.
[32] Decree of July 1, 1926, Article 98.

employers. Only when this procedure has failed can the dispute be submitted to a special section of one of Italy's sixteen courts of appeals, acting as a labor court. This section is composed of three magistrates and two citizens acquainted with the technical aspects of labor and production.

The labor courts have jurisdiction over all collective, as distinguished from individual, conflicts between workers and employers. They are empowered to apply the rules of collective contracts and, in the absence of such contracts, to establish norms for the regulation of labor conditions. The Ministry of Corporations always appears before the labor courts with the representatives of workers and employers. The verdicts of the labor courts are binding, and employers or workers who refuse to abide by them are subject to fine and imprisonment. Individual labor conflicts must be submitted to ordinary courts, assisted by two experts, one selected from the employers and one from the workers.[33]

The majority of collective labor conflicts have so far been settled without recourse to the labor courts, either by special conciliation commissions provided for in certain collective contracts, or by the Ministry of Corporations. Only two cases of national importance have been submitted to the labor courts. The first, decided on July 28, 1927, involved the interpretation of a contract regarding the remuneration of workers in rice fields. The second, decided on January 28, 1928, concerned the interpretation of a contract establishing the scale of wages for workers in maritime transportation. In both cases decision was in favor of the workers. The

[33] Decree of February 28, 1928, Regarding the Settlement of Individual Labor Conflicts.

labor courts, while directly subject to the control of the government, are, in general, regarded as impartial by both workers and employers.[34]

CRITICISM OF FASCIST LABOR POLICY

The general criticism directed against the syndical and corporative organization established by the Fascist government is that it replaces the free association of workers for the defense of their legitimate interests by a highly bureaucratized system subject to the control of the state which, in turn, is ruled by a single political party. Anti-Fascists assert that the practical exclusion of all but legally recognized syndicates from participation in the economic life of the country forces both workers and employers to join these syndicates, irrespective of the views they may hold regarding Fascism. Collective labor contracts, it is argued, tend to perpetuate, rather than improve, existing conditions of work, and to reduce the status of all workers, whatever their ability, to the same economic level. Critics of Fascism claim, moreover, that the labor courts in no sense achieve the practical results formerly attained by means of labor agitation and strikes, since their verdicts are dictated by Fascist interests, which do not necessarily coincide with those of the workers. Finally, it is claimed that the Fascist syndical organization, highly centralized and subject to close supervision by government organs, prevents the development of leadership on the part of the workers, and thus places them at a disadvantage in the class struggle which may eventually take place.[35]

Fascist spokesmen, for their part, are of the opin-

[34] Haider, *Capital and Labor under Fascism*, cited, p. 206.
[35] For a critique of the Fascist system, *cf. ibid.*

ion that no organizations, economic or political, can exist outside the state, and that therefore only Fascist syndicates should be permitted to participate in the regulation of production. Fascism prides itself on having transformed the syndical association, "critical and polemical in character," into a public institution devoted to national ends.[36] The interests of workers and employers, according to Fascism, must never threaten the economic equilibrium of the state, and syndical organization is justified on the ground that it maintains a just balance between the two groups. Fascism does not deny the existence of conflicts between workers and employers. It believes, however, that such conflicts, when permitted to develop, may cause incalculable injury to the state, and that they must in all cases be settled by resort not to violence, but to conciliation and judicial procedure. The class struggle, said Mussolini in 1923, is a luxury which a poor country like Italy cannot afford. He believes that only a long period of social peace will enable the country to overcome its natural inferiority: "Without this, we shall be irrevocably lost in the field of international competition."[37]

CHAPTER V

OPPOSITION TO FASCISM

THE opponents of Fascism in Italy—Liberals, Democratic Catholics, Socialists, Communists, Free-

---

[36] *L'Organisation Syndicale et Corporative Italienne,* cited, p. 159.
[37] Speech of December 20, 1923, *cf. La Nuova Politica,* cited, p. 136.

masons—have been effectively silenced by their exclusion from Parliament and by the restrictions imposed on the right of association and the freedom of the press. Any attempt to reconstitute the old political parties or create new ones is subject to severe punishment. "No tolerance, no indulgence," said Arpinati, Under-Secretary of the Interior on March 3, 1931, "will be conceded to those who, after nine years of the régime and after the titanic work accomplished by *Il Duce,* insist on regarding the Fascist revolution as a transitional episode." [1]

The Fascist press, which is uniformly laudatory, gives the impression that the entire population endorses the Fascist program without reservations or qualifications. Nevertheless, from time to time, official *communiqués* reveal the existence of some anti-Fascist plot, and indicate that the culprits will be tried by the Special Tribunal for the Defense of the State. The most spectacular of these plots, uncovered by the secret police (O.V.R.A.), concerned the National Alliance (*Alleanza Nazionale*). The latter had been founded in June 1930 by a young writer, Lauro De Bosis, formerly associated with the *Casa Italiana* in New York; its leading members were his mother, Signora De Bosis, an American by birth, and two prominent journalists, Mario Vinciguerra and Renzo Rendi. This group circulated a bulletin, for the most part written by Lauro De Bosis, who resided abroad. These bulletins were mimeographed by Signora De Bosis, and mailed to a list of persons, each of whom was requested to type six copies, and send them to six persons, always the same, at least two of whom were to be Fascists. The articles published in this bulletin invited patriotic

[1] *Il Giornale d'Italia,* March 4, 1931.

Italians to unite against Fascism under the leadership of the monarchy and the Church, and thus prevent monopolization of anti-Fascist opposition by the Communists. "Today," said the bulletin of July 15, 1930, "the National Alliance includes men of all non-subversive parties and can have only one enemy, Fascism." [2]

At the trial of the *Alleanza Nazionale* on December 22, 1930, the prosecutor accused its members of having represented the Church and the monarchy as antagonistic to the régime. Vinciguerra admitted that the bulletins were critical of Fascism, but denied that they advocated recourse to violence. The president of the tribunal interrupted him at this point and described the articles in the bulletins as "lies." Signora De Bosis, who had written Mussolini a letter from prison expressing penitence for her action and admiration for the Fascist government, was pardoned, while Vinciguerra and Rendi were condemned to fifteen years' imprisonment. [3]

ANTI-FASCIST TENDENCIES IN ITALY

It is the opinion of competent observers that there is little prospect at the present time of a violent overthrow of the Fascist government. Dissatisfaction with the government is found chiefly among industrialists and professional men. The industrialists, forced to maintain a prescribed scale of wages in the face of economic depression, accuse Fascism of undue leniency towards the workers. In general,

---

[2] *Alleanza Nazionale* (Paris, Imprimerie Vendôme, 1931). Nine bulletins were published by the *Alleanza Nazionale* between June 1 and November 1, 1930, when its members were arrested by the police.

[3] For an account of the trial, cf. *Corriere della Sera*, December 23, 1930.

however, the propertied classes, which welcomed
Fascism in 1922 in the hope that it would restore
public order, fear that the only alternative today
would be a return to revolutionary Socialism. Intellectuals and professional men oppose restrictions
on the liberty of association and of the press, and
complain of Italy's intellectual stagnation under
Fascism. Here again, however, there seem to be
no signs of concerted action. The workers, on the
whole, appear to have benefited by recent social
reforms, and with the exception of the Communists
have not openly attacked Fascism. Finally, the opposition of the Church, which might have proved a
serious obstacle, was in large part removed by the
conclusion of the Lateran accord in 1929. Nevertheless, the Pope has occasionally criticized Fascism
for the liberty accorded to Protestant sects, and the
Osservatore Romano, now published on Vatican territory, is the only Italian newspaper which takes
issue with the government.

MUSSOLINI'S PERSONAL INFLUENCE

The absence of any widespread active opposition
may be attributed, in part, to the political indifference of the population. In larger measure, however,
it appears to be due to the admiration with which
Mussolini is regarded in many circles otherwise opposed to Fascism. The fact that Mussolini enjoys so
great a degree of personal prestige has caused considerable speculation concerning the effects which
may be produced by his disappearance. The Fascist
party has been frequently divided on major questions of policy, the older, conservative elements advocating closer coöperation with capitalism, and the
former Socialists demanding radical reforms for the

benefit of the workers. Until now Mussolini has succeeded in preserving the unity of the party, with the result that the inner cleavage has not been reflected in the government's policy. It is as yet too early to say whether, in the absence of Mussolini, Fascism could be maintained indefinitely in its present form.

ANTI-FASCIST ACTIVITIES ABROAD

The anti-Fascist irreconcilables have for the most part transferred their activities abroad, and have established their headquarters in Brussels and Paris. The émigrés are divided into three main schools of political thought—Communists, Democratic Republicans and Democratic Monarchists. The Communists, rather numerous among the workers, have a widespread press which, according to their opponents among the émigrés, is subsidized by the Soviet government and by Italian *agents provocateurs*. The majority of the bourgeois émigrés are Democratic Republicans, but are further split into Right and Left Wing Socialists and Republicans. The Right Wing Socialists and Republicans form the so-called Anti-Fascist Concentration (*Concentrazione Antifascista*), which publishes a newspaper *Libertà* and, until 1932, issued a bulletin, *Italia*, both in Paris. In addition, the Concentration published a satirical paper, *Becco Giallo* (Yellow Beak), printed on very thin paper and smuggled every fortnight into Italy at the rate of some 7,500 copies. The Concentration has had among its leaders Professor Gaetano Salvemini and the late Filipo Turati, editor of *Italia*. Finally, the Democratic Monarchists, including Count Carlo Sforza, former Minister of Foreign Affairs, and ex-Premier Nitti, favor retention of the House of Savoy; in all other respects, they appear to agree, and actually collaborate, with the Democratic Republicans. The Fascist government professes nothing but contempt for the émigrés. On March 3, 1931, Arpinati, Under-Secretary of the Interior, described them as "people who make politics their profession, and who live on anti-Fascism as they once lived on subversive doctrines, people who have lost all notion of time and all sense of reality."[4]

SUMMARY

The émigrés charge the Fascists with the suppression of parliamentary government at a time when the latter not only had shown no signs of decadence, but was susceptible of further successful development. The Fascist government, they claim, has completely destroyed the spirit of the Italian constitution, while preserving a semblance of legality. The restrictions placed by Fascism on individual liberty, they argue, may have had some justification during a transitional period of political readjustment; subsequently, however, the government should have returned to normalcy—that is, apparently, restored the conditions which it set out to remove. The émigrés admit that such "normalization" would involve the disappearance of Fascism, but believe that this eventuality would redound to the benefit of the country. The anti-Fascists contend that at the present time the country's economic development is hampered by the control exercised by the state over production. They believe that, if order has been restored, it has only been at the expense of individual liberty, and that the govern-

[4] *Il Giornale d'Italia,* March 4, 1931.

ment has signally failed to solve the country's economic problems. Finally, they assert that the government has pursued an aggressive foreign policy which has injured Italy's prestige and credit abroad.

The Fascists, for their part, claim that parliamentary government was not an indigenous product, had never taken root in Italy, and had become completely impotent during the post-war years. They believe that a highly centralized government is alone capable of regulating the economic life of a country like Italy, poor in natural resources, and of insuring a just distribution of material goods among a rapidly growing population. The Fascists do not deny the suppression of individual liberty, but contend that they have introduced higher ethical values into Italian life by imposing on all groups of the population a discipline dictated by national, as contrasted with personal, interests. They assert that, as a result of this discipline, the Italian people have applied themselves with a new energy to the task of production, and that Italy's prestige among nations has thereby been restored and enhanced.

THE NAZI REVOLUTION
IN GERMANY

CHAPTER I

THE RISE OF GERMAN NATIONALISM

THE Hitler Third Reich is now an accomplished fact. Both democratic forms and terroristic methods have been used to destroy the Weimar Republic and set up a Fascist dictatorship. The National Socialist German Workers' party rules supreme in Germany, for after a year in office, Hitler and his lieutenants have dissolved or "coördinated" all other political parties; Germany has been completely unified; all opposition has been ruthlessly suppressed; and the ground has thus been cleared for the practical application of Nazi principles.

At the Reichstag election on March 5, 1933, more than 17 million Germans—comprising 44 per cent of the electorate—cast their votes for the National Socialist party, thus giving expression to an unparalleled unanimity of opinion in a country noted for particularist sentiment. These 17 million voters were drawn primarily from three sources: the youth of Germany who have come of age since the war, former supporters of the numerous conservative small bourgeois parties, and previous non-voters who were roused from political lethargy by economic disaster and National Socialist propaganda.

Despite the thoroughness and effectiveness of Nazi agitation, the success of the movement can only be explained by the psychological, physical and material suffering which the German people have undergone during the past two decades. The ideology and philosophy of the movement, however, have their roots far in the past. It is not only a mass protest against the hardships endured during and since the war, it is also a form of self-vindication for a people which, although trained and educated in a militarized state, were defeated in a great war. It is at the same time a national attempt to escape from the harsh realities of the present by resurrecting many of the attributes of the past which to a suffering people seems glorious in retrospect, and by introducing an undefined "socialism" which shall solve present-day economic and social problems.

In considering the present resurgence of German nationalism, it must be remembered that the Germans were the last great people to achieve national unity, and that the centuries-long history of the small kingdoms and principalities which made up the so-called "Germanies" was the record not of a united people but of Prussians, Saxons, Bavarians, and others. Even after Bismarck had founded the Empire in 1871, local patriotism was still predominant. The self-conscious nationalism which marked imperial Germany in the decades before the World War must be regarded as the manifestation of a people politically united but not sufficiently unified to take its national patriotism for granted.

The "Mission" of the German People

The movement for German political unity which finally bore fruit in 1871, had been profoundly influenced by German intellectuals—historians, philosophers and writers. The poetry of the Romanticists and the theories of the state expounded by Kant and Hegel had had a large share in developing that spirit of patriotic nationalism which finally won the battle of Leipzig in 1813 and liberated Prussia. Furthermore, the philosopher Fichte, in his *Reden an die deutsche Nation,* had set forth an exalted conception of the character and mission of the Germans, and put forward the idea of a geographically isolated and economically self-sufficient community as the ideal nation. Hegel particularly had glorified the state, declaring that "the State is God on Earth!" [1] He pictured mankind as progressing through the ages, steadily but unconsciously, toward the Germanic perfection of the nineteenth century. The German historians, meanwhile, developed the doctrine of the great "mission" of the German people and became leaders of nationalist thought. Histories lauding the Hohenzollerns, the glories of the German medieval period, German prowess in the crusades, and the deeds of the Teutonic knights contributed to nationalist fervor and did much to convince the Germans that Prussia and the Hohenzollerns were charged with a special "mission." The founding of the University of Berlin gave impetus to the development of glorious national history—past, present and future—supported by the Hegelian theory of the state. Most Prussian historians [2] shared Hegel's belief that civilization is spread only by war, and that the triumph of civiliza-

---

[1] Hegel, *Grundlinien der Philosophie des Rechts,* Vols. VIII–IX, sec. 258, p. 313.

[2] Duncker, Droysen, Leopold von Ranke, von Treitschke, von Sybel and Mommsen were the leading historians of this persuasion.

tion demanded the suppression of races less capable of or less advanced in culture by nations of a higher order. War and the doctrine of force thus became the embodiment of progress to many Germans.[3]

In addition to this glorification of the state and of force, a new "science" of race aided German nationalists in explaining the superiority of the German race over all others. The publication in 1854, of a work by a Frenchman, Count Joseph Arthur de Gobineau, entitled *Essai sur l'inégalité des races humaines,* did much to strengthen the cause of nationalism in Germany. The theories of Gobineau, moreover, furnish the "scientific" background for the anti-Semitism which forms a part of the intense Nazi nationalism. According to Gobineau, racial questions overshadow all other problems of history and hold the key to them. The inequality of races from whose fusion a people is formed explains the whole course of human destiny, Gobineau argued; and, further asserting the inherent superiority of the "Aryan" race, he held that racial degeneration was the inevitable result of the mixture of Aryans with inferior races.[4] This mystical glorification of Aryanism decisively influenced the growth of race vanity in Germany and the increasingly evident spirit of imperialism manifested after 1890.[5] Gobineau paved the way for the work of an Englishman,

[3] Mildred S. Wertheimer, *The Pan-German League, 1890–1914* (New York, Longmans Green, 1924), p. 13 *et seq.*
[4] Gobineau, *Essai sur l'inégalité des races humaines* (Paris, 1884, 2 vols., translated by Adrian Collins, New York, 1915, p. xiv, 33); *cf.* also Wertheimer, *The Pan-German League, 1890–1914,* cited; Frank H. Hankins, *The Racial Basis of Civilization, A Critique of the Nordic Doctrine* (New York, Knopf, 1931), p. 33 *et seq.*
[5] Hankins, *The Racial Basis of Civilization,* cited, p. 51.

Houston Stewart Chamberlain, whose *Grundlagen des neunzehnten Jahrhunderts* appeared in 1899. Chamberlain's main thesis was the assertion of the superiority of the Teuton family over all the other races of the world. "The awakening of the Teutonic peoples," he wrote, "to the consciousness of their all-important vocation and culture forms the turning point [in the history of Europe]." [6] Chamberlain's book was widely read and discussed in Germany; it became a best-seller and was popular with the Kaiser, who is said to have financed the distribution of thousands of copies.

It is impossible to estimate the extent to which such works as those of Gobineau and Chamberlain actually influenced historical events, but they were doubtless of considerable importance in nourishing German national egotism. [7] Mystical, abstract principles have always appealed to the German mind and have played a considerable rôle in German political life, as evidenced by the fact that all German parties in their official platforms outlined the broad philosophical bases of party dogma rather than policies on specific questions. Whether or not these theories had great influence on the German people before 1914, they established a most convenient foundation for Allied propaganda during the war

[6] H. S. Chamberlain, *The Foundations of the Nineteenth Century* (English translation by John Lees, London and New York, J. Lane, 1911), p. xv.

[7] Professor John Dewey has made the pertinent statement that "the philosopher sees movements, which might have passed away with change of circumstance as casually as they arose, acquire persistence and dignity because thought has taken cognizance of them and given them intellectual names. The witness of history is that to think in general and abstract terms is dangerous; it elevates ideas beyond situations in which they were born and charges them with we know not what menace for the future." (John Dewey, *German Philosophy and Politics*, New York, Holt, 1915, p. 12.)

and provided moral justification for the Versailles Treaty, particularly the "war guilt" article.

EVOLUTION OF THE NATIONAL SOCIALIST PARTY

It will be recalled, that the first post-war years in Germany were marked by the blackest disillusionment and discouragement. The Allied blockade, which was not lifted until after the signature of the peace treaty, increased the suffering of a people already starving and in the grip of revolution. The former German rulers had abdicated and the Kaiser had fled to Holland; the untried Social Democratic leaders who had taken over the government, were faced with the necessity not only of saving the country from Bolshevism, but of setting up a new democratic state. Added to this was the dislocation entailed by the demobilization of the German army. It was only with the aid of former officers of the imperial army that this demobilization was carried through and the Left revolution was crushed, while officials of the old régime stuck to their posts and carried on the administration of the country. As a result, the Republic incurred a large debt to these officials and officers, despite the fact that many of them paid only lip-service to the new régime and, as time went on, became openly antagonistic.[8] The seeds of counter-revolution were thus being planted even before the legal establishment of the Republic at Weimar on August 11, 1919. The new Republic also received a staggering blow in the Versailles Treaty. The German people, expecting a peace settlement based on Wilson's Fourteen Points, were

[8] Walter Gerhart, *Um des Reiches Zukunft* (Freiburg i/Br., Herder, 1932), p. 46 *et seq.;* Edgar Ansell Mowrer, *Germany Puts the Clock Back* (New York, Morrow, 1933), p. 17 *et seq.*

thunderstruck by the terms of a treaty which imposed huge reparation demands, losses of German
territory, occupation of the Rhineland and unilateral
disarmament of the Reich. The moral condemnation expressed in Article 231 of the treaty, which
was interpreted as placing the entire responsibility
for the war on Germany and its allies, the Reich's
loss of its colonies on the ground of German maladministration, and the demand that the so-called
war criminals be turned over to the Allies for trial
all seemed incomprehensible to the German people
who had believed Wilson's pronouncements. As a
result, the Weimar Republic was inextricably associated in popular opinion with the humiliation and
disappointment engendered by the Versailles Treaty.
The "stab-in-the-back legend" [9] so carefully nurtured by the Nazis—according to which the Weimar
coalition of Social Democrats, Catholic Centrists
and Democrats which founded the Republic was
held responsible for the German defeat—was thus
strengthened.

During the years 1919–1923, while the struggling
young Republic was endeavoring to consolidate its
position and pull the Reich out of the chaos caused
by war and revolution, its major task lay in the field
of foreign affairs, and was concerned primarily with
the reparation problem. This was the period of Allied ultimata, rejection of German counter-proposals,
Allied sanctions in the form of occupation of more
German cities, increasingly strict customs control
and recurring abortive reparation conferences.
Meanwhile the German mark sank deeper in the
mire of inflation. In January 1923, the French and
Belgians occupied the Ruhr, Germany countered
with measures of passive resistance, and by autumn

[9] *Dolchstoss Legende.*

of that year the value of the mark had sunk to zero and the life savings of the German lower middle class were wiped out. Furthermore, the Rhineland separatist movement—supported by the French [10]—seemed for a time to threaten the very unity of the Reich.

Under these circumstances it was all too easy to win support for an extreme nationalist movement of protest. This was particularly true in Bavaria which, after the murder of Kurt Eisner in Munich in February 1919 and the relatively short-lived Soviet interregnum which followed, had become the headquarters of German monarchist and militarist reaction. The brief Bavarian revolutionary episode had burned itself into the memory of the bourgeoisie; anti-Semitism has been strong in Bavaria ever since, for the conservatives blame all their troubles on the fact that Eisner and other revolutionaries were Jews. During the first post-war years, moreover, Germany was a veritable camp of so-called volunteer corps (*Freikorps*), composed of unemployed former officers and soldiers,[11] many of which had their headquarters in Bavaria. These groups were extra-legal, and although ostensibly organized only for defense purposes, were most reactionary in character. Their influence may be traced through the Kapp *Putsch* in 1920, the murders of Erzberger and Rathenau, as well as the many other political murders which marked the early years of the Republic.[12]

It was in such troublous times that the National

[10] G. E. R. Gedye, *The Revolver Republic* (London, Arrowsmith, 1930), *passim*.

[11] The Ehrhardt Brigade, the Baltic Defense Corps, the Bavarian *Einwohnerwehr*, the Black *Reichswehr*, etc.

[12] Mildred S. Wertheimer, "The Hitler Movement in Germany," Foreign Policy Association, *Information Service*, January 21, 1931.

Socialist party had its obscure birth. The party grew out of a group of six men who met during 1919, in a small back room of a Munich café. Adolf Hitler joined the group as its seventh member and almost immediately became its leading personality. In the autumn of 1919, these men founded the National Socialist German Workers' party in Munich. Among the earliest members were some of the leaders of the volunteer corps, notably General von Epp and Captain Röhm. The latter, who had close connections with the Reichswehr, brought into the party many of his friends, both officers and men, with the result that up to 1923, these army men were apparently the backbone of the movement.[13] Röhm is also reported to have been an important liaison officer between the volunteer corps and the militarist clubs and groups (*Wehrverbände*), which apparently furnished many recruits for the Reichswehr as well as for the Nazis. Meanwhile, Hitler by tireless speechmaking gained further supporters, and by the end of 1920, his party had 3,000 members; by November 1923, there were 5,000 paying members of the National Socialist party.[14]

Hitler's Beer-Hall Putsch

Hitler and his party first came into the limelight in 1923. By that time Hitler had attracted the attention of General Ludendorff and the latter's

[13] Konrad Heiden, *Geschichte des Nationalsozialismus* (Berlin, Rowohlt, 1932), p. 12 *et seq.*

[14] *Ibid.*, pp. 44, 143. A comprehensive description of the *Freikorps* movement in Bavaria is contained in Ernst Röhm, *Die Geschichte eines Hochverräters* (Munich, Eher Verlag, 1933). Captain Röhm, now Chief of Staff of the Nazi Storm Troops and Minister without Portfolio in the Reich government, was an important figure in the *Freikorps* movement. According to his own account, he acted as liaison between these illegal *Freikorps* and the legal German *Reichswehr* in which he was a staff officer.

nationalist followers. The crisis caused by the occupation of the Ruhr and the attendant growth of ultra-nationalist sentiment in Germany seemed to offer the psychological moment for Hitler's *Putsch.* On November 9, 1923, the combined forces of Hitler and Ludendorff attempted a coup d'état in Munich under Hitler's leadership, but it missed fire entirely. The attempt has gone down in history as the Beer-Hall *Putsch.*

As a result of this attempted coup, Hitler was arrested and on April 1, 1924, was sentenced to five years' imprisonment for treason. During his imprisonment, his followers had, against his will, joined forces with another extremist group—the German People's Freedom party (*Deutsch-Völkische Freiheitspartei*)—which managed to elect 32 members of the Reichstag at the general election on May 4, 1924. Hitler was released at the end of 1924 and at once renewed his political activity. In February 1925, he reorganized the National Socialist party, and assumed leadership over both this party and the German People's Freedom party.

After the stabilization of the mark, Germany enjoyed a period of comparative recovery and prosperity from 1924 to 1928, although even then there was considerable unemployment.[15] It was during this period that the great influx of foreign loans to Germany took place. Furthermore, this was the era of improved international relations, the Dawes Plan, Locarno, of Germany's entrance into the League of

[15] In January 1924 there were 1,900,000 unemployed in Germany; in January 1926, 2,221,000 were out of work. Even in the boom year 1928, there were 1,862,000 unemployed in January. (Institut für Konjunkturforschung, *Kurven und Zahlen in Deutschland,* Berlin, Reimer Hobbing, 1932, p. 8; also Mildred S. Wertheimer, "The Financial Crisis in Germany," *Foreign Policy Reports,* March 2, 1932.)

Nations, and the partial evacuation of the Rhineland. The domestic political situation was reflected in the results of the 1928 Reichstag election, when the moderate Social Democratic party made large gains, the middle bourgeois groups held their own fairly well, and the Communists showed only a small though steady growth. The Nationalists, however, lost 30 seats and the Nazis, who in the December 1924 election had dropped from 32 to 14, elected only 12 deputies in 1928.[16]

These four years of comparatively prosperous times proved to be merely a lull before the storm. German economic improvement, which was part of prevailing world prosperity had, however, been made possible largely by the great amounts of foreign capital, much of it borrowed at short-term, which had not only helped create an illusion of prosperity, but made it possible for the Reich to meet and transfer its reparation obligations. Nevertheless, Germany's reparation creditors, meeting in Paris early in 1929, drafted the Young Plan which replaced the Dawes Plan of 1924. The new arrangement was predicated on the continuation and expansion of world prosperity, which alone could assure the Reich a favorable trade balance sufficient to meet its obligations under the Young Plan. The world depression, which began even before the Young Plan had gone into effect, nullified the financial advantages which the Reich expected to derive from the plan, and eventually caused its demise for all practical purposes. German acceptance of the Young Plan, however, had freed the Rhineland from foreign occupation five years before the date stipulated in the Versailles Treaty. But

[16] *Statistisches Jahrbuch für das deutsche Reich, 1931*, p. 545.

when the evacuation of the Rhineland took place in June 1930, Germany was already in the grip of the depression. As a result, the salutary effects expected from the Rhineland liberation were not realized. On the contrary, the Hitler movement, of which little had been heard during the preceding years of relative prosperity, suddenly came once more into the limelight.

Hitler had coöperated with the Nationalist leader, Hugenberg, in the plebiscite on the Young Plan which was held late in 1929. On November 25, at the first poll, 4,135,300 votes were cast by Nazis and Nationalists, or only .02 per cent more than the 10 per cent of qualified voters necessary to force the Reichstag to introduce a bill against the Young Plan. The Reichstag rejected this bill on November 29 by an overwhelming majority and, when the actual plebiscite took place on December 22, only 5,825,082 votes, or less than one-third of the number necessary to prevent acceptance of the Young Plan, were cast by the combined forces of Hitler and Hugenberg.[17]

Economic Depression Fosters National Socialism

The fact that the Nazis and Nationalists together polled less than six million votes at the end of 1929, makes the success of Hitler at the Reichstag election on September 14, 1930, the more striking. Less than a year after the Young Plan plebiscite, the Nazis alone rolled up 6,401,210 votes and elected 107 members of the Reichstag. The Hugenberg Na-

---

[17] *Cf.* Cuno Horkenbach, *Das deutsche Reich von 1918 bis Heute* (Berlin, Verlag für Presse, Wirtschaft und Politik, 1930), p. 292 *et seq.* The popular vote polled by the Hugenberg Nationalists in May 1928, the last election before the plebiscite, was 4,380,200. The Nazis had polled only 809,000 at that election.

tionalists received only 2,458,497 votes, or slightly more than half of their 1928 following. The Nazi landslide had begun.

There were three principal causes for the tremendous Nazi increase. In the first place, the deepening depression had already thrown three million people out of work by September 1930.[18] Second, the inner political difficulties in the Reich created an increasing distrust and antipathy for the Republic and parliamentary government. The Reichstag, with its multiplicity of parties, seemed incapable of coping with the complex economic and financial problems confronting the country,[19] while the situation of the German people grew progressively worse. Both of these factors contributed to the third cause of Nazi growth—the success of the untiring agitation of the Hitlerites themselves. Between the autumn of 1929 and September 1930, the National Socialists staged meeting after meeting; [20] during the fortnight before the September elections, the *Völkische Beobachter,* official organ of the party, listed some 3,300 meetings; [21] many of these were held in small out-of-the-way villages, where few if any political gatherings had been held before. Hitler's stalwarts, clad in their brown uniforms, toured the countryside in trucks, unceasingly addressing the peasants and farm workers. In many small villages these meetings, well advertised beforehand, were much like a traveling circus to the inhabitants. The stage

[18] *Statistisches Jahrbuch für das deutsche Reich, 1931,* Graph VII.
[19] Mildred S. Wertheimer, "The Significance of the German Elections," *Foreign Policy Association Information Service,* September 3, 1930.
[20] Heiden, *Geschichte des Nationalsozialismus,* cited, p. 277 *et seq.*
[21] *Völkische Beobachter,* September 1–13, 1930, inclusive.

management of all Nazi gatherings has been dramatic in the extreme. Flags, bands, the marching of uniformed men appealed to a people which react *en masse* to the spectacular, especially in a Republic singularly devoid of colorful ceremonies which had succeeded an Empire with all its pomp and circumstance of kings, princes, courts and army.

CHAPTER II

THE NATIONAL SOCIALIST PARTY

THE Nazi agitation, from first to last, was based on denunciation of the Versailles "dictate," the Republic, its leaders, the Jews, the "Marxists," and the so-called "System." It followed Hitler's theories, expressed in his autobiography, that in propaganda the end justifies the means, and that all agitation should be directed solely to influence the masses. "Propaganda is not science," wrote Hitler, and while attempting to prove certain facts to the masses, "the appeal must be directed to the emotions and only in a very qualified manner to so-called intelligence." [1] The program of the party was sufficiently vague to allow Hitlerite orators to promise help to everyone, adjusting their remarks to suit their audiences. The Third Reich, which the Nazis told their followers would replace the hated Republic, appeared to many harassed Germans like the promised land, and Hitler himself became the Messiah of this new order.

[1] Adolf Hitler, *Mein Kampf* (Munich, Eher Verlag, 1930), p. 195 *et seq*. This was first published in 1924. At present German libraries are compelled to have several copies of this book on their shelves.

Negative propaganda was the cornerstone of all Nazi agitation. On the more positive side, stood the official program of the party which, vague and contradictory as it appears, must be considered as a possible guide to Nazi policy now that Hitler has taken complete control of the Reich. This program, which contains twenty-five points, was written by Gottfried Feder [2] in February 1920, and is prefaced by the following statement: "The program of the party is a program dedicated to the present (*Zeit-programm*)." After the aims set forth in the present program have been achieved, "the leaders decline to set themselves new goals which can only serve to make possible the continuation of the party by means of artifically heightened dissatisfaction among the masses." The official commentary published in the 1932 edition of the program contained the following further statement:

"We refuse to act as other parties do and, for reasons of opportunism, adapt our program to meet so-called conditions. We will on the contrary adapt conditions to square with our program in that we will master these conditions." [3]

THE TWENTY-FIVE POINTS

The Twenty-five Points, which are thus declared unalterable, are as follows:

I. We demand the union of all Germans by the right of self-determination of peoples, in one great Germany.

[2] Herr Feder was appointed Under-Secretary in the Reich Ministry of Economics on June 29, 1932. *New York Times,* June 30, 1933.

[3] This statement and the Twenty-five Points, as well as the following analysis of the program, are taken from the party's official program: Gottfried Feder, *Das Programm der N.S.D.A.P. und seine Weltanschaulichen Grundgedanken* (Munich, Verlag Frz. Eher Nachf. G.m.b.H., 1932).

II. We demand the equality of the German people with all other nations and the abrogation of the treaties of Versailles and St. Germain.

III. We demand land and territory (colonies) sufficient for the feeding of our people and for settlement by our surplus population.

IV. Only a member of our own people (*Volksgenosse*) may be a citizen (*Staatsbürger*). Our own people are *only* those of German blood without reference to confession. Therefore, no Jew may be a member of our people.

V. He who is not a citizen may live in Germany only as a guest and must be governed by laws regulating foreigners.

VI. Only citizens may decide on the leadership and laws of the State. Therefore, we demand that every public office, no matter of what sort, whether in the Reich, the States or the Communes, shall be filled only by citizens.

We fight against the corrupting parliamentary system which fills positions with people chosen only for their party politics without reference to character or ability.

VII. We demand that the State be obliged to provide working and living possibilities for its citizens. If it is not possible to feed the entire population of the State, all members of foreign nations (non-citizens) must be expelled from the Reich at once.

VIII. All further immigration of non-Germans must be stopped. We demand that all non-Germans who have immigrated to Germany since August 2, 1914, shall be ousted from the Reich.

IX. All citizens must have the same rights and duties.

X. It must be the primary duty of every citizen to engage in productive work, whether in physical or intellectual fields. The activities of individuals must not be such as to conflict with the general interest but, on the contrary, must be for the common good.

THEREFORE WE DEMAND:

XI. Abolition of all income acquired without work or trouble; DESTRUCTION OF THE SLAVERY TO INTEREST (ZINSKNECHTSCHAFT).

XII. Because of the tremendous sacrifice in goods and blood which every war demands of the people, personal enrichment through war must be branded as a crime against the people. We demand, therefore, complete confiscation of all war profits.

XIII. We demand the nationalization of all trusts.

XIV. We demand distribution of the profits of large industries.

XV. We demand an increase on a large scale in care for the aged.

XVI. We demand the building-up of a healthy middle class and its preservation; we demand immediate communalization of large department stores and further, that they be rented at moderate prices to small shopkeepers; the strictest control of all shopkeepers in their sales to the Reich, the States and the Communes.

XVII. We demand agrarian reform consistent with our national needs; the passage of a law to expropriate without compensation land which is to be used for common purposes; the abolition of interest on land debts (*Bodenzinsen*) and of all speculation in land values.[4]

XVIII. We demand a ruthless fight against those people who through their activities harm the common welfare. Dangerous criminals, usurers, profiteers, etc.,

[4] An "explanation" of this section of the program was added by Hitler on April 13, 1928, as follows: "In reply to the lying expositions of Point XVII of the program of the National Socialist party which our opponents have made, the following declaration is necessary. Since the National Socialist party stands firmly for the principle of private property, it is self-evident that the passage 'to expropriate without compensation' can only apply to the creation of laws concerning land which has been illegally acquired or which has not been administered according to the common good and which, therefore, should be expropriated when necessary. Such action is directed in the first place against Jewish companies engaged in land speculation."

must be punished with death without regard to religion or race.

XIX. We demand a German common law as a substitute for the Roman law which serves the materialistic world-order.

XX. To make it possible for every hard-working and capable German to secure a higher education and therefore the opportunity of attaining a leading position, the State has the responsibility of providing for a fundamental extension of our common educational system. The plans of instruction of all institutions of learning must correspond to the demands of practical life. An understanding of the theory of the State must be taught to the children at the earliest possible age. We demand special education at State expense of gifted children of poor parents, without regard to their profession or position.

XXI. The State must care for the improvement of the health of the people by protection of mother and child, by forbidding child labor, by making laws for the development of sport and gymnastics in order to build up the bodies of its citizens and by the most generous support of all clubs which work toward building up the bodies of the youth of the nation.

XXII. We demand the abolition of the mercenary army and the development of a people's army.

XXIII. We demand a legal (*gesetzlich*) battle against the conscious political lies and their propagation in the press. In order to make possible the creation of a German press, we demand that:

a. All editors and workers on newspapers which appear in the German language must be citizens.

b. Non-German newspapers require the specific permission of the State for publication. They may not be printed in the German language.

c. Any financial participation or influence in a German newspaper is to be forbidden by law and punished by confiscation of the paper as well as by the immediate expulsion from the Reich of the non-German in question.

Newspapers which work against the common good are to be prohibited.

We demand laws against tendencies in art and literature which have a bad influence on our life as a people, and the closing of institutions which conflict with this demand.

XXIV. We demand freedom for all religious sects in the State in so far as they do not endanger the State or work against the customs and morals of the German race. The party as such represents the point of view of a positive Christianity without binding itself to any particular confession. It fights the spirit of Jewish materialism in us and outside us and is convinced that a lasting convalescence of our people can only take place from the inner conviction that "common welfare comes before individual welfare."

XXV. In order to carry out all of this program, we demand the creation of a strong central authority in the Reich; unqualified authority of the political central parliament over the entire Reich and its organizations; the creation of professional chambers [like Soviets] to carry out the laws promulgated by the Reich in the several Federal States.

The leaders of the party promise to work ruthlessly for the fulfillment of the above [Twenty-five] Points even, if necessary, to the extent of staking their lives for the program.

OFFICIAL NAZI INTERPRETATION

The official commentary on the Twenty-five Points gives some further indication of the meaning of the program, declaring that the most important tenets in the Nazi program are those specifying that "the common welfare comes before individual welfare," and that "slavery to interest" must be abolished. The Nazi racial theories and anti-Semitism, however, form a connecting link between these apparently unrelated demands and the entire Nazi program as well. Thus the aim of the Hitlerites is said to be the creation of order out of the chaos caused by "a government fighting against the people, party against party, parliament against government, worker against employer, consumer against producer," with resulting "impoverishment, graft and betrayal." The cause of this state of affairs is the shattered and false spiritual foundations of society brought about by Marxists, capitalists, industrialists and public leaders, all of whom are motivated by the same individualist philosophy: personal individual aggrandizement. The Jews are the world enemy, responsible not only for Marxism but for large capitalism, for they hold the whip hand over the people in the form of interest on capital. Therefore, the Nazis contend, the "slavery to interest" must be broken, although the means by which this policy is to be carried out are not indicated.

Of primary importance in overcoming both "individualistic materialism" and "interest slavery" is the settlement of the Jewish question which is described as "the emotional foundation of the National Socialist movement." According to Nazi ideology, the Jewish "materialistic spirit" is the root of all evil. The Nazis envisage the struggle against this spirit as a battle between two philosophies: "the elemental, creative, productive spirit of the Aryans, firmly rooted in the earth; and the ravaging, rootless, self-seeking spirit of the Jews." Germany, say the Hitlerites, must be the home of the Germans and not the abiding place of "Jews, Russians (Communists), and Social Democrats who recognize no fatherland." In this statement is contained

Nazi foreign policy, the demand for political freedom of the Reich, all racial-political demands and citizenship requirements.

Main Principles of Nazi Foreign Policy

The primary object of Nazi foreign policy is to liberate Germany from "political and economic slavery." [5] Some indication of the measures by which this is to be achieved is given in Hitler's autobiography. Germany, he declared, must strengthen its position as a Continental power; this it can do only through alliances with Great Britain and Italy. France is the arch-enemy of Germany, and it is primarily against the French that Germany must fight. In his book Hitler envisages two wars with the aid of Great Britain and Italy—one against France and one against Russia. The fact that England does not seem particularly anxious to ally itself with Germany, Hitler ascribes to the influence of "international Jews," stating that in this "freest democracy [England] the Jews today dictate by the roundabout method of influencing public opinion, in a fashion which is practically unlimited. There is in England, almost uninterrupted coöperation between the representatives of the British state and the pioneer workers for a Jewish world-dictatorship." [6] As for Russia, Hitler contends that Germany needs territory on which its surplus population can settle; that territory is available only in the East, and therefore Germany must make war on Russia to obtain land.

[5] *Nationalsozialistisches Jahrbuch, 1931.* Hrsg. unter Mitwirkung der Reichsleitung der N.S.D.A.P., 5th year (Munich, Frz. Eher Nachf., 1931), p. 29.
[6] Hitler, *Mein Kampf,* cited, p. 721; for his foreign policy, *cf.* pp. 687-758.

Further light on Nazi aims in foreign policy is shed by the writings of Alfred Rosenberg, now head of the Foreign Affairs Bureau of the National Socialist party. Rosenberg proclaims that the Nazis desire "no *Mitteleuropa* without racial and national differences such as Naumann dreamed of, no Franco-Jewish Pan-Europa. A Nordic Europe is the solution of the future, together with a German *Mitteleuropa*. Germany as a racial and national state from Strassburg to Memel, from Eupen to Prague and Laibach, as the central power of the continent, as a guarantee for the South and Southeast. The Scandinavian states and Finland as a second alliance to guarantee the Northeast; and Great Britain as a guarantee in the West and overseas necessary in the interest of the Nordic race." [7]

The program commentary also contains further illuminating remarks regarding Nazi foreign policy. Thus in demanding "a self-sufficient national state comprising all Germans," Herr Feder, the official commentator, states that "all people of German blood, whether they live under Danish, Polish, Czech, Italian or French rule, must be united in a German Reich." And he adds: "We will not renounce a single German in Sudeten,[8] in Alsace-Lorraine, in Poland, in the League of Nations' colony Austria, or in the Succession States of old Austria." Moreover, in foreign policy in general, the Nazis demand that the "dust of the Foreign Office must be

[7] Alfred Rosenberg, *Der Mythus des 20 Jahrhunderts, Eine Wertung der seelisch-geistigen Gestaltenkämpfe unserer Zeit* (Munich, Hoheneichen-Verlag, 1930), p. 602. In a speech at Münster on May 13, 1933, Vice Chancellor von Papen attacked pacificism and declared that "the battlefield is for a man what motherhood is for a woman." *New York Times*, May 14, 1933.

[8] A mountain district in Prussia, Saxony, Silesia and Czechoslovakia.

swept out with an iron broom. There must be an end to the toadying of the Erzbergers and Stresemanns to foreigners and we shall soon see how a strong representation of German interests abroad will receive proper respect, and how German wishes will gain respect and consideration instead of kicks and blows."

NAZI RACIAL POLICIES

At home, however, the German Reich, comprising all Germans, is to be purely Teutonic. Nazi anti-Semitism is a racial and not a religious matter. It is based on the theory that no Jew is a German, regardless of how many centuries he and his ancestors may have lived in the Reich. Therefore, according to the Nazis, no Jew may be a German citizen. As a corollary, all Jews must be excluded from responsible positions in German public life. The official program commentary states in this connection:

"This demand is so much a matter of course to us Nazis that it requires no amplification. A person who regards Jews as 'German citizens of Jewish faith' and not as a foreign race, a strictly exclusive people of decidedly parasitic character, cannot understand the essentials of our demands."

Hitler himself may be listed as the primary source of Nazi anti-Semitism, and his autobiography is illuminating on this point. According to his own account, when he went from his childhood home in Linz to Vienna as a young man, he had already become an ardent nationalist, hating the Austro-Hungarian Empire because it was an empire of na-

tionalities and not a national empire.[9] In Vienna
he appears eventually to have found a job in the
building trades, and finally to have become a
draughtsman. He was asked to join the Social
Democratic party but refused. After listening to his
fellow workers for a time, he argued with them and
finally appears to have opposed them so hotly that
he was forced to leave his job. This happened
several times and, as a result, Hitler lived in great
poverty for a number of years. This may explain in
part his intense anti-Marxian feeling as well as his
anti-Semitism.[10] Since some of the Socialist leaders
were Jews, to Hitler the whole Socialist movement
was, and is, a plot of the "international Jews" to gain
control of the workers.

During the last decade of the nineteenth and the
first years of the twentieth century, Austria-Hungary
was a hotbed of anti-Semitism. Although by the
time Hitler reached Vienna the movement, which
had been largely political, was on the wane, the
prestige of the pan-German leader, Ritter von
Schoenerer, and of the notoriously anti-Semitic
Mayor of Vienna, Karl Lueger, was still great.[11]
Hitler was influenced by the views of both Schoenerer and Lueger,[12] although he apparently did not
always agree with their political tactics. It was
during his Vienna days, also, that Hitler for the
first time saw a Galician Jew in caftan and side
curls. His reactions, written many years later, are
significant. He noted:

[9] *Mein Kampf*, p. 8 *et seq. Nationalitätenstaat* as opposed
to *Nationalstaat*.
[10] *Ibid.*, p. 40 *et seq.*
[11] Lucien Wolf, "Anti-Semitism," *Encyclopedia Britannica*
(11th Ed., New York, 1910), p. 141 *et seq.*
[12] *Mein Kampf*, cited, p. 105 *et seq.*

"Once while I was going through the inner city I came suddenly upon an apparition in a long caftan with black curls. Is this also a Jew? was my first thought. Jews in Linz had not looked like that. I observed the man, furtive and stealthy, and the longer I stared at this foreign face and regarded it feature by feature, the more the question crystallized itself in my mind in another form: Is this a German as well?" [13]

Thus, even before the war, Hitler was a confirmed anti-Semite. After the war, when the National Socialist party was already active in Munich, Hitler met Alfred Rosenberg, the present head of the Nazi Foreign Affairs Bureau. It was apparently Rosenberg's influence which gave Hitler's anti-Semitism its "Black Hundred" [14] characteristics so evident since the Nazi accession to power, for Rosenberg, although of German ancestry, was born in Reval (Estonia); he spent the war years in Russia as a student and, like many other Russian emigrés, fled to Munich in 1919. [15]

BASES OF GERMAN ANTI-SEMITISM

It cannot be denied, however, that there had been considerable anti-Semitism in Germany even before Hitler's advent, and on several occasions feeling against the Jews reached large proportions. This was particularly the case during the last three decades of the nineteenth century. Anti-Semitism was started by a series of financial scandals involving prominent Jews as well as important Gentile aristocrats after the panic of 1873, which had resulted from wild speculation due to the rapid payment of the large French war indemnity. The publication at

[13] *Ibid.*, p. 59.
[14] The most reactionary elements in Tsarist Russia.
[15] Heiden, *Geschichte des Nationalsozialismus*, cited, p. 47.

this time of a pamphlet entitled *Der Sieg des Juden-
tums über das Germanentum* by an obscure jour-
nalist, Wilhelm Marr, fell on fertile soil. Marr was
imbued with Hegel's theory of nationality—namely,
that the nation should be a unit comprising individuals speaking the same language and of the
same racial origin, and demanding the elimination
of all elements which could not be reduced to the
so-called national type. The Jews, according to
Marr, were of course an element incapable of such
standardization. The exigencies of German party
politics added to the financial difficulties of the time,
fed the flame of this new pseudo-scientific anti-
Semitism which was based not on religious but on
racial grounds. Bismarck's breach with the National
Liberal party in 1879 was followed by a tremendous
growth of feeling against the Jews, which led to the
formation of a definitely anti-Semitic political group
—the Christian Socialist party—under the leadership of Adolf Stöcker, the court preacher. While
Stöcker's so-called Christian Socialism had appealed
to German conservative elements, a more popular
leader named Ahlwardt, whose name was connected
with many unsavory scandals, had gained a considerable hold on the masses as an anti-Semitic
agitator. Ahlwardt's propaganda was apparently
"wild, unscrupulous and full-blooded," and a prosecution and conviction for libel only seemed to increase his influence. Although eventually all this
agitation died down, there can be no doubt that the
wave of anti-Semitism left its mark on the German
people.[16]

The anti-Semitic sections of the National Socialist

---

[16] For a summary of anti-Semitism in Germany, *cf.* Wolf,
"Anti-Semitism," cited, p. 135 *et seq.*

program were thus not an entirely new thing in German politics. Furthermore, Nazi anti-Semitism offered the German people a welcome scapegoat on which to blame all their hardships since the war. Moreover, German youth, which today forms so important a section of Hitler's followers, was subjected to intense anti-Semitic propaganda almost from the beginning of its political consciousness.

COMPOSITION OF THE NATIONAL SOCIALIST MOVEMENT

The National Socialist movement is to a large extent a youth movement. The German birth rate during the fifteen years before the war was particularly high [17] and the children born during that period, now adults between the ages of 20 and 30, have undergone the severest hardships. First the war, with its attendant lack of proper food, lax discipline at school and at home, and overwrought emotional state; then the uncertainty of the Revolution and hunger intensified by the blockade. Later, at the time when youth should have been learning the value of money, came the inflation. Finally, when they were grown and ready to work, no jobs were available. As a result, these young people became completely disillusioned, and lost all hope regarding their future. Those young people who had any international sentiments became Communists; the large majority, attracted by the pomp and circumstance with which the Hitler movement surrounded itself, became National Socialists. Hotheaded and impulsive, these young Germans are tremendously idealistic. Since they had nothing to do with the war, they feel intensely that there is no

[17] *Statistisches Jahrbuch für das deutsche Reich, 1931,* p. ii.

reason why they themselves, and their children and grandchildren after them, should pay for it, and they have been told unceasingly that their Fatherland was humiliated by the Treaty of Versailles and betrayed into signing it. They have lost faith in their elders who, they believe, have made a complete failure of life: now it is their turn to set the world right and Hitler is their prophet.[18]

Among the older generation, the Nazi followers have come very largely from the ranks of the bourgeoisie. Many small white-collar people whose businesses have been completely disrupted by the depression, but who felt that it would degrade them to vote for one of the Left parties, turned National Socialist. This tendency was apparent also among farmers and agricultural workers, where Nazi propaganda was especially active. Finally, many people belonging to what has been called in the Reich the "non-voters' party"—people who had never voted before—went to the polls in the four Reichstag elections between 1930 and 1933 and voted for Hitler. Aroused by the Nazi propaganda, and utterly disillusioned with the older parties which apparently had been unable to help them out of their difficulties, these people also saw in Hitler their last hope.

Support of Hitler by the bourgeoisie and the younger generation caused a steady decline in all parties of the German Right except the Nazis, whose gains were correspondingly large. The Catholic parties managed to hold their own fairly well, while on the Left, the moderate Social Democrats declined somewhat, losing some supporters to the

[18] Hanns Heinz Ewers, *Horst Wessel* (Berlin, J. G. Cotta'sche Buchhandlung Nachf., 1933). This biography of the young Nazi "martyr," sympathetically written, attempts to portray the idealism and "pure patriotic feeling" of Hitler's young storm troopers.

Communists and failing to attract their proportion of the young workers who would normally have filled the Socialist ranks. The age distribution of the Social Democratic, Communist and Nazi deputies elected to the 1930 Reichstag as shown in the following table illustrates this situation: [19]

Age	Social Democrats	Nazis	Communists
Over 70	1	....	1
50–70	73	12	1
40–50	49	21	20
30–40	20	63	47
Under 30	...	9	8

The discipline of the older German workers, however, even at the elections on March 5, 1933, was demonstrated by the fact that at that poll, despite terror and suppression, the Socialists elected 120 Reichstag deputies, as compared with 121 at the previous election, while the Communists dropped from 100 to 81.

Paradoxically, the political discipline of the German workers during the whole period of the Republic proved of ultimate advantage to the Nazis: many important German industrialists and landowners saw in Hitler a means by which to crush organized German labor and the power of the trade unions, and thus free themselves from the expensive social insurances, fixed wage scales and compulsory labor arbitration. These magnates regarded the Nazis as the best bulwark against Socialism and Communism, despite the vague socialistic theories of the Hitlerites which they did not take seriously. As a result, many big industrialists gave the Nazis

---

[19] *Cf.* Sigmund Neumann, *Die deutschen Parteien* (Berlin, Junker and Dünnhaupt, 1932), p. 134. By 1933 this age distribution was even more marked.

financial assistance,[20] and the latter were enabled not only to carry on expensive propaganda campaigns, but also to support their increasingly powerful private army, the Storm Troops (*Sturm Abteilung-S.A.*) and the picked men who form the so-called *Schutzstaffel-S.S.*, a sort of party police and bodyguard of the Nazi leaders.[21] For more than two years there was virtual civil war in the Reich, the Nazi private army striving for "control of the streets" against the Republican *Reichsbanner* and the Communists.[22]

ORGANIZATION OF THE NATIONAL SOCIALIST PARTY

The organization of the National Socialist German Workers party [23] is based on the "leadership principle" which is a fundamental tenet of Nazi ideology. Hitler himself is the supreme leader of the party and of the Storm Troops. He has a Cabinet, however, consisting of seventeen men each of whom is in turn director of one of the major bureaus or divisions of the party. This cabinet is composed as follows: [24]

Rudolf Hess, Assistant to the Leader in all questions of party leadership; Director of the Political Central Commission.

Ernst Röhm, Chief of Staff of the Storm Troops.

[20] Heiden, *Geschichte des Nationalsozialismus,* cited, p. 144 *et seq.;* Richard Lewinson (Morus), *Das Geld in der Politik* (Berlin, Fischer Verlag, 1930), p. 146 *et seq.;* Mowrer, *Germany Puts the Clock Back,* cited, p. 142 *et seq.*

[21] It has been estimated that by the beginning of 1933, when Hitler came to power, the Nazi private army comprised between five and six hundred thousand men.

[22] The Nazi S.A. also had frequent encounters with the Nationalist *Stahlhelm,* the veterans' association, although the main riots were between the S.A. and the Communists.

[23] *Nationalsozialistische Deutsche Arbeiterpartei.*

[24] *Nationalsozialistisches Jahrbuch 1934,* Hrsg. unter Mitwirkung der N.S.D.A.P. (Munich, Eher Verlag, 1933.)

Heinrich Himmler, Reich leader of the *Schutzstaffel* (Protective Corps or Party Guard).

Franz Xaver Schwarz, Reich Treasurer of the party.

Philipp Bouhler, Reich Business Manager of the party.

Walter Buch, Chairman of the Reich Inspection and Arbitration Committee (*Untersuchungs und Schlichtungs-Ausschuss*).

Wilhelm Grimm, Chairman of the Second Chamber of the Reich Inspection and Arbitration Committee.

Dr. Robert Ley, Staff Director of the Political Organization.

Dr. Walther Darré, Director of the Agricultural-political Bureau.

Dr. Joseph Goebbels, Reich Propaganda Director.

Dr. Hans Frank II, Director of the Legal Department.

Dr. Otto Deitrich, Reich Press Chief.

Max Amann, Director of the Press Bureau.

Alfred Rosenberg, Director of the Foreign Policy Bureau.

Baldur von Schirach, Reich Youth Leader.

Ritter von Epp, Director of the Military Policy Bureau.

Karl Fiehler, Secretary of the National Socialist German Workers' Association. (*Nationalsozialistischer Deutsche Arbeiterverein.*)

Each of these bureaus or divisions has a complete organization under it which is responsible for various phases of German life. The Political Organization, for instance, which is the most important, and of which Hitler himself is the supreme commander, includes the Nazi Cell Organization which operates in industries and factories, the Nazi women's group, the Nazi civil servants' organization, all the so-called expert (*Fachschaft*) groups such as the Reich railways, post and telegraphs, tax administration, customs administration, workers' and charity bureaus, the Reichsbank, the police, justice, and education. The other divisions are less far-reaching in scope but all together, form a network which penetrates into every corner of German life.

Besides this all-inclusive organization of the party from the top, the Reich is divided in sections or *Gaue*, each of which is under the command of a so-called *Gauleiter* who is the party leader in that part of the country. There are 32 of these *Gaue* in Germany proper and a 33rd comprising Austria is listed in the official Nazi handbook.

Paralleling the civilian organization of the National Socialist party is Hitler's private army, the *Sturm Abteilung* or Storm Troops and the smaller but more selected *Schutzstaffel* or guard. Both these groups are organized on a strictly military basis, the various Storm Troop companies now bearing the divisional, regimental and battalion numbers of the corresponding sections of the old imperial German army. Moreover, the divisional organization of the Storm Troops corresponds almost exactly with that of the present German army, the Reichswehr. The following table shows the set-up of the Nazi Storm Troops.[25] (See p. 158.)

The Storm Troops possess an aviation escadrille in the Nazi *Luftsportsverband* (Air Sports Union) and *Luftschutzbund* (Air Protection League), both under the ægis of General Goering. The Air Sports Union is an unofficial organization designed to train

[25] Müller-Jabusch, *Handbuch des öffentlichen Lebens* (5th edition, Leipzig, Kohler Verlag, 1930), p. 111 *et seq.;* Leland Stowe, *Nazi Germany Means War* (London, Faber and Faber, 1933), p. 22 *et seq; Nationalsozialistisches Jahrbuch 1934,* cited, p. 157 *et seq.*

GROUPS	NUMBER OF MEN	LEADERS
Rotte (Squad)	4–8	*Rottenführer*
Schar (Platoon)	10–16	*Scharführer*
		Oberscharführer
Trupp (Troop)	30–48	*Truppführer*
composed of 3 *Scharen* .		*Obertruppführer*
Sturm (Company)	150–250	*Sturmführer*
		Obersturmführer
		Sturmbannführer
Sturmbann (Battalion) ...	600–1,000	*Obersturmbannführer*
		Sturmbannführer
Standarte (Regiment)	3,000–3,500	*Standartenführer*
		Oberführer
Brigade (*Division or Brigade*)	10,000	*Brigadeführer*
Gruppe (Region)	40,000–100,000	*Gruppenführer*
Obergruppe (Super-regions as in the Reichswehr) ..		*Obergruppenführer*

pilots and operates throughout the Reich, which has
been divided into fourteen aviation regions, two for
each storm troop *Obergruppe*. At least one flying
school is situated in each region, where the Storm
Troop fliers receive complete instruction in flying
and aërial warfare from war aces and veteran commercial pilots. The Air Protection League, on the
other hand, is designed not only to make the Germans air-minded but also to teach them how to
defend themselves against air-raids.[26]

CHAPTER III

HITLER AND THE GERMAN POLITICAL CRISIS

DEEPENING economic depression and increasing
inability of the German political system to cope
with the crisis provided a fertile field for the Hitler

[26] Stowe, *Nazi Germany Means War*, cited, p. 49 *et seq.*

movement with its elaborate, all-inclusive organization. The Treaty of Versailles, furthermore, gave the Nazis a popular basis for their agitation which carried out the following sentiments of Hitler: "What a means to an end this instrument of unlimited oppression and shameful degradation [the Treaty of Versailles] could become," he wrote in his autobiography, *Mein Kampf*,[1] "in the hands of a government which desires to whip up national passions to the boiling point. . . ." As a result, millions of Germans rallied to the Nazis. This swing to the extreme Right, however, was made at the expense of the more moderate bourgeois parties of the Right and the Middle. The two Republican Catholic parties of the Middle nevertheless managed to maintain their strength practically unchanged, while within the proletarian Left there was a large shift with the continued growth of the extreme Communist party whose support was drawn from the more moderate Social Democrats. Thus, as the following chart indicates, there was a marked trend toward extremism on both the Right and the Left during the fourteen years of the German Republic.

THE POLITICAL SITUATION, APRIL TO JULY, 1932

The tide of Hitlerism had apparently reached a peak in the summer of 1932. In the four major elections held between March 10 and July 31, 1932, the movement registered heavy gains although in a slightly reduced tempo. Thus, in the first presidential poll on March 10, Field Marshal von Hindenburg received 18,654,244 votes to Hitler's 11,341,-

[1] Adolf Hitler, *Mein Kampf* (Munich, Eher Verlag, 1930), p. 714.

119.[2] In the "run-off" election on April 10, the President was reëlected by a clear majority of 53 per cent, rolling up a total of 19,361,229 votes to Hitler's 13,-418,676.[3] President von Hindenburg, therefore, remained the one stable element in the German political situation.

This fact became even more apparent after the state elections in Prussia, Bavaria, Württemberg, Anhalt and Hamburg—comprising five-sixths of the Reich—which took place on April 24. Although the National Socialists received an average of about 35 per cent of the votes in these polls, nowhere were they able to obtain a majority. The Nazis almost entirely absorbed the smaller conservative parties, the Social Democrats lost heavily, and the Communists made slight gains. Coalition government in large sections of the Reich became impossible; it was therefore necessary, for the most part, to retain the old Cabinets to carry on the administration of the government.

The situation in Prussia, a state which comprises three-fifths of Germany, was especially serious, for, as a result of the April elections, the Nazis and the Catholic Center party controlled a majority in the Prussian Diet, and negotiations for a possible coalition between these two parties were unsuccessful. The government of Otto Braun—consisting of Social Democrats, Centrists and Democrats, which had ruled Prussia since 1925—remained to administer affairs.

The Braun government in Prussia had long been

[2] *Der Heimatdienst,* XIIth year, No. 6, 2nd Märzheft 1932. There were three other candidates also running.

[3] *Ibid.,* No. 8, 2nd Aprilheft 1932. Vera Micheles Dean and Mildred S. Wertheimer, "The Political Outlook in Germany and France," *Foreign Policy Reports,* Vol. VIII, No. 4, April 27, 1932.

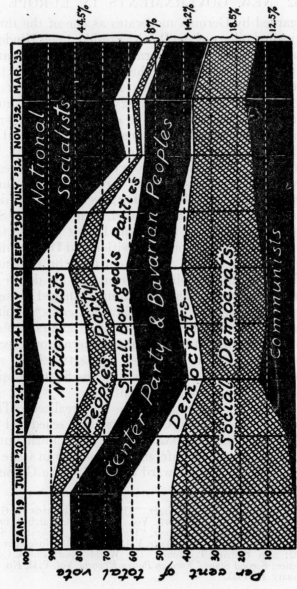

CHANGES IN PARTY POWER IN GERMANY [4]

Per cent of total vote

JAN. '19 | JUNE '20 | MAY '24 | DEC. '24 | MAY '28 | SEPT. '30 | JULY '32 | NOV. '32 | MAR. '33

National Socialists — 44.5%

Nationalists

Peoples Party

Small Bourgeois Parties — 87%

Center Party & Bavarian Peoples

Democrats — 14.2%

Social Democrats — 18.5%

Communists — 12.5%

[4] Based on graph published in *Die Tat* (Jena, Eugen Diederichs Verlag), September 1932

regarded by German moderates as one of the three principal pillars of the Reich; President von Hindenburg, impelled by his stern sense of duty to maintain his oath to uphold the Constitution, was the second; the third was the Reich government of Chancellor Heinrich Brüning who, although governing entirely by means of drastic decrees issued under Article 48 of the Weimar Constitution, had at least preserved the forms of that Constitution by securing indirect parliamentary assent to his measures. This was possible only through Social Democratic toleration of the Brüning government in which that party was not represented. The National Socialists, at that time the second largest party in the Reichstag, were in noisy opposition and Dr. Brüning made no attempt to force them into the responsibilities of office, probably because of his desire to retain foreign confidence. Brüning managed to steer Germany through the 1931 financial crisis,[5] hoping that a major success in foreign affairs would strengthen his hand and that international economic action, along the lines of the two Basle reports, would pull Germany out of the financial mire and deflate the Nazi movement.

Dr. Brüning's hopes were not realized. The Lausanne Reparation Conference, first scheduled to convene in January 1932, was postponed until June; the Disarmament Conference dragged on in Geneva and made no move toward recognizing the German claim for equality.[6]

[5] *Cf.* Mildred S. Wertheimer, "The Financial Crisis in Germany," *Foreign Policy Reports,* Vol. VII, No. 26, March 2, 1932.

[6] *Cf.* Mildred S. Wertheimer, "The Lausanne Reparation Settlement," *Foreign Policy Reports,* Vol. VIII, No. 19, November 23, 1932; also William T. Stone, "The World Disarmament Conference: Second Stage," *Foreign Policy Reports,* Vol. VIII, No. 23, January 18, 1933.

Meanwhile political tension and bitterness in the Reich had greatly increased. Despite Hitler's defeat in the presidential poll, the state elections in the spring of 1932 registered the continued growth of the National Socialist movement. More and more voices were raised against the "Brüning system"— the all-embracing epithet of the Hitlerites for everything against which their agitation was directed. Political riots and bloodshed increased, and there was latent civil war. In an attempt to restore order, General Groener, Minister of Defense and of the Interior in the Brüning Cabinet, decreed the dissolution of Hitler's private army on April 13.

On May 12 the Reichstag defeated a motion of non-confidence in the Brüning government by a margin of 30 votes, but on the same day General Groener resigned as Defense Minister—although he remained as Minister of the Interior. It was evident that Groener had been forced out because he had lost the confidence of the Reichswehr Ministry, particularly General Kurt von Schleicher, the permament chief [7] of that Ministry.[8] On May 30 the storm broke and Chancellor Brüning and his entire Cabinet resigned.

Brüning fell, not because of the withdrawal of Reichstag confidence, but due to the increased pressure which was brought to bear on President von Hindenburg. The immediate reason for the President's refusal, on the eve of the Lausanne Conference, to accord his Chancellor a free hand in directing German policy was von Hindenburg's opposition to a projected emergency decree. This

[7] *Chef des Ministeramtes.*
[8] *Cf. Der deutsche Volkswirt,* May 20, 1932; also Kurt Caro and Walter Oehme, *Schleicher's Aufstieg* (Berlin, Rowohlt, 1933), p. 222 *et seq.*

measure undertook to secure small land allotments for the unemployed by dividing up many large, bankrupt East Prussian estates. The underlying reason for Brüning's dismissal, however, was the President's conviction, reinforced by the arguments of influential conservative advisers,[9] that the Brüning government no longer represented the German people. Dr. Brüning, at the urgent request of von Hindenburg, had taken office in March 1930 as a conservatively inclined chancellor.[10] The course of events during the next two years, however, particularly the rising tide of Hitlerism, had forced him to rely increasingly on the Socialists and the Catholic Center for support. In May 1932, President von Hindenburg was persuaded that the time had come to part with Brüning, despite the fact that the latter was primarily responsible for Hindenburg's re-election to the presidency, and without regard for the Reichstag's recent vote of confidence in the Chancellor. The German conservatives felt that by harnessing the Nazis to governmental responsibility the Reich might secure a strong and stable national government,[11] which alone, they were convinced, could win concessions abroad and keep order at home. Furthermore, it seemed apparent that the Reichswehr no longer had confidence in the Brüning government, a factor which no doubt especially disturbed the old Field Marshal.

[9] The President's son, Major Oscar von Hindenburg, his Chef du Cabinet, Dr. Otto Meissner, and General von Schleicher were apparently the real actors in the drama, although behind the scenes. *Cf.* Caro and Oehme, *Schleicher's Aufstieg,* cited.

[10] *Cf.* Mildred S. Wertheimer "The Significance of the German Elections," Foreign Policy Association, *Information Service,* Vol. VI, No. 13, September 13, 1930.

[11] *Cf. Frankfurter Zeitung,* May 29, 30, 31, June 1, 2, 1932; *Der deutsche Volkswirt,* June 3, 10, 1932.

Papen-Schleicher Government

As a result, after conversations with most of the parliamentary leaders—a proceeding which somewhat preserved constitutional forms—President von Hindenburg on May 31 asked Colonel Franz von Papen, then a right wing Centrist, to form a government of "national concentration," apparently hoping to assure the toleration of the Catholic Center party for the new Ministry.[12] The Center, however, smarting under the dismissal of its leader, Dr. Brüning, went into opposition and von Papen resigned from the party.

The Papen-Schleicher government took office with little or no apparent parliamentary support. It was designated as a presidial Ministry responsible to the President alone, and was entirely satisfactory to the Reichswehr. The new Cabinet, which for the most part consisted of non-party aristocrats of the class which before the war ruled Germany, was announced on June 2, as follows: [13]

Chancellor:	Colonel von Papen
Interior:	Baron von Gayl
Foreign:	Baron von Neurath
Finance:	Count Schwerin von Krosigk
Commerce:	Professor Warmbold
Defense:	General von Schleicher
Justice:	Dr. Gürtner
Agriculture:	Baron von Braun
Transportation:	Baron von Eltz-Rübenach
Labor:	Dr. Schaeffer

[12] It was evidently hoped to secure the services of Dr. Brüning at the forthcoming Lausanne Conference; however, he refused the offer of the Foreign Ministry in the Papen Cabinet. Cf. *Frankfurter Zeitung*, May 31, 1932.

[13] *Frankfurter Zeitung*, June 3, 7, 1932. The Papen government was often called the Cabinet of Barons.

The Nazis, it will be noted, were not represented. It was reported, however, that a gentlemen's agreement had been reached between Hitler and the new rulers of the Reich, to the effect that in return for certain concessions the Nazis would not oppose the government. These concessions were said to be dissolution of the Reichstag and new elections—which could not fail to result in greatly increased Nazi representation in the new Parliament—and the removal of the ban on the Hitler Storm Troops.[14]

Events bore out the report that an effort would be made to propitiate the Nazis. On June 4, President von Hindenburg dissolved the Reichstag, which was not in session, on the ground that state elections during the past months had shown that the Parliament no longer represented the will of the people, and new Reichstag elections were announced for July 31.[15] The Papen-Schleicher government had not dared to risk its official life by facing the Reichstag, in which, under the circumstances, it could have counted on the support of less than one-tenth of the deputies.

Nevertheless, the Reich government, despite pressing political and financial tasks, had at once taken steps to break the Prussian deadlock. This action not only aroused opposition and resentment in Catholic and Social Democratic circles in Prussia, but was viewed with particular alarm in South Germany. On June 7, Chancellor von Papen attempted to bring financial pressure to bear on Prussia, and also requested the Nazi president of the Prussian Diet to convene that body as soon as possible.

[14] *Cf.* p. 163. *New York Herald Tribune,* June 4, 1932; *Frankfurter Zeitung,* June 7, 1932.
[15] *Frankfurter Zeitung,* June 4, 7, 1932.

Papen's move was ostensibly based on the need for a responsible Prussian government with which financial questions could be settled, but rumors at once began to circulate that the Chancellor was actually seeking to provoke open conflict as an excuse for installing a Reich Commissioner. Such a development, from the point of view of the Papen-Schleicher régime would have had the advantage of removing the liberal Braun government from office and placing the powerful Prussian police in the hands of the Reich. It was intimated, moreover, that a clarification of the situation in Prussia might be looked on with favor by Hitler.[16]

It should be noted that plans to abolish the dual régime by bringing the Prussian administration under the Reich authorities had long been discussed.[17] In fact, the relations of the Reich and its component states had always been recognized as a major German problem. Its solution, however, was envisaged as possible only by democratic methods, with due consideration of local feeling in all parts of the Reich. The energetic moves of the Papen government in the matter of Prussia at once inflamed particularist sentiment in South Germany. The situation was further aggravated on June 16 by the government's action in lifting the ban on the Hitler Storm Troops—the second major concession of the Reich government to the Nazis. Disturbances and riots, with many casualties, immediately increased throughout the Reich. The South German states, jealous of their authority and genuinely concerned with the difficulty of maintaining order within their

---

[16] *Frankfurter Zeitung,* June 8, 9, 10, 1932.
[17] *Cf.* particularly H. Höpker-Aschoff, "Reichsreform," *Der deutsche Volkswirt,* August 21, 1931; also *ibid.,* August 28, 1931.

borders, met the situation by renewing the ban on
political uniforms within their territories.[18]   On
June 22, at a conference between the Reich Minister of the Interior, von Gayl, and the Interior Ministers of the states, von Gayl "urgently requested
the states to adapt their political legal measures
to those of the Reich." [19] Two days later, however,
Bavaria took even stronger measures to preserve
order. Finally, on June 28, the Reich government
issued a second emergency decree "to protect public
order," providing similar legal measures for the entire Reich and abrogating state decrees which were
not consistent with this action. State officials, however, were given the right to prohibit political meetings "in case of unquestionable danger to public
safety." [20]

Thus, during its first month in office, the Papen
government succeeded in stirring up South German
particularism without either propitiating the Nazis
or clarifying the Prussian situation. Political bitterness had increased and the campaign preparatory to
the July 31 elections was marked by a mounting
casualty list. The most serious riot took place on
July 17, in Altona, where a National Socialist parade
through the Communist section of the city caused
severe fighting in which 15 were killed and 70
wounded.[21] As a result, the Reich government on
July 18 decreed a ban on demonstrations throughout the Reich, forbidding all open-air meetings and
parades, and imposing severe punishments for offenses against the decree.

[18] *Frankfurter Zeitung,* June 23, 1932; *Der deutsche Volkswirt,* June 24, 1932.
[19] *Cf. Frankfurter Zeitung,* June 23, 1932.
[20] *Ibid.,* June 30, 1932.
[21] *Ibid.,* July 19, 20, 1932.

The Prussian Coup D'État

An even more important result of the Altona riots was von Papen's action in ousting the Braun government and installing a Reich Commissioner in Prussia. This move was as radical as it was sudden. Without warning, Chancellor von Papen issued on July 20 an emergency decree under Article 48, paragraphs 1 and 2, naming himself Reich Commissioner and Prussian Minister of the Interior, and appointing Dr. Bracht, the chief mayor of Essen, as his permanent representative to administer these offices. Simultaneously, the Reich government dismissed from office Minister President Otto Braun [22] and Minister of the Interior Severing—both Socialists—and placed Berlin and the province of Brandenburg under martial law. Herr Severing refused to desert his post and was temporarily arrested by a Reichswehr lieutenant and two men. At the same time, the Socialist police president of Berlin, Grzesinski, the Commandant of the Berlin police, Colonel Heimannsberg, and the Socialist vice-president of the Berlin police, Dr. Weiss, were forced out of office. These officials refused to submit and were promptly arrested by Lieutenant-General Rundstedt who, under the martial law decree, was in command of Berlin and Brandenburg, and who appeared at Police Headquarters with fifteen soldiers armed with hand grenades. The deposed officials were released after some hours and filed suits with the Reich Supreme Court against the government.

The reason given by the Reich government for its drastic action was the alleged inability of the Prus-

---

[22] Herr Braun was absent from Berlin on sick leave, and Dr. Hirtsiefer, a Centrist, was Acting Minister President of Prussia.

sian authorities to cope with the so-called Communist menace which, von Papen declared, had been responsible for the terror and latent civil war of the past weeks.[23] It was, however, generally admitted by impartial observers that before the ban on the Hitler Storm Troops had been lifted the Prussian police had had no difficulty in keeping order. Other motives seem to have actuated the events of July 20.

The attitude of the Papen government in the Prussian question had been considered vacillating by both the Nazis and the Hugenberg Nationalists, who were bending every effort to gain control of that all-important state. In a speech on July 18, Geheimrat Hugenberg had brought pressure on Papen by stating:

"We [the German Nationalist People's party] expect the Reich government at this moment to make an immediate end of the Marxist scum in Prussia and to install a Reich Commissioner armed with all necessary powers. We Nationalists have no responsibility toward the Papen government, but we will be willing to support it in anything which would lead to the ending of the present impossible situation in Prussia."

The Hitlerites, for their part, also demanded the appointment of a Reich Commissioner, and the Nazi president of the Prussian Landtag, Kerrl, wrote an open letter to von Papen on July 18, blaming the Socialists and the Communists for the Prussian deadlock, and stating that the existing situation was fostering an increase in Marxian propaganda which threatened to undermine the very foundations of the state.[24] This pressure evidently stiffened

[23] *Cf.* radio speech of von Papen on July 20. Text in *Frankfurter Zeitung,* July 21, 1932.
[24] *Frankfurter Zeitung,* July 20, 1932.

the determination of the Papen-Schleicher régime.

From the government's point of view, the coup d'état of July 20, in addition to being a bid for Nazi and Nationalist support, had many advantages. The powerful Prussian police was removed from Socialist control and placed in the hands of the Reich. It could now be relied on, it was felt, as a reserve for the Reichswehr in case of serious internal disorders. The government's position was thus consolidated by concentrating power in its hands. Furthermore, the Prussian deadlock had been broken and the dualism between the Reich and Prussia abolished, clearing the way for the abrogation of much administrative duplication.

The first general reaction to the coup d'état was stunned amazement. The Hitlerites, however, were jubilant, many of their leaders stating publicly that the government's move was the direct result of Nazi pressure; in their eyes, the first decisive step against the "November traitors"[25] had been taken. The Social Democrats and the Catholic Center party were of course not only incensed but gravely apprehensive over the consequences of the events of July 20. Nevertheless, with great self-control, the leaders confined themselves to strongly worded resolutions of protest, while exhorting their followers to maintain discipline and avoid disorder. Word went out to concentrate all efforts on demonstrating to the Papen-Schleicher government, through a peaceful revolution at the polls on July 31, that German democracy could not be trampled on.

In non-Prussian Germany there was not only bit-

[25] A Nazi term of opprobrium for the Socialists, whom they accuse of betraying the Fatherland in the November 1918 revolution.

terness against the government, but great uneasi-
ness. As in Prussia, the particularistic, democratic
South German states were administered by provisional "business governments" because the parliamentary deadlock had made it impossible to form
new ministries. These states, furthermore, had already crossed swords with the Papen government in
the matter of the prohibition of the Nazi Storm
Troops. They therefore saw in the events of July 20
a possible precedent for action against themselves
and were correspondingly alarmed despite the Reich
government's denial of any such intention.

Meanwhile, the deposed Prussian Ministers had
appealed to the Reich Supreme Court in Leipzig for
a temporary injunction to restrain further removals
of Prussian officials from office, and to restrict von
Papen as Reich Commissioner for Prussia in the internal administration of the state. The Court handed
down an interim decision on July 25, declining to
grant this request. The real issue as to the constitutional right of the Reich government to intervene
in the affairs of a state was not settled, however,
the Court stating that a decision on this important point would be given later after a full investigation.[26] The legal aspects of the Papen government's action in Prussia remained completely
obscure, and relations between the Reich and the
state governments were greatly aggravated.

THE POLITICAL DEADLOCK, JULY TO NOVEMBER, 1932

The German people went to the polls on July 31
with passions roused to fever pitch.[27] The only party

[26] *Frankfurter Zeitung,* July 26, 1932.
[27] *Der deutsche Volkswirt,* August 5, 1932.

backing the Cabinet—the Hugenberg Nationalists —suffered a loss of four seats.[28] The National Socialist vote amounted to something more than one-third of the electorate. While it showed an immense increase compared with that cast in the 1930 Reichstag election, it was only slightly larger than the vote polled by the party in the April 1932 state and presidential elections. Many observers believed that the movement had now reached its peak, and later events seemed to justify this opinion. The Hitlerites were not only unsuccessful in massing a majority of the German people under their banner, but lacked a majority even with the coöperation of the other Right parties, although the latter groups had gained strength. The combined Middle parties, on the other hand, remained exactly the same size. There were, however, shifts within the group, the democratic State party dwindling almost to nothing, while the two Catholic parties showed gains. On the Left, also, there was practically no change in the total proletarian vote. The Communists, however, made large gains at Socialist expense.

The large Communist vote was, in fact, the chief surprise of the election, for in previous polls during 1932, it had fallen off considerably. The success of the Communists on July 31 has been directly attributed to the lukewarm resistance of the Social Democrats to the action of the Papen Ministry in deposing the Prussian government. The Social Democrats had been faced with the difficult choice of resisting the Reich government through the proclamation of a general strike in coöperation with the Communists, or accepting a *fait accompli*. In March 1920, at the time of the Kapp *Putsch*, a general

[28] *Cf.* p. 192 for table of 1930–1932 Reichstag election returns.

strike had defeated the attempted *coup*. In 1932,
however, with more than five million unemployed
in the Reich, the moderate Social Democrats felt
that they dared not risk throwing the country into
further economic chaos by provoking civil war.
As a result, many of these erstwhile supporters lost
patience with this attitude, and apparently turned
to the Communists.[29]

The Nazis and Governmental Responsibility

The problem of inducing the Nazis to accept governmental responsibility reappeared in even more
pressing form after the elections. The only possibility for coalition government appeared to be
through Nazi-Center coöperation, for these two
groups together commanded a bare majority in the
new Reichstag. The Centrists were apparently willing to enter such a combination in the hope of re-
establishing constitutional government. Back-stage
negotiations between the two parties were carried
on early in August, but it soon became apparent
that Hitler would accept nothing less than the
Chancellorship. Meanwhile, despite von Hindenburg's proclamation of a political truce, a veritable
reign of terror, involving murders, bomb outrages
and riots, had broken out. In view of the danger-
ously disturbed situation, Hitler's aspirations for
sole power seemed incongruous to many Germans.

On August 9 the Reich government finally took
drastic action to restore public safety and order.
After several warnings, emergency decrees were promulgated extending the ban on demonstrations until
August 31, 1932, and setting severe penalties for its
infraction, including sentence of death for political

[29] *Cf. Der deutsche Volkswirt,* August 5, 1932.

murders, arson, destruction of property by explosives, or the endangering of railway traffic. Imprisonment of not less than ten years for slightly less extreme cases was decreed, and even for minor offenses the penalties were severe. Special courts were set up to administer these laws.

On the night the new decrees came into force, a gang of Nazis shot and killed a Communist in Beuthen, Upper Silesia, and brutally mistreated the body. One of the new special courts promptly tried those concerned in the affair and sentenced five Nazis to death. The verdict was the occasion for a mob demonstration against the liberal newspapers and Jewish department stores in Beuthen. The Nazi press took up the cause of the condemned men and Hitler himself telegraphed them: "From this moment your freedom is a question of our honor and a fight against the government under which this sentence has been possible is our duty." Strong Nazi protests were sent to the President and von Papen urging immediate pardon, but the government insisted that impartial justice must be done.[30]

Meanwhile, with public feeling aroused to the highest pitch by the terror and general uncertainty, negotiations to bring Hitler into the government were continued. Apparently the Catholic parties, under certain conditions, were willing to enter a coalition with the Nazis—even with Hitler as Chancellor; the Hitlerites, however, would not accept these conditions. On August 10 President von Hindenburg is reported to have expressed himself

---

[30] The sentence was eventually commuted to life imprisonment, on the ground that the new decrees had gone into force only 90 minutes before the murder was committed.

as opposed to allowing Hitler to become Chancellor.[31]

On August 13 the long-awaited interview between the President and the Nazi leader took place in Berlin. It lasted fifteen minutes. President von Hindenburg asked Hitler whether he and his followers were ready to enter the Papen Cabinet. Hitler refused the proffered Vice-Chancellorship, demanding leadership of the Reich government and entire power. In reply the President stated that his conscience and his duty to the Fatherland would not allow him to give complete power to the National Socialist movement, and expressed regret that Herr Hitler did not find it possible to support the national government as he had promised before the Reichstag elections. The interview closed with the earnest appeal of the President that Hitler carry out his announced opposition to the government in a chivalrous manner and realize his (Hitler's) responsibility to the Fatherland and to the German people.[32]

Thus despite the gentlemen's agreement,[33] the attempt to induce the Nazis to coöperate positively with the government had failed again. Hitler, backed—or forced—by his advisers, demanded "all or nothing."

Dissolution of the Reichstag

As a result, the Papen-Schleicher Cabinet had no opportunity to secure the confidence or toleration of the Reichstag which was to convene on August 30, and the government therefore announced that it would dissolve the Reichstag and call new elections. The Reichstag, nevertheless, met on schedule, and

[31] *Frankfurter Zeitung*, August 11, 1932.
[32] *Ibid.*, August 14, 1932, official communiqué.
[33] *Cf.* p. 166.

elected as its president the National Socialist deputy, Captain Hermann Goering. The session was surprisingly orderly, and the shadow of impending dissolution led the Nazis—traditional foes of constitutional government—to become the champion of a parliamentary régime, protesting that the Reichstag was capable of "constructive" work and should not be excluded from its share in governing the Reich. The parliament then adjourned until September 12, hoping to be able to convince President von Hindenburg in the interval that there was no need for dissolution.

This, however, proved impossible. Continued negotiations between the Center and the Nazis were unsuccessful. The Reichstag reconvened on September 12 and, after a stormy session during which there was great confusion in regard to constitutional procedure and rules of order, was dissolved by the government before the Chancellor had presented his program. A Communist motion of non-confidence, however, was unexpectedly brought to a vote and passed by the huge poll of 512 to 42, only the Hugenberg Nationalists and the People's party supporting the Cabinet. Although the motion was later declared null and void, having been enacted by an already dissolved parliament, it nevertheless gave striking evidence of the unpopularity of the Papen régime.

Thus, by the use of rather questionable constitutional methods, a government with the support of less than one-tenth of the German electorate remained in office. The Cabinet's official reason for dissolving the Reichstag and calling new elections, which were later fixed for November 6, was its conviction that the newly announced economic program had to be put into effect and that the Papen Ministry, therefore, must remain to carry out the task.

The government's economic program as promulgated in the emergency decree of September 5, provided for indirect credit inflation by the issue of tax credit certificates acceptable from 1934 to 1938 for the partial payment of all except income taxes. These certificates were to be used to refund part of the taxes paid by industrialists which had been regarded as especially crippling to industry. The decree further provided bonuses in the form of tax credit certificates for employers who hired additional workers. Provision was made for large appropriations for public works and virtually full power was given the Reich government to revise the social insurance legislation and the collective wage agreements, as well as the compulsory wage arbitration system.[34] The decree also envisaged the introduction of agricultural import contingents.

The reception of this decree was mixed. Industrialists were strongly in favor of it, since its provisions were undoubtedly to their advantage. Nevertheless, they entertained grave doubts regarding its promise to introduce agricultural contingents. The workers, on the other hand, were highly skeptical as to its success, and fearful that it would be the means of nullifying most, if not all, of their hard-won privileges—notably the social insurances, the fixed wage system and the arbitration of labor disputes.[35] The decree also proved unacceptable to the Nazis, either from the point of view of social welfare or from pique against the Cabinet.

[34] Text of the September 5, 1932, decree in *Frankfurter Zeitung,* September 6, 1932.

[35] *Cf Frankfurter Zeitung,* September 9, 1932.

The serious differences of opinion regarding the Papen government's energetic action in the economic field were paralleled by the general reaction to statements by various Cabinet members forecasting extensive constitutional and social reforms. The parliamentary impasse which had furnished the *raison d'étre* for the introduction of presidential government emphasized the need for constitutional reforms; however, the depth of German political passions—both cause and effect of the deadlock— made it equally difficult, if not impossible, to institute the necessary changes. Thus, in his first Ministerial Declaration on June 4, von Papen immediately antagonized and embittered the Left as well as part of the Middle parties by stating that German financial difficulties were due mainly to mounting social costs. Despite the partial truth of this statement, his further remark that the Reich had become a "charity state" [36] and that the moral forces of the nation had been weakened by steadily increasing state socialism did not enhance his prestige except in the eyes of big industry and agriculture. Von Papen's forcible removable of the Socialist Ministers in Prussia on July 20 seemed further evidence of anti-labor tendencies, and the government's economic program reinforced this impression. The unpopularity of the "Cabinet of Barons" was further increased by the speech of Minister of the Interior von Gayl on August 11, the anniversary of the signing of the Weimar Constitution, in which he indicated the amendments to that instrument which the Cabinet felt were essential. The suggested changes were designed to increase the power of the Executive, and strengthen the federal government *vis-à-vis* the states. Many of these re-

[36] *Wohlfahrtsstaat.*

forms had been thoroughly studied and discussed in the Reich, and for years had been considered necessary. The fear that they would be summarily forced on the people by decree, however, motivated the unfavorable reception which they were generally accorded. The events of July 20 in Prussia, moreover, seemed to many, particularly in South and Southwest Germany and among the workers, to be symptomatic of the Cabinet's intentions in other matters.

The position of the Papen government was further weakened by a final decision of the Supreme Court of the Reich in the Prussian question, handed down on October 25.[37] The Court ruled that the suspension of the Prussian government and appointment of a Reich Commissioner for Prussia were constitutional under Article 48, since, in its opinion, law and order in Prussia had been endangered on July 20. The Court held, however, that the suspension of the Prussian Cabinet was constitutionally valid only as a temporary measure; and, further, that the suspension deprived the Prussian Ministers of their administrative functions only. The Cabinet's right to represent Prussia in the Reichsrat (Federal Council) and in Prussia's relations with the other German states could not be abrogated. The Braun Ministry, therefore, remained the constitutional Prussian government while the acts of the Reich Commissioner for Prussia and his deputy were deemed valid only in the field of administration. In general, both sides were able to claim the decision as a victory and it contributed little to an immediate clarification of the situation.[38] Moreover, von Pap-

---

[37] *Cf.* p. 169.
[38] *Cf. Preussen contra Reich vor dem Staatsgerichtshof* (Berlin,

en's action in replacing Social Democratic Prussian officials with more conservative men indicated that the Reich government did not regard the existing order in Prussia as temporary despite the decision of the Supreme Court.

NOVEMBER 6 ELECTIONS FAIL TO BREAK DEADLOCK

Although markedly unpopular throughout the Reich because of its domestic policies, the Papen Ministry hoped that its strong stand in foreign affairs would serve to win it support at the polls on November 6. Von Papen's undoubted success at the Lausanne Conference, which had virtually wiped out German reparation,[39] and the government's renewed and energetic demands for equality in armaments [40] were calculated, from the internal political point of view, further to steal Hitler's thunder and add to the prestige and strength of the Papen Ministry. The latter, however, had been formed as a non-party government, and was definitely backed by only one party—the Hugenberg Nationalists. In order to register support of the Papen policies at the polls, it was therefore necessary to vote for the Nationalists, a conservative Protestant party which appealed, for the most part, only to large agricultural and industrial interests. Thus, in a sense, the election of November 6 was fought in a vacuum without either clearly defined issues or sharply drawn fronts.

J. H. W. Dietz Nachf. Verlag, 1933). This volume contains the complete stenographic report of the hearings before the Court from October 10 to 14 and on October 17, 1932, as well as full text of the decision and an explanatory foreword by Dr. Arnold Brecht, counsel for Prussia in the proceedings.

[39] Wertheimer, "The Lausanne Reparation Settlement," cited.

[40] *Cf. Stone,* "The World Disarmament Conference: Second Stage," cited.

While the poll on November 6 did not serve to break the parliamentary deadlock, it reflected two major shifts in German public sentiment: the Nazis lost 34 seats, and the Communists gained 11. At the same time, the Nationalists regained 14 mandates, apparently at Hitler's expense. The terror which obtained immediately after the July 31 elections and Hitler's defense of the Storm Troopers convicted in the Beuthen murder case had evidently frightened and alienated many of the Nazi leader's former supporters. Furthermore, Hitler's refusal to accept the proffered post of Reich Vice-Chancellor on August 13, 1932 [41] and his subsequent critical remarks about President von Hindenburg had made a bad impression. Finally, there had been considerable dissatisfaction among the younger and more radical Hitler followers, who were impatient with his "legal tactics." Recognizing that some of their relatively moderate bourgeois supporters were returning to the government camp and hoping to prevent further defections among the younger radicals, the Nazis had appealed primarily to the workers during the campaign. A transit strike in Berlin on the election day week-end, put through under combined Nazi and Communist leadership, was an example of their tactics.

Despite the election agitation of the Hitlerites, however, the Nazi losses on November 6 do not seem to have accrued to the Communists. On the contrary, the latter's gain of 11 seats was apparently made at the expense of the Social Democrats who lost 12 mandates. Beside the changes in the Nazi, Social Democratic and Communist camps, the No-

[41] *Cf.* p. 176.

vember 6 election showed a continued shrinkage in the representation of the smaller parties.[42]

The election had shown conclusively that the great majority of the German people were opposed to the Papen government; the feeling against the Ministry and in particular against the Chancellor was unmistakable. As a result, von Papen felt it necessary after the election to state that the way was now clear for the formation of a "real government of national concentration," and that for his part the question of personalities would not be allowed to block such development. President von Hindenburg on November 10, therefore, charged von Papen to sound out the various party leaders with a view to ascertaining which groups were ready to support the government's political and economic program. These conversations brought out the fact that only the Hugenberg Nationalists and the People's party were willing to back von Papen; the Catholic parties withheld their support, while the Social Democrats refused even to negotiate. The Nazis, however, declared themselves willing, under certain circumstances, to engage in written negotiations with the Chancellor. Realizing the hopelessness of its position, the Papen Cabinet resigned on November 17.

The Schleicher Government

President von Hindenburg thereupon took over the task of setting up a government. On November 19 the President received Adolf Hitler, who assured him that he could form a government acceptable to the Reichstag. On November 21, at a

[42] *Cf.* table, p. 192 for results of July 31 and November 6 elections.

second meeting, von Hindenburg charged Hitler, "as the leader of the largest German party," to determine whether and under what conditions he could be sure of a "secure, positive majority for a strong, unified program." On the same day the President laid down in writing several conditions which he considered a *sine qua non* for the formation of such a Ministry. These included the formulation of a workable economic program, no attempt to return to the former dual relationship between the Reich and Prussia, and no tampering with Article 48 of the Constitution. Furthermore, in the matter of personnel, the President insisted that he must have the final decision regarding the list of Ministers, and reserved the right to appoint the Foreign Minister and the Minister of Defense as consistent with his legal position as head of the Reich and Commander-in-Chief of the army. Following this communication, there was a further exchange of letters between Hitler and the President's Secretary of State, Dr. Meissner, regarding the definition of presidial government, in which it was stated that von Hindenburg could not appoint as Chancellor, in a government responsible to the President alone, the leader of a party which demanded sole power for itself. Despite this statement, Hitler wrote von Hindenburg on November 23 requesting the latter to commission him to form a presidial Ministry with full powers. The President flatly refused this demand on November 24, stating that he could not reconcile it with his oath of office or his conscience.[43] A second direct attempt to bring

---

[43] Text of the Hindenburg-Hitler exchange of notes in *Frankfurter Zeitung*, November 25, 1932; *cf.* also *ibid.*, November 12 to 24, 1932; *Der Zeitspiegel*, 1st year, No. 23, December 3, 1932.

the Nazis into the government had failed; Hitler still insisted on "all power or nothing."

After thus rebuffing Hitler, President von Hindenburg on December 2 named General von Schleicher Chancellor, although the old Field Marshal had apparently endeavored to reappoint von Papen in whom he still had the highest confidence. It is reported that the declaration of several important Ministers [44] that they would not serve in a new Papen Cabinet, added to von Papen's earnest request to the President to release him from responsibility, finally forced von Hindenburg to appoint von Schleicher.

The new presidial Cabinet, as finally constituted, had the following membership: [45]

Chancellor, Minister of Defense, and Reich Commissioner for Prussia, General von Schleicher;
Interior, Dr. Bracht;
Labor, Dr. Syrup;
Foreign Affairs, Baron von Neurath;
Finance, Count Schwerin von Krosigk;
Justice, Dr. Gürtner;
Posts, Baron von Eltz-Rübenach;
Reëmployment, Dr. Gereke;
Agriculture, Baron von Braun;
Commerce, Professor Warmbold;
Without Portfolio, Dr. Popitz.

The composition of the new government showed that consideration had been given to the factors

[44] The Ministers were: Baron von Neurath, Foreign Minister; Dr. Bracht, deputy Reich Commissioner for Prussia and member of the Reich government without portfolio; the Finance Minister, Count von Krosigk; and Dr. Popitz, a financial expert and also Minister without portfolio. Cf. *Der Zeitspiegel,* 1st year, No. 24, December 17, 1932; *Frankfurter Zeitung,* November 29 to December 3, 1932; also *Der deutsche Volkswirt,* December 9, 1932.
[45] *Frankfurter Zeitung,* December 4, 5, 1932.

which had discredited von Papen's régime; namely, its outspoken anti-labor tendencies, which had resulted in many strikes and contributed to the increase in the Communist vote; the introduction of agricultural import contingents designed to benefit the bankrupt East Elbian landowners, which jeopardized Germany's already precarious foreign trade with the threat of serious retaliation; and the government's attempts to establish a strongly centralized state and to reform the constitution, which aroused animosity throughout South Germany and Prussia. The von Schleicher Cabinet attempted to remedy the situation by appointing a Minister of Labor more sympathetic to the workers; dropping the system of import contingents; and replacing the former Minister of the Interior, Baron von Gayl, with a man less conspicuously associated with schemes for constitutional reform.

Von Schleicher was reputed to be more conciliatory than his predecessor and slightly more acceptable to labor. The Ministerial Declaration of the new government, announced in a radio speech by the Chancellor on December 15, bore out this prediction. In this statement the new government's policy was summarized in one outstanding point: creation of work.

For the rest, von Schleicher both by omission and commission, attempted to allay the fears of the German people. He declared himself opposed to a military dictatorship, saying that one cannot "sit comfortably on bayonet points"; expressed himself in favor of increased settlement of unemployed on the land; and stated that he was neither a "capitalist nor a socialist." The Ministerial Declaration, moreover, contained nothing in regard to "authoritative government," there was no mention of "abolishing the state as a charity organization," and no word about reforming the constitution or the "divine and historical misson" of the government.[46]

As an earnest of its conciliatory intentions, the government indicated to the trade unions immediately upon taking office that it would not be unwilling to renounce the blanket powers for revision of the social insurances which had formed a part of von Papen's September 5 emergency decree.[47] The Reichstag, which met from December 6 to 9, repealed this section of the decree and reinstituted the system of wage agreements.[48]

During the first month after von Schleicher assumed office, there was apparent a noticeable relaxation throughout Germany. Political passions appeared to have somewhat subsided; there were a few visible signs of improvement in the economic situation; the year-end summaries of conditions were relatively optimistic; [49] the German people seemed to yearn for peace and stability after the financial and political crises of the past two years.

---

[46] Text of Ministerial Declaration in *Hamburger Fremdenblatt,* December 16, 1932.

[47] *Cf.* p. 178.

[48] *Der deutsche Volkswirt,* December 16, 1932.

[49] *Cf. Der deutsche Volkswirt,* December 23, 1932; *Frankfurter Zeitung,* December 31, 1932; *Berliner Handelsgesellschaft,* confidential reports, Berlin, December 23, 30, 1932; Deutsche Bank und Disconto Gesellschaft, *Wirtschaftliche Mitteilungen,* January 14, 1933; *Vierteljahreshefte zur Konjunkturforschung,* Hrsg. vom Institut für Konjunkturforschung, 7th year, Heft 3, Berlin, December 1932, Parts A and B.

CHAPTER IV

THE NATIONAL REVOLUTION

SUDDENLY, on January 28, 1933, the Schleicher government resigned when President von Hindenburg refused it power to dissolve a hostile Reichstag. On January 30 a new Cabinet took office, with Hitler as Chancellor and von Papen as Vice-Chancellor and Reich Commissioner for Prussia.

Von Schleicher's endeavors to gain the confidence of both Right and Left had been unsuccessful. He had not only failed to induce the Nazis to accept governmental responsibilities, but his flirtation with the trade unions—although it strengthened his position to a certain extent—completely alienated the big industrialists and the Junkers. The Schleicher government, therefore, would have faced the Reichstag without the support of a single party. The President's refusal to retain von Schleicher might appear to have been a logical step toward reintroduction of parliamentary government.

For some weeks backstage negotiations between industrialists and Nazis had been in progress to induce Hitler to depart from his uncompromising position of "all power or nothing." The reported indebtedness of the National Socialist party to its industrialist friends, estimated at some twelve million marks, was probably a factor in the situation. Moreover, the large East Elbian landed interests had found it increasingly difficult to extract concessions from the Schleicher government, and the discovery by a Reichstag committee of financial graft in the administration of the *Osthilfe* fund[1] added to the Junkers' grievances against von Schleicher. News had leaked out of a meeting in Cologne, January 4 between Hitler and von Papen, at which a government of "national concentration" was admittedly discussed, although the participants flatly denied that they were trying to undermine von Schleicher's position. Von Papen's easy access to President von Hindenburg undoubtedly made it possible for him to persuade the aged Field Marshal of the necessity for a change of government, and to convince him of Hitler's qualifications.

His efforts evidently met with complete success: not only was von Schleicher forced out, but the new government represented the most conservative elements in the Reich. The Cabinet, in addition to Hitler and Papen, was composed as follows:

Hermann Goering (Nazi), Aviation and Acting Prussian Minister of the Interior
Wilhelm Frick (Nazi), Interior
Alfred Hugenberg (Nationalist), Agriculture and Commerce
Franz Seldte (Nationalist), Labor
General von Blomberg, Defense
Count von Eltz-Rübenach, Posts and Communications
Dr. Gereke, Commissioner for Reëmployment
Baron von Neurath, Foreign Affairs
Count Schwerin von Krosigk, Finance

The outstanding feature of the Cabinet was its balance of Nazi and Nationalist Ministers, although

[1] The money appropriated to assist bankrupt eastern agriculturists at Reich expense. *Cf. Der deutsche Volkswirt,* January 27, 1933.

the non-party Ministers were known to be close to the Nationalist party.

Since the new government could count definitely on only 247 votes in the Reichstag, and, even with the aid of the smaller Right groups, lacked a majority by a margin of at least 25 votes, the support or toleration of the Catholic parties was indispensable. Negotiations between Hitler and Monsignor Kaas, the Centrist leader, were initiated on January 31. The next day, the Center party addressed a series of questions to Hitler to ascertain the government's intentions regarding observance of the constitution; assistance to industry; possible reactionary social measures; and sound currency. Without replying to these inquiries, Hitler suddenly broke off negotiations and on February 1 the government announced the dissolution of the Reichstag, with new elections on March 5. Elections for the Prussian Diet—which was summarily dissolved on February 6 after President von Hindenburg had appointed von Papen head of the state government, apparently in direct violation of the constitutional principles defined by the Reich Supreme Court on October 25 [2]—were also scheduled for March 5.

Hitler's accession to power on January 30, 1933, as Chancellor of Germany marked the beginning of the so-called National Revolution. Despite the fact that the new government was supposedly a coalition of Hitlerites and Nationalists, containing only three Nazi Ministers, it soon became apparent that the latter were the driving force in the Cabinet. Backed by a party organization which covered every phase of German life and in reality constituted a

[2] *Cf.* p. 180.

state within a state,[3] and uninhibited by scruples of any sort, the Nazis were able to dominate the government completely and put through the revolution. Their task was facilitated not only by Hitler's Chancellorship but also by the fact that his lieutenants, Frick and Goering, were respectively Reich and Prussian Ministers of the Interior, and thus controlled the police in the entire country. Furthermore, the non-Nazi members of the Hitler government were apparently willing that the major share of the election campaign preparatory to the March 5 Reichstag poll should be carried on by the Nazis, who were universally recognized as excelling in propaganda of this sort. The Nationalists hoped thus to consolidate their own position and ride to power, as it were, on the shoulders of the Hitlerites.

The campaign as directed by the Nazis was used to stir up an immense Communist scare in the Reich, culminating in the burning of the Reichstag building on the night of February 27 by alleged Communists. This incident gave the Nazis an opportunity to effect complete suppression of Socialist and Communist election meetings and press, to arrest the Communist leaders, to institute a drastic censorship, and to abolish all forms of personal liberty in general. A decree proclaimed by President von Hindenburg on February 28, 1933, rescinded until further notice all the articles of the Weimar constitution providing for liberty of the person; freedom of opinion, including freedom of the press; right of assembly; secrecy of postal, telegraphic and telephonic communication; inviolability of dwellings; and sanctity of private property. Furthermore, under this decree the Reich government was given

[3] *Cf.* p. 155.

the right to enforce its provisions in the federal states, and the penalties for infraction were made very severe. The death sentence, life or long imprisonment were specified for particular crimes including high treason, poisoning, arson, conspiracy against the life of the Reich President, the members of the Reich government or Reich Commissioners. The execution of the decree was placed entirely in the hands of the police, with no appeal.[4] As a result of this decree and of Nazi terrorism, the opposition was prevented from carrying on its campaign. The actual election, however, apparently took place without incident, although the atmosphere throughout the Reich was tense in the extreme. The following table gives the results of the voting on March 5,

Parties	Mar. 5, 1933 Seats	Nov. 6, 1932 Seats	July 31, 1932 Seats	Sept. 14, 1930 Seats
National Socialist	288	196	230	107
German National People's *	52	51	37	41
German People's	2	11	7	30
Economic	...	1	2	23
Other Parties	7	12	9	55
Catholic Center	74	70	75	68
Bavarian People's	18	20	22	19
State	5	2	4	14
Social Democratic	120	121	133	143
Communist	81	100	89	77
Totals	647	584	608	577

* The German National People's party fought the March 1933 election under the designation *Schwarz-Weiss-Rote-Front*—Black-White-Red Front.

[4] For English text of the decree, *cf.* J. K. Pollock and H. J. Heneman, *The Hitler Decrees* (Ann Arbor, George Wahr, 1934), p. 10. German texts in Werner Hoche, *Die Gesetzgebung des Kabinetts Hitler: Die Gesetze in Reich und Preussen seit dem 30 Januar 1933*, vol. I, p. 236 *et seq.; Reichsgesetzblatt I*, p. 83 (1933). The articles of the Constitution which have been rescinded are: 114, 115, 117, 118, 123, 124 and 153. For texts of the articles, *cf.* p. 259 *et seq.*

as well as the returns in the three previous elections, thus presenting a complete picture of the rise of the Nazis.[5]

THE BROWN TERROR

Thus the Nazis, with 44 per cent of the total vote, and their Nationalist colleagues in the government, who polled 8 per cent, achieved a working majority of the German electorate on March 5. The so-called National Revolution must be characterized, however, as the consolidation of complete Nazi control of the Reich.

Following the example of Soviet Russia and Fascist Italy, the accession of the Nazis to power—known as the "National Revolution"—was accompanied by a reign of terror. Responsible Ministers in the Hitler Cabinet repeatedly stated that no revolution was ever consummated with less bloodshed. This contention may be accurate, since the Nazis came to power originally by constitutional means and not by an actual coup d'état; nevertheless, the consolidation of their rule, after the manner of most revolutions, was accomplished by suppressing constitutional guarantees and by systematic action against persons whom the Nazis considered enemies of the "new Germany," including all "Marxists," such as Communists and Socialists; all "internationalists," including liberals and pacifists; and all Jews. More recently Catholics and even Nationalists have not been exempted.[6]

As early as February 24, Nazi Storm Troopers and

[5] Der Zeitspiegel, March 19, 1933; Der Heimatdienst, Jahrgang XII, No. 16, August 2, 1932; Frankfurter Zeitung, August 16, 1932; Reichstagshandbuch V. Wahlperiode, 1930, Hrsg. vom Bureau des Reichstags (Berlin, Reichsdruckerei, 1930).
[6] Cf. p. 226.

some members of the Steel Helmet veterans' organization had been inducted into the police as auxiliaries[7] and the control of law and order throughout the Reich was therefore virtually in the hands of the Nazis. Even before the election on March 5, many terrorist acts had been perpetrated by Nazis. A well-informed foreign observer stated on March 1: "The last few weeks have looked very much like a cold-blooded, long-drawn-out, diluted St. Bartholomew's Eve."[8] The election itself passed off without disturbances, but in the succeeding weeks more and more acts of violence by uniformed Nazi Storm Troopers against Jews and "Marxists" were reported abroad. In the Reich the Nationalist *Deutsche Allgemeine Zeitung* ventured to say on March 13:

"Certain sections of the population in the large towns have been in a state of panic and terror. . . . Whoever is guilty today of breaking into houses, of kidnapping, of threats, or of any other crimes and offenses punishable by law must immediately be handed over to the police.

"The houses where 'political prisoners' are supposed to have been locked up by private individuals must, if the police do not know of them already, be immediately indicated to the police authorities. . . . Private revenge in blood must no longer be taken."[9]

The occasion for this statement in the *Deutsche Allgemeine Zeitung* was an appeal issued by Hitler

---

[7] *The Times* (London), February 25, 1933.

[8] *Ibid.*, March 2, 1933.

[9] *Deutsche Allgemeine Zeitung,* March 13, 1933. This paper, supported by the heavy industries, was eventually banned on May 30 for three months; but was permitted to re-appear on June 16 after the editor, Dr. Fritz Klein, had been forced to resign. *Cf. New York Times,* June 17, 1933; *The Times* (London), March 14, 1933; and *Manchester Guardian Weekly,* March 17, 1933.

on March 10 to his followers to refrain from molesting individuals and disturbing business. On the same day Captain Goering [10] declared, in a speech rejecting the idea of using the police to protect Jewish stores: "We have been saying to the people for years that they might settle accounts with the traitors. We stand by our word: accounts are being settled." [11] Hitler's command to the Storm Troopers to cease acts of political terror, however, was broadcast over the government radio on March 12. [12] It was immediately stated in Berlin that the Storm Troops had been restrained by Hitler's action, although reports of outrages against Jews and "Marxists" continued. The government attempted to convince the world that such terrorization as had occurred was perpetrated by "Communist impostors clad in Nazi uniform." In many statements government officials denied even the existence of a terror, [13] despite the virtual admission contained in Hitler's order to the Storm Troops and the fully authenticated accounts sent out by all responsible foreign journalists. In response to strong American protests, Secretary of State Hull asked the American diplomatic and consular agents in Germany for a full report and, in an official statement issued on March 26, declared that "a reply has now been received indicating that whereas there was for a short time considerable mistreatment of Jews, this phase may be considered virtually terminated.

---

[10] At that time Deputy Minister of the Interior for Prussia, Federal Commissioner of Aviation and Minister without Portfolio in the Reich Cabinet. On April 11 Hitler appointed Goering to the post of Prussian Premier responsible only to the Regent (*Staathalter*) for Prussia, a post held by Hitler.

[11] *The Times* (London), March 13, 1933.

[12] *New York Times*, March 13, 1933.

[13] *The Times* (London), March 27, 1933.

There was some picketing of Jewish merchandising stores and instances of professional discrimination. These manifestations were viewed with serious concern by the German government." [14]

Reports of terrorization and further "preventive arrests" continued, the Nazis having set up concentration camps for political prisoners before the end of March.[15] Goering's promised action against the Jews apparently made a deeper impression at home and abroad than Hitler's appeals to his Storm Troopers. Large meetings protesting Nazi persecution of the Jews were held in the United States and elsewhere, at which both Jewish and non-Jewish leaders voiced their condemnation of Nazi actions. Within the Reich, the Nazis retaliated by using German Jews as hostages to force the cessation of anti-Nazi protests abroad. On March 27, it was officially announced that the "National Socialist movement will now take the most drastic legal counter-measures aimed against the intellectual authors and exploiters of this treasonable agitation which is mainly conducted abroad by Jews formerly resident in Germany." The same official statement announced the formation of Nazi "Committees of Action" to take measures against atrocity reports abroad by organizing a boycott of Jewish business men in Germany, and forecast the introduction of a *numerus clausus* for Jewish doctors and lawyers.[16]

The Jewish Boycott

National Socialist party headquarters issued a manifesto on the night of March 28, proclaiming a

[14] Department of State, *Press Releases*, April 1, 1933.
[15] *The Times* (London), March 25, 1933.
[16] *Frankfurter Zeitung*, March 28, 1933.

national boycott of Jewish goods and Jews in the professions to start on April 1, as a counter-action to the "lies and defamations of absolutely shocking perversity which have been let loose about Germany." This official declaration stated categorically that "Communist and Marxist criminals and their Jewish-intellectual instigators, who managed in good time to escape abroad with their money, are now conducting a conscienceless, treasonable propaganda campaign against the German people . . . from the capitals of the former Entente countries." [17] The manifesto was accompanied by an official order organizing the boycott as follows: [18]

(1) "In every local branch and unit of the N.S.D.A.P.,[19] Committees of Action must be appointed immediately to carry out a systematically planned boycott of Jewish businesses, Jewish doctors and Jewish lawyers . . .

(2) "The Committees of Action are responsible for the most careful protection of all foreigners without regard to confession, origin or race. The boycott is a purely defensive measure which is directed solely against German Jewry.

(3) "The Committees of Action must immediately popularize the boycott by propaganda and enlightenment. Its keynote is that no German shall buy from a Jew. . . . The boycott must be all inclusive. It shall be undertaken by the whole people and must strike Jewry in its most sensitive spot.

(4) "In doubtful cases, boycotting of the concerns in question may be dispensed with until the Central Committee in Munich can make a definite decision.

---

[17] *Ibid.*, March 29, 1933.
[18] Translated from the *Frankfurter Zeitung,* March 29, 1933.
[19] *National Sozialistische Deutsche Arbeiter Partei* (National Socialist German Workers' party).

Party Comrade Streicher [20] is appointed chairman of the boycott committee.

(5) "The Committees of Action must watch the newspapers closely and observe how strongly they participate in the campaign of enlightenment of the German people against Jewish atrocity agitation abroad. Papers which do not participate or do so only to a limited extent are to be immediately removed from every German home. No German and no German business shall give advertising to such papers. They must be ruined by public contempt and may be written only for their Jewish racial comrades but not for the German people.

(6) "The Committees of Action in cooperation with the Work Cells organization of the party, must carry enlightenment into the factories as to the consequences of the Jewish atrocity agitation to German work and therefore to German workers. In particular, the workers must be enlightened as to the necessity for a national boycott as a defensive measure to protect German work.

(7) "The Committees of Action must penetrate into the smallest villages in order particularly to strike at Jewish traders in the country. It must always be explained that this action has been forced upon us as a defensive measure.

(8) "The boycott is not to start in a scattered fashion but must begin at one stroke and all preparations are now to be toward this end. Orders will be issued to the Storm Troops to stand guard, beginning the

---

[20] Julius Streicher had been a school teacher in Nuremberg. In 1920 he became known as an agitator for a small group calling itself "German Socialists" and strongly agrarian in sympathy. He was particularly notorious as an anti-Semite and as publisher of *Der Stürmer,* a sheet with a large circulation devoted primarily to so-called Jewish scandals, treated in a fashion bordering on the pornographic. Streicher in the earlier years of the so-called *Voelkische* movement in Germany was a bitter enemy of Hitler, always striving to attain leadership in the movement. *Cf.* Konrad Heiden, *Geschichte des Nationalsozialismus* (Berlin, Rowohlt, 1932), pp. 29, 53–55, 122, 178.

second at which the boycott starts, in order to warn the people from entering Jewish businesses. The start of the boycott will be announced by placards, by the press, by handbills, etc. The boycott will begin at one stroke on Saturday, April 1, at 10 A.M. sharp. It will continue until an order of the party executive decrees its end.

(9) "The Committees of Action shall immediately organize tens of thousands of mass meetings which shall reach into the tiniest hamlets and which shall demand the introduction of a quota system for Jews in all professions. . . . In order to intensify the effect of this action, these demands shall be confined for the present to the following three categories: (a) Attendance at German middle and higher schools (colleges); (b) Doctors; and (c) Lawyers.

(10) "The Committees of Action have the further task of seeing to it that every German who has any connections whatsoever in foreign countries shall make use of them to spread the truth in letters, telegrams and telephone messages: that peace and order prevail in Germany, that the German people has no more ardent wish than to live in peace with the rest of the world and that it is conducting its struggle against Jewish atrocity agitation as a purely defensive battle.

(11) "The Committees of Action are responsible that the entire struggle be conducted in complete peace and strictest discipline. Not a hair on any Jewish head shall be touched. We will cope with this agitation only by means of the decisive pressure of these measures."

As a result of this order, individuals and organizations in the United States and abroad having contacts with Germans were flooded with denials of the existence of a terror in the Reich and assured that German Jews could and did go about their affairs as usual. Nevertheless, foreign protests and reports of atrocities did not cease. The Hitler government, through the medium of the strictly censored German press, announced on March 31, that the "foreign atrocity agitation" was waning and therefore the boycott would be put into effect for one day only—April 1. It threatened to resume the boycott on April 5, if by that date the "foreign agitation" had not entirely ceased.[21]

Thus the boycott, originally proclaimed by the National Socialist party as distinct from the Hitler government, was actually carried out by the latter. On April 1, all Jewish concerns, with the exception of banks and newspapers, were placed under guard by Storm Troopers from ten o'clock in the morning until midnight. The Storm Troopers not only tried to keep out the few who attempted to enter boycotted establishments, but pasted up signs announcing that "no German buys from Jews," smeared windows with the word "Jew" in large red or white letters, and similarly decorated the name plates of doctors and attorneys. In Berlin the regular police were apparently inactive, and "groups of Nazis with heavy, weighted riding-crops strode about . . ."[22] Besides boycotting Jewish places of business, Storm Troop pickets kept Jewish judges, lawyers and jurymen out of the courthouses, admittance to the grounds of the University of Berlin was denied to Jewish students, and the Prussian State Library refused to admit Jewish readers.[23]

While the Jewish boycott was a strictly official matter, the terror which existed in the Reich during March was apparently due in large part to individual actions by Storm Troopers. This is evident from the contradictory statements made during March by

[21] *Frankfurter Zeitung*, April 1, 1933.
[22] *The Times* (London), April 2, 1933.
[23] *New York Times,* April 2, 1933.

Hitler in attempting to restrain his private army, and by Goering who, while exhorting the Storm Troopers to preserve discipline, openly incited them to fresh violence against the Jews. In the early stages of the Revolution, the Storm Troopers were kept busy for a time hoisting the red, black and white Imperial flag and the Nazi swastika on all public buildings in place of the black, red and gold Republican colors.[24] This relatively harmless task did not satisfy the Storm Troopers, whose leaders had promised them for a decade that once Hitler came to power they could revenge themselves on all their enemies, particularly the Jews. Thus the anti-Jewish boycott was an earnest of the government's intentions to put into effect the Nazi program, of which anti-Semitism forms such an important part,[25] and also provided an occupation for the Storm Troops. The Nazis, in consolidating their power, had met with little or no opposition. Their opponents collapsing like a house of cards, the Nazis found themselves within a short time in complete control, and concentrated much of their fury and surplus energy on the Jews—who offered a convenient scapegoat. By placing the responsibility for spreading so-called atrocity stories on the Jews, the Nazis hoped to convince the German people that the reports of excesses perpetrated by Storm Troopers were false, and thus to clear themselves. By making German Jews hostages for the "good behavior" of the world, the Nazis apparently expected to control public opinion abroad as they controlled it within the Reich.

---

[24] The flag was officially changed on March 12 by a decree of President von Hindenburg. *New York Times,* March 13, 1933.

[25] *Cf.* pp. 140–144.

Revolution or Staatsstreich?

Although Hitler's consolidation of power was generally called a revolution by the Nazis themselves, some doubt may be expressed of the technical accuracy of the term as applied to German developments during the early months of 1933. Furthermore, while the Nazi leaders on the one hand protested that never in history had so bloodless a revolution been achieved, they strove, on the other hand, to give the impression that this revolution had been carried out by constitutional methods—obviously a contradiction in terms. Hitler, moreover, on taking office on January 30, 1933, had solemnly sworn to uphold the constitution and defend the law and, since the Nazis laid great stress on the so-called "old German virtue" of fidelity, the bad psychological impression involved in a purported breach of his oath was doubtless a factor in the situation.

It would probably be more accurate to term the establishment of the Third Reich a *Staatsstreich,* or coup d'état. The Nazis did not achieve power by fighting as in an out-and-out revolution, but instead Hitler took office in a constitutional manner. Once in control of the government, however, the Nazis consolidated their power and set up the Third Reich by effecting changes which appear to have been in violation of existing constitutional law. The principal instrument under which these changes were made was the Enabling Act, and the question of the authority of the rump Reichstag which accepted that Act is therefore of importance. This question was never settled by recourse to a competent court.

Nevertheless, it appears that the exclusion of all the Communist deputies and several of the Socialists from the Reichstag sessions of March 21 and 23, was a breach of the constitution.[26] These members of the Reichstag had been duly elected on March 5, but had been arrested and put in custody despite their parliamentary immunity. Apparently this immunity had not been done away with previously by the government; in any case, under German law, only the Reichstag itself was entitled to set it aside. Therefore the exclusion of 81 Communists and 16 Social Democrats was doubtless unconstitutional. The problem was and is, however, primarily of academic importance.[27] The Enabling Act itself was apparently constitutional as an amendment to the Weimar instrument for it was passed by the requisite two-thirds majority of the Reichstag.

The Weimar constitution still forms, theoretically at least, the legal basis of the German state,[28] although many official acts and decrees of the government and the Reichstag have already considerably altered or suspended the provisions of the old constitution. Nevertheless, in order to comprehend fully the changes in the structure of the German state which have taken place during the first year of Nazi rule, it is essential to review briefly the chief provisions of the Weimar constitution.

The German constitution, drawn up by the Weimar Assembly, was described as the most democratic in the world. Article I stated that "The

[26] *Cf.* p. 225.

[27] Even if all the 647 duly elected Reichstag deputies had been present, the Hitler government would probably have been able to achieve a two-thirds majority in favor of the Enabling Act. Doubtless only the 81 Communist and the 120 Social Democratic deputies would have voted against the bill. Actually, only the 94 Socialists present voted against it.

[28] The official *Nationalsozialistisches Jahrbuch, 1934,* published after the Nazis came to power, still gave the form of government in Germany as a "Republic."

German Reich is a Republic. The political power emanates from the people." A Reichstag, elected by universal suffrage, according to the principles of proportional representation, was the chief legislative body of the Republic. A second chamber, the Reichsrat, representing the component states or *Länder* of the Reich, had subordinate legislative powers. The executive was composed of a President, elected for seven years by popular vote, and a cabinet of ministers appointed by the President and responsible to the Reichstag. Under the Empire, the power of Prussia had been supreme; the Weimar constitution limited Prussia's votes in the Reichsrat —the successor of the old Bundesrat—to two-fifths of the total votes. The powers of the Reichsrat were also greatly reduced.

The Weimar constitution thus established parliamentary government on a broad democratic basis and introduced some interesting experiments. Committees of investigation and permanent committees of the Reichstag watched over the government when the Reichstag was not in session. The constitution provided for the initiative and referendum; it made possible the recall of the President and provided as well that all his acts had to be countersigned by a responsible minister. In the field of socialization, the constitution had several novel provisions, chief among them having been an important attempt to establish an advisory body of representatives of occupations. Factory Workers' Councils, District Workers' Councils and a Workers' Council for the Reich were provided for, the original intention having been to give labor an actual participation in the control of industry and government, although a subsequent law gave these bodies only advisory power. The Councils, however, were empowered to name one or two members to the boards of directors of industrial enterprises, and under some circumstances they also had access to the books of such concerns. The constitution further provided for the representation of economic interests in an advisory capacity in political matters. Drafts of bills of a political-social nature which were of fundamental significance had to be submitted to the Economic Council of the Reich for consideration before they were introduced into the Reichstag. This Council included representatives of all important economic groups and had power also to initiate bills.

The constitution contained far-reaching and very liberal provisions for the protection of the rights of individuals; [29] the State church was done away with; the constitution provided for a school system and all schools were placed under governmental control; private preparatory schools were abolished.

The constitution greatly altered the relations of the various provinces of Germany to the Reich. It no longer spoke of them as states, but as territories (*Länder*), and the powers which might be exercised solely by the central government were greatly increased. The intense jealousy of the south German states, particularly Bavaria and Württemberg, toward Prussia made the drafting of the constitution exceptionally difficult and complicated domestic politics in Germany during the entire republican era.

The constitution was finally adopted on July 31, 1919, and came into force on August 11. The Weimar constitution provided that each of the German states must have a republican constitution,

[29] For text of these articles, *cf.* p. 256 *et seq.*

and as a result the units of the German Reich all had constitutions modeled largely on the Weimar instrument itself.[30]

Although, as has been pointed out, the Weimar constitution was one of the most democratic in the world, ironically enough the German republican governments felt forced by stress of circumstances to make increasing use of one of its least democratic provisions—Article 48. This article provided:

"If a state fails to carry out the duties imposed upon it by the national constitution or national laws, the President of the Reich may compel performance with the aid of armed force.

"If public safety and order be seriously disturbed or threatened within the German Reich, the President of the Reich may take the necessary measures to restore public safety and order; if necessary, with the aid of armed force. For this purpose he may temporarily suspend in whole or in part the fundamental rights enumerated in Articles 114, 115, 117, 118, 123, 124 and 153.[31]

"The President of the Reich must immediately communicate to the Reichstag all measures taken by virtue of Paragraph 1 or Paragraph 2 of this Article. On demand of the Reichstag these measures must be abrogated.

"Detailed regulations shall be prescribed by a national law." [32]

From October 1919, through September 1932, no less than 233 emergency decrees were issued under Article 48. During the troubled early years of the Republic from 1919 to 1925, there were 135 such decrees promulgated. In contrast, only 16 emergency decrees were issued between 1925 and 1931, no recourse to Article 48 having been necessary during the year 1929. By the beginning of 1931, however, the deepening economic depression, with the attendant growth of the National Socialist and Communist parties, made it increasingly difficult for the Reich governments to put necessary legislation

[30] Cf. Gerhard Anschütz, Die Verfassung des Deutschen Reichs von 11 August 1919 (4th edition, Berlin, Stilke, 1933).
[31] Cf. p. 259.
[32] This law was never passed.

through the Reichstag directly, and Article 48 was invoked more and more frequently. Thus in 1931 the proportion between emergency decrees and regular laws passed by the Reichstag was 42 to 35; in 1932 there were only 5 laws as compared with 59 emergency decrees.[33] Nevertheless, the Reichstag, which was incapable of legislating directly because the deputies felt unable to accept the political onus involved, did not refuse its assent to the emergency decrees as provided in Article 48.

The increasing reliance placed on Article 48 by governments of the Weimar Republic as the political deadlock continued provided a convenient precedent for the Nazis after the formation of the Hitler ministry on January 30, 1933. Hitler merely substituted out-and-out dictatorship based on dubious constitutional changes for an indirect dictatorship under Article 48.[34]

The ideal toward which the Nazis worked consistently after their assumption of power was the erection of a totalitarian state,[35] and during their first year in office they went far toward achieving this goal. All political parties in the Reich, with the exception of the National Socialist, were outlawed or dissolved. The state assumed control of every aspect of cultural life and even of some aspects of family life. Moreover, agriculture and organized labor were put completely under the ægis

[33] For list of emergency decrees promulgated between October 1919 and the end of September 1932, cf. Lindsay Rogers and others, "German Political Institutions II: Article 48," in *Political Science Quarterly*, December 1932. The proportion of laws to decrees is given in Dr. Franz Albrecht Medicus, "Programm der Reichsregierung und Ermächtigungsgesetz," No. 1 of *Das Recht der nationalen Revolution* (Berlin, Carl Heymanns Verlag, 1933).
[34] Cf. Chapter "Hitler and the German Political Crisis," p. 158.
[35] Cf. Chapter "The Attack on Democracy," p. 15.

of the state, although industry remained relatively independent. The legal structure of the nation, furthermore, was changed by alteration of the relations of the federal states with the Reich, abolition of the state diets and the Reichsrat, and introduction of Reich regents appointed by Hitler, at the head of all state administrations. The final form of the Reich, however, has not as yet been decreed, although it has been indicated that the Nazis plan to re-divide the country into more or less arbitrary divisions which would not correspond with the present states. Such a measure, if it materializes, would be a drastic attempt to abolish the centuries-old particularism and separatism of the German states and principalities which has already received a death-blow through the practical abolition of the states as sovereign political entities. Finally, the legislative function was given to the Reich government for a period of four years, and the civil service law was fundamentally changed.

THE ENABLING ACT

The Reichstag elected on March 5, 1933, held a solemn opening session on March 21, at the Garrison Church in Potsdam, which was marked by a ceremony at the tomb of Frederick the Great, participated in by President von Hindenburg and Chancellor Hitler. The Potsdam meeting was followed by an organization session in Berlin on the afternoon of the same day, when Minister Goering was reëlected President of the Reichstag. On March 23, the parliament assembled once more and listened to a speech by Chancellor Hitler in which he outlined the policy of the government and introduced an Enabling Act which was promptly passed by a vote of 441 to 94, only the Social Democrats opposing the bill.

The Enabling Act, officially entitled "Law to Combat the Misery of People and Reich," went into force on March 24, 1933. It concentrated practically complete power in the hands of the Reich government through the following provisions:

"The Reichstag has enacted the following law which, with the consent of the Reichsrat [36] and after determining that the requirement for laws changing the constitution have been complied with, is hereby promulgated:

ARTICLE 1.

"National laws can be enacted by the Reich cabinet as well as in accordance with the procedure established in the constitution. This applies also to the laws referred to in article 85, paragraph 2,[37] and in article 87 [38] of the constitution.

ARTICLE 2

"The Reich laws enacted by the Reich cabinet may deviate from the constitution in so far as they do not affect the position of the Reichstag and the Reichsrat. The powers of the President remain undisturbed.

ARTICLE 3

"The Reich laws enacted by the Reich cabinet are prepared by the Chancellor and published in the *Reichsgesetzblatt*. They come into effect, unless otherwise specified, upon the day following their publication. Articles 68 to 77 [39] of the constitution do not apply to the laws promulgated by the Reich government.

ARTICLE 4

"Treaties of the Reich with foreign states which concern matters of national legislation do not require the consent of the bodies participating in legislation. The Reich cabinet is empowered to issue the necessary provisions for the execution of these treaties.

[36] The Reichsrat met immediately after the adjournment of the Reichstag session and adopted the Enabling Act on the same day, March 23, 1933. Medicus, "Programm der Reichsregierung und Ermächtigungsgesetz," cited, p. 14.

[37] *Cf.* p. 258.

[38] *Cf.* p. 259.

[39] For text of these articles, *cf.* pp. 256–257. Article 77 was not abolished.

ARTICLE 5

"This law becomes effective on the day of its publication. It becomes invalid on April 1, 1937; it further becomes invalid when the present Reich cabinet is replaced by another.[40]

"Berlin, March 24, 1933.

> The Reich President
> von Hindenburg
> The Reich Chancellor
> Adolf Hitler
> The Reich Minister of the Interior
> Frick
> The Reich Minister of Foreign Affairs
> Freiherr von Neurath
> The Reich Minister of Finance
> Graf Schwerin von Krosigk"[41]

The official commentary on the Enabling Act states that its purpose is first of all to mark a definite departure from "negative parliamentarianism. Anonymous responsibility is replaced by consciousness and joy of the responsibility of leaders. . . . This law signifies the manifestation of the special confidence of an overwhelming majority of the Reichstag in the government of national concentration." Moreover, it is pointed out that the ordinary legislative organs provided in the Weimar constitution are in no way abolished, although in practice there is little expectation that they will be made use of.[42] The possibility of issuing emergency decrees under Article 48 continues in existence also,

[40] The following analysis of the Enabling Act is based on the official commentary published in *Das Recht der nationalen Revolution* No. 1, Medicus, "Programm der Reichsregierung und Ermächtigungsgesetz," cited.

[41] English text in J. K. Pollock and H. J. Heneman, *The Hitler Decrees* (Ann Arbor, George Wahr, 1934). German texts: Medicus, "Programm der Reichsregierung und Ermächtigungsgestez," cited; *Die Gesetzgebung des Kabinetts Hitler: Die Gesetze in Reich und Preussen seit dem 30 Januar 1933,* Hrsg. von Dr. Werner Hoche, Vol. 1 (Berlin, Vahlen Verlag, 1933), p. 23 *et seq.; Reichsgesetzblatt,* I (1933), p. 141.

[42] Actually they have been superseded and the Reichsrat has been abolished.

although that too will probably seldom be exercised.

According to the official commentary, the Enabling Act allows the Reich government to promulgate measures which extend beyond the limits imposed by the constitution and the "chief significance of the new act lies above all in the fact that the Reich government may create new constitutional law which departs from previous constitutional law." Thus it is contended that the Reich government may legally set aside articles of the Weimar instrument. As an example, moreover, the official commentary declares that the article of the constitution [43] providing that all individuals are equal before the law and that men and women shall have the same civil rights and duties, may be abolished by the Hitler government.

There are apparently no limitations on the government's power of legislating by decree under the Enabling Act except that the Act is to remain in force for a period of four years only. During that time, the government may do anything that it sees fit in order "to combat the misery of people and Reich." Despite the provision in the Act that it will become invalid when the present national cabinet is replaced by another, the resignation of Dr. Hugenberg from the Ministries of Economics and Agriculture on June 27, 1933, in no way changed the status of the Hitler government. The German Nationalists maintained at the time of Dr. Hugenberg's resignation that this action voided the Enabling Act but their protests were disregarded. Moreover, on March 13, the government had created a new Ministry of Propaganda and Public Enlightenment headed by Dr. Goebbels, who was given

[43] Article 109, paragraphs 1 and 2.

a seat in the Reich cabinet. On December 1, two more Nazis—Captain Roehm and Rudolf Hess—were appointed Ministers without Portfolio in the Reich government. The official commentary explains at some length that it would minimize the strength and importance of the government of national concentration to consider that the resignation of one or another minister might invalidate the Enabling Act. Apparently the same interpretation applies to the appointment of new Ministers.

In financial matters, the Enabling Act sets aside the provision of the constitution which states that "the budget shall be adopted by law before the beginning of the fiscal year," [44] the official commentary pointing out in this connection that the budget law was only law in "form" but in reality merely an administrative measure. The same interpretation is applied to the borrowing power of the state,[45] which the Enabling Act also places in the hands of the government. Thus the entire control of the elected legislature over finances has been abolished.

In the same way, the authority of the Reichstag in foreign affairs over ratification of treaties was abrogated by the Enabling Act.[47] According to the official commentary, the further question of putting treaties with foreign states into effect by legislative action was left open in Article I of the Enabling Act. If the carrying out of treaties between states requires the passage of legislation by the Reichstag or the Reichsrat, according to Article 4, paragraph 2 of the Enabling Act, this function may now be undertaken by the Reich government.

[44] Article 85, paragraph 2. For text, cf. p. 258.
[45] Article 87. For text, cf. p. 259.
[47] Cf. Article 4 of the Enabling Act.

There is no mention made in the official commentary of the important second paragraph of Article 45 of the Weimar constitution—"Declaration of war and conclusion of peace shall be made by national law." Doubtless, the Reich government has the supreme power here also, although since the Reichstag, as at present constituted,[48] consists almost entirely of members of the National Socialist party, its consent would be a foregone conclusion. Moreover, although the President of the Reich must still abide by Article 50 of the Weimar constitution, which provides that all his orders and decrees must be countersigned by the Chancellor or by the competent national minister, under the Enabling Act the Chancellor was empowered to promulgate laws without any counter-signature. The official commentary points out, however, that "nevertheless, the Reich government evidently intends to follow the former procedure of counter-signature by the responsible minister or ministers concerned."

Finally it appears that, at the time the Enabling Act was enacted, the Hitler government intended as far as possible to keep the Reichstag and Reichsrat in existence even though these bodies were shorn of their power. Hitler called the Reichstag together several times after March 23, 1933, to listen to important pronouncements on foreign policy. On February 14, 1934, however, the government issued a decree abolishing the Reichsrat, which, as the direct representative of the German states (*Länder*), had become superfluous.[49] The constitutionality of the abolition of the Reichsrat is dubious, since the Enabling Act had stated explicitly that the position

[48] *Cf.* p. 214.
[49] *Voelkischer Beobachter,* February 15, 1934.

of the Reichstag and the Reichsrat must not be affected by the laws enacted by the Reich government.

COÖRDINATION OF THE GERMAN STATES

The abolition of the Reichsrat was only one indication of the revolutionary changes which were made during the first year of the Hitler government in the relations between the Reich and its component states. As a result of various measures culminating in a law passed on January 30, 1934—the first anniversary of Hitler's accession to power—Germany became a completely unified and centralized state, offering a great contrast to the federal character of the old Empire and the Republic. Within the short space of one year, Hitler apparently completed the task of German unification inaugurated by Bismarck with the proclamation of the German Empire at Versailles in 1871. The Nazis accomplished what neither the Empire nor the Republic were able to bring about: the political, if not the territorial, abolition of the German states.

Four measures promulgated by the Nazis form the main constitutional bases for the unified German Reich, namely: the provisional law coördinating the states with the Reich (March 31, 1933); the second law coördinating the states with the Reich, known as the Reich Regents Law (April 7, 1933); the law concerning the new structure of the Reich (January 30, 1934); and the decree abolishing the Reichsrat (February 14, 1934). Only the third of these measures was passed by the ordinary legislative organs of the Reich, the others having been promulgated by the Hitler government under the power vested in it by the Enabling Act. All four laws indicated, however, the increasing centralization of power in the hands of the Reich government.

Provisional Law for Coördinating of the States with the Reich [50]

This law, which was promulgated by the Reich government on March 31, 1933, came into force on April 3. As the title states, it was conceived as a first step toward centralization. Under its provisions the state cabinets were empowered to enact state laws in the same manner as the Reich government acting under the terms of the Enabling Act.[51] Moreover, the state governments were also allowed to promulgate measures deviating from the state constitutions, although according to the official commentary on this law, departures from the Reich constitution were not to be undertaken. Thus the state governments were in reality limited to taking measures which concerned administrative matters only. Furthermore, the state legislatures or diets, as such, were to remain intact, but, with the exception of the Prussian Diet, which was elected on March 5, 1933, all of them were dissolved and ordered newly constituted "according to the number of votes which, in the election to the German Reichstag on March 5, 1933, were cast within each state for each party list." The law stated explicitly, however, that the Communist seats would not be apportioned and that the same ruling applied to "lists of electoral

[50] English text in Pollack and Heneman, *The Hitler Decrees,* cited, p. 14 *et seq.;* German texts: *Das Recht der nationalen Revolution,* no. 2; Georg Kaisenberg, "Gleichschaltung der Länder mit dem Reich" (Berlin, Carl Heymanns Verlag, 1933); Werner Hoche, *Die Gesetzgebung des Kabinetts Hitler, Die Gesetze in Reich und Preussen seit dem 30 Januar 1933,* cited, Vol. I, p. 23 *et seq; Reichsgesetzblatt,* I (1933), p. 153.

[51] *Cf.* p. 211.

groups which are regarded as appendages of the Communist party."[52] Furthermore, the diets in many of the states were reduced in size in order to simplify legislation and effect economies. In the same fashion the local representative bodies were dissolved and reconstituted and both the state legislatures and the local administrative groups were, according to the provisional law, chosen for a period of four years. The life of the state and local diets was automatically terminated in case of dissolution of the Reichstag. Thus the Nazis secured the proportion of mandates in the state and local groups which they held in the Reichstag elected on March 5 and, with the exclusion of the Communists, had a majority throughout the Reich. "The execution of the law with respect to details rests with the Reich Minister of the Interior in so far as national questions are concerned, and with the state cabinets in state matters. The Reich Minister of the Interior can decree general provisions and, upon proposal of a state cabinet, may permit exceptions to the law."

The Reich Regents Law

This first law laid the foundations for coördination of the states with the Reich. The second law, promulgated on April 7, 1933, and bearing the same title as the first with the exception of "provisional," represented an even more important step toward the goal of complete unification of the Reich. This law, which places the states under the control of regents appointed by Hitler, is therefore

[52] The *Kampfgemeinschaft der Arbeiter und Bauern* and the *Sozialistische Kampfgemeinschaft* are cited in the official commentary as organizations coming under this ban. The official commentary forms a part of *Das Recht der nationalen Revolution,* no. 2. Georg Kaisenberg, "Gleichschaltung der Länder mit dem Reich," cited.

known as the Reich Regents law and contains the following provisions: [53]

1

In the German states, with the exception of Prussia, the Reich President, upon the proposal of the Reich Chancellor, is to name the Reich regent. The Reich regent has the function of requiring the observance of the general policy laid down by the Reich Chancellor.

The following powers of state authority appertain to him:

(1) Appointment and removal of the head of the state cabinet, and upon his proposal, the other members of the state cabinet;

(2) Dissolution of the legislature and designation of new elections;

(3) Preparation and publication of state laws, including the laws which are determined upon by the state cabinet according to . . . the temporary law of March 31, 1933. . . . Article 70 [54] of the Reich constitution of August 11, 1919, applies accordingly;

(4) Upon the proposal of the state cabinet, appointment and dismissal of higher state officials and judges, so far as this formerly was accomplished by the highest state officials;

(5) The power of pardon.

(2) The Reich regent may preside over the meetings of the state cabinet.

(3) Article 63 [55] of the Reich constitution of August 11, 1919 remains unaltered.

2

(1) A Reich regent may not be, at the same time, a member of a state cabinet. He shall belong to the state whose sovereign powers he exercises. His official residence is at the seat of the state cabinet.

(2) For several states, in each of which there are less than two million inhabitants, a common Reich regent, who must be a resident of one of these states, may be named. The Reich President shall designate the regent's official residence.

[53] English text in Pollock and Heneman, *The Hitler Decrees*, cited. German texts: *Das Recht der nationalen Revolution*, no. 3. Carl Schmitt, "Das Reichsstatthaltergesetz" (Berlin, Carl Heymanns Verlag, 1933). *Die Gesetzgebung des Kabinetts Hitler: Die Gesetze in Reich und Preussen seit dem 30 Januar 1933*, cited, vol. I, p. 29 *et seq.*, *Reichsgesetzblatt*, I (1933), pp. 173, 225, 293.

[54] Article 70. The President of the Reich shall proclaim the laws constitutionally enacted, and shall publish them within a month in the *Reichsgesetzblatt*.

[55] Article 63: The states shall be represented in the Reichsrat by members of their ministries. But one-half of the Prussian representatives shall be appointed, in accordance with a state law, from among the Prussian administrative authorities.

3

(1) The Reich regent is appointed for the duration of a state legislative period. He can be recalled at any time by the Reich President on the proposal of the Chancellor.

4

Votes of no confidence of the state legislature against the head and the members of the state cabinet are not permitted.

5

(1) In Prussia, the Reich Chancellor exercises the rights specified in section 1. He may transfer the rules in Article I, paragraph 1, number 4 and 5 to the state cabinet.

(2) Members of the Reich cabinet may, at the same time, be members of the Prussian state cabinet.

6

This law goes into effect on the day after its proclamation. Conflicting provisions of the Reich constitution of August 11, 1919, and of the state constitutions are suspended. So far as state constitutions provide for the office of a state president, these provisions go out of force with the naming of a Reich regent.

Berlin, April 7, 1933   The Reich Chancellor
                                          Adolf Hitler

                              The Reich Minister of the Interior
                                          Frick

With the promulgation of the two laws for coordinating the Reich and the states, all possibility of political opposition or even of individual policy on the part of a state government was done away with. "Sovereignty of the states" as it had existed under both the Empire and the Republic was abolished: [56] the Reich Chancellor determines policy for both Reich and states. Therefore, as the official commentary points out, with the promulgation of the Regents law, German "federalism" ceased to be. The separate states, however, continued to

[56] Official commentary on the Regents law in *Das Recht der nationalen Revolution*, no. 3, Dr. Carl Schmitt, "Das Reichsstatthaltergesetz," cited.

exist as administrative units, although in so far as their sovereign rights are concerned, the Regents law in practice transferred them to the Reich.

The regents themselves were regarded as political appointees and not as civil servants; they were paid by the Reich,[57] not by the state in question, and are responsible to the Reich Chancellor. "The regent is a political subordinate leader of the political leader. It accords with the structure of the present state that *Gauleiter* [58] of the National Socialist German Workers' party should be appointed as regents. The Reich regent is to a particularly high degree an instrument of coördination and therefore is bound to the Reich Chancellor by special discipline and loyalty. His service and office take on significance and dignity through his discipline and loyalty to the political leadership of the Reich Chancellor." [59] According to the official commentary, the authority of the regents has a three-fold legal basis: In the first place, through his primary task of coördination, he must see to it that the Reich Chancellor's policies are carried out, and thus in his person he forms the connecting bond between Reich and state. Through the regent, moreover, "the state now has a second means of presenting its problems to the Reich, a

[57] The salaries were fixed by a decree of June 2, 1933, the provisions of which were retroactive to April 1, 1933. Reich regents in Bavaria, Saxony, Würtemberg, Baden, Thuringia, Hesse, Oldenburg-Bremen, Hamburg, Brunswick-Anhalt, Mecklenburg-Schwerin-Mecklenburg-Strelitz-Lübeck receive remuneration equal to the official salary of a Reich cabinet minister. The Regent for Lippe and Schaumburg-Lippe receives an amount equal to the basic salary of a secretary of state in the Reich. The Reich regents are assigned an official residence but in cases where that is not possible they receive rent allowances. *Cf.* Pollock and Heneman, *The Hitler Decrees,* cited, p. 20; *Reichsgezetzblatt,* 1933, no. 60, p. 330.

[58] The Nazi leader of a *Gau* or section of the Reich. *Cf.* p. 157.

[59] Official commentary, cited.

means which, depending on circumstances, may be even more satisfactory than the Reichsrat." In the second place, the regent holds authority over the state government through his power to appoint and dismiss the president of that government, and, upon the latter's recommendations, the other members of the cabinet. Furthermore, the regent has the right to appoint and dismiss lower officials and judges on the recommendation of the state government, and the power of pardon. The official commentary states that these rights enable him to prevent political abuses. In the third place, the regent has the power to prepare and proclaim the state laws, both those passed by the legislatures and those promulgated by the state governments. Finally, the relations of a state with the *Reichswehr* or national army are exclusively in the hands of the regent. In contrast to the situation obtaining under the Weimar constitution which gave a state government no right to call on the *Reichswehr,* the regent now has the following power: [60] "In case of public emergency or of a threat to public order the military forces [of the Reich] must render assistance at the request of the Reich regent or, in the case of Prussia, of the Reich Chancellor or officials designated by him."

The general situation in Prussia, comprising three-fifths of the Reich, is exceptional in that it has no regent, the Reich Chancellor exercising the rights and prerogatives of the regent. In this way, the republican "dualism," as it was called in the relations of the Reich with Prussia, is done away with. In its place there is apparently a return to the "personal union" between the two régimes such as ex-

[60] According to the *Reichswehr* law of July 20, 1933 (*Reichsgezetzblatt,* I, p. 526).

isted under the Empire. The Reich Chancellor may, however, delegate his powers of legislation, appointment and pardon to a Minister President of Prussia who in return is enabled to delegate them further.[61] The delegation of power by the Chancellor is, however, revocable by him at any time. Prussia, moreover, differs from the other states in that members of the Reich government may at the same time be ministers in the Prussian cabinet which makes it possible to avoid considerable administrative duplication by a "personal union" of Reich and Prussian ministries. In general, the law is interpreted to mean that the historical rôle of Prussia as "the political destiny of the Reich" has been recognized and that Prussia is now an indissoluble part of the Reich. In a sense the two political entities—Reich and Prussia —appear to have become one.[62]

It is plain that the two laws coördinating the states with the Reich have fundamentally altered the previous constitutional structure of the Reich. The official commentary states that new constitutional law was created by these measures which cannot be regarded merely as supplementing and amplifying the provisions of the Weimar instrument, but which formally and materially replaced the old law and put the relations of the Reich with its component states on a new foundation. Besides the changes which have already been pointed out, the new laws did away with the fundamental principle of Article 5 of the Weimar constitution which provided that "political power shall be exercised, in

[61] On April 11, 1933, Hitler appointed General Goering to be Minister President of Prussia.

[62] *Das Recht der nationalen Revolution,* no. 6. Professor Otto Koellreutter, "Die nationale Revolution und die Reichsreform" (Berlin, Carl Heymanns Verlag, 1933).

matters pertaining to the Reich, through the organs of the Reich on the basis of the national constitution, and in matters pertaining to the states, through the organs of the states on the basis of the state constitutions." Furthermore, under the new system of political coördination, there can be no question of constitutional controversies between the Reich and a state or states. Thus as the official commentary points out, Article 19 of the Weimar constitution which empowered the Supreme Court of the Reich to decide such questions "is no longer of interest." [63] On the whole, however, German state and constitutional law remained in flux and the Nazi commentators themselves declare that a fundamental revision of German constitutional law is necessary.

The two laws coördinating the states with the Reich were promulgated shortly after the Nazis came to power. The dissolution of the Reichstag on October 14, 1933, was of course automatically accompanied by dissolution of all the state diets under the provisions of the provisional coördination law.[64] No new elections were decreed for the state legislatures, however, although a new Reichstag was elected on November 12 simultaneously with the plebiscite on foreign policy. When this Reichstag met on January 30, 1934—the first anniversary of Hitler's accession to power—to listen to the Chancellor's account of his stewardship, the Reich Min-

[63] Article 19. If constitutional controversies arise within a state, for the decision of which there is no competent court, or should controversies of a public nature arise between different states or between the Reich and a single state, the Supreme Judicial Court of the German Reich shall decide the controversy on the appeal of either of the contesting parties, if no other court of the Reich is competent. The President of the Reich shall execute the decisions of the Supreme Judicial Court.

[64] *Cf.* p. 215.

ister of the Interior, Dr. Frick, introduced a bill finally regulating the relations of the Reich with the states. This measure was promptly voted unanimously by the Reichstag and on the same day by the Reichsrat as well,—apparently the last official act of the Reichsrat before it was abolished on February 14. The new law, which completes the process of transferring to the Reich all the sovereign powers of the states, provides as follows: [65]

Law Concerning the New Structure of the Reich

"The plebiscite and the Reichstag elections of November 12, 1933, have proved that the German people has been blended into an indissoluble unity which has done away with all inner political barriers and differences.

"The Reichstag has therefore unanimously accepted the following law, which, with the unanimous consent of the Reichsrat is herewith proclaimed, after it has been determined that the requirements for legislation changing the constitution have been complied with.

"Article 1. The popular representation of the states is abolished.

"Article 2. (1) The sovereign rights of the states are transferred to the Reich.

"(2) The state governments are subordinate to the Reich government.

"Article 3. The Reich regents are subordinate to the Reich Minister of the Interior.

"Article 4. The Reich government may determine new constitutional law.

"Article 5. The Reich Minister of the Interior issues the orders and regulations necessary to carry out the law.

"Article 6. This law goes into force on the day of its proclamation.

"Berlin, January 30, 1934.

Hitler, Dr. Frick, Hess, Seldte, etc."

Thus the German states are to all intents and purposes abolished as political units, remaining only as administrative and, for the present, territorial entities: Germany has become, on paper at least, a politically centralized Reich. The Reich Minister

[65] *Voelkischer Beobachter,* January 31, 1934.

of the Interior, Dr. Frick, explaining the new law over the radio on January 31, 1934, declared that "The historical task of our times is the creation of a strong national unitary state to replace the former federal state. There is no longer room in the new Germany for states (*Länder*) in the former sense or for state frontiers. . . . The state governments from today on are merely administrative bodies of the Reich. . . . According to the so-called Enabling Act . . . the Reich government was empowered to make certain constitutional changes, but was at the same time restricted to some extent. . . . The law concerning the new structure of the Reich does away with these restrictions and gives the Reich government complete power to undertake the constitutional reconstruction of the Reich." [66] The question, therefore, as to the present status of the Weimar constitution may be answered as follows: portions of it apparently remain in force; other sections have been entirely suspended or changed beyond recognition. In actual fact, Hitler and the National Socialist party under his leadership determine the German law and the German constitution.

FORMATION OF A ONE-PARTY NATION

Meanwhile, before the complete constitutional reorganization of the Reich was completed, the Hitler government had effected absolute political consolidation of its power by abolishing all the German parties except the National Socialist. The Communist party was banned on March 31, 1933, by the provisional law for the coördination of the states with the Reich [67] which voided the Communist

---

[66] *Frankfurter Zeitung,* February 1, 1934.
[67] *Cf.* p. 215. According to Article 10 of this law.

mandates in the Reichstag and Prussian Diet elected on March 5. Actually, however, no Communists had attended the sessions of the Reichstag held before the law of March 31 was promulgated by the government, for a large portion of the Communist deputies were in prison or refugees abroad.[68] The Social Democrats were the next to come under the Nazi axe; 94 of the 120 Socialist deputies elected to the Reichstag on March 5 had been present and had voted against the Enabling Act on March 23. The party received its death-blow, however, when on May 2 the Nazis seized control of the German trade unions, occupied the buildings and offices of the unions, arrested their principal leaders, seized the labor banks and coöperatives and impounded the funds of leaders and unions. A government de- cree of July 7, 1933, abolishing the Socialist man- dates in the Reichstag and the Prussian Diet,[69] and in all state and local organizations as well, legally terminated the existence of the once powerful Social Democratic party, which had already been officially banned on June 22, by an order issued by Reich Minister of the Interior Frick.[70] The smaller State party (*Staatspartei*), which had been allied with the Socialists for the March 5 elections, was also wiped out [71] by the July 7 decree. The grounds for the

[68] All property and funds of the Communist party and its affiliated organizations were seized by the state under a law of May 26, 1933. *Reichsgesetzblatt*, I (1933) p. 293; Werner Hoche, *Die Gesetzgebung des Kabinetts Hitler: Die Gesetze in Reich und Preussen seit dem 30 Januar, 1933*, cited. Vol. 2, p. 224, *et seq;* Vol. 3, p. 374 *et seq.*

[69] *Reichsgesetzblatt*, I (1933) p. 462; Werner Hoche, *Die Gesetzgebung des Kabinetts Hitler: Die Gesetze in Reich und Preussen seit dem 30 Januar, 1933*, cited, vol. 3, p. 49 *et seq.*

[70] *Der Zeitspiegel*, July 2, 1933.

[71] *Das Recht der nationalen Revolution*, no. 1; Medicus, "Pro- gramm der Reichsregierung und Ermächtigungsgesetz," cited.

abolition of all these Left and Liberal groups were given by the Nazis as "high treason."

The dissolution of the less radical German parties which occurred during the same period was on a slightly different basis: the Right and Middle political groups may be said to have committed suicide under pressure. During June 1933, repressive measures against the Nationalist *Stahlhelm* were reported in different parts of Germany, many of the *Stahlhelm* leaders were arrested and local units of the organization dissolved. On June 21 the independent existence of the entire Nationalist veterans' association (the *Stahlhelm*) was terminated and it was placed under Hitler's command. At the same time Nationalist organizations were dissolved by the Nazis because of "absolute proof that the Communists and other enemies of the state had joined these groups in large numbers." [72] Finally, on June 27, the Nationalist leader, Dr. Hugenberg, resigned from his post as Reich and Prussian Minister of Agriculture and Economics and on the same day the German National Front, which had taken the place of the Nationalist party soon after Hitler's accession to power, declared itself dissolved. The act of dissolution was stated to have been taken "in full understanding with the Reich Chancellor and in recognition of the fact that the state based on political parties is no longer in existence."

The end of the other important German political parties followed almost immediately. The Nazis had already taken repressive action against the Catholic parties—the Center and the Bavarian People's party. Catholic organizations had been dissolved by the

[72] *Der Zeitspiegel,* July 2, 1933.

secret police, meetings had been disrupted and some of the Catholic leaders had been taken into custody. Finally on July 4, the Bavarian People's party voted to dissolve itself, and on the following day the important Catholic Center party, which had held the balance of power in almost every Republican ministry and had played a great rôle under the Empire, followed suit. The German People's party, once led by Dr. Stresemann, also terminated its life on July 4.[73]

As a result of the Nazi dissolution of the Communist, Social Democratic and State parties and of the suicide of the other political groups in the Reich, the law promulgated by the Hitler government on July 14, 1933, which prohibited the formation of new political parties merely recorded an already accomplished fact. This law provides as follows: [74]

Law Prohibiting the Formation of New Political Parties

1

"The National Socialist German Workers' party is the only political party in Germany.

2

"Whoever undertakes to maintain the organization of another political party, or to form a new political party, is to be punished with imprisonment in a penitentiary up to three years or with confinement in a jail from six months to three years unless the act is punishable by a higher penalty under other provisions."

Thus the Nazi party, to all intents and purposes, became the German state after Hitler had been in power only six months. The Nazi leaders waited an-

[73] *Der Zeitspiegel,* July 23, 1933.
[74] English text in Pollock and Heneman, *The Hitler Decrees,* cited p. 34; German texts: *Reichsgesetzblatt,* I (1933) p. 479; Werner Hoche, *Die Gesetzgebung des Kabinetts Hitler: Die Gesetze in Reich und Preussen,* cited, vol. 3, p. 66 *et seq.*

other five months, however—until December 1933—
before promulgating a further law which legalized
this existing situation and clarified the relations between the Nazi party organizations and the state
itself.[75] The provisions of the law, announced on
December 1 and which went into effect on December, 2, 1933, follow: [76]

Law for Safeguarding the Unity of Party and State

1

"(1) After the victory of the National Socialist Revolution
the National Socialist German Workers' party has become the
carrier (*Trägerin*) of the government and is inseparably connected
with the state.

"(2) It is a corporation of public law. Its constitution is
determined by the leader (*der Führer*).

2

"To secure the closer coöperation of the officers of the party
and the Storm Troops with the public officials, the assistant of
the leader [77] and the chief of staff of the Storm Troops [78] are
to be members of the Reich cabinet.

3

"(1) Members of the National Socialist German Workers' party
and of the Storm Troops (including affiliated organizations) have,
as the leading and moving power of the National Socialist state,
increased duties toward the people and the state.

"(2) For violation or neglect of these duties the members are
subject to special party and Storm Troop jurisdiction.

"(3) The leader may extend these regulations to the members
of other organizations.

4

"Violations or neglect of duty may mean any action or neglect
which may attack or endanger the stability of the organization, or

[75] This justification of the law was published in the official
Reichsanzeiger, no. 284, 1933.

[76] English text in Pollock and Heneman, *The Hitler Decrees*,
cited, p. 34 *et seq.*; German texts: *Reichsgesetzblatt*, I (1933)
p. 1016; Werner Hoche, *Die Gesetzgebung des Kabinetts Hitler:
Die Gesetze in Reich und Preussen seit dem 30 Januar*, cited,
vol. 5, p. 60 *et seq.*

[77] Rudolf Hess.

[78] Captain Ernst Roehm.

the authority of the National Socialist German Workers' party, and in case of members of the Storm Troops (including affiliated organizations) any violation against discipline and order.

5

"Besides the customary disciplinary measures, arrest and imprisonment may be decreed (*verhängt*).

6

"Public authorities must, within their power, give assistance to party and Storm Troop officials who are vested with party and Storm Troop jurisdiction in rendering justice and legal redress.

7

"The law governing penal authority over members of the Storm Troops (S.A.) and Special Guards (S.S.) of April 28, 1933, is declared inoperative.[79]

8

"The Reich Chancellor, as leader of the National Socialist German Workers' party and as supreme chief of the Storm Troops, issues orders and regulations necessary for the execution and extension of this law, especially regulations concerning the formation and procedure of the party's and Storm Troops' jurisdiction. He determines the date on which the regulations concerning this jurisdiction are to become effective."

THE PLEBISCITE AND REICHSTAG ELECTION
OF NOVEMBER 12, 1933

The enactment of the above law, which merely legalized an already existing situation, was facilitated by the result of the "election" of November 12, 1933. On that date 96 per cent of the qualified German electorate went to the polls and cast their votes on two propositions: support of the Hitler government's foreign policy as expressed in Germany's resignation from the Disarmament Conference and

[79] Text of this law in Werner Hoche, *Die Gesetzgebung des Kabinetts Hitler: Die Gesetze in Reich und Preussen seit dem 30 Januar,* cited, vol. II, p. 38.

the League of Nations, and "election" of a new Reichstag to replace the body chosen on March 5 which had been dissolved by decree on October 14 simultaneously with the Reich's departure from Geneva. On November 12, 93 per cent of the electorate supported the government's foreign policy, while in the Reichstag poll one million less votes were cast and 92 per cent of the qualified voters backed the government. Three million of the ballots cast were invalid—the only way in which opposition to the Hitler régime could be expressed. Instead of the usual twenty or more party lists of candidates which had been presented to the voters at all previous German elections, on November 12 there was one unified list only: the National Socialist. Several of the former Nationalist leaders were allowed to run, but they were included in the Nazi list.

REFORM OF THE CIVIL SERVICE

In considering the rapidity with which the Hitler régime was able to transform the Reich into a totalitarian state, one important factor must not be overlooked: the civil service. In the 1918 Revolution, the victorious Republican forces had never undertaken a thorough weeding-out of the reactionary elements from the civil service,[80] an omission which seriously weakened the Republic from its inception. The Nazis, however, made no such mistake. One of the first important measures promulgated by the Hitler government under the terms of the Enabling Act was a law for the restoration of the civil service, which formed the basis for most of the subsequent restrictive action of the Nazis against the Jews, liberals, pacifists, Socialists, Communists

[80] *Cf.* p. 131.

and others regarded by the Hitlerites as "enemies of the state."

The Civil Service Law was promulgated on April 7, 1933, and went into force on the following day.[81] The Ministers of Finance and the Interior subsequently issued several decrees designed to carry out the law and defining its provisions exactly.[82] The law and the supplementary decrees are stated to apply, even when they conflict with previously existing laws, to all officials of the Reich, the states and the municipalities, including not only the regular civil servants but also employees in semi-public enterprises and undertakings in which the government had a 50 per cent or larger financial interest. It applied as well to employees in the social services having the rights and duties of officials, while the Reichsbank and the German Railway Company were empowered to enforce its provisions. Furthermore, the following persons were included in the German civil service: judges; all court officials; notaries; teachers in schools, including teachers and instructors in scientific universities (*Hochschulen*); all professors; officials of the old and new army (*Wehrmacht*); members of the police forces of the

[81] *Gesetz zur Wiederherstellung des Berufsbeamtentums.* This law was promulgated directly by the Reich government under the authority of the Enabling Act of March 24, 1933, which vested full legislative power in that government for a period of four years. Published on April 7, 1933, in the *Reichsgesetzblatt,* I, p. 175.

[82] The following summary of the provisions of the Civil Service Law, and excerpts from the official commentary on it are taken from Hanns Seel, "Erneuerung des Berufsbeamtentums," no. IV in *Das Recht der nationalen Revolution* (Schriftenreihe Hrsg. von Dr. Georg Kaisenberg und Dr. Franz Albrecht Medicus; Berlin, Carl Heymanns Verlag, 1933). This series on the law of the National Revolution is the official publication concerning the new laws, etc., promulgated by the Hitler government. The amplifying decrees are dated April 11. 1933 (*Reichsgesetzblatt,* I, p. 195); May 4, 1933 (*ibid,* I, p. 233); May 6, 1933 (*ibid.,* I, p. 245).

states, not including officers, army doctors or veterinarians; elected municipal officials; and office employees and workers in public enterprises.[83]

RESTRICTIONS IMPOSED BY CIVIL SERVICE LAW

The Civil Service Law provided that "officials who are of non-Aryan descent must be retired; in so far as concerns honorary officials, the latter must be dismissed from their positions." A "non-Aryan" was then defined as "a person descended from non-Aryan, particularly Jewish, parents or grandparents.[84] It suffices if one parent or grandparent is a non-Aryan. This applies especially if one parent or grandparent has professed the Jewish religion." Every official was required to fill out a detailed questionnaire giving information as to the names, professions, addresses, places and dates of birth, religion, and places and dates of death and marriage of himself, his wife, and their respective parents and grandparents. Proof must be offered by presentation of such documents as birth and marriage certificates of parents or military papers. If Aryan descent was questionable, a ruling must be secured from the "expert on racial research" attached to the Ministry of the Interior. Moreover, if the official was an Aryan married to a "non-Aryan," he rated as "non-Aryan" himself and was dismissed.[85] All officials whose Aryan antecedents were in doubt had to swear to the following statement:

[83] *Frankfurter Zeitung,* June 30, 1933.
[84] In the decree of April 11, 1933. A decree of September 16 provides that any official can be regarded as "non-Aryan" whose great-grandfather belonged to the Jewish faith, even if he were baptized in the Christian church. *New York Times,* September 17, 1933.
[85] *Frankfurter Zeitung,* July 4, 1933.

"I herewith testify on oath that: despite careful examination, no circumstances are known to me which could justify the supposition that I am not of Aryan descent or that one of my parents or grandparents at any time professed the Jewish religion. I am aware that I am liable to legal prosecution and dismissal from service if this declaration does not contain the truth." [86]

The "Aryan paragraph" of the Civil Service Law contained provisions exempting certain "non-Aryan" officials from dismissal. Thus the law did not apply to persons "who held office on or before August 1, 1914, or who fought in the World War at the front for the German Reich or its allies, or whose fathers or sons fell in the war." Army service during the war was defined as

"participation with a fighting troop in a battle, a fight, a struggle for position or a siege. It does not suffice if the military service during the war was performed without having actually met the enemy, if, for instance, the person was merely in the war zone on official business or in the service at home or behind the lines. The promotion lists (*Rangliste*) and war service records (*Kriegsstammrollen*) are the only valid documentary proofs in determining whether the individual in question was actually a front-line soldier. A person possessing a wound certificate is always to be regarded as a front-line soldier without further proof.

"Participation in the fighting in the Baltic, in Upper Silesia, against the Sparticists and Separatists, as well as against the enemies of the national resurgence, counts equally with participation in the World War."

Besides stipulating immediate dismissal of "non-Aryan" officials, the Civil Service Law contained other far-reaching provisions. Thus "officials may

[86] *Reichsbesoldungsblatt,* Reichsfinanzministerium, June 12, 1933, p. 31.

be dismissed from service who because of their previous political activities do not offer surety that they
will at all times act unreservedly for the national
state." "Previous political activities" were further
defined as membership in the Communist party or
in its affiliated organizations; moreover, officials
who have been connected with the so-called
"Schwarze Front"—the extreme "National Bol-
shevist" wing of the Nazis—were dismissed as
"unsuitable." It was further provided that every official must report to the proper authorities the parties to which he had belonged, and "parties" were
defined for the purpose of the law as including the
republican Reichsbanner Black-Red-Gold, the Union
of Republican Judges, the League for the Defense
of the Rights of Man, the Union of Republican Officials, and the Iron Front.[87] Furthermore, political
unreliability was stated to be present "particularly
when an official in word, writing or other conduct
has come out in an odious fashion against the national movement [Nazi], has insulted its leaders
or has misused his official position to persecute, to
slight or otherwise injure nationally-minded officials.
In such case, the fact that the person in question has
joined since January 30, 1933, a party or organization supporting the government of national resurgence will not suffice to clear him."

The Civil Service Law further provided that officials who lack requisite education and training
may be dismissed, and that an official may be transferred to a post lower in rank and salary—which allowed the Nazis to demote "non-Aryan" and other

---

[87] The latter organization was one of the principal supporters
of President von Hindenburg at the last presidential election
in 1932.

officials who, because of war services, etc., could not be dismissed. Officials who were dismissed or retired might be prosecuted and punished for any dereliction of duty during their tenure of office. Persons dismissed on the grounds of insufficient training, "non-Aryan" descent or political unreliability were liable to be sued until April 7, 1934.

Finally, the new law contained detailed provisions concerning pensions. Officials dismissed on grounds of insufficient education and training did not receive pensions save in exceptional cases of destitution. Those ousted because of previous political activities were entitled to three months' salary and thereafter, provided they had held office for at least ten years, to three-fourths of their normal legal pensions,[88] while a proportionate allowance was to accrue to their families after death. The same regulations applied to ousted Jewish officials except that they were to receive full pension.

As a result of these measures, any civil servant in whom the Nazis lacked confidence, against whom they bore a grudge, or whose position some member of the party coveted might be dismissed on the ground that his politics in the past showed he could not be trusted as an official of Nazi Germany. In order to comprehend the radical changes effected by the new Civil Service Law, it is necessary to recall that in Germany under both the Empire and the Republic, officials held a specially favored position and the public administration always enjoyed an enviable reputation for integrity, efficiency and stability. Before the war, in practice if not in law,

---

[88] After only ten years' service, however, salaries are small; the pension allowance is also small, since it is based on the last actual salary received.

higher officials were recruited from the upper classes of society and few Jews were admitted. Under the democratic Republic, however, the Weimar constitution laid down the principle that "citizens without discrimination shall be eligible for public office in accordance with the laws and their capacities and merits." [89] It stated that "officials shall be appointed for life except as otherwise provided by law," and specified the rights and protective measures applying to them.[90] The Weimar instrument declared that "officials are servants of the whole community and not of a party," and granted them "freedom of political opinion and freedom of association." [91]

The new Civil Service Law offered a great contrast to previous legislative and constitutional regulations concerning the German civil service. In explanation, the official commentary on the new law declared that the

"government of national resurgence, in fulfillment of its tasks, requires above all the strength of the German civil service. The latter, however, once so highly respected throughout the entire world, has not remained unaffected by the influence and consequences of the revolution of 1918. With an eye to party politics, numerous members of the November parties [92] were allowed to enter the public administration without the required education and preparation. These people in many instances have not only displaced professional civil servants but through their incompetence, self-interest and,

[89] Article 128.
[90] Article 129.
[91] Article 130. For a discussion of the question of rights, duties, privileges and status of officials in Republican Germany, cf. F. F. Blachly and M. E. Oatman, *The Government and Administration of Germany* (Baltimore, Johns Hopkins, 1928), p. 371 et seq.
[92] The Social Democratic, Catholic Center and Democratic parties.

in fact, criminal acts have terribly damaged the prestige of the German civil service.

"Only by cleansing the civil service of these elements, part of which are of an alien race, can a national civil service be created which will not be primarily interested in material advantages but, as formerly, will recognize that its highest goal is uncompromising fulfillment of duty and will prove worthy of the national honor which is placed in its hands."

The commentary stressed the special importance of the "Aryan paragraph" and pointed out that this created a "completely new law which was a conscious antithesis to the previous law." Specifically this paragraph and the regulations connected with it became the model for a series of other laws such as those for the admission of lawyers to the bar, the decree dealing with admission of doctors to practice under the social insurance laws and the law directed against the over-crowding of German universities [*Hochschulen*] and schools.[93] The commentary added that these radical measures were essential for the welfare of the state and declared that they were not conceived in a spirit of hate but had become necessary because of the increasingly dangerous alienization (*Ueberfremdung*) of the German people.

CHAPTER V

THE JEWS IN THE THIRD REICH

THE Nazi charge that the Jews had caused a "dangerous alienization" of the German people must be considered in relation to the actual position occu-

---

[93] Many doctors and lawyers and all professors have the status of officials in Germany.

pied by the Jews in Germany before the National Revolution.

According to the last German census for which figures are available, June 16, 1925, the total population of the Reich was 62,410,619, of which 564,379 were Jews,[1] who thus comprised 9/10 of one per cent.[2] The anti-Jewish measures of the Nazis, however, affected not only those listed as Jews, but also a newly created class of "non-Aryans."[3] Although no official figures are available, it has been estimated that this "non-Aryan" category comprised approximately two million Germans,[4] making a total of 2½ million persons in the Reich who, according to Nazi standards, were classified as Jews. In analyzing the rôle of the Jews both under the Empire and the Republic, the available data concerns only those officially listed as Jews.

In Imperial Germany almost no Jews held posts as officials in the civil service, the army or the navy. As a result of their position, the largest number of Jews turned to commerce, industry and banking.[5] Those Jews desirous of entering professional life became for the most part doctors or lawyers, the two branches most readily open to them, which accounts in part for the relatively greater percentage of Jews in the liberal professions. During the war 96,327 Jews, or 17.3 per cent of the Jewish population, served in the German army and navy. The

[1] *Statistisches Jahrbuch für das deutsche Reich, 1931* (Berlin, Reimer Hobbing, 1931), p. 15 *et seq.*

[2] *Ibid.,* p. 15. The above percentage is calculated on the same territorial basis as that for 1925.

[3] Persons one of whose parents or grandparents were Jewish. C^4 p. 179.

[4] *Jewish Daily Bulletin,* July 18, 1933.

[5] Heinrich Silbergleit, *Die Bevölkerungs- und Berufs- Verhältnisse der Juden im deutschen Reich* (Berlin, Akademie Verlag, 1930), Vol. I, p. 89.*

percentage of Germans with the colors was slightly higher, 18.73 per cent, but the fact that the Jewish birth rate had been falling steadily [6] for some time was apparently responsible for the existence of fewer Jewish than non-Jewish males of military age. Of the 96,000 enlisted Jewish soldiers and sailors, approximately 12,000 were killed, 78 per cent were at the front, and 12 per cent of those with the colors were volunteers. These figures are particularly important in view of the Nazi contention that most of the Jews who fought in the war held soft posts.[7]

The establishment of the Weimar Republic undoubtedly improved the status of the Jews. The largest proportion still found its way into commerce and industry, although many more than formerly entered the public administration. There are no reliable figures available for the occupational distribution of the Jews in the entire Reich. For Prussia, however—a state comprising three-fifths of Germany—statistics compiled from official sources give a full picture of the situation: of the Jews in Germany in 1925, 71.6 per cent lived in Prussia, where they formed 1.5 per cent of the population as compared with 9/10 of one per cent in the Reich as a whole.

According to the 1925 census, on which the following data is primarily based, the working population in Prussia totaled 21,267,033, of which 225,523 were Jews, or 1.06 per cent.[8] Of the Jews gainfully employed, 71.7 per cent were engaged in commerce and

---

[6] The Jewish birthrate fell from 32.26 per thousand in 1880 to 16.55 in 1910. The total birthrate for the same period fell from 41.05 per thousand to 33.05. *Ibid.*, p. 14.

[7] Jakob Segall, *Die deutschen Juden als Soldaten im Kriege, 1914–1918* (Berlin, Philo-Verlag, 1922), p. 11 *et seq.*

[8] It must be stated again, however, that the latter figure comprises only the Jews, and not the so-called "non-Aryan" class created by the Nazis.

industry, as compared with 51.7 per cent of the gainfully employed non-Jews. Only 7/10 of one per cent of Jews gainfully employed found their way into public administration, in contrast to 2.3 per cent of the gainfully employed non-Jews. The other professions, however, accounted for 10 per cent of the gainfully employed Jews, and 6.8 per cent of the gainfully employed non-Jews. The occupational distribution of both Jews and non-Jews is shown in the following table:

OCCUPATIONAL DISTRIBUTION OF JEWS AND NON-JEWS
GAINFULLY EMPLOYED IN PRUSSIA

	Jewish workers	Non-Jewish workers	Total workers	Per-centage of Jews
Commerce and transportation	112,188	3,135,957	3,248,145	3.4
Industry	49,318	7,722,481	7,771,799	0.63
Professional class [1]	9,761	422,572	432,333	2.3
Health, medicine and charity [2]	8,297	348,119	356,416	2.3
Domestic service	6,338	1,085,097	1,091,435	0.58
Agriculture, truck farming, forestry, fishing	3,324	5,589,820	5,593,144	0.06
Public administration, officials of the law, army and navy [3]	1,563	487,152	488,715	0.32
Without profession [4]	34,734	2,250,312	2,285,046	1.08
Totals and average percentage	225,523	21,041,510	21,267,033	1.06

[1] This group includes:
    a. All clerics, workers in religious institutions and associations with religious aims. b. All teachers, professors, etc., in universities, colleges, private and public schools, scientific institutes and art centers. c. Lawyers and legal trustees. d. Artists, scholars, editors, writers, persons connected with theaters, opera houses, music centers, cinemas, radio. e. Persons in physical training centers.
[2] This group included:
    a. All doctors and dentists. b. All persons connected with hospitals, clinics, asylums, public and private. c. All persons connected with bathing and swimming pools, masseurs, barbers. d. All persons connected with life-saving and first aid stations, ambulance service. e. Veterinarians, meat inspectors. f. Disinfection service. g. Street cleaning, canalization, garbage collection and comfort stations. h. Undertakers. i. Druggists. j. Social services.
[3] This group included:
    a. Diplomacy. b. All officials of the Reich, states and municipalities. c. All court officials in so far as they have civil service rank. d. Army and navy, and military and naval administration, including military hospitals.
[4] This group included:
    a. Persons living from private fortunes, *rentiers* and persons living on pensions. b. Persons living from outside support (inmates of poorhouses, etc.). c. Inmates of insane asylums. d. Students not living with their families. e. Persons serving prison sentences.

The percentage of Jews in commerce and in the liberal professions was higher than their relation to the total population. They comprised, however, only 3.4 per cent of all persons engaged in commerce and business in Prussia, and 2.3 per cent of the professional classes. The Jews in public administration and government, on which the Nazis have laid so much emphasis, comprised only .32 of one per cent of all officials in Prussia.

In their anti-Semitic agitation the Nazis continually stressed the fact that great numbers of Eastern Jews (*Ostjuden*) entered Germany during and since the war and, in a period of severe economic crisis, secured good jobs which should have gone to deserving Germans. Whether or not this Nazi charge can be substantiated, undoubtedly a large number of Jewish emigrants came into the Reich after the war, many if not most of them coming from territory which had formerly been German. Thus between 1910 and 1925 the number of Jews in Prussia increased by 37,093 [9] despite the war, the economic difficulties and a continually falling Jewish birthrate. There were, in 1925, 601,779 non-citizens in Prussia; of this number 76,387 [10] were Jewish. According to figures prepared by the Nazis, 12,500 Eastern Jews became citizens in Prussia between 1919 and 1931.[11]

THE "COLD POGROM"

Despite the relatively small percentage of Jews in the Reich, Hitler told his followers for ten years

[9] Silbergleit, *Die Bevölkerungs- und Berufs- Verhältnisse der Juden im deutschen Reich*, cited, p. 37 * et seq. The figures are: 1910—366,876; 1925—403,969. These compilations were made on the territorial basis of 1925.

[10] This figure is included in the 564,397 Jews in the Reich.

[11] *Frankfurter Zeitung*, August 12, 1933.

and more that the Jews were responsible for all German difficulties, and promised that once in power he would eliminate "Jewish influence" from all phases of German life. The first step toward achieving this end was the Jewish boycott on April 1, 1933. The second was the promulgation of the Civil Service Law which, as has been stated, formed the basis for all subsequent anti-Semitic action as well as action against Socialists, liberals, etc. The effects of this law must now be considered.

Lawyers

At the time of the general boycott, Jewish judges and lawyers were excluded from the courts although the procedure adopted varied in different sections of the Reich.[12] In Prussia, Nazi Commissioner of Justice Kerrl issued instructions that all Jewish judges were to be granted immediate leave of absence and that the powers of Jewish court officials were to be cancelled at once. The declaration added: "Any Jewish judge refusing to apply for leave shall be forbidden to enter the court building on the basis of the law of trespass." Jewish commercial arbitrators, jurors, etc., were no longer to be appointed, Jewish states' attorneys and other officials were to be granted leave of absence, and only certain Jewish lawyers, not to exceed in numbers the percentage of the Jewish population to the total population, were to be allowed to enter the courts.[13] On April 7[14] matters were regularized by the promulgation of a law concerning the admission of lawyers

[12] Calvin B. Hoover, *Germany Enters the Third Reich* (New York, Macmillan, 1933), p. 128.
[13] *Frankfurter Zeitung,* April 1, 1933.
[14] The date on which the Civil Service Law was promulgated.

to the bar,[15] which provided that all "non-Ayran"[16] lawyers might be disbarred up to September 30, 1933. The exceptions to this ruling were the same as those stipulated in the Civil Service Law: no "non-Ayrans" might be admitted to the bar; lawyers who had been engaged in Communist activities must be disbarred immediately; and disbarment was recognized as a basis for cancelling contracts already made with the persons in question.

As a result of the exemptions for front-line soldiers and pre-1914 appointments, however, a large number of "non-Aryan" lawyers were eligible to practice and Nazi lawyers, especially in Berlin, were incensed. On May 13, therefore, the Prussian Ministry of Justice published statistics concerning the situation as it then stood: before the "cleansing" of the bar there had been 11,814 lawyers in Prussia, of whom 3,515 were Jews and 8,299 "Aryan." Of the 3,515 Jewish lawyers, 1,383 had been admitted to the bar before 1914 and 735 had been at the front during the war. Nine hundred and twenty-three Jews and 118 Communists were ousted and in future, 2,158 Jewish lawyers were to have the right to practice in Prussia, the number of Jewish lawyers allowed to practice in Berlin being 1,203.[17]

The situation of the Jewish lawyers in Prussia and throughout the Reich was far different from what these figures might imply. Early in July the Berlin Federation of Lawyers issued an order prohibiting Aryan lawyers from entering into partnership or sharing offices with Jewish lawyers, and dissolving partnerships of Aryans and Jews entered

[15] *Reichsgesetzblatt* No. 86, April 10, 1933, p. 188.
[16] According to the Civil Service Law definition.
[17] *Frankfurter Zeitung*, May 13, 1933.

into since September 1930, even though the Jewish partner was entitled to exemption because of war service.[18] The press continued to report the dismissal of large numbers of notaries and lawyers.[19] Equally serious was the fact that an actual boycott was enforced against Jewish lawyers who theoretically were eligible to practice. Early in June the Berlin section of the Association of National Socialist Lawyers sent a protest to the presidents of all Berlin courts against the appointment of Jewish lawyers as attorneys for the poor, official defendants, trustees and executors. These appointments, it was stated, were acts of sabotage against the measures enacted by the national government to restore German law, and gave proof that the judges who made such appointments were not ruthlessly enforcing the provisions of the Civil Service Law.[20]

Doctors and Dentists

The situation in regard to the medical profession was similar to that of the legal profession, since the Jews had been especially prominent in both fields. Most German medical men derived 80 to 90 per cent of their income from membership in the so-called panels of the health insurance offices. "Non-Aryan" panel doctors were directly affected by the provisions of the Civil Service Law and even though many were exempt because of war service, etc., their position became rapidly worse. A special law of June 2, 1933, excluded dentists and dental technicians from panel

[18] *The Times* (London), July 5, 1933.

[19] A further list of 214 dismissed notaries was published on July 8 by the Prussian Ministry of Justice, and on the same day an order was issued ousting 150 lawyers. *Le Temps,* July 13, 1933.

[20] *Frankfurter Zeitung,* June 8, 1933.

practice on the basis of the Civil Service Law,[21] and in the social insurance clinics and offices patients could refuse to be examined by a "non-Aryan" physician.[22] It was reported that 1,500 Jewish physicians were expelled from the health insurance clinics in Berlin alone, and that at least 6,000 were ousted in Prussia,[23] while practically all "non-Aryan" doctors in private health insurance institutions were dismissed.[24]

The situation in private practice was just as serious. The medical association issued a regulation according to which German and "non-Aryan" doctors were forbidden to substitute for one another; German doctors might not send patients to "non-Aryan" physicians or call "non-Aryans" into consultation.[25] Furthermore, partnerships with "non-Aryan" doctors were forbidden.[26] As a result of these prohibitions, plus the tacit boycott to which doctors as well as lawyers were subjected, large numbers of "non-Aryan" physicians and dentists faced a black future and many emigrated from Germany.

Professors and Students

The measures enacted by the Nazis against "non-Aryan" lawyers and doctors had far-reaching effects on the status of law and medicine in the Reich, but the real foundations of the Third Reich were laid in the realm of education. Not only is the rising generation taught by "pure" Aryans, but there is no possibility for German youth to become tainted by

[21] *Reichsgesetzblatt*, June 10, 1933, p. 350.
[22] *Frankfurter Zeitung*, June 28, 1933.
[23] *Le Temps*, July 11, 1933.
[24] *Frankfurter Zeitung*, July 9, 1933.
[25] *Ibid.*, August 15, 1933.
[26] *New York Times*, August 20, 1933.

exposure to the hated doctrines of liberalism and democracy. Instruction is given in racial questions; great emphasis is laid on the glorious history of Germany and the "shame" of the years 1919 to 1932; *Wehrsport, i.e.,* military sports, have a prominent place in the curriculum for both students and teachers; and youth is imbued with real fighting spirit and extreme nationalism as the primary object of education.[27] Fact-finding, painstaking research is no more; the Nazis "must think with their blood."

To put these theories into practice, German professors, instructors and teachers, including many of the most eminent, were ousted from their positions. The Civil Service Law applied to them directly and, in cases where the "non-Aryan" paragraph was not applicable, the provisions in regard to "political unreliability" were often used. "Non-Aryan" professors who might have been exempt as war veterans or who had been appointed before 1914 were forced to resign by Nazi students who organized demonstrations against them and made their positions untenable.[28]

While professors and teachers, theoretically at least, were regulated by the Civil Service Law, students were selected under the terms of a law promulgated on April 25, 1933, "against the overcrowding of the German universities." [29] This meas-

---

[27] *Prospectus of Hochschule für Politik, 1933–1934.*

[28] Hoover, *Germany Enters the Third Reich,* cited.

[29] "Gesetz gegen die Ueberfüllung der deutschen Schulen und Hochschulen," April 25, 1933, *Reichsgesetzblatt,* April 26, 1933, I, p. 225. The text of the law, as well as the texts of the various orders issued by Rust, the Prussian Minister of Science, Art and Popular Education, are given with official commentaries in Joachim Haupt, "Neuordnung im Schulwesen und Hochschulwesen," No. V in *Das Recht der nationalen Revolution,* cited.

ure was designed, it was officially stated, to rebuild
German education along the lines of the German
heritage, by molding the youth through discipline
and comradeship. The new laws introduced a complete educational reformation, which "is worthy of
the desire and the struggle of the German people
during the past decades for inner unity and
strength."

To achieve these ends, liberal hypotheses have
been replaced by popular national (*voelkische*)
hypotheses. As a first step, admission of students
was based on entirely different standards from heretofore. According to the new law, students were
admitted only in numbers consistent with the opportunities in the professions for which they wish to
prepare themselves. New applicants of "non-
Aryan"[30] descent were admitted according to a
numerus clausus which limited the total of such
newly entered students in any school and any faculty
of a school to the proportion of "non-Aryans" in
the total population of the Reich. A decree issued
simultaneously with the School Law placed this
proportion at 1½ per cent of the students in a given
institution of learning. If the percentage of "non-
Aryan" students already enrolled exceeds 5 per cent
of the total, it must be lowered to that percentage
by dismissal of "non-Aryans." The law did not
apply to students whose fathers fought at the front
during the war or to children one of whose parents
or both of whose grandparents were "Aryans," if
the marriage took place before the promulgation of
this law. Obviously, the full effect of these regulations will not be felt for several years. Further regulations for candidates for the general *Abitur* ex-

[30] In accordance with the definition of the Civil Service Law.

amination, which must be passed before entrance to any German university, made possible the exclusion of candidates for alleged political heresy. All "Marxist" and "anti-National" students were ousted from Prussian universities.[31]

Once admitted to a college or university, the students were officially organized in a National Socialist Association recognized by the government.[32] Only students of "German descent and mother tongue" may belong to this organization which represents the student body and has as its purpose "the fulfillment by the students of their duty to people, state and university." A decree issued in Prussia on April 12, 1933, by the Ministry of Education defined "German descent" according to the standard Civil Service Law terms. This decree also stressed the Nazi principle of "leadership," and declared that one of the purposes of the students' association is "the education of the students for military service and for coöperation with the German people as a whole by means of military and labor service and physical exercises," a provision obviously contrary to the terms of the Versailles Treaty. "Non-Aryans" are not admitted to the inner student life of the university, while German-speaking students from Austria and those countries which have German minorities are to be received into the fold. Two major planks of the Nazi program are here in process of fulfillment.[33]

[31] Decree issued August 9, 1933, by Rust, Prussian Minister of Education. *New York Herald Tribune,* August 10, 1933.

[32] According to a law of April 22, 1933, *Reichsgesetzblatt,* I, p. 215. Included in *Das Recht der nationalen Revolution,* no. V, cited.

[33] Wertheimer, "Forces Underlying the Nazi Revolution," cited.

Nazi Cultural Activities

The cultural aspects of the Nazi revolution were exemplified by the *auto-da-fé* held on May 10, 1933, when books by Jewish authors, pacifists, so-called "Marxists" etc., were publicly burned by students.[34] An even more illuminating example is found in the "Theses" posted prominently on the bulletin boards of German universities, which stated: [35]

"Our most dangerous enemy is the Jew and everyone connected with him. The Jew can only think Jewish. If he writes German, he lies. The German who writes German but thinks un-German is a traitor. We censor Jewish works. We wish German students to destroy Jewish intellectualism. We demand that students and professors should be chosen from Germans and that the German spirit should be thus safeguarded."

A further indication of this "safeguarding" of the German spirit is to be found in the law ousting all Jewish actors, directors, producers, cameramen, authors and conductors from the German film industry[36] and the German theatre. Most "non-Aryans" were expelled from orchestras,[37] both as conductors and as musicians, and in principle no "non-Aryan" soloists may appear in concerts or on the radio;[38] so-called Jewish influence was thus removed from music, literature and art. In the field of journalism, many eminent writers have been dismissed because of their race, and the confiscation of the entire Socialist and Communist press has thrown large num-

---

[34] A fairly complete list of the books banned is to be found in the *Essener Volks-Zeitung,* May 18, 1933.

[35] *The Times* (London), August 15, 1933.

[36] *New York Times,* July 1, 1933.

[37] *Ibid.,* July 5, 1933.

[38] The "Aryan" paragraph of the Civil Service Law is the definition used.

bers out of work. Furthermore, during the process of "coördinating" the non-Nazi press, numerous "non-Aryans" have been ousted.[39]

Commerce and Industry

Nazi opposition to Jewish "intelligence" was apparent in these measures which not only made it practically impossible for Jews in the liberal professions to earn a living, but also limited the possibilities, especially in higher education, for "non-Aryan" youth to acquire training and knowledge. The fear and hatred of the Hitlerites for so-called Jewish business acumen was undoubtedly just as great, as indicated by their constant references to "Jewish materialism."[40] The thoroughness with which the Nazis acted in economic life was perhaps not quite so marked as in the professions, where definite laws were promulgated regulating Jewish participation. While the measures taken in regard to business were far-reaching, there were some indications that concern over the grave economic situation tempered Nazi ardor to "cleanse" business.

The effects of the boycott of April 1 on commerce, however, outlasted the one day to which it was officially limited. This was reported to be especially the case in small towns and cities, for on June 30, 1933, the city of Dortmund staged a private anti-Jewish boycott of its own which was declared a great success;[41] a week or so later the local *Dortmunder*

[39] The National Press Law promulgated by the Hitler government on October 5 provided that every working newspaper man in Germany is to be regarded as a servant of the state, and will be held morally and legally responsible for his professional activities. The "Aryan" provisions of the Civil Service Code are incorporated in the press law.

[40] Wertheimer, "Forces Underlying the Nazi Revolution," cited.

[41] *The Times* (London), July 11, 1933.

Generalanzeiger warned all members of the National
Socialist party and related organizations not to enter Jewish business premises.[42] Instances of persecution can be multiplied many times. On July 20 in
Nuremberg 300 Jews, chiefly shop-keepers but including several well-known lawyers and doctors, were
arrested. Their houses were searched and they were
made to march through the streets in a procession,
flanked on either side by Storm Troopers, treated
with derision and brutality, and finally interned in
a large public barracks.[43] In Berlin the municipal
authorities excluded Jewish merchants from the public market; [44] in Munich the municipal council decreed that no Jewish merchants may be permitted
in the auction room of the city pawnshop or allowed
to participate in the October Fairs; [45] in Hamburg
no "non-Aryans" may have public telephone booths
in their shops.[46] The National Association of German Shoe Merchants demanded the exclusion of
"non-Aryans" from the shoe trade, and that shoe
shops owned by Jews shall be closed on Saturday
as well as Sunday.[47] A final instance was the an-
nouncement that the government on September 30,
1933, would rescind all permits to trade on the Stock
Exchange. Only those persons who fulfilled the necessary "moral" and "technical" requirements were
readmitted.[48] While these were scattered incidents,
they showed clearly the temper of the Nazi rank
and file.

During the first weeks of the Nazi revolution,

[42] *Ibid.*, July 20, 1933.
[43] *Ibid.*, July 21, August 1, 1933.
[44] *Le Temps*, July 15–16, 1933.
[45] *Frankfurter Zeitung*, August 13, 1933.
[46] *Ibid.*, p. 19.
[47] *Le Temps*, July 20, 1933.
[48] *Voelkischer Beobachter*, July 6, 1933.

many Jewish members of boards of directors and managements of important firms were forced out in the general coördination, or *Gleichschaltung,* of every aspect of German life. Even the powerful Association of Germany Industry [49] was "coördinated" early in March 1933, and the coördination of all other trade associations, large and small, wholesale and retail, followed.[50] Nazi commissars were installed in almost all firms and zealously worked to purify business. As the first flush of the Revolution passed, many of the Nazi leaders apparently began to realize that business and industry in the Reich was being harmed by these tactics, with consequent detriment to employment. In July, in a series of speeches by Hitler and other Nazis, it was announced that the revolution was over, that there would be no second revolution, and Nazi followers were exhorted to refrain from meddling in industry. Hitler, on July 7, went so far as to say that "an industrial leader cannot be removed if he is a good business man merely because he is not yet a Nationalist Socialist, especially if the National Socialist being put in his place knows nothing about industry." [51] In a decision of July 14, 1933, the Cabinet laid down a policy in regard to government contracts to be awarded "non-Aryan" firms. If bids made by German firms equal bids by firms whose owners or directors are "non-Aryan," the German firm is to be preferred.[52] On September 27, however, Dr. Kurt Schmitt, Minister of Economics, declared that discrimination between Aryan and non-Aryan

[49] *Reichsverband der deutschen Industrie.*

[50] Hoover, *Germany Enters the Third Reich,* cited, p. 137 *et seq.*

[51] *New York Herald Tribune,* July 8, 1933.

[52] *Frankfurter Zeitung,* August 4, 1933.

business establishments would hamper economic recovery, and should therefore be discountenanced. Furthermore, many similar statements were made subsequently as it became evident that complete exclusion of Jews from German economic and financial life would seriously hamper economic recovery.

The situation of Jewish industrial and office workers was also difficult and uncertain. All labor, including the white-collar class, had been organized in the so-called "German Labor Front," and "non-Aryans" [53] were excluded from this organization.[54] There were reports that only members of the Labor Front would be able to secure jobs. The situation was greatly complicated by the fact that a large proportion of German workers were "Marxists," against whom the Nazis have been as violent in their repressive measures as against the Jews. On October 2 the Hitler government promulgated the Hereditary Homestead Law creating a "peasant aristocracy," which consists of "Germans, Aryan and honorable." Under this law, "Aryans" are those whose families have been free of Jewish blood since 1800.[55] While very few Jews in the Reich were engaged in agriculture,[56] this was nevertheless a significant move.

The problem of citizenship for German Jews has received the attention of the Hitler government, which has thus acted in accordance with the official program of the National Socialist party.[57] On

[53] According to the civil service definition.
[54] *Frankfurter Zeitung,* July 7, 13, 1933.
[55] *New York Herald Tribune,* October 3, 1933.
[56] *Cf.* table, p. 240.
[57] Wertheimer, "Forces Underlying the Nazi Revolution," cited. This program states: "IV. Only a member of our own people (*Volksgenosse*) may be a citizen (*Staatsbürger*). Our own people are *only* those of German blood without reference to con-

July 14, 1933, the Reich Cabinet decided to withdraw German citizenship at its discretion from "undesirables" naturalized within the last fifteen years—between November 9, 1918, and January 30, 1933. Citizenship is to be withdrawn from Germans who have fled abroad if they conduct anti-German propaganda or if they do not return to the Reich at the request of the German government. The property of all such persons is to be confiscated,[58] as well as the property of all "anti-state" elements, the Ministry of the Interior having the power to establish which persons and what actions are "anti-state" in character.[59]

In conclusion it must be said that the position of all "non-Aryans" in the Reich is uncertain and precarious, for, aside from the humanitarian and social aspects of the situation, their economic future appears black. The younger generation of "non-Aryans" will not only be unable to earn a livelihood, but the educational opportunities open to them are strictly limited.

CONCLUSION

The National Socialists, after a full year in office, are firmly in the saddle. They have ruthlessly suppressed all internal opposition to their régime

fession. Therefore no Jew may be a member of our people." "V. He who is not a citizen may live in Germany only as a guest and must be governed by laws regulating foreigners." "VI. Only citizens may decide on the leadership and laws of the state. Therefore, we demand that every public office, no matter of what sort, whether in the Reich, the States or the Communes, shall be filled only by citizens."

[58] In the case of thirty-three persons, these regulations have already been enforced. *The Times* (London), August 26, 1933.

[59] *Frankfurter Zeitung,* July 15, 1933.

and have already gone far toward realizing many
of the essential planks in the Nazi program. The
complete unification of Germany with absolute
centralization of power in the hands of the Reich
government stands out as Hitler's most important
achievement. On the debit side, however, must be
noted the suppression of all personal liberty and
freedom of thought in the Reich. Furthermore,
two major questions of future Nazi policy remain
unanswered. As yet no steps have been taken to
carry out the party program and the promises of the
leaders indicating that German "socialism" would
be introduced which would benefit the masses of
the workers. On the contrary, big industry in Nazi
Germany appears to have retained its hold on the
economic system of the country and the hard-won
concessions gained by the trade unions and the
Social Democrats have been vitiated to a large
extent.

In foreign affairs, also, wide uncertainty exists.
The policy of Hitler does not entirely square with
his previous promises to carry out the first and
most important point in the Nazi program: the
unification of all Germans in one great Germany.
Although some steps have been taken in this
direction, notably in Austria, Hitler has made several
peace speeches and has signed a ten-year truce with
Poland which is equivalent to stabilization of the
hotly contested Polish-German frontier during that
period. On the other hand, the militarization and
rearmament of the Reich is proceeding apace. In
general, the realization of equality in armaments
is still the primary object of German foreign policy.
After that has been attained, it remains to be seen
whether the Nazis will actually attempt to realize

their more ambitious ultimate aims or become more moderate.

Article 45: The President of the Reich represents the Reich in international relations. In the name of the Reich he makes alliances and other treaties with foreign powers. He accredits and receives diplomatic representatives.

Declarations of war and conclusion of peace shall be made by national law.

Alliances and treaties with foreign states which relate to subjects of national legislation require the consent of the Reichstag.

Article 68: Bills shall be introduced by the National Ministry, or by members of the Reichstag. National laws shall be enacted by the Reichstag.

Article 69: The initiation of a bill by the National Ministry shall require the consent of the Reichsrat. If the National Ministry and the Reichsrat fail to agree, the National Ministry may, nevertheless, introduce the bill but must present therewith the dissenting opinion of the Reichsrat.

If the Reichsrat passes a bill to which the National Ministry fails to assent, the Ministry must introduce such bill in the Reichstag accompanied by an expression of its views.

Article 70: The President of the Reich shall proclaim the laws constitutionally enacted, and shall publish them within a month in the *Reichsgesetzblatt.*

Article 71: National laws, unless otherwise provided, shall be effective on the fourteenth day after the day of publication in the *Reichsgesetzblatt* in the capital of the Reich.

Article 72: Publication of a national law shall be deferred for two months on request of one-third of the members of the Reichstag. Laws which the Reichstag and the Reichsrat declare to be urgent may be published by the President of the Reich regardless of this request.

Article 73: A law passed by the Reichstag shall, before its publication, be subject to a referendum, if the President of the Reich, within a month so decides.

A law, the publication of which has been deferred on the request of one-third of the members of the Reichstag shall be subject to a referendum upon the request of one-twentieth of the qualified voters.

A referendum shall also take place, if one-tenth of the qualified voters petition for the submission of a proposed law. Such petition must be based on a fully elaborated bill. The bill shall be submitted to the Reichstag accompanied by an expression of its views. The referendum shall not take place if the bill petitioned for is accepted by the Reichstag without amendment.

Only the President of the Reich may order a referendum concerning the budget, tax laws, and salary regulations.

Detailed regulations in respect to the referendum and initiative shall be prescribed by a national law.

Article 74: Laws enacted by the Reichstag shall be subject to veto by the Reichsrat.

The veto must be communicated to the National Ministry within two weeks after the final vote in the

Reichstag, and within two additional weeks must be supported by reasons.

In case of veto the law must be presented to the Reichstag for reconsideration. If no agreement upon the matter is reached between the Reichstag and the Reichsrat, the President of the Reich may within three months submit the matter in dispute to a referendum. If the President fails to exercise this right, the law shall be considered as of no effect. If the Reichstag overrules the veto of the Reichsrat by a two-thirds majority vote, the President shall within three months publish the law in the form adopted by the Reichstag or shall order a referendum.

Article 75: A resolution of the Reichstag shall not be annulled unless a majority of the qualified voters participate in the election.

Article 76: The constitution may be amended by legislative action. However, resolutions of the Reichstag for amendment of the constitution are valid only if two-thirds of the legal members are present and if two-thirds of those present give their assent. Moreover, resolutions of the Reichsrat for amendment of the constitution require a two-thirds majority of all the votes cast. If by popular petition a constitutional amendment is to be submitted to a referendum, it must be approved by a majority of the qualified voters.

If the Reichstag adopts a constitutional amendment over the veto of the Reichsrat, the President of the Reich shall not publish this law if the Reichsrat within two weeks demands a referendum.

Article 85, paragraph 2: The budget shall be adopted by law before the beginning of the fiscal year.

Article 87: Funds may be procured on credit only for extraordinary needs and as a rule only for expenditures for productive works. Such a procurement as well as the assumption of any liability by the Reich may be undertaken only by authority of a national law.

Article 114: Liberty of the person is inviolable. A restriction upon, or deprivation of, personal liberty, may not be imposed by public authority except by law.

Persons who have been deprived of their liberty must be informed no later than the following day by what authority, and upon what grounds, the deprivation of liberty was ordered; without delay they shall have the opportunity to lodge objections against such deprivation of liberty.

Article 115: The dwelling of every German is his sanctuary and is inviolable. Exceptions may be imposed only by authority of law.

Article 117: Secrecy of postal, telegraphic, and telephonic communication is inviolable. Exceptions may be permitted only by a national law.

Article 118: Every German has the right within the limits of the general laws, to express his opinion orally, in writing, in print, pictorially, or in any other way. No circumstance arising out of his work or employment shall hinder him in the exercise of this right, and no one shall discriminate against him if he makes use of such right.

No censorship shall be established, but exceptional provisions may be made by law for cinematographs. Moreover, legal measures are permissible for the suppression of indecent and obscene literature, as well as for the protection of youth at public plays and exhibitions.

Article 123: All Germans have the right to assemble peaceably and unarmed without notice or special permission.

By national law notice may be required for meetings in the open air, and they may be prohibited in case of immediate danger to the public safety.

Article 124: All Germans have the right to form societies or associations for purposes not prohibited by the criminal code. This right may not be limited by preventive regulations. The same provision applies to religious societies and associations.

Every association has the right to incorporate according to the provisions of the civil code. Such right may not be denied to an association on the ground that its purpose is political, social, or religious.

Article 153: Property shall be guaranteed by the constitution. Its nature and limits shall be prescribed by law.

Expropriation shall take place only for the general good and only on the basis of law. It shall be accompanied by payment of just compensation unless otherwise provided by national law. In case of dispute over the amount of compensation, recourse to the ordinary courts shall be permitted, unless otherwise provided by national law. Expropriation by the Reich over against the states, municipalities, and associations serving the public welfare may take place only upon the payment of compensation.

Property imposes obligations. Its use by its owner shall at the same time serve the public good.

STABILITY IN THE BALTIC STATES

INTRODUCTION

THIS study embraces a survey of salient events occurring since the end of the World War in each of the succession states of the Russian Empire, with a view to forming an objective judgment on the forces at work for stability and internal peace in each.[1] To estimate the degree of stability in any given region involves an analysis of the interplay of those cohesive and disintegrative forces entering into the internal structure of each state. Stability is, then, the resultant of the social structure and conditioning environment—the product of domestic forces. While it is virtually impossible in a complex world completely to dissociate internal from external factors entering into any given situation, the principal objective here is the appraisal of the elements of strength and weakness in the respective countries at the present time.

FINLAND

COMMUNIST ACTIVITY

THE emergence of Finland from the Russian fold in 1918 was not effected without a short, but intensely bitter, civil war. Because of its position

[1] For a more detailed study of the Baltic states, *cf.* Malbone W. Graham, *New Governments of Eastern Europe* (New York, Holt, 1927).

in adjacence to the group of northern neutrals, Finland was felt to form an excellent base from which revolution could be spread westward into Europe. To convert the former Grand Duchy into a Soviet republic became, accordingly, one of the initial missionary enterprises of the Communist faith. But the effort to spread Communism by fire and sword among a basically democratic people, steeled in defense of their native institutions by the excesses of Czarism, proved a distinct failure. The bourgeois classes of Finland, along with the land-owning peasantry, crushed the imported revolution in the field, thanks to German assistance. The civil war, however, left a legacy of social bitterness between the bourgeoisie and peasantry on the one hand, and a large part of the Social Democratic urban population and a small rump of Communists on the other, which a decade of political independence and stable, orderly government were not able totally to efface. After the civil war the Finnish Social Democratic party returned to the fold of evolutionary methods and abandoned subversive tactics. It devoted its attention to strengthening its parliamentary position, becoming, as in Germany, easily the largest political party, and endeavored through comprehensive social legislation and a fostering of the trade union movement to consolidate its position with the working classes. The rump of Communists, in definite political alliance with the Third International, separated from the Social Democrats, organized as a Communist party, and until 1923 carried on typical Communist activity. Following the discovery of a plot against the security of the state in 1923, their activity as a party was officially outlawed, but in subsequent elections, under one pseudonym or other, a Communist ticket was presented. In the parliamentary elections of July 1–2, 1929, held at a time of economic depression which has since become intensified, the Communist contingent conquered twenty-three seats out of a Diet comprising 200 members.[2] Strengthened by this success, the Communist groups set out to control the trade unions if possible and, where successful, to restrict union membership to Communists. This type of activity was bitterly resented by workers of other political inclinations as "terrorism." A final step taken by the Communists, obviously at the instigation of Moscow, was the introduction in 1929–1930 of active anti-religious propaganda as a means of breaking down the resistance of the strongly pietistic Finns to revolutionary ideas. Under a liberal press régime, which dealt with press offenses through presidential ordinance, propaganda against Finnish institutions was allowed considerable leeway. The decision of the Communist leaders to select the town of Lapua, for over eighty years the stronghold of a pietistic Lutheran sect, as the center of an anti-religious demonstration-festival at the end of November 1929, was the culminating factor in arousing and mobilizing latent psychological resistance, and galvanizing it into an effective countermovement.

ANTI-COMMUNIST ACTIVITY: THE LAPUA MOVEMENT

The demonstration planned for Lapua was not permitted to take place, not because of official police prohibitions, but because of the emergence from the countryside of a volunteer vigilantist group which dispersed the attempted gathering of four

[2] *Bulletin périodique de la presse scandinave*, No. 204, p. 6.

hundred Communist atheists. Following this, a mass meeting of farmers and peasants, under Lutheran auspices, gathered in Lapua on December 1, 1929 to present demands to the government for the effective suppression of Communism. Beginning in the province of Ostrobothnia, this movement, under the fiery leadership of Vihtori Kosola, who has been described as a Finnish Mussolini, finally spread throughout the country.[3] Delegations bearing the demands of the movement descended upon Helsingfors to put their memorials before the government and demand action.

The response of the Kallio cabinet, composed of Agrarians sympathetic to the Lapua movement, Progressives looking askance at its illegalities, and Social Democrats who held the balance of power in the Diet, could hardly be vigorous. A bill was introduced to enlarge the powers of the government over the organization and dissolution of societies, and was quickly passed. When, however, a second bill aiming to control the press by legislative action came up for discussion, the Social Democrats, in response to the demands of their central organization, succeeded in killing it.[4] The hope of the leaders of the Lapua movement, that it might be possible to proceed by lawful means against what they deemed subversive elements, now seemed doomed to disappointment.

It was not long before direct action followed. On March 28, 1930, the Lapua leaders wrecked the plant

[3] For a review of the beginnings of the movement, cf. Goeteborgs Handels-Tidning, April 23, 1930, and Lauri Ingman, The Lapua Anti-Communist Movement in Finland (Helsingfors, 1930), p. 3.

[4] Ingman, The Lapua Anti-Communist Movement in Finland, cited, p. 10.

of the *Työn Ääni* (The Voice of Labor), a Vaasa Communist sheet,[5] on account of "the license of its articles." This inaugurated a period of sporadic vigilantism, which presently assumed the form of systematic kidnapping of Communist leaders and their detention for a few days under harrowing circumstances, followed as a rule by release at some point distant from the scene of the abduction, or by ejection across the eastern border. In the face of these acts of normally law-abiding citizens, the police, the civic guards and the frontier patrols were impotent, and an administrative paralysis, which crept from Vaasa to Helsingfors, became patent. The movement next assaulted the judiciary; it was a simple expedient to abduct the attorney for the plaintiffs when vigilantist activities came under judicial scrutiny.[6] With the local government authorities and the judiciary subject to effective pressure, the next objective of the movement became the influencing of the national government.

FINNISH LOCK MOVEMENT

While the Lapua movement proper, which proceeded on a purely emotional basis, was undertaking these capricious activities in various parts of Finland, a second and more closely knit movement came into being, with far more consciously directed objectives. If Pastor Kares, father-confessor to the Lapuans, could proclaim with all sincerity

[5] *Hufvudstadsbladet,* March 29, 1930.
[6] In the trial of the *Työn Ääni* case, the chief attorney for the owners of the paper, Mr. Asser Salo, was kidnapped and taken over the border into Sweden on June 4. This disrupted the trial, which was postponed to July 9. By that time the Lapua movement had reached such proportions that the case could not be disposed of. For the full documents in the case, *cf. Suomen Sosialidemokraatti,* June 7, 1930.

that "the Lapua movement was national and religious merely, and that there was nothing of an economic theory in it," [7] the same could not be said of the *Suomen Lukko* (Finland's Lock) movement, which assailed the economic power of Communists by appealing to patriots to discharge Communist employees and not in the future to employ in any capacity those who subscribed to Communist principles. In addition it favored the education of public opinion to its view of individual political and economic liberty.[8]

The convergence of these two movements took place in July 1930, when Kosola and his lieutenants organized, with the support of the *Suomen Lukko*, an imposing mass demonstration for a "March on Helsingfors" mildly imitative of the famous Italian exploit. But before the arrival of the contingents of picked Lapua men in the capital, two significant events took place: (1) on the assembling of the Diet in extraordinary session on July 1, Premier Kallio secured from that body a "bill of immunity" for the government to cover its admitted illegalities in the suppression of Communist newspapers; [9] and (2) laid before it certain proposals for constitutional

[7] *New York Times,* August 31, 1930.

[8] *Bulletin périodique de la presse scandinave,* No. 212, May 29, 1930; Ingman, *The Lapua Anti-Communist Movement in Finland,* cited, pp. 10–13; *New York Times,* August 26, 1930.

[9] The convocation of the Diet followed closely a mass meeting of the Lapua leaders which called upon the government to close Communist printing establishments and suspend their journals, liquidate Communist organizations under whatever guise they might appear, imprison Communist leaders, agitators and their supporters, and enact laws validating such action. (*Cf. Hufvudstadsbladet,* June 12, 1930.) Kallio immediately announced the drafting of laws on the press and the defense of the state, and authorized provincial governors to suppress Communist newspapers if they thought it necessary for the maintenance of order and peace. (*Bulletin périodique de la presse scandinave,* No. 214, August 7, 1930, p. 7.)

reform which, in his opinion, would give to the government adequate powers to deal with the Communist movement. Having been officially vindicated by the Diet, Kallio thereupon resigned to permit the formation of a broader all-bourgeois coalition cabinet.[10] After the reference of the bills to the Constitutional Commission of the Diet, members of the Lapua movement on July 5 openly entered the Diet building, invaded the commission's sessions and abducted the two Communist members. These events demonstrated the powerlessness of the government to maintain law and order, as well as the strength of the popular movement. It was manifestly necessary to bring the government into accord with the masses.[11]

When, therefore, Kosola and twelve thousand of his followers marched upon Helsingfors on Sunday, July 7, and openly presented their demands to the government, they were met by President Relander, who expressed general approval of their actions, by General Mannerheim, the *père de la victoire* of the Finnish Civil War, who added his benediction, and by a cabinet almost entirely recast [12] to include strong nationalists and extra-parliamentary leaders, and headed by the Grand Old Man of Finland, Judge Svinhufvud.[13] It was plain that the period of governmental temporizing which had doomed the Kallio ministry was over.

[10] *Helsingin Sanomat,* July 3, 1930.
[11] Ingman, *The Lapua Anti-Communist Movement in Finland,* cited, p. 14; *Talonpoikan Marssi,* p. 4.
[12] *Hufvudstadsbladet,* July 4, 1930.
[13] Ingman, *The Lapua Anti-Communist Movement in Finland,* cited, p. 14; *Helsingin Sanomat,* July 5, 1930. Of the thirteen ministers, only seven belonged to the Diet. At no time were the Lapua leaders brought into the government, however, nor did they put forward any demand to that end (*Uusi Suomi,* July 5, 1930). Foreign Minister Procopé was the sole survivor of the

THE CONSTITUTIONAL CRISIS

The Svinhufvud government was forced to give its attention to the constitutional measures laid before the Diet by its predecessor. The first of the reforms proposed by Kallio was openly anti-Communist, seeking to "forbid the entrance into parliament of members of a party working for the overthrow of the state, likewise their right to sit in municipal councils"; [14] another was intended to "restrict the possibilities of a misuse of the freedom of the press for subversive propaganda"; [15] a third—the so-called Law for the Defense of the Republic—sought to give the government power to deal with an emergency by ordinance.[16] Inasmuch as these provisions clearly conflicted with the Bill of Rights, they partook of the nature of constitutional amendments which require a two-thirds vote for their enactment, a dissolution or delay until the meeting of the next Diet, and then repassage by a two-thirds majority. It was a simple enough matter to put the bills through the first two readings and then to bring

Kallio ministry, his inclusion in the new cabinet being due to the desire to impress foreign countries with the purely domestic character of the Lapua movement and the continuity of Finnish foreign policy.

[14] According to the *Helsingin Sanomat,* July 2, 1930, the bill deprived of eligibility to public office anyone belonging to a society, organization or other association whose aims included the direct or indirect overthrow, by violence or by any other illegal manner, of the social and governmental order in Finland, or representing such a society, organization or association, or who in any other manner showed himself favorable to acts tending to such ends. Its enforcement was to be left to the central electoral commission from whose decisions appeal could be made to the supreme administrative court.

[15] *Ibid.* This involved "the modification of certain articles of the law on the liberty of the press and of Article 24 of Chapter 16 of the penal code."

[16] Such ordinances, issued on the basis of the new law, were to be brought immediately to the attention of the Diet and to be abrogated in so far as it might decide. (*Ibid.*)

them, by interparty caucus and negotiation, into a form representing the composite views of the bourgeois coalition backing Svinhufvud and the Social Democrats led by Mr. V. Hakkila. As thus agreed to, the measures were reported for third reading. The Social Democrats had fought inch by inch, however, against the extreme extension of governmental powers demanded by Svinhufvud, and their substitute amendments had considerably tempered the bills. They were prepared, if the government assented to their proposals, to accept urgency procedure, which involved a vote by a five-sixths majority. Svinhufvud, however, was insistent upon the passage of the bills in the form in which he favored them, so that although they easily received a two-thirds majority—the twenty-three Communist seats being vacant [17]—the Social Democrats were able effectively to prevent their adoption under urgency rules.[18] Svinhufvud might have allowed the matter to rest until the next election, which would normally have come in 1932, but in the face of the demands of the Lapua leaders, he had no other choice than to dissolve the Diet. This he did on July 15, 1930, with the full consent of President Relander, setting the date for the new elections for October 1 and 2, and for the assembling of the new Diet on October 20.[19]

[17] On July 8 the Svinhufvud cabinet ordered the arrest of all the Communist deputies; on the following day the Diet gave its approval. (*Helsingin Sanomat,* July 10, 1930.)

[18] One bill, on the reform of municipal elections, actually passed and was not held up by a sufficient number of votes to force a dissolution; the others were able to obtain only a vote of 105 to 66. In the opinion of the *Helsingin Sanomat,* the substitute measures sponsored by M. Kivimäki would have counteracted the criminal activity of Communists as efficaciously as the government bills, and on a surer juridical foundation. (*Ibid.,* July 15, 1930.)

[19] *Uusi Suomi,* July 15, 1930.

The outstanding problem in the post-dissolution period was whether the government parties could muster a two-thirds majority out of the elections wherewith to complete the constitutional reform. It was obvious that no Communist ticket would be in the field, as most Communists were under cover, many had voluntarily gone to Russia, and others had been forcibly assisted across the frontier. All forms of exit and intimidation could not, of course, dispose of the 128,000 votes that had been cast for the Communist ticket in the elections of 1929, and it was generally agreed that any Communists participating in the elections would cast their votes for the Social Democratic list. With a normal Socialist membership of 59 out of a Diet of 200, and with 25 Communist seats to be disposed of, the chances seemed extraordinarily good for the Social Democrats to control at least 67 votes after the election, an eventuality which would give them the power permanently to block Svinhufvud's desired reforms. If this were the case, an impossible situation would arise, opening the possibilities of civil war; if, on the other hand, the bourgeois coalition should command the necessary 134 votes, the Lapua movement would emerge successful from the electoral campaign and be able to enact its basic program into law.

THE ELECTORAL CAMPAIGN

Between July and October the force of the Lapua and Finnish Lock movements was brought to bear upon the political parties. Within a fortnight of the dissolution, prominent men in the Lapua movement kidnapped the Social Democratic leader, Mr. Vaino Hakkila, took him to a wild spot in northern

Finland and ordered him to prepare for his execution. After protracted parleying, during which he
managed to clear the Social Democrats of complicity
in Communist propaganda, he was released, but it
was clear from that moment that the Lapua movement would make short shrift of the Social Democrats also, if it were necessary to do so to carry out
its program. Thereafter systematic abductions of
all Communist members of municipal and local government bodies took place, with here and there a
Socialist as well, and the government was finally
forced, early in September, to appeal to the leaders
to keep their cohorts in control, and to return to the
paths of legality.[20]

Meanwhile efforts to build a solid bourgeois electoral cartel proved unavailing. The result was that
the parties ran individual tickets, hoping for some
distinct benefits out of the electoral mêlée.[21] The
Lapua movement did not attempt to enter the field
with a ticket of its own. Indeed Kosola issued, the
day after the dissolution of the Diet, a manifesto
declaring that members of the movement should
hold aloof from appearing "in party formation," and
announcing that the leaders would curb the activity
of those attempting to do so. The real activity of
the Lapua movement consisted in creating electoral
committees in the cities and communes to "supervise the electoral lists" by striking off the names of
Communists.[22] This, although clearly illegal, was

[20] *Bulletin périodique de la presse scandinave*, No. 216,
October 16, 1930, p. 8, and *Hufvudstadsbladet*, September 5, 1930.
The kidnappers of Hakkila were given suspended sentences of
eight months on December 17, 1930. *Cf. New York Times*, December 19, 1930.
[21] *Bulletin périodique de la presse scandinave*, No. 216,
October 16, 1930, pp. 8–10.
[22] *Le Temps* (Paris), September 27, 1930.

done with impunity.[23] Such disfranchisement was considered an effective re-insurance against Communism. At the same time the Svinhufvud ministry by a mere cabinet decision prohibited all Communist activity, forbade "meetings and outdoor celebrations as well as parades and other manifestations of Communist associations, organizations and individuals," and authorized the police to prevent all private gatherings and manifestations of Communists.[24]

The elections after an intense campaign were held quietly on October 1 and 2, with a vote 25 per cent greater than at the preceding elections. Thanks to the cumulative effect of the various restrictive measures taken officially and unofficially, and even despite the non-formation of a cartel, a bourgeois majority for the reforms was produced, as indicated by the following table: [25]

FINNISH NATIONAL ELECTION, 1930

Party	Number of Seats	Number of Votes in 1930	Number of Votes in 1929
Progressive	11	64,914	53,301
Agrarian	59	308,003	248,762
Unionist	42	208,090	138,008
Swedish	21	122,579	108,886
Small Farmers	1	19,919	10,154
Social Democrats	66	385,820	260,254
Communists	0	11,503	128,164
Total	200	1,120,828	947,529

From the moment that the results were announced, the passage of the constitutional amendments was a foregone conclusion.

THE CONSTITUTIONAL REFORMS

When the Diet assembled on October 20, it found the government deeply concerned over the illegalities

[23] This would have been legalized by the Kallio proposals as passed by the Diet.
[24] *Helsingin Sanomat*, July 18, 1930.
[25] *Ibid.*, October 10, 1930.

born of the Lapua movement. Although the political objectives had all but been attained, the kidnappings continued, culminating in the abduction of a former President of the republic and outstanding Progressive leader, Dr. Kaarlo J. Stahlberg, and his wife. The plot was one in which both the *Suomen Lukko* and the highest officers of the Finnish army, including General Kurt Wallenius, chief of staff, were implicated, and if carried through might have caused grave international complications.[26] The vigilantist movement here overreached itself and produced an inevitable reaction. The leaders of the Lapua movement thereupon called upon the vigilantists to surrender to the courts and admit their illicit doings, and some 400 immediately avowed their participation in various acts of violence. This permitted the Finnish government to proceed against such individuals in the normal judicial manner.[27] Svinhufvud was forced to admit to the Diet, on October 23, that "political unrest had been so intense that strong measures by the government would have resulted in civil war and bloodshed, as the Lapuans were determined to accomplish their objects." [28] In the face of this situation the cabinet, he declared, "preferred a policy of moral pressure." The government having been vindicated in this attitude by the Diet, in a strict Socialist versus non-

[26] That Russia was aware of the activities of General Wallenius is indicated by the concern shown by *Izvestia* on May 14, 1930, over Wallenius' visit to the Polish military authorities, which it regarded as evidence of a recrudescence of anti-Soviet activity. (*Cf. Bulletin périodique de la presse russe,* No. 197, June 24, 1930, and *New York Times,* October 20, 1930.)

[27] After the passage of the constitutional amendments, judicial procedure was begun at once against many Communists already under arrest. More than 200 cases were in process on November 14, 1930, with fifty-seven already disposed of. (*Cf. New York Times,* November 15, 1930.)

[28] *The Times* (London), October 24, 1930.

Socialist vote, the anti-Communist bills were passed by a vote of 134 to 66 on November 11, 1930.[29] This brought to a close the official legislative and constitutional phase of the struggle.

PRESIDENTIAL ELECTION OF 1931

One of the immediate results of enhancing presidential authority through the widening of the ordinance power was to focus public attention upon the holders of the presidential office. As the six-year term of President Relander drew to an end, the country was plunged into a presidential campaign of unexampled bitterness in which the proponents and opponents of the Lapua movement sponsored the candidacies of Svinhufvud and Stahlberg respectively. The first phase of the presidential contest involved the balloting for an electoral college of 300 members on January 16, 1931. Here the Socialists secured 90 electors, the Agrarians 69, the Progressives 52, the Unionists 64, and the Swedish People's party 25. Computation by comparison with the figures in October elections shows that both the Agrarians and Socialists had lost approximately 10 per cent of their followings, the Lapua movement had barely maintained its strength, and the Swedish party had lost 2 per cent of its supporters. The gain came to the Progressives, and was accounted for by the enormous moral prestige of Stahlberg.[30] It was impossible, however, for a pure coalition of Socialists and Progressives—such as has frequently mustered

---

[29] *Helsingin Sanomat,* November 12, 1930. In its opinion there was every reason to believe that in the light of the solution reached the public activity of Communists could be considered terminated and the objectives of the patriotic majority of the country attained.

[30] For the data, *cf. The Times* (London), January 24, 1931.

sufficient scattered support to maintain a cabinet in power—to elect a President over the combined Unionist, Swedish and Agrarian groups. On February 16, Premier Svinhufvud was chosen President by the electoral college by 151 votes to 149 for Stahlberg.[31] The coalition of the Agrarians, the Unionists and the Swedes was almost complete.[32] As in the case of the constitutional reforms, the vote was just within the limits of legality. Svinhufvud resigned as Premier on March 1, 1931, to assume the presidency. Finland thus entered a new phase in its internal political development with the elevation of its Grand Old Man—a national hero in Czarist days, the main bastion of the White government during the civil war, and dictator-regent in the days of monarchist orientation—to the position of supreme power in the republic.

With the removal of Svinhufvud from party politics, the cabinet was recast under Agrarian and Unionist leadership after removing all personalities tainted by sympathy or affiliation with the Lapua movement. With new hands at the helm in the ministries of Foreign Affairs, the Interior and Labor, Premier Sunila set about to undertake a non-partisan solution of the economic crisis, subsequently continued by his successor, Kivimäki, and "the absolute reëstablishment of legality and of law, and a resolute repression of all intrigues and attempts at extra-parliamentary excitation, from whatever source."[33]

[31] *New York Times,* February 17, 1931.
[32] On the eve of the elections it was necessary for Svinhufvud to suspend the Lapuan paper *Aktivisti,* edited by Kosola, on account of its "abusive articles" and hints of assassination of Stahlberg, should he be elected. Warrants were issued for the arrest of the assistant editors, but not of Kosola. (*Cf. New York Times,* February 16, 1931.)
[33] *Suomen maa* (Agrarian), March 21, 1931.

Notwithstanding the new ministry's zeal for orderly
public life, kidnappings of Socialists and of journalists who pried too closely into the past of the
Lapua movement occurred sporadically throughout
1931, while demonstrations of "patriotic" societies
against Soviet deportations of Finnish residents
from Ingria threatened, for a time, to disturb the
peaceful relations between Finland and the U.S.S.R.[34]
Moreover, despite the efforts of M. Kivimäki, the
Minister of Justice, to procure the conviction of
General Wallenius, he was acquitted by the Finnish
Supreme Court on July 15, 1931, whereupon he became secretary-general of the Lapua movement.
After a new period of quiescence and conspiracy,
deeply implicating the Civic Guard, the Lapua
movement again showed itself in an ill-starred uprising at Mäntsälä on February 27, 1932, which
nearly brought the nation to civil war.

THE MÄNTSÄLÄ AND NIVALA REVOLTS

Preceded by bombings of Socialist quarters at Abo
in mid-February, the Mäntsälä affair was the product of long Lapua agitation directed by General
Wallenius, who succeeded in persuading armed peasants, along with veterans of the War of Independence and members of the Civic Guard, to participate
in terroristic acts directed against Socialists and
trade unions and, finally, against the local administrative authorities, leaving them helpless. Thereupon Kosola demanded of Svinhufvud the resignation of the cabinet. The aged president appealed to
the Civic Guard not to forget its oath of allegiance,

---

[34] For the correspondence which passed between Finland and
the U.S.S.R. on these points, *cf. Bulletin périodique de la presse
scandinave*, No. 224, June 25, 1931, and No. 226, August 8, 1931.

and besought the adventurers by radio to return to
their homes. The moral prestige of Svinhufvud suf-
ficed to break the "Lapua front" and, as amnesty
was offered to all except the leaders, the malcontents
rapidly dispersed. On March 6, the last handful of
insurgents and their leaders, Kosola, Wallenius and
others, surrendered unconditionally and were imprisoned. A resolute government, invoking against
the radicals of the Right the legislation they had
enacted for use against the radical Left, emerged
strengthened and victorious. Nevertheless, while
temporarily forbidding assemblies of the suspect organizations, the government did not dissolve them,
and the Lapua movement blossomed out with new
leaders in April, resolved to continue "the struggle
against Marxism." [35] Another outbreak and attempted coup at Nivala, June 11–14, 1932, demonstrated that the Lapua movement was still unre-
pentant, and that the infection of Lapuaism with
which the Civic Guard was tainted had not been
completely cured. This time, however, there was no
vacillation on the part of the government and eighteen ringleaders were imprisoned at Uleaborg, while
116 persons involved in the Mäntsälä uprising were
brought to trial at Abo. [36] These actions, while failing to crush the Lapua movement, definitely broke
its internal solidarity, produced several off-shoots, [37]

[35] *Dagens Nyheter,* April 19, 1932.

[36] Of these 52 were convicted and sentenced to prison terms
of from two to thirty months, 32 were given suspended sentences
—among them Kosola and Wallenius—24 were acquitted, and
20 others were amnestied. *Hufvudstadsbladet,* July 13, and
November 21, 1932.

[37] These were: The Finnish National Socialist Party, purely
Hitlerite in character, founded by Professor Yrjö Ruutu of the
University of Helsingfors in April, 1932; the Finnish Popular
Movement Party, "further to the Right than the Lapua move-

and forced a third reorganization of the movement—
this time along military lines—which has since assumed a definitely anti-Swedish [38] as well as an anti-
Communist character. Calling itself the "Popular
Patriotic Movement," Lapua now developed racist
and pagan [39] tendencies not unlike those in contem-
porary Germany. That the movement overreached
itself and lost prestige when it undertook conspiracies against the Svinhufvud régime was evident
long before a new anti-inflationist cabinet, headed
by Kivimäki, went to the country in the parliamentary elections of 1933.

ment" and criticizing it for not copying Hitlerite tactics, with
a program broadly comparable to that of the Nazis imported
by its leader, Captain Kalsta, from Germany; the Finnish National Party, recruited from non-Marxist workers; and the
Finnish Workers' Party, claiming that it represents the "Whites"
among the organized labor movement. Two anti-Marxist factions
in the Agrarian Party, one advocating legal repression of socialism, the other proposing even more extreme measures, also
deserve attention. *Cf. Bulletin périodique de la presse scandinave,*
No. 240, April 27, 1933, p. 11.

[38] This is attributed to the fact that the Swedish population
in the vicinity of Mäntsälä refused to support the Lapua revolt.
Thereafter the Lapua leaders characterized them as being "a
direct danger to Finland" (*Dagens Nyheter,* April 19, 1932). This
attitude has since been persistently reflected in the efforts of the
conservative Finns to demote Swedish from its position of equality with Finnish as a state language.

[39] "Lapua and its affiliated groups and competitors lay stress
on a racism impregnated with religiosity. Influence here comes
from Pastor Kares, who eloquently defends kidnapping and
the use of illegal means; and from another, Pastor Annala, the
promoter of projects of linguistic unification in the university
of Helsingfors at the expense of the Swedes. But a third, new,
essential complement to these two is furnished by a third leader,
ex-chaplain of the Whites in the Civil War, a popular writer,
Pastor Arvi Järventaus. At a recent meeting of young patriots
he recently launched the new battle-cry: Back to Jumala, to the
cult of the primitive god common to the Finns, the Esths and
the Hungarians, a pagan god, master of the tribes of Karelia as
Jehovah was of the Hebrews. This ethnic paganism preaches a
break with Western Liberalism which Järventaus characterizes
as the 'spiritual tuberculosis of the civilization of the West.'"
(Professor Estlander in *Finsk Tidskrift,* April 1, 1933.)

ELECTIONS OF 1933

In striking contrast of the elections of 1930, in which the bourgeois parties closed ranks against the radical Left, the elections of July 1st and 3rd, 1933, saw a marked shift of public opinion to the Left. There was heavy balloting and the vote polled was the second largest in the history of Finland. The significant feature of the elections, which were fought out on the issue of activism versus constitutionalism, was the defeat of all the extremist Right parties, from which the dangers to public liberties had come. The two quasi-Nazi parties together polled less than .0035 of the popular vote, indicating that the break with Germanophil tendencies in politics was complete. The principal gains, as shown in the accompanying table, were made by the Social Democrats at the expense of the Agrarians and the Unionists, with whom the Lapua party made common cause. In the Riksdag of 1933–1936, therefore, Finland has reached a new normalcy, which marks the defeat of ideas of a dictatorship or of racialism, and a return to the paths of legality. In the words of Premier Kivimäki, "Finland, where serfdom never existed and where one may observe the development of democratic legality for nearly ten centuries, is incapable of submitting to any sort of slavery." [40]

RESULTS OF THE ELECTIONS TO THE FINNISH RIKSDAG, JULY 1-3, 1933.*

Party	Votes 1933	Votes 1930	Seats 1933	Seats 1930
Social Democrats	412,360	386,026	78	66
Agrarians	248,973	308,280	53	59
Unionists and Patriotic National Movement	186,815	203,958	32	42
Swedish Party	115,385	122,589	21	21
Progressives	81,391	65,830	11	11
Small Farmers	37,607	20,883	3	1
National Party	9,387	......	2	0
Other parties	11,533	22,462	0	0

* Bank of Finland Monthly Bulletin, July 1933, No. 7, p. 33.

[40] Turun Sanomat, June 27, 1933.

ESTONIA

CONSTITUTIONAL DEVELOPMENT

FOLLOWING its separation from Russia in February 1920, the Estonian Republic in June of that year adopted a democratic constitution which provided for a unicameral State Assembly of 100 members; a system of ministerial responsibility vesting in the Prime Minister all the attributes normally given to a chief of state, for whom no provision was made; an independent judiciary; and democratic local government. As a safeguard against possible abuses, popular initiative and legislative referendum were provided, although financial matters were rigorously excluded from the sphere of direct legislation. A decade of experience with this instrument of government witnessed only one application of the initiative, that relative to religious education, by which the conservatism of an overwhelmingly Lutheran population defeated the secular program of the ministry of the day. Otherwise, fluctuations in policy were registered by easy transitions from one cabinet to another without formal constitutional change.[41]

COMMUNIST ACTIVITY

The unsuccessful attempt of a small band of native Communists, supported by Russian nationals of Estonian race, to overthrow the government by force in December 1924 demonstrated the over-

---

[41] Subsequent demands for constitutional change will be discussed under the Estonian Lapua movement, which brought them to the fore.

whelming solidarity of the democratic peasantry and their intense nationalism. After judicial trials had sentenced to death or to long terms in jail the persons guilty of this revolutionary activity, the only procedure necessary for control of Communism was police surveillance, and occasional search and seizure. In the early spring of 1930, however, the assassination of the head of the Tallinn garrison, General Uut, as an act of Communist terrorism, aroused nation-wide resentment, the reaction of the press and public opinion clearly indicating that "the people were in no mood for Eastern experiments." [42] In addition to planning and trying out experimental military manœuvres for the defense of the capital in the event of any possible uprising, the government undertook a new round-up of Communists, discovering an interesting liaison with Moscow,[43] and proceeded to the dissolution of the parliamentary Communist Labor party of Estonia—the so-called Kaaver-Socialists—and the proportional distribution of their six mandates among the remaining parliamentary groups.[44] Without need of further political action, and solely through administrative vigilance, the Communist movement in Estonia was thus reduced to such insignificant proportions that it does not constitute a serious factor in the development of the country's constitutional life. Here the constructive effect of a policy of land reform has been most noteworthy in cutting the ground from under potential Communism.

[42] *Baltische Monatsschrift*, Vol. 61, No. 4 (April 1930), p. 258.
[43] According to the Helsingfors *Hufvudstadsbladet* (April 5, 1930), the Estonian security police discovered "a vast organization of Communist espionage even in the offices of the Ministry of War."
[44] *Baltische Monatsschrift*, Vol. 61, No. 6 (June 1930), p. 396.

ESTONIAN LAPUA MOVEMENT

Without the presence of factors such as operated to produce the Lapua movement in Finland, and in default of any attacks upon their religious institutions, the Estonians witnessed in July 1930 the beginning of a movement among the peasantry which acquired vitality contemporaneously enough to receive the epithet of an Estonian Lapua movement.[45]

In reality the movement would appear to have originated in a general dissatisfaction with the prolonged economic crisis, discontent with certain party intrigues in the parliament and with the electoral[46] system, and resentment at the apparent impotence of the government. Following a series of meetings of farmers in certain south Estonian communes, written memorials were sent to the Prime Minister setting forth demands for protection of agriculture, economies in the governmental administration and specific changes in the Constitution. These aimed at the establishment of a presidency, the reduction of the number of deputies in the State Assembly and the withdrawal of the right of franchise from those not paying state and communal taxes.[47] The latter

[45] These symptoms of agrarian dissatisfaction are not comparable to the Finnish movement. "While doubtless suggested by the events in Finland," says a French observer, "this attitude of the Estonian peasants presents fundamentally no analogy with that of the Finnish peasants. Rather it may at most be interpreted as a sign of political dissatisfaction. . . ." (*Bulletin périodique de la presse scandinave,* No. 216, October 16, 1930, p. 17.)

[46] *Cf.* the Tartu *Postimees,* August 5, 7, 1930.

[47] *Baltische Monatsschrift,* Vol. 61, No. 10 (October 1930), p. 629. Undoubtedly the problem of instituting a presidency— a move which would certainly involve constitutional amendment —is the most important of these demands, and the one most likely to affect the internal stability of the country.

"At the time of the elections to the Fourth State Assembly," declares a leading Democratic journal, "we showed how we could not hope for the reconstruction of our political life and the or-

demand elicited a violent protest from an assembly of poorer peasant-farmers and homesteaders, which declared that such "machinations . . . aimed at undermining the democratic order in the state." Other demands for change voiced in the press included "breaking the strong-willed absolutism of parliament" and the confining of the legislative assembly to its proper functions of law-making and control, with a view to freeing the government, the electors and the representatives of the people from the oppressive tutelage of the party bureaus. The existing State Assembly long remained impervious to demands for change. Just before it expired, it voted, on March 31, 1932 [48] to submit to the electorate an amendment reducing the membership of the Assembly to 80, and creating an elective five year presidency with considerable discretionary authority. The

ganization of our national economy by means of an active economic policy until after effecting serious political reforms. The strengthening of governmental power demands constitutional amendments, the instituting of a President of the State elected by the people. The President should have the right to dissolve parliament in case of need and to appeal to the people for new elections—a thing which would tend to check the arbitrariness of party conduct. The people's representatives ought to conform more closely to the will of the people, hence the necessity of modifying the organic law of parliament." (Tartu *Postimees*, August 7, 1930.) Such is the "revisionist" program. On the other hand, it is argued that:

"At the Constituent Assembly where the practical intelligence and vital instinct of the people showed their solidity in spite of the difficult times, the presidential question was debated in all its aspects. In reality there were very practical, well-founded arguments which led the Constituent Assembly overwhelmingly to reject the presidential institution. In simple and logical words our greatest statesman, Jaan Poska, showed that the Republic of Estonia did not need a president. The practice of ten years has demonstrated that his point of view was correct. Other States, in which presidents hold office, have passed through rude upheavals. The life of Estonia, without a president, has, on the whole, developed normally." (Tallinn, *Vaba Maa*, September 9, 1930.)

[48] *New York Times*. April 1, 1932. 1:3

referendum, held August 19, 1932 resulted in the rejection of the proposal by the close margin of 341,000 to 330,000 votes. The opposition consisted of Socialists who considered the measure anti-democratic, and of war veterans who felt that it still left too many matters to the caprice of parliament.[49] A year later, on June 11–12, 1933, another referendum was invoked on amendments seeking "to introduce a presidency on the German and Finnish patterns." It resulted in their decisive rejection by a vote of 333,045 to 161,089 by the combined forces of the Right and Left—"the Socialists, radicals and war veterans." [50] The latter now organized along Lapuist lines throughout the country and, despite governmental dissolution of their formations, brought about a third referendum on amendments reducing the State Assembly membership to 50, breaking parliamentary omnipotence, and establishing a strong presidency, comparable to that of the United States save for the coexistence of ministerial responsibility to parliament. The projects carried, on October 14–16, 1933, by a vote of 450,000 to 170,000.[51] Estonia's transition to the new constitution, however, involves various stages, as the amendments went into force only 99 days after the results of the referendum were announced.

[49] *Bulletin périodique de la presse scandinave,* No. 242, July 29, 1933.

[50] Professor Antonius Piip to the author, from Tallinn, June 16, 1933.

[51] A counter-project, sponsored by Professor Piip, proposed to safeguard parliament while stabilizing executive power by making the cabinet elective by parliament for a three year term but, like the Swiss, irremovable. This ingenious compromise was necessarily defeated by the vote for the war veterans' proposals. A full account of the constitutional reforms, with a slight Nazi bias, is found in Axel de Vries' "Neue Entwicklungen in Estland" (*Ost-Europa,* 9. Jhrg., Heft 3, pp. 157–165, December, 1933).

Provisionally, Premier Konstantin Päts became acting President, pending the election, after another 100 days (*i.e.*, in mid-May, 1934) of a new parliament and president. The new presidential election law is patterned closely on that in force in Germany under the Weimar constitution, and permits the choice of a new chief executive by a plurality if a run-off election is needed.

Estonia thus brings to a close a period of parliamentary supremacy and opens a new chapter of republican government under stabilized executive leadership.

PROTECTION OF MINORITIES

Estonia, on entering the League of Nations, gave a declaration signed at Geneva [52] that it would accord equitable treatment to its racial, religious and linguistic minorities—principally Russians, Germans and Swedes. In pursuance of this declaration, the Estonian State Assembly on January 5, 1926 passed a law on cultural autonomy [53] for minorities which has been commended as the most liberal in Europe. The only complaints arising from "minorities" in Estonia are those put forward by the Baltic barons whose estates were expropriated under the terms of the Agrarian law of September 19, 1919. [54] At the suggestion of the German government, these individuals, who, by every canon of international

---

[52] Declaration of August 31, 1923, *League of Nations Official Journal*, Vol. 4, November 1923, p. 1311.

[53] *The Estonian Year Book, 1929*, pp. 28–30. When, however, the German-Balt party, late in 1933, reorganized itself as a National Socialist Party along German lines, the Estonian government promptly dissolved all its organizations and prohibited its newspapers, considering, in the light of intercepted evidence, that the Balts were engaged in a conspiracy against the state.

[54] *Ibid.*, pp. 83–86.

law, were Estonian nationals, withdrew from Estonia and acquired German nationality. The German
government then put forward their special preferen-
tial claim to cash compensation for their losses.
After wearisome negotiations on both sides, the Estonian government, on December 8, 1931, concluded
an agreement with the former landlords according
them a compensation of four million Estonian
crowns.[55]

LATVIA

POLITICAL AND ECONOMIC DEVELOPMENT

The Republic of Latvia, with a less homogeneous
population than Estonia, and an enormous capital
city to support, came into existence under even
more grievous circumstances than either Finland or
Estonia. Devastated by both German and Czarist
armies, visited by two Bolshevik invasions, and
made the stamping ground of the residual monarchist armies of the German and Russian counter-
revolutions, Latvia was compelled to delay its
constitutional reconstruction until peace had been
restored with Russia in August 1920. Under steady,
practical leadership in both domestic and foreign
policy Latvia established its constitutional structure through an instrument of 1922, which differed
from that of Estonia chiefly in that it created an independent Presidency. Reforms in land distribution,
colonization of the soldiery on plots of ground taken
from the detested Baltic barons, and the building-up
of institutions of local self-government have proceeded largely parallel with those in Estonia. Under

[55] *Ost-Europa,* 7 Jhrg., Heft 4, January, 1932, p. 238.

more auspicious circumstances, a valorization of the currency and the establishment of the *lat* as the monetary unit was effected by 1922, to the great benefit of the middle class of security holders and merchants. In its treatment of minorities Latvia likewise followed the lead of Estonia, giving an analogous declaration at Geneva [56] and executing it by appropriate legislation. The complaints of the barons whose lands were expropriated have been few, and have not secured the backing of any great power. Owing to the presence of an appreciable number of Catholics in Latgallia, once a province of historic Poland, Latvia has reached, through a concordat with the Vatican,[57] a satisfactory adjustment of the position and obligations of this religious element, and political life is now singularly free from any religious vicissitudes. Conscious of its rôle as an *entrepôt* country, Latvia has endeavored by calm, objective negotiation to increase its exports of goods to the Soviet Union and has managed to secure the placing of large orders from the U.S.S.R. in its territory.[58] Possessing ports more free of ice than those of Estonia, Latvia has likewise increased its transit commerce despite the marked difficulties for the economic hinterland arising from the closed Polish-Lithuanian "frontier." The country has suffered little from Communist conspiracies or agitation, owing in part to the rigor-

[56] Declaration of July 7, 1923, *League of Nations Official Journal,* Vol. 4, November 1923, p, 1275.

[57] The text of the concordat is given in the *League of Nations Treaty Series,* Vol. XVII, p. 365, No. 443, and in G. Albat, *Recueil des principaux traités conclus par la Lettonie avec les pays étrangers, 1918–1928,* Vol. I, pp. 71–75.

[58] *Cf.* Oswald Zienau, "Die sowjetrussisch-lettischen und estnischen Handelsbeziehungen," *Ost-Europa,* Vol. 5, No. 4 (January 1930), pp. 250–260.

ous administrative vigilance of the police,[59] but largely because its undisturbed existence as the mediary between East and West in commerce has been indispensable to Soviet Russia.

INTERNAL POLITICAL LIFE

Latvia's internal political life has fluctuated between the policies of Agrarian and Socialist coalitions, dependent for the execution of their respective programs upon the moderating support of the numerous bourgeois factions in the *Saeima*. On the whole, the Conservative-Agrarian groups have enjoyed the preponderance of power. The last parliamentary elections, held on October 7, 1928, indicated a trend "away from Kerenskism," [60] and evicted from power the Socialist coalition led by Felix Cielens, replacing it by an Agrarian-Conservative coalition under the premiership of Mr. Hugo Celmins, which has proceeded with extraordinary stability in its legislative and administrative program. Its position was strengthened in April 1930, when Mr. Albert Kviesis, vice president of the *Saeima* and an influential member of the Peasants' Union, was elected President of the republic for a three-year term by a vote of 55 to 36; the vote represented the approximate strength of the Right-Center against the Left parties.[61] The

[59] It is also attributable in part to the rigorous administrative vigilance of the Latvian police. (*Cf. Baltische Monatsschrift,* Vol. 61, No. 9, September 1930, p. 562.)

[60] The radical ministry of Cielens was frequently compared by its opponents to that of the equally mild Socialist, Kerenski, in 1917 in Russia. The election, according to the semi-official *Messager Polonais* (October 11, 1928), indicated the reaction against a socialistic policy and the concentration of the forces of the moderate parties.

[61] *New York Times,* April 10, 1930. Kviesis, according to the *Polska Zbrojna,* a semi-official military journal, is a member of

Celmins ministry was in power for over two years with the Social Democrats as its principal opponents. In March 1931 it was replaced by a new Conservative-Agrarian coalition headed by Karl Ulmanis, five times previously Prime Minister. Following the elections of October 3–4, 1931, which reinforced the conservative parties, the Ulmanis cabinet gave way in November to a new all-bourgeois ministry under Margirs Skujenieks of the New Farmers' Party, which, under pretexts of effecting economies, vigorously attacked the cultural and educational privileges of the different minorities, principally German and Russian, and inaugurated a stringent policy of Lettification. This exhibition of intransigeant nationalism continued under the cabinet of Adolfs Blodnieks (also New Farmers' Party) which succeeded to power in March 1933. Toward the end of 1933 there developed a Latvian National Socialist movement of pronounced anti-Semitic tendencies, with which the German minority showed itself in sympathy, and two rival varieties of Latvian Fascism: the "aissang" or militant bourgeois organization, and the "Perkonkrusts," [62] a militant nationalist group not without traces of atavistic paganism. In sharp contrast to Estonia, Latvia has not thus far curbed the activities of such groups.

the order *"Polonia Restituta"* and is regarded as very intimate with Poland. His opponent was Mr. Kalnins, the president of the *Saeima* and leader of the Latvian Social Democratic party. The victory of Kviesis, according to the *Wilno Slowo* (April 11, 1930), was attributable to his large personal following and his personal integrity. The President, it adds, "follows clearly the . . . policy of polonophilism." President Kviesis was reëlected for a three year term on April 4, 1933, *Ost-Europa,* 8 Jhrg., Heft 8, p. 487, May, 1933.

[62] *Izvestia,* August 26, 1933; *L'Europe Nouvelle,* 16e annee, No. 824, November 25, 1933, p. 1137; *Ost-Europa,* 9. Jhrg., Heft 3, pp. 178–179, December, 1933.

The influence of constitutional developments in Estonia has not been lost upon Latvia. At the time of the first plebiscite in Estonia, in 1932, reform of the constitution to give greater independence to the President by electing him directly and reducing the size of the legislative body was widely discussed. With the triumph of the revision movement in Estonia, Ulmanis and the Peasants' Union championed a replica for Latvia and, in November 1933, presented draft amendments to the *Saeima*. As in Finland and Estonia, the movement for greater executive authority has been closely connected with the repression of Communism and a certain disregard for the rights of national minorities.[63]

LITHUANIA

CONSTITUTIONAL DEVELOPMENT, 1922–1926

THE post-war history of Lithuania is roughly divisible into two periods of almost equal length: the period of government under the Constitution passed by the Constituent Assembly on August 1, 1922,[64] which was in operation until December 1926; and the period of dictatorship which followed the coup d'état at the end of that year, and extends to the present. During the first period, the country, operating within the framework of a democratic instrument, was under the control of a coalition government composed of Clerical and Agrarian parties down to May 1926; then a ministry of radically

[63] *Ost-Europa, loc. cit.*, and Heft 4, p. 258, January, 1934.
[64] Text in M. W. Graham, *New Governments of Eastern Europe* (New York, Henry Holt and Company, 1924), pp. 720–735.

different nature supported by the Socialist-Populists and the organized national minorities (Jewish, Polish, White Russian and German) took office. This government, under the leadership of Dr. Mikolas Slezevicius, followed a policy of distinct friendship to Russia, which even permitted the dissemination of Communist propaganda in the few industrial establishments in the country, while fighting the Clerical-Agrarian bloc in parliament with the aid of its minority allies. Such a situation threatened to carry the country further to the Left than a stolid and devout peasantry and a highly nationalist army desired, with the result that resort was had on the night of December 17, 1926, to a bloodless coup d'état. The government, installed with military support, virtually evicted the Left parties from Parliament, received a formal lease of power from a bare majority of the rump parliament,[65] and shortly afterward dissolved the legislative body without ordering new elections. From December 1926 to September 1929 the government was in the hands of Professor Augustinas Voldemaras, an ultra-Nationalist, supported by a group of Lithuanian intellectuals of relatively high ability, whose convictions were more Nationalist than Socialist or Clerical. In due season, however, this dictatorship of the intelligentsia became government of, by, and for Voldemaras, in that the fiery Nationalist Premier, whose successes lay primarily in the field of foreign policy, fought both the conservative Right and the radical Left and quarreled with his own Nationalist entourage. The persecution and imprisonment of many of the parliamentary leaders weakened the general prestige of the government, and on his re-

[65] *Ibid.*, pp. 404–405.

turn from Geneva in September 1929 Voldemaras
was forced by his colleagues to resign. Power now
reverted to the President, Dr. Smetona, profes-
sionally a philosopher, and to the new premier,
Mr. Juozas Tubelis, theretofore a moderate Nationalist, who now also became the official leader of the
Tautininkai party.

From September 1929 to July 1930, Voldemaras
refused to vacate his official quarters, hoping that
a turn in the affairs of Lithuania would permit his
resumption of power. Meanwhile, the Tubelis government liquidated the political heritage from
Voldemaras and began the release of political prisoners of the Right and Left, while rounding up Communists into an internment camp, in order that the
Ninth Fort at Kaunas should not be comparable to
the Polish prison at Brest-Litovsk.[66] When it became apparent to the government that Voldemaras
contemplated a return to power with the assistance
of a personal following in the army and the possible
diplomatic support of a powerful eastern neighbor,
he was arrested and interned, subsequently tried
and sent into exile in France.

With the problem of Voldemaras disposed of,
temporarily at least, the government has centered
its attention on various means for the improvement of agricultural conditions and the widening of
Lithuania's markets as the primary bases for building up its power in the country. The government
of Lithuania today rests upon the support of the
army, which is strongly Nationalist, peasant in
origin and virtually casteless, and the commercial
classes whose property is bound up with the maintenance of monetary stability and the modernization

[66] *Cf.* p. 302.

of the country. By a system of subsidies to agriculture, it strives to retain the support of the farming classes brought into being by the partitioning of large estates under the agrarian reform laws. The government itself is in the hands of a small nationalist intelligentsia neither military nor commercial in its inclinations. Legislation rests upon presidential ordinances and the courts enforce without hesitancy the decrees of the Nationalist régime. The formal basis of legal authority is the Constitution of May 25, 1928, promulgated by Voldemaras, and legitimating much that was the early work of the dictatorial régime.[67] It differs from the instrument of 1922 chiefly in its explicit reference to Vilna, taken by Poland in 1920 and still held by that country, as the national capital, and in its provisions for the legislative body. No elections have been held under the dictatorship, since there is scant probability that the Nationalist régime would survive a free consultation of the populace; first, because in its earlier phases it unquestionably alienated the national minorities, and second, because of the predominantly clerical trend of the country.[68]

THE KULTURKAMPF

One of the most recent acute phases in Lithuanian politics, which brings into clear relief a basic factor in national stability is the struggle of the Nationalist dictatorship with the organized Roman

[67] Text in *Vyriausbes Zinios*, No. 275, May 25, 1928.

[68] This statement refers, of course, only to the legislative body. In virtue of a law of November 25, 1931, promulgated by him, Smetona convoked an electoral college, largely made up of Nationalist representatives, which, on December 11, 1931, re-elected him to the presidency for a term of seven years, as provided by the constitution of 1928. (*Ost-Europa*, 7. Jhrg. Heft 4, January 1932, p. 236).

Catholic Church. Except for a small portion of her people living in the Memel area and in the east of the country, Lithuania is overwhelmingly Catholic; her Polish minorities and even a large portion of her White Russian minorities profess the forms of Christianity which they have inherited from the Western Church. The efforts at dissociation of church and state attempted by certain members of the Constituent Assembly in 1920–1922 proved a failure, and in the end a union of church and state was authorized. The political crisis of May 1926 was definitely connected with the effort of the Holy See to use its concordat with Poland as a political weapon against Lithuania, and only laboriously was a *modus vivendi* arrived at in 1928 between the Vatican and Voldemaras.[69] Since then, continuous difficulties have arisen in the application of the Lithuanian concordat, inasmuch as the Vatican has insisted on complete control of disbursements to its clergy made from the national treasury, while the Voldemaras régime insisted on retaining financial control. Under such arrangements, which have continued since the fall of the dictator, the Nationalist lower clergy have been treated with signal consideration by the government, whereas the higher clergy, regarded as polonophil, have fared less well.

Late in 1930, a new development came to light in the effort of the higher clergy to utilize theological students for political propagandist purposes among the younger generation, and in various student clubs

[69] *Cf.* Ladas Natkevicius, *Aspect politique et juridique du différend polono-lithuanien,* pp. 199–204, citing the *Acta Apostolicæ Sedis,* Anno XIX, Vol. 29, No. 15, p. 425 *et seq.,* and the *Osservatore Romano,* December 14, 1927, for the text of the concordat with Lithuania. *Cf.* also *Vyriausbes Zinios,* No. 264, December 20, 1927.

throughout the country. As a result, the government decreed the dissolution of the student clubs, in return for which the lower clergy received orders from their bishops, at the beginning of 1931, to cease completely all connection with the government. In retaliation, the government placed under internment the secular leaders of the Christian Democratic party and certain prelates,[70] and forbade the broadcasting of church services. The outcome of the struggle is by no means clear, and it may well be that a protracted contest is in prospect.

FASCIST TENDENCIES

In the presence of the schism between Church and State, Lithuanian nationalism has tended to evolve in a steadily Rightward direction, being largely influenced by fear of Poland on the one hand, and by a conscious desire to pattern after Italian Fascism and establish a corporative state on the other. In the absence of representative institutions, neither agitation nor referenda are essential to the process; most measures of a Fascist stamp are quietly undertaken through administrative channels. In a peculiar sense Lithuania, since the elimination of Voldemaras from public life, presents the curious spectacle of a régime, whose outstanding characteristic is presumed to be leadership, actually functioning without ostentatious leaders and attempting no slavish imitation of either Berlin or Warsaw.

MINORITY PROBLEM

Lithuania is less homogeneous in population than either Estonia or Latvia, having fallen heir, *inter*

---

[70] *Chicago Tribune,* January 5, 1931; *Berliner Tageblatt,* January 7, 1931.

alia, to a large part of the Jewish population forced by Czarist ukase to live "within the pale." However, in making peace with Russia in 1920, Lithuania refrained from claiming extensive territorial regions historically but not ethnologically Lithuanian. Within its present confines Lithuania has an appreciable German minority at Memel, actively supported by the *Reich* government; large Jewish populations in the principal towns; White Russian minorities, practically all of Roman Catholic religion, in the easternmost part of the country, and appreciable Polish groupings in the south and west. Like Estonia and Latvia it gave a declaration at Geneva with reference to minorities, but went further in agreeing to apply in its own territory, *mutatis mutandis,* the stipulations of the minority guarantee treaties.[71] A major difficulty in relation to minorities arose through rigorous application of the Sunday closing law in the cities, which operated to the economic detriment of the Jewish population. A recent change in the law, has, however, practically abolished Sunday closing.[72] Grievances arising from the land reform have affected principally Russian and Polish proprietors, but the Soviet government does not push such claims of its nationals,[73] and the Polish government, owing to the absence of diplomatic relations with Lithuania, is not in a position to act on behalf of Polish claimants.

[71] This wider declaration has made it possible for the League of Nations to apply to Lithuania the procedure on minority petitions not involved in the commitments of Estonia and Latvia. Declaration of May 12, 1922, *League of Nations Official Journal,* Vol. 3, June 1922, pp. 584, 588.

[72] Trading is permitted, except at Kaunas, on Sundays and other holidays, with the exception of six national holidays. (*Cf.* the Lithuanian Telegraph Agency Service, *Economic and General Bulletin,* No. 9, October 1930, p. 19.)

[73] *Ibid.,* No. 6, June–July 1930, pp. 8–9, 16.

The basic problems of Lithuania are political, not economic; their settlement is more dependent on the international situation than is the case in any other country in Eastern Europe. So long as the Polish-Lithuanian controversy remains unsettled, so long as there are threats to Lithuania's territorial integrity, the internal stability of the country cannot be high, nor can it be entirely dissociated from the major problem of security. That is why Lithuania is obliged to defer a number of internal political adjustments until final disposition of pressing external problems.

POLAND

POLITICAL DEVELOPMENT

The political reconstruction of Poland following the World War was not a simple task. With traditions of chronic political disorder behind her, resurrected Poland returned to the fold of nations seemingly predestined to conform to the pattern of behavior she had followed in the years before the partitions. That policy, historically associated with the famous *liberum veto* of an omnipotent Diet and an extraordinarily weak executive, might have been reënacted in the Polish Republic, had it not been for the forceful personality of Marshal Pilsudski. In his capacity of Chief of State in the formative years of the Republic, Pilsudski successfully prevented such an ascendancy on the part of the Polish *Sejm* as would have attenuated completely the power of the executive. To prevent the recrudescence of anarchy, Pilsudski was prepared to curb the Diet by the use of force, if necessary.

From the end of the Russo-Polish War to 1926, Pilsudski's principal attention was devoted to safeguarding the army from what he believed to be excessive parliamentary control. When such independence of the military from the civil branch of the government seemed threatened in 1926, Pilsudski marched his legionaries into Warsaw and made himself master politically, although refusing the presidency. The ensuing constitutional reforms were clearly intended to reinforce the authority of the President and to give him a position of vigor and independence. With ordinance power in safe hands, and most legislation enacted by presidential decree, Pilsudski has directed, from his position of either Premier or Minister of War, the main course of Polish politics since 1926, striving to render the *Sejm* impotent without entirely dispensing with it, and endeavoring to govern, in so far as possible, by means of a group of administrators—the successive "cabinets of colonels"—drawn from the ranks of the army. The results of such a policy have been to produce a bitter clash between the elements represented in the *Sejm* and the new nucleus of bourgeois industrialists who have come to the support of the Pilsudski régime. In the process, the dissident minority elements unrepresented in the government have hardly fared well.

A veiled dictatorship by Pilsudski, acting through President Moscicki, with the assistance of the leading officials of the army, irrespective of the wishes of Parliament, characterized the situation in Poland in the middle of 1930. Since that time the controversy between Pilsudski and the *Sejm* has been marked by a dissolution of the legislative body, and the imprisonment of many of its members, followed by a heated electoral campaign, an election accompanied by unusual violence, and a new ordering of forces in both branches of the legislative body. The period covered by the latter half of 1930 was also characterized by a drastic treatment of the Ukrainian minorities in Eastern Galicia and the German minorities in Polish Upper Silesia.[74]

THE DOWNFALL OF THE DIET

The constitutional quarrel between the government and the Diet concerning the power of the President over that body was renewed on June 21, 1930, when President Moscicki, without allowing the Diet the opportunity to assemble, prorogued the extraordinary session and set no date for the resumption of its deliberations.[75] Almost simultaneously he postponed for one month the convocation of the Senate, which had been requested by a petition of 38 of the 111 Senators in accordance with the Constitution.[76] By this action, the constitutional controversy, which had theretofore involved only one house, was broadened to embrace both. In support of his position, Moscicki declared that the existing constitutional precedents dictated the convoking of each chamber by a separate act, and that the criticisms made by the Senators were "inadmissible." From the time of this unilateral interpretation of the Constitution by the President, it was plain that reconvocation of the chambers would ac-

[74] The reconstruction of Poland was treated in detail by Mildred S. Wertheimer, "The Reconstruction of Poland," Foreign Policy Association, *Information Service*, Vol. VI, No. 7, June 11, 1930. The account here given is supplementary thereto.

[75] *Bulletin périodique de la presse polonaise,* No. 205, July 11, 1930, p. 13.

[76] Articles 25 and 37.

complish nothing; after June 23, a dissolution was inevitable.[77]

In the face of the suppression of the representative bodies, the deputies and senators of the Socialist, Radical Populist, Moderate Populist, Christian Democratic and National Workers' parties organized a "Congress for the defense of the rights and liberties of the people," convoked at Cracow on June 29, 1930, despite every form of intimidation attempted by the government.[78] At this congress

[77] In reply to Moscicki's action the National party issued a declaration noting that "the impossibility evidenced in the last two years of collaboration between the government of Mr. Pilsudski and the majority of the *Sejm* imposes the constitutional necessity of appealing to the will of the nation and ordering new elections. The present *Sejm,* a third of whose mandates were obtained by frauds and violence attested by the Supreme Court, must be dissolved without delay after having deferred to the next Diet the right of constitutional revision." (*Gazeta Warszawska,* June 26, 1930.)

[78] "The mystery surrounding the intentions of the government," declared the congress, "the unremitting campaign against the Diet, the violation of the laws and of the constitution, the open and unpunished threats of a coup d'état, the use made, by the governing, of the means and resources of the state for their personal ends . . . keep the country in a perpetual state of unrest and uncertainty, throw the population into anarchy . . . stop economic initiative, increase immeasurably the risks of industry and commerce, alienate foreign capital and cause Polish capital to flee. . . . The *de facto* dictatorship of Joseph Pilsudski, hidden behind the façade of parliamentarism . . . cannot continue longer without bringing the state to a catastrophe. . . . The well known declaration of Joseph Pilsudski that he had 'kept three Diets from working' must appal all citizens, whatever their convictions and their views on the rôle of parliamentarism in reconstituted Poland. We note with sadness that the Chief of State has associated himself with the efforts which tend to render fruitless at all costs the work of the Diet and Senate." (*Robotnik,* June 21, 1930.) The principal means of endeavoring to prevent the Congress were the issuance by government party circles of false manifestoes indicating the break-up of the *Centrolew* coalition, the blocking of highways, the stopping of vehicles bound for Cracow and rigorous police patrol at the gates of the city. Seizure of the principal Opposition newspapers also took place. (*Cf. Bulletin périodique de la presse polonaise,* No. 206, August 16, 1930, p. 1.)

the coalition, known as the *Centrolew*, made open demands for the resignation of both Pilsudski and Moscicki, and a return to the paths of constitutional legality. The reply of the government was to issue warrants for the arrest of the organizers, under the provisions of an old Austrian law penalizing written, printed or graphic attacks on the emperor, the integrity of the state, or the form of government or administration of the state.[79] The Cracow tribunals declared, however, that such indictments as had been submitted to it lacked all juridical foundation.[80] The stopping of judicial action did not, however, prevent the continuance of administrative repressions.

The action of the government in dealing with the organizers of the Cracow congress caused a dispute in the ranks of the Polish legionaries, indicating that the solidarity of the military groups upon which Pilsudski has so depended was not totally unshakeable. A renewal of the agitation of the Center-Left bloc immediately after the Legion congress at Radom brought matters to an open issue: the Slawek cabinet resigned, Pilsudski assumed office with but one change of portfolio, and a militant cabinet was in power, ready to cope alike with the *Centrolew* coalition in domestic politics, and with blustering Hitlerism, and treaty revision in foreign policy.[81]

Undaunted by this move of Pilsudski, the *Centrolew* coalition called for a mass rallying of the democratic groups in twenty-one of the principal cities

[79] *Bulletin périodique de la presse polonaise,* No. 206, August 16, 1930, p. 5.

[80] *Gazeta Warszawska,* July 11, 1930.

[81] *Bulletin périodique de la presse polonaise,* No. 207, October 7, 1930, pp. 1–5; *cf.* also *Messager Polonais,* August 26, 27, 1930.

of the republic on September 14, to demand the convocation of the Diet and the overthrow of the dictatorship.[82] The immediate countermove of the government was to dissolve both houses, as of August 30,
1930, setting the date of elections to the *Sejm* for
November 16, and of those to the Senate for November 23.[83]

"After mature reflection," declared Moscicki in the
decree of dissolution, "I have concluded that the most
important thing for the work of all citizens of Poland is
the reform of the fundamental laws which govern the
Republic, the laws constituting the base of all those
which exist in the State. The reform is necessary, inasmuch as it has hitherto been impossible to remedy the
juridical chaos in which the Republic finds itself. Having
convinced myself that I would not be able, in spite of all
my efforts, to effect this reform with the aid of the
present Diet, I have decided to dissolve the *Sejm* and
the Senate."

In so doing, Moscicki and Pilsudski put an end to
what even the Opposition declared to be "a state
of intolerable incertitude"[84] and opened an electoral battle unparalleled in the history of the Republic.

THE ELECTIONS

Ten days elapsed before the hand of Pilsudski
fell upon the *Centrolew,* which had shown its in-
capacity to retain a united front in the campaign.
Forthwith the leading deputies of all factions were
arrested and sent to the well-known fortress of
Brest-Litovsk,[85] while police likewise rounded up

[82] *Robotnik,* August 22, 1930.
[83] *Messager Polonais,* August 30, 1930.
[84] *Robotnik,* August 31, 1930.
[85] *Messager Polonais,* September 11, 1930.

over a thousand of their principal supporters
throughout the country.[86] The hand of the military
dictatorship fell heaviest, in some respects, upon
the Ukrainian deputies from Galicia and the fiery
young nationalists of Ukrainian extraction, who resorted throughout the electoral campaign to widespread acts of violence, burning of farms, etc., as
a means of attracting international attention and
bringing about a change in the Polish attitude
towards the Ukrainian minority.[87]

Although twenty-one electoral tickets were put
into the field for the *Sejm* and twelve for the Senate,
only three major groupings need to be noted: the
"Independent bloc of collaboration with the Government" or Government bloc,[88] the "Union for the
defense of the rights and liberties of the people" or
the *Centrolew*,[89] and the National party,[90] constituting the Right Opposition. In addition, three Jew-

[86] *Bulletin périodique de la presse polonaise*, No. 207, October 7, 1930, p. 6.

[87] *Ibid.*, p. 7, and *ibid.*, No. 208, November 4, 1930, pp. 7–8.

[88] The Government bloc consists of those radicals, conservatives, clericals, and anti-clericals who are "united in the
conviction that Marshal Pilsudski is accomplishing a work of
public welfare." It has been characterized as made up of "former
anti-Russian legionaries, former Austrophil and Germanophil
Activists, former revolutionary socialists, great landed proprietors, Catholics, Free Masons, Jewish merchants and heavy
industrialists." *Ibid.*, p. 4.

[89] This coalition lost its Christian Democratic faction during
the campaign and found its Populist elements at complete logger-
heads, its "beautiful moral and social program" being thereby
vitiated. The arrest of the principal leaders and the persecution
of the party press further militated against active coöperation
of the Opposition. *Ibid.*, p. 5.

[90] This grouping, seriously disciplined since the elections of
1928, forms "a homogeneous party with modern organization,
having a single program and obeying a unified command"; is
profoundly "republican, anti-German, anti-Semitic, uncompromis-
ingly hostile to the present régime," and untainted by any
affiliation with the Left Bloc. *Gazeta Warszawska*, October 8,
1930.

ish factions and one joint White Russian-Ukrainian grouping presented parliamentary lists.[91]

The result of the elections to both the *Sejm* and the Senate was the triumph of the government bloc, the marked progress of the Right Opposition and the crushing defeat of the parties of the Left and the national minorities.

In the words of the chief spokesman for the "cabinet of colonels": "The verdict of November 16 definitively struck down the vampire of party oligarchy and parliamentary domination." [92] But while the elections produced a remarkable gain for the Government bloc, it gained that victory by a large scale process of disfranchisement. The electoral lists of a number of groups were annulled on the eve of the elections, and large numbers of citizens were given either the privilege of abstention—noticeable in the reduced total vote—or that of voting for a different ticket—a process which in large part accounts for the remarkable increase of the National party. When examined in some detail, the electoral figures demonstrate that the Government bloc was most successful in the easternmost portions of the country, and polled the fewest votes on the borders of Germany.[93] The phenomenal success in the east is explained by the government·press as due to a rapid rallying to the Polish Republic and its acting government on the part of the allogeneous minor-

[91] *Bulletin périodique de la presse polonaise,* No. 208, November 4, 1930, p. 6.

[92] *Gazeta Polska,* November 18, 1930.

[93] "The victory of the government list, often feeble or totally ineffective in the western provinces where the ethnologically Polish element is very dense, was crushing in the territories of the East, where, in many places, it gained 100 per cent of the votes cast." (*Bulletin périodique de la presse polonaise,* No. 209, December 23, 1930, p. 4.)

POLISH PARLIAMENTARY ELECTIONS OF 1930

PARTY	SEJM VOTE (in thousands) 1928	1930	Loss or gain	SEJM SEATS 1928	1930	Loss or gain	SENATE SEATS 1928	1930	Loss or gain
Government bloc	2,740	5,272	+ 2,532	125	248	+ 123	48	76	+ 28
National	925	1,418	+ 493	38	63	— 25	9	12	+ 3
Centrolew	3,986	1,861	— 2,125	161	80	— 81	27	14	— 13
Piast	.....	.....	.....	21	15	— 6	.....	.....	.....
National Workers	.....	.....	.....	14	8	— 6	.....	.....	.....
Peasant	.....	.....	.....	26	18	— 8	.....	.....	.....
Wyzwolenie	.....	.....	.....	40	15	— 25	.....	.....	.....
Socialists	.....	.....	.....	65	25	— 40	.....	7	.....
Minorities	2,134	1,517	— 617	81	33	— 14	15	7	— 8
Ruthene	.....	.....	.....	49	21	— 28	11	4	— 7
White Russian	.....	.....	.....	19	5	— 14	4	1	— 1
German	.....	.....	.....	13	7	— 6	4	3	— 1
Jewish	.....	.....	.....	14	14	0	.....	.....	.....
Christian Democrats	936	343	— 593	7	5	— 2	3	2	— 1
Communists	266	170	96	.....	.....	.....	9	0	.....
Miscellaneous	.....	.....	.....	.....	.....	.....	.....	.....	.....

ities in the eastern provinces [94]—an explanation which also covers the crushing of the *Centrolew* bloc. In Opposition circles astonishment was expressed that the election should have reversed the expression of opinion in the partial elections in the eastern provinces ordered by the Supreme Court in May 1930, after the mandates of 1928 were held by it to have been fraudulently obtained.[95] It is clear that the electoral methods of the administration in power must be taken into account before attributing to a

[94] "The people have learned," declared *Polska,* a Catholic journal (November 26, 1930), "that the game was dangerous and this time they have not supported the fomenters of anarchy. That is the real cause of the failure of the minority lists."

[95] *Gazeta Warszawska,* November 18, 1930; *Glos Narodu,* November 18, 1930. Imprisonment of candidates, confiscation of newspapers, prohibition of meetings and annulment of electoral lists obtained in the Upper Silesian elections on a more extensive scale than elsewhere. (*Cf. Bulletin périodique de la presse polonaise,* No. 209, December 23, 1930, pp. 5–10.)

The adjournment, *sine die,* on July 1, 1930, of the Silesian Dietine elected in May 1930, and not previously convoked, precipitated another, though less serious, controversy between the deputies of that body on the one hand and the President of the Republic and M. Grazynski, the *voyevod* of Silesia, on the other. It was charged by supporters of the Dietine that the budgets for 1929 and 1930 had been "steam-rollered" through by a select "Council of the Voyevodship." (*Cf. ibid.,* No. 204, p. 10; No. 206, p. 8.) Subsequently, on September 25, 1930, President Moscicki dissolved the Dietine, which had not been allowed to meet, and ordered new elections for November 23.

RESULTS OF ELECTIONS TO THE SILESIAN DIETINE

Groups	1928	1930
Government bloc	10	19
Christian Democrats	16	19
Polish and German Socialist bloc	5	3
German bloc	15	7
Communists	2	0

There was 90 per cent participation in the elections. (*Messager Polonais,* November 24, 1930.)

The treatment of the German population during this period was the subject of extended discussion by the League of Nations Council in its meeting in January 1931.

moral reformation of minorities the crushing victory of the government bloc.

THE MARSHAL AND THE CONSTITUTION

Having brought Poland through the electoral period, and obtained a clear-cut majority for the Government bloc in both houses, Pilsudski left the task of constitutional reform to his colleagues, and on November 29, 1930, resigned both his membership in the *Sejm* and his position as Premier, turning the government back to Colonel Slawek. On the eve of his departure for an extended rest, Pilsudski outlined once more the character of the new constitution he desired.[96] Pilsudski's colleagues considered, however, that alteration of the existing instrument would suffice. In consequence a compromise text was drafted which was presented to the *Sejm* on March 2, 1931.[97]

Due to the deadlock between the Government and the Opposition, only desultory discussion of the proposed changes took place, at intervals, between 1931 and 1934. Finally, on January 26, 1934, the draft elaborated by the Government bloc and approved by the Constitutional Committee of the *Sejm* was discussed in plenary session. Both Right and Left Opposition parties declared irregular if not unconstitutional the endeavor of the Government to pass

[96] For a summary of the plan laid before the *Sejm* by the Government bloc in the spring of 1929, *cf.* Wertheimer, "The Reconstruction of Poland," cited, p. 148. For Pilsudski's proposed reforms, *cf. Gazeta Polska,* November 27 and 29, 1930.

[97] *New York Times,* March 4, 1931. Debate on the Government bloc proposals began on March 3, 1931, in the *Sejm.* The representatives of all the Opposition parties announced at that time that they would refuse to coöperate in amending the Constitution, inasmuch as they believed economic matters demanded prior consideration. (*Cf. The Times,* London, March 4, 1931.)

the new constitutional draft as an ordinary bill, and accordingly left the chamber. The Government thereupon moved the passage of the draft, which was effected in three immediately consecutive readings.

The new instrument is clearly one intended to concentrate executive power in the presidency, which is exalted from the position given it under the constitution of 1921, to a powerful office superior to any and all the other branches of government. The president is to be elected for a seven year term by the people acting directly, if the retiring executive and an electoral college consisting of 80 persons [98] are unable to agree upon a common nominee; otherwise the person selected by the electoral college is declared elected. The President thus becomes the highest representative of the power of the Polish State and is no longer dependent for either election or power upon Parliament, either in peace or war. Endowed with a far-reaching ordinance power, which in time of war supersedes the legislative function, with the power of convoking and dissolving Parliament, vetoing laws passed by it, appointing ministers and judges, signing and ratifying treaties without the consent of Parliament, and disposing of the armed forces at any time,[99] he be-

[98] The College of Electors is composed of the Marshal of the Senate, the Marshal of the *Sejm,* the President of the Council of Ministers, the Chief Justice of the Supreme Court, the Inspector-General of the Armies, and of 75 electors, of whom 50 are to be selected by the *Sejm* and 25 by the Senate from among the most worthy citizens. *Polish Press Information Bulletin,* Vol. IV, No. 58, January 15, 1934, p. 6.

[99] "The President of the Republic decides the use of the armed forces for the defense of the State. . . . In case of war the President of the Republic, without authorization of Parliament, has the right to issue decrees in the province of State legislation, excepting amendments to the Constitution, to prolong the term

comes a constitutional autocrat, centralizing in his person most of the attributes of national sovereignty.

The principal innovations effected by the new instrument bear on the relationship of the President to the Cabinet and of the Cabinet to the legislature. The Cabinet is made responsible solely to the President, and not to Parliament. Should the latter, by resolution, demand the removal of the Prime Minister or one of his colleagues, it is left to the President, at his discretion, either to comply or to dissolve both chambers. With this threat perennially before it, the *Sejm* is, therefore, hardly in a position to challenge the executive. Its rôle is, therefore, secondary and subsidiary, but not altogether superfluous, as it is possible for one half of the members of the *Sejm* to force the President to convoke it within 30 days in extraordinary session for such purposes as they may desire. The *Sejm,* whose composition and method of election are left unchanged, is given an annual life-span of at least four months, unless it passes the budget at an earlier date,[100] permitting prorogation, or clashes with the

of office of the *Sejm* until the conclusion of peace, and to open, postpone or close sessions of the *Sejm* and Senate in a manner adjusted to the necessities of the defense of the State. . . . The term of office of the President is seven years. In case of war this period is prolonged until three months after the conclusion of peace." *Ibid.,* pp. 6, 8.

[100] "For the consideration of the budget the *Sejm* is given 90 days from the date of its submission by the Government; the Senate, twenty days from the expiration of the date prescribed by the *Sejm*. The President shall declare the budget passed: (*a*) in the version adopted by both houses of Parliament if the *Sejm* and the Senate have considered the budget within the dates prescribed for them; (*b*) in the version adopted by the *Sejm,* in case the Senate did not consider the budget within the stipulated time; (*c*) in the version adopted by the Senate, if the *Sejm* did not consider the Senate's amendments within the stipulated time; (*d*) in the version of the Government project, if neither the *Sejm* nor the Senate examined the budget within the stipulated time." *Ibid.,* pp. 7–8.

President, inviting dissolution. The Senate, hitherto wholly elective, is entirely reconstituted, its term being lengthened from five to six years, two-thirds of its membership being elected, the remaining third appointed by the President, one-half of each category retiring every three years. The right to elect to the Senate was left by the new constitution to be defined by future legislation, save that it is constitutionally restricted to "those citizens who are deemed leaders in the activities for the benefit of the commonwealth." Some indication of what the makers of the new fundamental law conceived this to mean is found in the provision that the first Senate chosen under the reformed constitution is to be elected by those citizens who are holders of the decorations of *Virtuti Militari* or the Cross of Independence. This provision is signally indicative of the prestige value attached in Poland to the military, as no State in modern times, not even Riverist Spain, ever deliberately established pretorian government so openly. The Polish Senate, it would appear, is to be raised constitutionally to the level of the Cabinets of Colonels.

Viewed objectively, the new fundamental law introduces little else that is new in Polish constitutional practice. Much that it legalizes has for the past eight years been implicit in the existing alignment of political forces. The changes are, therefore, not psychological, but formal, completing and rendering legal and sacrosanct the changes begun in 1926, when the Legions marched upon Warsaw.

PRESENT PROBLEMS CONFRONTING POLAND

Poland has passed more than a decade in complete independence—almost eighteen years in some degree of autonomy. In that time her institutions have undergone only superficial evolution; parliamentarism and democracy have not struck root. Beset by the problems of alien and unassimilated minorities, she has followed the course of coercion and oppression. The preponderance of strength on the side of the Polish elements in the state, backed by the organized might of the bureaucracy and the army, is so great that a policy of open resistance seems destined to be uniformly unsuccessful. It is altogether likely that the passive loyalty of the devoutly Catholic or Orthodox populations in her Eastern provinces is partly induced by the fact of the intense suffering of their co-religionists on the other side of the Soviet frontier; in the case of the German and Ukrainian minorities such forces are not nearly so operative, and the happier lot of their co-nationals in Germany [101] and Czechoslovakia respectively serves as a constant standard of unfavorable comparison. The structure of the Polish state today is still in flux, inasmuch as Poland is undergoing a type of renovation, socially and economically, which cannot be effected overnight. That is why a bureaucracy and a military hierarchy serve as the principal pillars of the state, which is neither the paradise of landed magnates that it was before the World War, nor the full-rounded industrial commonwealth that may yet be in the making. In this period of basic social and economic transition, Poland finds her governmental functioning still dependent upon the tradition of racial supremacy, militant nationalism, bureaucratic omnipotence and ecclesiastical politics that was the mainstay of a now ex-

[101] This generalization, of course, characterizes the situation of minorities previous to the triumph of Hitlerism in Germany.

tinct Austria-Hungary. Such are, at least, among the principal bases of power in the Polish Republic.

The major fact of the post-war period in the region embraced by the succession states of the Russian Empire is their inclusion in the life of Western Europe. Heretofore borderlands of empire, suffering under oppression yet quick with nascent nationalism, they have come into their own in the past decade and swung into the orbit of Europe, not of Moscow. This shift in their orientation has pushed eastward the boundaries of Europe proper and forced a readjustment of retarded regions to the ideology and cadence of Westernism. Emerging from a common historical experience of subjection to Russia, they have travelled radically different paths from those traversed by the peoples and communities making up the Soviet Union. To attain and maintain stability in a region bordering a land of revolution has involved a fundamental change in the culture pattern of these peoples.

In the foregoing pages the principal devices used by each in the quest for stability have been noted: the constitutional mechanism, intended to inaugurate a régime of liberal legality; the agrarian reform, designed to produce a stable, land-owning class content with semi-pastoral existence; the weaving of a national character on the loom of common experience in school, in field, in army and in church. The product, given the different strands in the stuff and fabric of each nation, has been far from uniform. Stability is not inertia or stagnation; it is the product of practical correlation of the various elements operative in national life. Stability may still exist in the presence of conflicting forces, barely held within the bond of legality by the constitutional mechanism: here it requires marked adaptability to solve the problems of the day without the use of brute force. Again, high stability may exist where there is homogeneity in the body politic and little diversity in the social structure. In such a case the very absence of conflicting elements creates balance. Finally, there is the sham stability of external order maintained by authoritarianism, unconstitutionality and sheer force. Where such conditions subsist, there can scarcely be appeal to the conceptions of legality; force creates counterforce and instability.

One evanescent thread runs through the pattern of the collective behavior of the border peoples: Bred in resentment of autocratic authority, they first endeavored, by constitutional restrictions, to whittle governmental power down toward the vanishing point; then, even when the necessity of efficient action was borne in upon them by the hard lessons of experience, they endeavored to delay by every means the growth of strong—and therefore (to them) irresponsible—executives. The quest of the last half decade has been a mental groping for a new conception of executive authority, for the vesting of power in an administration that can keep pace with the tempo of a changing age. It is largely as the power of efficient governmental action is brought into cadence with the march of economic life that the question of authority can be settled. If the harmonization is consciously facilitated by the collaboration of cabinets and parliaments, stability is attained by constitutional means. It is where the hope of collective salvation is mistakenly placed by parliaments and peoples in the historic policy of attrition that constitutional authority gives way and authoritarianism rides roughshod over public liberties in the attempt to trail the careening chariot of economic life. To attain stability and balance, to solve within the framework of legality the major aspects of their respective adjustment to the complex of an independent life, to perfect from indigenous resources the culture pattern of liberated nationality—these have been the basic problems of the new commonwealths of Eastern Europe.

THE
POLITICAL STRUCTURE OF
THE SOVIET STATE

INTRODUCTION

IN 1933, sixteen years after the Bolshevik *coup d'état,* the Soviet Union is still in the throes of a profound economic and social revolution. In the face of innumerable handicaps the Soviet government has unremittingly pursued the gigantic task of socialization and industrialization. It has had to rely almost exclusively on the country's own resources of capital and raw materials. It has had to employ on giant undertakings labor which lacks the technical experience and discipline of Western labor. It has had to combat and suppress the hostility of important groups of the population, most formidable of which has been the passive resistance of the peasants. Much of the work accomplished under these circumstances has inevitably been hasty, crude, ill-devised; much has been of high quality, and has revealed at their best the imagination, resourcefulness and selfless zeal of Soviet leaders.

No generalization can adequately encompass the maelstrom of new ideas, new experiences, new aspirations in the midst of which the Russian people is working out its destiny. The state, far from "withering away" as predicted by Marxist doctrine, has daily encroached more and more on the individual. The abolition of class distinctions based on wealth, and the drastic social leveling intended to pave the

315

way for the classless society of the future have failed to prevent class differentiations based on control of power. The suppression of organized religion, regarded as synonymous with ignorance and superstition, has been accompanied by an almost religious worship of the machine and the material benefits it is expected to produce.

The pace set by the Five-Year Plan has been feverish, has created serious tension between workers and peasants, has strained the nerves of even the iron young generation, has resulted in startling contradictions. Side by side with enthusiasm and unlimited faith in human progress which surpasses that of the Victorians, one finds depression and that kind of apathy which can be more dangerous than active opposition. Side by side with sincere concern for the improvement of living conditions, care of mother and child, a new humanitarian spirit, one finds readiness to sacrifice human lives to the achievement of plans dictated from above. Side by side with a materialistic conception of life, constant emphasis on scientific method, deprecation of sentimentality, one finds a mystic exaltation of socialism and its prophet Lenin, embalmed for posterity not unlike the saints exposed to public ridicule in anti-religious museums. The Soviet Union is still in a state of profound ferment and it would be hazardous to predict the ultimate outcome of its manifold undertakings. One thing can be said with assurance: state socialism—state control over industry, trade, transportation, banking and, ultimately, agriculture—is firmly established. Whatever changes may be effected in the near future will be directed not at the overthrow of the existing system, but at its consolidation and further adaptation to the needs of the U.S.S.R. It is therefore par-

ticularly important to examine the political structure of a state which, for the first time in world
history, has undertaken to control and direct both
production and distribution in accordance with a
clearly defined program of social readjustment.

The autocratic rule of the Romanov dynasty established in 1613 remained unchallenged until the
Napoleonic wars, which brought the Russian armies
in contact with the theories of nationalism and constitutionalism then ripening in Western Europe.
The spiritual ferment created by this glimpse of a
new world of political thought found an outlet in
the abortive Decembrist revolution of 1825, organized by a handful of nobles and army officers. Far
from heeding this warning, however, Nicholas I
sought to crush social unrest by a policy of severe
repression. The weakness of his method, which
stifled political initiative without uprooting opposition, was dramatically revealed by Russia's defeat
in the Crimean war, which convinced the government that the country's prestige as a great power
could be restored only by internal reforms. The
reign of Alexander II, who succeeded Nicholas I
in 1856, was consequently marked by a series of
measures designed to improve agriculture, develop
industry and establish the rudiments of civil liberty.[1]

---

[1] For the history of Russia, 1825–1917, *cf.* the following works:
R. Beazley, N. Forbes and G. A. Birkett, *Russia from the
Varangians to the Bolsheviks* (Oxford, Clarendon Press, 1918);
Michael Karpovich, *Imperial Russia, 1801–1917* (New York, Holt,
1932); V. O. Kluchevsky, *A History of Russia* (four volumes,
New York, Dutton, 1911–1926); Bernard Pares, *A History of
Russia* (second edition, New York, Knopf, 1926); *Idem., Russia
and Reform* (London, Constable, 1907); George Vernadsky,
A History of Russia (revised edition, New Haven, Yale Uni-
versity Press, 1930); M. N. Pokrovsky, *Russkaya Istoriya s
Drevneischich Vremen* (Russian History since the Most Ancient
Times), fifth edition, Moscow, State Publishing House, 1923.
For additional works on this period, *cf.* the bibliographies con-
tained in the above volumes.

The first step toward agrarian reform was taken in 1861 with the promulgation of the Emancipation Edict, by the terms of which twenty million household and peasant serfs received personal freedom without compensation to their former masters. The distribution of land which accompanied emancipation, however, proved unsatisfactory to the peasants, who for the most part received smaller allotments than those they had previously leased from the landowners and had to purchase land at a price usually in excess of its actual value. The ownership of land, moreover, was vested not in individual farmers, as in Western Europe, but in the village community (*mir*), which the peasants could leave only with the greatest difficulty. The peasants consequently developed little or no sense of private property and, with the exception of a small group of *kulaks*—rich peasants who had succeeded in buying land other than that assigned to the *mir*—suffered from "land-hunger," intensified by the steady growth of the agricultural population. They regarded the Emancipation settlement as essentially unjust, and believed that the government should correct this injustice by dividing among them the estates of the gentry and the nobility.[2]

Despite these grievances, which constituted a potential danger to the established order, the peasants, who were for the most part illiterate, remained politically passive. Their principal spokesmen were drawn not from the village, but from the educated classes—gentry and intelligentsia—which advocated

[2] For a detailed analysis of the agrarian problem before the Bolshevik revolution, *cf.* G. T. Robinson, *Rural Russia under the Old Régime* (New York, Longmans, Green, 1932); Vera M. Dean, "Russia's Agrarian Problem," Foreign Policy Association, *Information Service*, Vol. VI, No. 10, July 23, 1930.

recognition of the peasants' right to land and civil liberty. This group of idealistic men and women, inspired by romantic devotion to the peasants and by a desire to go "to the people," formed the nucleus of the Social Revolutionary party organized about 1900. The Social Revolutionaries regarded the peasants as the keystone of the Russian state, and sought to arouse them by education and propaganda to revolt against autocracy.[3]

THE RISE OF THE PROLETARIAT

Beginning with the nineties, however, the activities of the Social Revolutionaries were overshadowed by the rise of a class-conscious proletariat. Industrialization, which had made a modest start under Peter the Great, received fresh impetus after the Crimean war, when the government not only encouraged, but frequently subsidized, the construction of factories and railways and the exploitation of natural resources. Like all undeveloped countries, Russia had to finance its industry with foreign capital, imported chiefly from France, which after the conclusion of the Franco-Russian alliance in 1893 invested heavily in strategic railways, mines and other enterprises.

Russia's industrialization was fraught with far-reaching political and social consequences. The growth of industry hastened the emergence of an educated middle class, roughly divided into two groups—the "big" bourgeoisie, composed of bankers and industrialists, and the "small" bourgeoisie and

[3] *Cf.* Katerina Breshkovskaia, *Hidden Springs of the Russian Revolution* (Stanford University, Stanford University Press, 1931), the memoirs of one of the leading figures in the Social Revolutionary party, and Vera Figner, *Memoirs of a Revolutionist* (New York, International Publishers, 1927).

intelligentsia, recruited from merchants, technical experts and the liberal professions. The "big" bourgeoisie, which enjoyed the advantages of cheap labor and of a high protective tariff, allied itself with the autocracy in demanding the preservation of order, and in turn received aid from the government for suppression of labor conflicts. By contrast the "small" bourgeoisie, which derived less tangible economic benefits from the Tsarist régime, opposed the forces of reaction and cherished a romantic longing for political liberty. While the more radical members of the intelligentsia pledged their allegiance to various revolutionary groups, the majority of the "small" bourgeoisie supported the Constitutional Democratic party (*Cadets*), led by professors and liberal landowners, which advocated universal suffrage, constitutional monarchy, and solution of the agrarian problem by expropriation of the landowners, who were to receive money compensation.

The rise of the middle class was paralleled by the transformation of many landless peasants, who had been absorbed by the new industries, into a class-conscious proletariat which numbered 3,000,000 on the eve of the Bolshevik *coup d'état* in 1917. The proletariat suffered the usual hardships of an industrial revolution—long hours of work, low wages, intolerable living conditions and brutal treatment on the part of employers and police. Deprived of all opportunity to voice their grievances through trade unions, prohibited by the government until 1906, the workers resorted to illegal "underground" organizations which eventually became affiliated with the Social Democratic party formed in 1898 by a group of radical intellectuals, notably Georgyi Plekhanov, who had popularized the writings of

Marx in Russia, and V. I. Lenin. Unlike the Social Revolutionaries, who devoted their attention mainly to the peasants, the Social Democrats concentrated their efforts on the industrial workers, whom they regarded as shock troops of the coming revolution. At the London Congress of 1903 the Social Democratic party split into two factions—the Bolsheviks, led by Lenin, and the Mensheviks, among whom was Lenin's former collaborator, Leon Trotzky. The Bolsheviks, who were in a minority in Russia but had a majority at the congress, favored a thoroughgoing revolution to be effected by violent means, while the Mensheviks advocated evolutionary methods and cooperation with the bourgeoisie for the overthrow of autocracy.

The ultimate success of the Bolsheviks appears to have been determined less by their numbers, which remained relatively small until 1917, or even by their close-knit organization, than by the driving force of Lenin, who combined an iron will and a profound knowledge of economic theory with a keen sense of political expediency, and whom neither defeat nor defection among his adherents could divert from preparations for the revolution. Born in 1870 of a family of well-to-do intellectuals, Lenin early in his youth discovered a lifelong source of inspiration in the writings of Karl Marx. Arrested in 1896 for revolutionary activities, and later deported to Siberia, he utilized his enforced leisure to analyze Russia's economic conditions in the light of Marxist doctrine. In 1900 he left Russia and settled in Zürich, where he founded a newspaper, *Iskra* (The Spark), which became the organ of the Bolsheviks. Except for a brief visit to Russia during the 1905 revolution, he remained abroad until 1917, immersed in studies which often appeared academic to his followers and practically isolated from direct contact with Russian workers.[4]

THE 1905 REVOLUTION

The various currents of social unrest which Tsarist repression had failed to subdue converged in the revolution of 1905, precipitated by Russia's defeat in the Japanese war. This revolution reached its climax in the general strike of October 1905, which completely paralyzed the country's economic life. The government, faced by determined opposition on the part of the liberal bourgeoisie, the proletariat and the peasants, issued a manifesto which promised a number of fundamental reforms, including the establishment of a *Duma* elected by democratic suffrage and the recognition of civil liberties. The October manifesto revealed a fatal lack of unity among the revolutionaries: the liberals, while pressing for a constitution, feared further acts of terrorism and were for the most part content to accept the government's program, while the Social Democrats, who under Trotzky's leadership had organized the first Soviet[5] of Workers' and Soldiers' Deputies in St. Petersburg, demanded the overthrow of the monarchy. This divergence of aims, which created an irreparable breach between bour-

[4] No definitive biography of Lenin has yet been published in English. The best available works are Valeriu Marcu, *Lenin* (New York, Macmillan, 1928); D. S. Mirsky, *Lenin* (Boston, Little, Brown, 1931); Leon Trotzky, *Lenin* (New York, Minton, Balch, 1925); and George Vernadsky, *Lenin, Red Dictator* (New Haven, Yale University Press, 1931). For other works on this period, *cf.* also V. I. Lenin, *The Iskra Period* (New York, International Publishers, 1929); Leon Trotzky, *My Life* (New York, Scribners, 1930); *idem., The History of the Russian Revolution* (New York, Simon & Schuster, 1932), 3 vols.

[5] The word *soviet* means council.

geoisie and proletariat, proved the death blow of the revolution. The army, which had meanwhile returned from the Far East, remained loyal to the government, and the country gradually returned to a state of political apathy from which it was not aroused until the industrial strikes of 1913–1914.

The 1905 revolution, however, was not entirely barren of results. While representation in the *Duma* was practically restricted to the propertied classes, and while its powers were constantly whittled down by the autocracy, this assembly nevertheless constituted Russia's first experiment in self-government since the *zemstvos*.[6] The agrarian disorders of 1905, moreover, had demonstrated the danger of a property-less peasantry. By the Stolypin reforms, 1906–1910, the peasants were consequently permitted to separate themselves from the *mir* and to take personal possession of land without compensation to the community. On the eve of the World War, nearly 25 per cent of the peasants in European Russia had left the *mir* and had received individual properties.

RUSSIA DURING THE WORLD WAR

The World War, which in Western states rallied all parties to the support of their respective governments, produced the opposite effect in Russia where, after the first outburst of patriotism, the bourgeoisie as well as the proletariat were soon alienated by the autocracy's incompetent military organization. The weak and obstinate character of Nicholas II de-

[6] The *zemstvos* were provincial councils established in 1864, on which the nobility, the town intelligentsia and the peasants were represented, and which exercised a certain degree of autonomy with respect to education, health and road construction.

feated the efforts of his more able collaborators to formulate a unified policy. A series of reactionary and ignorant ministers, who were at the mercy of Court circles dominated by Rasputin, Empress Alexandra's favorite, flitted rapidly across the political scene. Neither industry nor transportation proved equal to the demand for war material. All attempts of the liberal *zemstvos* and of civil organizations to supplement the government's inadequate preparations were viewed with suspicion and promptly suppressed. Hoarding of foodstuffs by the peasants, which became widespread after 1916, caused an acute food shortage in the cities, and increased the dissatisfaction of the army, whose morale had been shaken by military reverses. The bourgeoisie, which had hitherto opposed extreme measures, began to advocate the overthrow of the monarchy. Bread riots in the principal cities culminated in the revolution of March 1917. The Emperor was forced to abdicate, and power passed into the hands of the Provisional Government, composed of Constitutional Democrats and *zemstvo* leaders, with one Social Revolutionary, Alexander Kerensky, in its ranks.[7]

THE BOLSHEVIK COUP D'ETAT, 1917

The rule of this government of liberals who, content with political revolution, contemplated no fundamental social changes, was promptly challenged by the Soviets of Workers' and Soldiers' Deputies, which had been simultaneously organized by Social Revolutionaries and Social Democrats,

[7] For a study of Russia's political and social conditions on the eve of the March 1917 revolution, *cf.* Michael T. Florinsky, *The End of the Russian Empire* (New Haven, Yale University Press, 1931).

chiefly Mensheviks. The Provisional Government, undismayed by the fact that Russia lacked political experience and was then in the throes of a disastrous war, referred the solution of all pressing problems, including the land question, to a Constituent Assembly, to be elected by universal suffrage and convened in the autumn of 1917. Constitutionalism and democracy, however, had no meaning for the peasants, workers and soldiers, who demanded land, bread and peace at any price. The soviets, which after Lenin's return from exile in April had been gradually converted to the Bolshevik point of view, adopted the slogan "All power to the soviets!" and advocated withdrawal from a war in which, they claimed, the proletariat was being needlessly sacrificed to selfish capitalist schemes. The disorganization of the army, which had been subjected to able Bolshevik propaganda, practically suspended military operations after June 1917. Kerensky, who had meanwhile become Prime Minister, was unable either to control the soviets or to elaborate a concrete program which would have met the demands of the masses. The bourgeoisie failed to assume the leadership in this crisis, and offered no effectual resistance to the Bolshevik *coup d'état* of November 1917, which established the "dictatorship of the proletariat." The new government immediately announced its intention to terminate the war, nationalized land, took possession of banks and factories, separated the church from the state and the school from the church. The Constituent Assembly, which finally convened in January 1918 after perfunctory elections, was unceremoniously dissolved, despite the protests of Mensheviks and Social Revolutionaries.

The authority of the Soviet government, controlled by the Bolsheviks—who assumed the name of Communist party in 1918 [8]—was at first paramount only in Great Russia, notably the two capitals, Petrograd (rechristened Leningrad) and Moscow. No sooner had the government obtained a "respite" in the West by concluding a separate peace with Germany at Brest-Litovsk in March 1918 than it found itself confronted by several hostile "White" armies. These armies, recruited chiefly from officers, the bourgeoisie and the old bureaucracy, and aided by Allied expeditionary forces, disputed Soviet rule in North and South Russia and in Siberia until their final defeat in 1920.[9] The dangers of civil war and intervention were further increased by the threatened disruption of the Russian Empire, whose two hundred races and nationalities, differing widely in education, religion and economic development, had been held together before 1914 largely by a brutal policy of "Russification." [10] Finland had become an independent republic in 1917; the new states of Poland,

[8] The original name, "All-Russian Communist party (Bolsheviks)," was changed to "All-Union Communist party (Bolsheviks)" after the establishment of the Soviet Union in 1923.

[9] For a detailed account of this period, cf. A. L. P. Dennis, *The Foreign Policies of Soviet Russia* (New York, Dutton, 1924); Louis Fischer, *The Soviets in World Affairs* (two volumes, New York, Cape and Smith, 1930), Vol. I, Chapters I–VIII; General William S. Graves, *America's Siberian Adventure* (New York, Cape and Smith, 1931); United States, *Papers Relating to the Foreign Relations of the United States, 1918, Russia* (2 volumes, Washington, Government Printing Office, 1931), Vol. I.

[10] The population of the Soviet Union is at present composed as follows: Russians, 52.9 per cent; Ukrainians, 21.2 per cent; White Russians, 3.2 per cent; Kazaks, 2.7 per cent; Uzbeks, 2.6 per cent; Tartars, 2 per cent; Jews, 1.8 per cent; Georgians, 1.2 per cent; Azerbaidjan Turks, 1.2 per cent; Armenians, 1.1 per cent. Other racial and national groups constitute less than one per cent of the total population. American-Russian Chamber of Commerce, *Economic Handbook of the Soviet Union* (New York, 1931), p. 3.

Estonia, Latvia and Lithuania had been established on Russia's Western border; [11] Rumania, Russia's World War ally, had seized Bessarabia; White Russia, the Ukraine, the various peoples of the Caucasus, had sought to erect national states with foreign assistance. The spirit of local autonomy swept in the wake of civil war.

FORMATION OF THE SOVIET UNION

The disintegration of the former empire was not only contrary to Soviet doctrine, which envisaged a union of the world proletariat irrespective of national boundaries, but seriously threatened Communist plans for the economic reconstruction and industrialization of the country. This tendency had been partially stemmed in 1918 by the "free and voluntary union" of "the laboring classes of all nationalities" of Great Russia in the Russian Soviet Federated Socialist Republic, which became the nucleus of the future Soviet Union. The danger of territorial break-up was further lessened in 1920, when White Russia and the Ukraine, which had failed to secure independence, concluded treaties providing for military and economic union with the R.S.F.S.R. Similar agreements with the R.S.F.S.R. were signed in 1921 by Georgia, Armenia and Azerbaidjan, which a year later jointly organized the Transcaucasian Soviet Federated Socialist Republic. The Communist party, however, believed that the political bonds uniting the four soviet socialist republics were not yet sufficiently close. At the Tenth All-Russian Congress of Soviets in 1922, Joseph

[11] *Cf.* M. W. Graham, "Security in the Baltic States," *Foreign Policy Reports,* Vol. VII, No. 25, February 17, 1932.

Stalin, then People's Commissar for Nationalities, consequently urged the formation of a Union of Soviet Socialist Republics on the ground that economic reconstruction and the danger of capitalist attack necessitated a strong centralized government. The congress promptly adopted a declaration and a treaty of union, both of which were ratified by the first All-Union Congress of Soviets on December 22, 1922, and were promulgated on July 6, 1923.[12] This federation, originally composed of the R.S.F.S.R., White Russia, the Ukraine and the Transcaucasian S.S.R., was subsequently enlarged by the admission of the Turkmen and Uzbek Soviet Socialist Republics in 1925, and of Tadjikistan in 1929. The territories of the Russian Empire were thus united in "the first workers' republic of the world," from whose name all reference to its predominantly Russian character had been intentionally omitted.

The treaty of 1923, which is also the constitution of the U.S.S.R., established a federation now composed of seven Union republics, whose respective territory, population and principal administrative divisions are shown in the following table: [13]

[12] For the Russian text of the declaration and the treaty of union, cf. Union of Soviet Socialist Republics, *Sbornik Postanovlenii i Rasporiazhenii Raboche-Krestianskovo Pravitelstva S.S.S.R.* (Collection of Decrees and Regulations of the Workers' and Peasants' Government of the U.S.S.R.), Moscow, 1923, No. 1, p. 16. For an English text of these documents, cf. Walter R. Batsell, *Soviet Rule in Russia* (New York, Macmillan, 1928), p. 300. Since 1923 the laws of the Soviet Union have been published annually in *Sobranye Zakonov i Rasporiazhenii Raboche-Krestianskovo Pravitelstva S.S.S.R.* (Collection of Laws and Regulations of the Workers' and Peasants' Government of the U.S.S.R.), which appears in two parts, the first part containing laws and decrees, while the second contains administrative regulations and treaties with foreign states.

[13] *Sovetskoe Stroitelstvo* (Soviet Construction), a monthly magazine published by the Central Executive Committee of the U.S.S.R., December 1930, p. 39.

THE UNION OF SOVIET SOCIALIST REPUBLICS [14]

Union Republics	Area (square kilometers)	Popu- lation	Republics	Auton- omous Republics	Auton- omous Regions
Russian S.F.S.R.	19,667,900	110,932,500	..	11	15
White Russian S.S.R. .	126,800	5,246,400	..	..	..
Ukrainian S.S.R.	452,000	31,403,200	..	1*	..
Transcaucasian S.F.S.R.	185,500	6,426,700	3†	3	2
Uzbek S.S.R.	176,100	4,685,400	..	..	..
Turkmen S.S.R.	491,200	1,137,900	..	..	..
Tadjik S.S.R.	141,600	1,174,100	..	..	1
	21,241,100	161,006,200	3	15	18

* Moldavia.   † Georgia, Armenia and Azerbaidjan.

By the terms of the constitution, the Union government is entrusted not only with powers usually reserved to the central organs of a federation—conduct of foreign affairs, national defense, administration of the Union budget—but controls foreign and internal trade, and is authorized to establish a general plan of national economy, to formulate the general principles of education, to issue fundamental labor laws and to define the principles governing the development and use of land. These powers are vested in the All-Union Congress of Soviets which, according to the constitution, exercises "supreme authority." In practice, however, the Congress delegates its legislative powers to a Central Executive Committee which it elects, and its executive powers to a Council of People's Commissars, appointed by the Central Executive Committee. The Union republics, whose respective governments are similar

[14] The autonomous republics which are found in the R.S.F.S.R., the Ukrainian S.S.R. and the Transcaucasian S.F.S.R. are little more than administrative divisions established on an ethnographic basis. While these republics enjoy a considerable degree of cultural autonomy, they are politically and economically subordinated to the government of the Union republic in which they are situated, and ultimately to the government of the U.S.S.R. The autonomous regions which are found in the R.S.F.S.R., the Transcaucasian S.S.R. and the Tadjik S.S.R. occupy an even less important position in the structure of the Union, and for the most part serve merely as organs of local administration.

to that of the Union, with a congress, central executive committee and council of people's commissars, retain the right of "free withdrawal" from the Union and sovereign authority over all matters not specifically reserved to the federal organs, including the administration of justice, health, education and social welfare. Despite this provision, all activities of the republics must conform with the policies of the Union government and the Communist party, and decrees of republican organs which infringe on the Union constitution may be repealed by the All-Union Congress.

The political centralization of the Union, which has been denounced by some critics as another form of "Russification," is justified by Soviet spokesmen on the ground that, while all national groups have a right to self-determination, this right must always be subordinated to the interests of the class struggle, which demands a centralized government during the period of socialism.[15] The Communist party, however, has always maintained that centralization should be "democratic" in character and should be accompanied by a wide degree of cultural autonomy. Unlike the Tsarist régime, the Soviet government encourages every nationl group, no matter how small, to develop its own language and literature, in the hope that education will strengthen the consciousness of proletarian solidarity. Obscure languages have been revived and transcribed, alphabets have been devised for dialects which formerly possessed no written literature, native languages have

[15] *Cf.* V. I. Lenin, *Izbrannye Statyi po Nazionalnomu Voprossu* (Selected Articles on the National Question), Moscow, State Publishing House, 1925; Joseph V. Stalin, *Nazionalnye Momenty v Partyinom i Gosudarstvennom Stroitelstve* (National Questions in Party and State Construction), Moscow, State Publishing House, 1925.

been introduced in the schools, courts and government institutions of various regions, and an effort has been made to select local officials from the native population. This policy which, according to Stalin, will facilitate the eventual assimilation of proletarian groups irrespective of nationality, has been hampered, on the one hand, by the chauvinism of the Great Russians, who demand the "liquidation" of all national cultures and the adoption of a single language for the whole Union and, on the other, by a drift toward local "nationalism" on the part of national groups in which "petty bourgeois" elements retain considerable influence. At the Sixteenth Congress of the Communist party in 1930 Stalin denounced both tendencies as deviations from the "party line," and demanded their eradication by the party.[16]

Despite the government's efforts to equalize the economic and cultural opportunities of the national groups composing the Union, the R.S.F.S.R., with ninety per cent of the country's territory and sixty-eight per cent of its population, continues to occupy a dominant position in the federation, while the Great Russians, who form sixty-five per cent of the Communist party, enjoy a marked preponderance in the federal administration.

CHAPTER I

MARXIST POLITICAL THEORY

THE political system established by the 1923 treaty has been, at one and the same time, de-

[16] All-Union Communist Party, *Shestnadzatyi Syezd Vsesoyuznoi Communisticheskoi Partyi* (Sixteenth Congress of the All-Union Communist Party), Stenographic Report, Moscow, State Publishing House, 1930, pp. 54–57.

nounced as a ruthless dictatorship and acclaimed as the only real democracy in the world. No general conclusions regarding the character of the Soviet government can be reached without a preliminary analysis of the theory, organization and functions of the Communist party, which occupies a pivotal position in the Soviet state.[1]

Russian communism, while daily adapted to the needs of the Soviet Union by timely interpretation, continues to derive its theoretical content from the works of Lenin,[2] which in turn are based on those of Karl Marx and his collaborator, Friedrich Engels. Lenin's principal contribution to political theory was not the introduction of new concepts, but his re-interpretation of Marxism, which he rescued from the sterile discussions of Marxist Socialists, and his practical application of a doctrine originally devised for highly industrialized states to a country pre-

---

[1] For the official history of the All-Union Communist party, cf. Emelyan Yaroslavsky, editor, Istoriya VKP (History of the All-Union Communist Party), four volumes, Moscow, State Publishing House, 1926–1930. Cf. also Gregorii Zinovyev, Istoriya Rossiiskoi Communisticheskoi Partyi (History of the Russian Communist Party), Moscow, State Publishing House, 1923.

[2] The first edition of Lenin's works, begun in 1920 and completed in 1926, consists of twenty volumes, published by the State Publishing House as Sobranye Sochinenyi (Collected Works). A second edition, which includes posthumous and hitherto unpublished material, known as Sochineniya (Works), was begun by the Lenin Institute in Moscow in 1926, and will consist of twenty-five volumes when completed. A translation of the second edition, authorized by the Lenin Institute, is now in progress under the auspices of International Publishers, New York. Current bibliographies of all publications relating to Lenin and Leninism are contained in Leniniana, published annually by the Lenin Institute. Moreover, a number of Soviet periodicals, of which the fortnightly Bolshevik is the most important, publish articles devoted to interpretation of Lenin's writings. The outstanding exposition of Lenin's doctrines is found in Joseph V. Stalin, Leninism (London, Allen and Unwin, 1928). Cf. also Mirsky, Lenin, cited, p. 191 et seq., and Max Eastman, Marx, Lenin and the Revolution (London, Allen and Unwin, 1926).

dominantly agricultural. The essential features of a workers' state may be found in Marx and Engels. It remained for Lenin to translate theory into action.

Unlike Hegel, who viewed the state as a mystical entity, the product of "the general progress of the human mind," Marx believed that the character of the state is determined primarily by the existing "material forces of production." The development of these forces, which shape not only the economic but the social and political structure of society, offers, according to Marx, the principal clue to the understanding of history. The forces of production, however, are not static: they undergo constant change and eventually conflict with existing property relations, within whose framework they have hitherto developed, but which now act as intolerable fetters. This conflict precipitates a revolution, in the course of which the entire structure of society is eventually transformed.[3]

Applying Hegel's dialectical method to the analysis of social problems, Marx argued that history consists of class struggles, each social system, based on existing forces of production, creating an antithesis by which it is ultimately destroyed. Throughout the ages, he contended, freeman and slave, baron and serf, burgess and journeyman— "oppressor and oppressed"—have been arrayed each

---

[3] For Marx's only direct statement of the materialist conception of history, cf. Karl Marx, A Contribution to the Critique of Political Economy (Author's Preface), translated from the second German edition by N. I. Stone (New York, International Library Publishing Company, 1904). Cf. also, N. I. Bukharin, Historical Materialism (New York, International Publishers, 1925). For a recent commentary on Marxist theory, cf. Sidney Hook, Towards the Understanding of Karl Marx (New York, John Day, 1933).

against the other.[4] The capitalist system, itself
founded on the ruins of feudalism, merely inten-
sifies the class struggle by dividing society into
two irreconcilable camps—the bourgeoisie, which
owns the means of production, and the proletarians,
who must sell their labor to gain a precarious livelihood. Capitalism, the thesis, calls into being its
antithesis, organized labor, by introducing collective
methods of production, strict industrial discipline
and universal literacy.[5] The establishment of large-
scale industry, the expansion of commerce and navigation, the struggle of industrialized states for markets and raw materials, all tend to concentrate economic and political power in the hands of a few
great capitalists, while the ranks of the proletariat
are constantly swelled by the impoverishment of the
lower middle class. Despite its power, however,
the bourgeoisie fails "to cope with the abundance
of the wealth which it has created," [6] and proves
unable, during recurring periods of overproduction
and unemployment, to provide security "for its
slaves even within the confines of their slavish existence." [7] The proletarians, who "have nothing to
lose but their chains," cannot hope to alter existing
conditions by other than violent means. To seize
the political machinery is not sufficient: the workers,
under the leadership of their vanguard, the Com-

[4] Karl Marx and Friedrich Engels, *The Communist Manifesto*
(New York, International Publishers, 1930).

[5] Karl Marx, *Capital, a Critique of Political Economy,* translated from the fourth German edition by Eden and Cedar Paul
(two volumes, New York, Dutton, 1930), Vol. II, p. 846;
V. I. Lenin, *Gosudarstvo i Revolutzia* (The State and Revolution), Petrograd, "Life and Science," pp. 94–95. For an English
translation of the latter work, cf. V. I. Lenin, *The State and
Revolution* (London, Communist Party of Great Britain, 1925).

[6] Marx and Engels, *The Communist Manifesto,* cited.

[7] *Ibid.*

munist party, must abolish the economic conditions which give rise to capitalism—private property and the exploitation of labor.[8] "The knell of capitalist private property sounds. The expropriators are expropriated." [9] The capitalist system is supplanted by its antithesis, the "dictatorship of the proletariat." Out of this conflict, according to Marx, a final synthesis—classless society—is evolved, with whose establishment "pre-history ends and history begins."

THE DICTATORSHIP OF THE PROLETARIAT

The appearance of a classless society, which is synonymous with communism, is preceded, according to Marx and Lenin, by a transition period known as socialism, when the dictatorship of the proletariat gradually socializes natural resources and means of production, and may use all means at its disposal, including violence, to extirpate the last remnants of capitalism. During this period which, it is expected, will be marked by bitter struggles between "a dying capitalism and a communism which is being born," [10] the state, conceived primarily as an instrument of the ruling class, will continue to exist. Only when classes have been completely destroyed will the state become obsolete and slowly "wither away," until it is relegated, in Engels' phrase, to the museum of antiquities, along with the bronze axe and the spinning-wheel.[11] Economic inequalities between intellectual work and manual labor will like-

---

[8] *Ibid.*
[9] Marx, *Capital,* cited, pp. 846–847.
[10] V. I. Lenin, "Economics and Politics during the Period of the Dictatorship of the Proletariat," *Sochineniya,* cited, Vol. XV, p. 347.
[11] *Idem., Gosudarstvo i Revolutzia,* cited, p. 16.

wise persist under socialism; consequently goods will be distributed among the citizens not according to need, but on the basis of work actually performed.[12]

Both Marx and Lenin argued that the dictatorship of the proletariat, while resorting to compulsion, will differ from its predecessor, the bourgeois state, in one important particular: in contrast to the latter, where a majority, the proletariat, had been oppressed by a minority, the former will organize the masses of the people for the oppression of a small group of exploiters. The workers' state, they claimed, will thus be more truly democratic than so-called Western democracies, where legal provisions guaranteeing liberty and equality of workers and employers alike are nullified in practice by the control which the propertied classes exercise over the schools, the courts, the press and the ballot-box.[13] Nor is the "democratic" character of the dictatorship of the proletariat modified, in their opinion, by the restrictions which it places on the freedom, not only of former exploiters, but even of the ruling class. These restrictions are regarded as a temporary expedient, which will be abandoned at the termination of the class struggle.[14]

Neither Marx, nor Lenin before 1917, attempted to describe the political structure of the socialist state in any detail, beyond referring in laudatory terms to the type of government established by the Paris Commune of 1871, which both regarded as

[12] *Ibid.*, p. 87.
[13] *Ibid.*, p. 82.
[14] Program of the All-Russian Communist Party, *Vossmoi Syezd Rossiiskoi Communisticheskoi Partyi* (Eighth Congress of the Russian Communist Party), March 18–23, 1919 (Stenographic Report, Moscow, "Communist," 1919), p. 341.

the first step toward proletarian revolution.[15] Marx expressed particular enthusiasm regarding the fact that the Commune had been "not a parliamentary, but a business corporation," combining executive and legislative functions, and that deputies had been selected not for their political views but for their technical qualifications. Lenin indicated a preference for a state organized on the model of a business enterprise, in which the class of professional "rulers"—civil servants and politicians—would be rapidly replaced by technical experts selected by the laboring masses, in which all public functions would be simplified and brought to the level of the average citizen's capacity, and whose defense would be entrusted to an army drawn exclusively from the proletariat.[16]

The Marxist conception of political organization in the "classless" society which will succeed socialism has as yet been even less definitely formulated. Inequality between intellectual and physical labor will presumably disappear, production will be greatly expanded, and social wealth will be distributed on the principle of "from each according to his ability, to each according to his needs."[17] The population, trained in the methods of collective production, will learn to observe the elementary rules of collective life, and the machinery of the state, designed primarily for compulsion, will be discarded in favor of unqualified freedom and equality.[18] National barriers will disappear as proletarian revolution spreads from

[15] Karl Marx, *Der Bürgerkrieg in Frankreich* (Berlin-Wilmersdorf, *Die Aktion*, 1919); Lenin, *Sochineniya*, cited, Vol. XII, p. 163.
[16] Lenin, *Gosudarstvo i Revolutzia*, cited, p. 46.
[17] *Ibid.*, p. 90.
[18] *Ibid.*, p. 84.

state to state, and the proletariat of the world, liberated from the capitalist yoke, will unite in one vast community of producers.[19]

MARXISM AND THE SOVIET "CLASS" STATE

The development of the Soviet state during the sixteen years of its existence has, on the whole, followed the course indicated by Marxist doctrine. The dictatorship of the proletariat, controlled by the Communist party, has socialized industry and over eighty per cent of agriculture, and has transformed the state into a vast business enterprise operated by a hierarchy of soviets which combine executive and legislative powers. During this period, regarded as transitional, the class struggle, far from abating, has been intensified by the sharp distinction drawn between four main social classes: the proletariat—workers and "poor" peasants; the "middle" peasants, potential allies of the proletariat, who have not yet been entirely won over to the socialist cause; employees and professional men, drawn chiefly from the old intelligentsia; and the former "exploiters"—aristocrats, bourgeoisie, private traders, priests and, since 1930, *kulaks*—who are known as the "disfranchised" (*lishentzi*).

The proletariat, composed of factory workers and farm laborers, is recognized as the ruling class, and is accorded various privileges with respect to food rations, housing, medical aid, recreation and education. This class, however, has not yet produced its own intelligentsia, and the government has consequently been forced to rely on the services of "bourgeois" technical experts, the majority of whom are

[19] No attempt is made in this book to give an analysis of the economic theories of Marxism.

non-Communists, and who until recently were suspected of nurturing counter-revolutionary sentiments. Distrust of the technical intelligentsia weighed like a millstone on Soviet industry: experts whose tasks called for the greatest initiative hesitated to make important decisions which, if unsuccessful for technical or other reasons, might lead to prosecution for counter-revolutionary crimes, and eventual imprisonment, exile or death. Stalin attempted to remedy this situation in June 1931, when he declared that the government should henceforth seek not to suppress but to attract the technical experts who, in his opinion, were no longer as hostile to the Soviet régime as in the past. "It would be stupid and senseless," he said, "if we were now to look upon practically every engineer of the old school as if he were a potential criminal or 'wrecker.' " [20] Following Stalin's speech, a large number of engineers accused or convicted of counter-revolutionary activities were released from prison and encouraged to resume their work, with assurance that they would not be willfully prosecuted for technical errors. While many specialists now enjoy a standard of living equal or even superior to that of the workers and are urged to display greater initiative, they remain for the most part agents, rather than collaborators, of the proletariat. Finally, the "disfranchised" have been penalized for their connection with the Tsarist régime by deprivation of civic rights and social ostracism: they and their older children are practically barred from active participation in Soviet life and are doomed, as a class, to slow extinction.

[20] *Cf.* Stalin's speech on "New Economic Problems," *The Soviet Union Review,* July-August 1931, p. 152.

This class demarcation which, according to Western critics, is the direct antithesis of democracy, is regarded by leading Communists as an inevitable corollary of the transition period, which must witness the final destruction of capitalist elements both in the economic system and in "the consciousness of men." Communist spokesmen declare that the progress of economic planning and the consequent growth of socialism have already mitigated the class struggle, and predict the abolition of all classes under the second Five-Year Plan, scheduled to end in 1937. The fundamental political problem of the second Five-Year Plan, in their opinion, will be "the transformation of all the working population of the country into conscious and active builders of a classless socialist society." The "liquidation" of classes, however, will temporarily require an increase in the powers of the proletarian state,[21] which as yet gives no signs of withering away.

LIBERTY UNDER THE SOVIETS

The dictatorship of the proletariat, as prophesied by Marx and Lenin, has not abandoned the use of force during the period of socialism, and the rights of all individuals, irrespective of class, have been subordinated to collective interests as interpreted by the Communist party. A vigilant secret police is charged with the task of checking all attempts to overthrow or openly criticize the government. Workers and technical experts are subject to "mobilization" and may be transferred at short notice from one weak "sector" of the industrial or agricultural

[21] *Cf.* report on the second Five-Year Plan by Vyacheslav Molotov, president of the Council of People's Commissars of the U.S.S.R., at the Seventeenth Conference of the All-Union Communist party, February 4, 1932, *Izvestia,* February 5, 1932.

"front" to another.[22] While Soviet legislation permits the existence of religious associations of all sects and denominations, in practice religious groups constantly encounter serious obstacles to the prosecution of their activities. The right of association is granted only to professional or social groups which have the government's approval, and attempts to form non-Communist political organizations or even independent Communist factions are promptly suppressed. The expression of unorthodox political or economic views is barred in schools and universities. The press, the radio, the publication of books, are controlled solely by the government. Even literature and art are judged less by their intrinsic quality than by their willingness to depict the class struggle.

Stifling as these restrictions on individual liberty may appear to Western observers, they are justified in Soviet opinion by the exigencies of the class struggle and the wartime tension resulting from the application of the Five-Year Plan. It should be noted, moreover, that liberty as conceived in Western states played little or no part in the pre-revolutionary life of the Russian proletariat. The sense of individual dignity which the West inherited from the Renaissance and the Reformation was practically unknown to the Russian masses, brought up in a tradition of Byzantine subservience to autocracy and orthodoxy. Far from resenting the absence of rights they had never enjoyed, the workers now derive a real sense of power from the economic benefits which they receive and from their participation in

[22] For a translation of some Soviet labor laws, *cf.* Great Britain, *A Selection of Documents Relative to Labour Legislation in Force in the Union of Soviet Socialist Republics* (London, H. M. Stationery Office, 1931), Cmd. 3775, *Russia No. 1,* 1931.

innumerable conferences and elections. Furthermore, while even the workers must abstain from
criticism of the government and the Communist
party, they are encouraged to flay economic short-
comings under the guise of "self-criticism."

While the structure of the Soviet state thus em-
bodies the principal features of Marxism, the special problems of the Soviet Union have necessitated
considerable modification of Marxist doctrine. Of
the various modifications introduced by Lenin and
his successor, Joseph Stalin, none has provoked such
bitter controversy within the Communist party as
that concerned with the solution of Russia's agrarian
problem. Convinced that the proletarian revolution
would first occur not in a highly industrialized state,
as predicted by Marx, but in a state where capitalism
was weakest, Lenin did not hesitate to proclaim the
dictatorship of the proletariat in a country eighty
per cent of whose population was composed of peasants eager to obtain private ownership of land. He
clearly perceived, however, that the rule of the
proletariat—workers and farm laborers—could be
successfully maintained in Russia only with the co-
operation of the "middle" peasant (*seredniak*), distinguished from the so-called rich peasant (*kulak*)
by the fact that he is not an exploiter of labor.[23]

To achieve this end, Lenin advocated the industrialization and voluntary collectivization of agriculture which, in his opinion, would not only raise
agrarian productivity, but create an identity of interests between workers and peasants, and exter-

[23] Lenin, *Sobranye Sochinenii*, cited, Vol. XVI, p. 146;
Vol. XX, p. 361.

minate the seeds of capitalism in the village.[24] The Communist party, however, was divided regarding the policy best calculated to secure peasant participation in this program. Trotzky, who after Lenin's death in 1924 feared that the concessions granted to the peasants by the New Economic Policy would consolidate agrarian capitalism, urged drastic measures of repression against the *kulaks,* as well as intensive collectivization.[25] Stalin, Secretary-General of the party, contended in 1927 that Trotzky's policy, which he denounced as "Left Opposition," was premature, and would merely foment class war in the villages. Nevertheless, with the introduction of the Five-Year Plan in 1928, Stalin sought to hasten collectivization and to restrict *kulak* activities by methods strikingly similar to those advocated by the exiled Trotzky. These measures, in turn, were criticized by the more moderate elements of the Communist party, known as the Right Opposition, under the leadership of Rykov, president of the Council of People's Commissars, who wished for the time being to protect the interests of the more prosperous peasants. Stalin, however, denounced the protests of the Right Opposition as inspired by "petty bourgeois sentiments," obtained the recantation of Rykov and his associates in 1929, and proceeded to carry through his policy of collectivization and "liquidation" of the *kulaks,* with the result that over seventy per cent of the country's farms had been collectivized by the end of 1933.[26]

[24] *Ibid.,* Vol. XVI, p. 106; Vol. XVIII, Part I, pp. 143, 200.
[25] Leon Trotzky, *The Real Situation in Russia* (New York, Harcourt, Brace, 1928), p. 60 *et seq.*
[26] For Stalin's attack on Trotzky and "Trotzkyism," *cf.* Joseph V. Stalin, *Ob Opposizii: Statyi i Rechi, 1921–1927* (Regarding the Opposition: Articles and Speeches, 1921–1927), Moscow, State

CHAPTER II

THE COMMUNIST PARTY

INTERNAL conflicts and resulting modification of Marxist doctrine, however, have not impaired the outward unity of the Communist party, preserved by a close-knit organization, an iron discipline and a strict enforcement of the "party line." The Communist party has at present a total membership of 2,500,000. The relatively slow growth of the party is due, in part, to the rigid conditions required of candidates for admission, and in part to the searching control which the party exercises over its members through periodic investigations of their activities, known as "purges," which frequently result in the censure or expulsion of politically "alien" or passive elements.

THE COMMUNIST PARTY

The constitution of the party, adopted at its Fourteenth Congress in 1925,[1] draws a sharp dis-

Publishing House, 1928, and his political report to the Fifteenth Congress of the Communist Party in 1927, *Piatnadzatyi Syezd VKP* (Fifteenth Congress of the All-Union Communist Party), Stenographic Report, Moscow, State Publishing House, 1928, p. 68 *et seq.* Cf. also N. I. Bukharin, *Partiya i Opposizionnyi Blok* (The Party and the Opposition Bloc), Leningrad, "Priboi," 1927. For a detailed study of Soviet agrarian policy, *cf.* Vera M. Dean, "Russia's Agrarian Problem," Foreign Policy Association, *Information Service*, Vol. VI, No. 10, July 23, 1930.

[1] *Ustav VKP s Resolutziami Partsyezdov, Conferenzii i TSK VPK po Voprossam Partyinovo Stroitelstva* (The Constitution of the All-Union Communist Party with the Resolutions of Party Congresses, Conferences and of the Central Committee of the

tinction between the workers who, according to Communist doctrine, must serve as the vanguard of the proletariat and must form at least fifty-one per cent of the party,[2] and other groups of the population. Applicants for membership are consequently divided into three categories: 1. workers and Red Army soldiers (subdivided in turn into two groups —industrial workers engaged in physical labor, and non-industrial workers, including farm hands); 2. peasants and private handicraftsmen; 3. employees, professional men and others. Qualifications for admission range from a six months' period of probation, accompanied by two recommendations from party members of two years' standing for the first group of the first category, to a two-year period of probation and five recommendations from party members of five years' standing for the third category.

In recent years, however, the percentage of factory workers has declined, while that of peasants and other social groups has slightly increased. Of the total membership of the party in 1933, 50 per cent were workers, 20 per cent were peasants and

Party on Questions of Party Construction), Moscow, State Publishing House, 1926. For discussion of various questions concerning the organization of the party, *cf.* the stenographic reports of the sixteen party congresses, as well as the following: *Rossiiskaya Communisticheskaya Partiya v Postanovleniach ye Syezdov, 1903–1921* (The Russian Communist Party in the Resolutions of its Congresses, 1903–1921), Moscow, State Publishing House, 1921, and *Rossiiskaya Communisticheskaya Partiya v Resolutaziach ye Syesdov i Conferenzii, 1898–1927* (The Russian Communist Party in the Resolutions of its Congresses and Conferences, 1898–1927), Moscow, State Publishing House, 1927. For discussion of current questions of party organization, *cf. Partiynoe Stroitelstvo* (Party Construction), a semimonthly organ of the Central Committee of the party; *Pravda* (The Truth), the party's daily organ; and such periodicals as *Bolshevik.*

[2] *Cf.* resolution of the Thirteenth Party Congress, 1924, *Ustav VKP,* cited, p. 106.

the rest were drawn from employees and intellectuals.[3]

Members of the Communist party are required not only to obtain a thorough knowledge of Marxist doctrine and to participate in all civic and party activities, but to observe a certain standard of personal conduct. They must abstain from excessive drinking and other indulgences, and must in general serve as an example to the rest of the population. The Communists, regarded as the governing *élite,* are industriously trained for their manifold tasks in a series of special educational institutions ranging from local schools of "political grammar" to the Communist Academy and the Marx-Engels and Lenin Institutes in Moscow. While both careerists and incompetents may be found in the ranks of the party, the Communists have on the whole shown sustained zeal and enthusiasm, and have willingly served as shock troops in the new enterprises launched under the Five-Year Plan.

The Comsomol

The members of the Communist party will gradually be relieved at their posts by the new "shift" now trained in the Communist League of Youth (*Comsomol*), composed of 5,000,000 boys and girls between the ages of fourteen and twenty-three. The constitution[4] of the *Comsomol,* like that of the

[3] In 1930, 68.2 per cent of the party were industrial workers, 18.7 per cent peasants, and the rest employees and intellectuals. *Calendar-Ezhegodnik Communista na 1931 God* (Calendar of the Communist for 1931), Moscow, "The Moscow Worker," 1931, p. 351.

[4] *Ustav i Programma Rossüskovo Leninskovo Communistecheskovo Soyuza Molodiozhi* (Constitution and Program of the Russian Leninist Communist League of Youth), Moscow, State Publishing House, 1926. *Cf.* also Balashov and Nelepin, *VLKSM za Desyat Let v Tzifrach* (Ten Years of the Russian Leninist Communist League of Youth in Figures), Moscow, "The

party, draws a distinction between proletarian and non-proletarian elements. Young workers and peasants are admitted without recommendations or previous probation, while youths of non-proletarian origin must undergo a year's probation, and present two recommendations from party or *Comsomol* members of two years' standing. The *Comsomols* are regarded as a leavening element in the young generation, whose vanguard they are destined to become. They are consequently encouraged to perfect their knowledge of Communist doctrine, to improve their health by sports and physical culture, to participate collectively in the political and economic activities of the community in which they live, and to prepare themselves for the defense of the country. While promotion from the *Comsomol* to the party is not automatic, young Communists trained under the Soviet régime, who know little or nothing of the country's pre-revolutionary history and are fired with enthusiasm for the Five-Year Plan, now predominate in the ranks of the party, bringing youthful energy and a boundless faith in ultimate success.

The Young Communists direct the work of their juniors, the Pioneers, an organization of children aged ten to sixteen, numbering 6,000,000 in 1933, which in turn leads a still younger group, the "Octiabrists," [5] which includes children from eight to

Young Guard," 1928; Andrei Shokhin, *Kratkii Ocherk Istoryi Comsomola* (Short Sketch of the History of the *Comsomol*), Moscow, "The Young Guard," 1926; Thomas Woody, *New Minds: New Men?* (New York, Macmillan, 1932), Chapter VI. The *Comsomol* has its own official organ, *Comsomolskaya Pravda,* modeled on the party *Pravda,* as well as a number of other newspapers and periodicals.

[5] The "Octiabrists," often referred to as "children of the revolution," are named in honor of the October (old style) revolution of 1917. The Pioneers were organized in 1922, and the "Octiabrists" in 1923.

ten years of age.[6] The work of the Pioneers and "Octiabrists," like that of the Young Communists, emphasizes the study of Communist principles, the performance of "socially useful labor," and elementary military training.

PARTY ORGANIZATION

The nucleus of the party is the cell (*yacheika*), which must include not less than three party members, and which may be formed in factory, village or office, or by Communists who are attached to no organized production unit. The function of the cell is to carry out party policies and decisions, to recruit and educate new members, to assist local party committees in propaganda work, and to participate actively in the country's political and economic life. Of a total of 39,321 party cells in 1928, 25.4 per cent were found in factories, 52.7 in villages, 18.5 in offices and enterprises, and 1.8 in educational institutions.[7]

Party cells elect delegates to the higher organs of the party, which correspond to the administrative divisions of the country. From the provincial and regional party congresses delegates are elected to the All-Union party congress, which is usually convoked once every two years [8] and which, according to the

[6] *Cf.* N. K. Krupskaya, *Deti Revolutzii* (The Children of the Revolution), Moscow, "The Young Guard," 1929; Woody, *New Minds: New Men?* cited, Chapter V. A certain overlapping of ages is allowed in all Communist groups, in order that a number of Young Communists may remain as leaders of the Pioneers, and that a number of Pioneers may serve as leaders of the "Octiabrists."

[7] All-Union Communist Party, Statistical Department of the Central Committee, *VKP v Tzifrach* (The All-Union Communist Party in Figures), Moscow, State Publishing House, 1929, p. 13.

[8] In the intermediate year the party usually holds an All-Union party conference, which is distinguished from the party congress principally by the fact that, while the latter is com-

party constitution, acts as the supreme organ of authority. The Congress, however, delegates its powers to a Central Committee which it elects, and which represents it during intervals between sessions. The Central Committee is at present composed of seventy-one members, and is divided into three sections: a secretariat; an organization bureau (*Orgbureau*), which is entrusted with administrative functions; and a Political Bureau (*Politbureau*) of ten members, which is concerned with the formulation of party policies.[9] The members of the *Politbureau* are nominally appointed by the Central Committee. In practice, however, their selection is determined by Stalin, Secretary-General of the party since 1922, himself a member of the *Politbureau*. While Stalin occupies no important post in the government of the Union, he exercises a decisive influence on both party and government policy. The *Politbureau* has no published statutes; its meetings, like those of the party congress, are not open to the public; and only its decisions, usually embodied in decrees countersigned by Soviet officials, appear in the Soviet press. It is generally known, however, that all fundamental problems of party and gov-

posed of delegates elected by the various party organizations. the former is attended only by party officials.

[9] The *Politbureau* is at present composed as follows: Joseph Stalin, Secretary-General of the Central Committee of the Communist Party; Michael Kalinin, senior chairman of the Central Executive Committee of the U.S.S.R.; Valerian Kuibyshev, president of the State Planning Commission; A. A. Andreyev, People's Commissar for Transportation; Vyacheslav Molotov, president of the Council of People's Commissars; Klimentyi Voroshilov, People's Commissar for Military and Naval Affairs; Sergey Kirov, Secretary of the Leningrad Regional Committee of the party; Lazar M. Kaganovich, Secretary of Central Committee of Communist party and of the Moscow Communist party committee, and Stanislav Kossior, General Secretary of the Executive Committee of the party in the Ukraine.

ernment policy are first threshed out in the *Polit-bureau,* and the latter's decisions regarding the "line" which the party will follow on all current questions are reported by the press. Such far-reaching developments as the introduction of the Five-Year Plan, the "liquidation" of the *kulaks* and the inauguration of a milder policy toward technical experts originated not with the organs of the Soviet government, but with the *Politbureau,* and were actually formulated by Stalin and his closest associates. This predominance of the party over the government, however, creates no real political conflict, since all leading Soviet officials are members of the party, while the majority of the members of the *Politbureau* occupy responsible government positions.[10]

At the Seventeenth Congress of the Communist party held in January and February 1934, it was proposed to obliterate all outward distinction between party and government by officially welding the two together and centralizing authority in the hands of party organs. The program of proposed reforms was submitted by Lazar M. Kaganovich, secretary of the Moscow Communist party committee and a close collaborator of Stalin, who is generally regarded as Stalin's most probable successor. According to this program, the Central Control Committee of the party and the Commissariat of Workers' and Peasants' Inspection—the control organ of the Soviet government [11]—will be abolished. They

[10] The organization of the *Comsomol* is modeled on that of the party, with cells, rural, county, economic district, provincial and regional committees and an All-Union *Comsomol* Congress. The Pioneers are organized in brigades and detachments, while the "Octiabrists" are organized in divisions.

[11] *Cf.* p. 377.

will be replaced by a Party Control Committee attached to the Central Committee of the party and a Soviet Control Committee attached to the Council of People's Commissars. The significant point of this reform is that both committees will be elected by the congress of the Communist party, and that the Soviet government will thus be directly subordinated to party control. Kaganovich also proposed to abolish party cells—with a view to centralizing authority in higher party organs—and to create a category of "sympathizers" drawn from the ranks of those who, although not yet ready to shoulder the responsibilities of party membership, are willing to cooperate loyally with the party.[12]

The constitution of the party describes party organization as "democratic centralism," and provides for "complete freedom" of discussion regarding controversial questions.[13] Once a decision has been reached, however, party discipline demands the cessation of discussion, and all party organs, as well as Communist "fractions" in non-party organizations (soviets, trade or professional unions, and cooperative associations), must immediately give effect to party mandates. Failure to follow party directions, and "other offenses recognized as criminal by the public opinion of the party," are investigated by a Central Control Committee, and are subject to penalties ranging from censure to expulsion from the party. Thus when Trotzky condemned Stalin's policies in 1927, he and some of his associates in the Left Opposition were expelled from

---

[12] *Cf.* theses of Kaganovich, *Izvestia,* December 31, 1933.
[13] *Cf.* also resolution of the *Politbureau* and of the Central Committee, December 5, 1923, *Ustav VKP,* cited, p. 86.

the party,[14] and subsequently exiled. Similarly, when Nicholas Bukharin, editor of the Communist organ *Pravda*, supported the Right Opposition, he was ousted from the *Politbureau* in 1929, and his fate was shared in 1930 by Rykov and Tomsky, chairman of the All-Union Council of Trade Unions, despite their recantation of the "Right heresy."

THE "PARTY LINE"

The severe treatment meted out to dissenters by what Trotzky described as the "party bureaucracy" is justified by Communist leaders on the ground that the "monolithic unity" of the party, which serves as a bulwark against capitalist reaction, can be maintained only by strict enforcement of the "Leninist party line." This line is not a rigid program which takes no cognizance of change of circumstances, but a flexible set of formulas determined by a concrete "historical situation" and designed to meet the special problems which each situation creates. Competent observers believe that the party line, while invariably supported by numerous quotations from Lenin's works, represents the policy which Stalin and his associates consider best adapted to existing conditions.

The centralization of party authority in the hands of the *Politbureau*, which Trotzky denounced as contrary to "inter-party democracy," [15] is regarded by

[14] *Cf.* resolution of the Fifteenth Party Congress, approving the decision of the Central Committee to expel Trotzky and his associates from the party. *Piatnadzatyi Syezd Vse-Soyuznoi Communisticheskoi Partyi* (Fifteenth Congress of the All-Union Communist Party), Stenographic Report, Moscow, State Publishing House, 1928, p. 1317.

[15] Trotzky, *The Real Situation in Russia,* cited, p. 111 *et seq.*

Communist leaders as the only method calculated to establish the leadership of the party, and consequently of the proletariat, among less class-conscious elements of the population. Only a disciplined, united party, they claim, can give effect to the aspirations of the laboring masses and lead them to decisive victory over capitalism.

THE THIRD INTERNATIONAL

The All-Union Communist party forms a "section" of the Third (Communist) International (*Comintern*), established in 1919 with headquarters in Moscow, in which fifty-eight Communist parties from as many states or colonies are represented.[16] The object of the Third International, according to its constitution, is to struggle with all means at its disposal, including violence, "for the overthrow of the international bourgeoisie and the establishment of an international Soviet republic, as a transitional stage toward complete annihilation of the state."[17] The Third International regards the dictatorship of the proletariat as the only institution capable of liberating mankind "from the horrors of capitalism," recognizes the Soviet government as "the historic form" of the dictatorship, and undertakes to support every Soviet republic, "wherever established."[18] The program adopted at the close of the Sixth Congress of the Third International in 1928 declared that Communist aims "can be accomplished only through

[16] The *Comsomol* similarly forms a "section" of the Communist Youth International, which is affiliated with the Third International.

[17] Constitution of the Third International adopted at its Fifth Congress in 1924, *Ustav VKP,* cited, p. 165.

[18] *Ibid.*

an overthrow by force of the whole existing social order." [19]

The supreme organ of authority in the Third International, according to its constitution, is the World Congress—which last met in 1928—in which the All-Union Communist party, despite its minority position, exercises a predominant influence. This congress delegates its powers to an Executive Committee of fifty-nine members, which it elects. Of the ten members of the *Politbureau* only Stalin, Secretary-General of the Communist party, is a member of the Executive Committee of the Third International, but others, including Molotov, president of the Union Council of People's Commissars, served as delegates to the Sixth World Congress of the *Comintern*. The decisions of the Executive Committee are binding on all "sections" of the Third International, including the All-Union Communist party, as well as on individual Communists throughout the world. While the All-Union Communist party, like other "sections," contributes dues to the Third International, there is no evidence that the latter receives financial aid from the Soviet government.

[19] *Izvestia,* September 5, 1928. Reports of the first two congresses of the Third International are available in Russian: *Pervyi Congress Communisticheskovo Internatzionala* (First Congress of the Communist International), March 2–19, 1919 (Petrograd, 1921); *Vtoroi Congress Communisticheskovo Internatzionala* (Second Congress of the Communist International), 1920 (Petrograd, 1921). Abridged reports of the Fourth and Fifth Congresses have been issued in English by the Communist Party of Great Britain. *Cf.* also *The Communist International between the Fifth and Sixth World Congresses, 1924–1928* (London, The Communist Party of Great Britain, 1928). *The Communist International,* the organ of the Third International, is published simultaneously in Russian, German, French and English. *Cf.* also A. Tivel and M. Kheimo, *Dessyat Let Cominterna v Resheniach i Tzifrach* (Ten Years of the *Comintern* in Decisions and Figures), Moscow, State Publishing House, 1929.

SOVIET FOREIGN POLICY AND THE COMINTERN

The internal conflicts of the All-Union Communist party, the *Comintern's* most active and powerful "section," have been reflected in the Third International, many of whose constituent parties, less disciplined than that of the Soviet Union, have split into Trotzky, Stalin and other factions. The policy of the Third International, however, has in recent years been determined by the Stalin "party line," notably with respect to the imminence of world revolution. The Communist conviction that the World War marked the beginning of a period of world revolution, which would witness the intensification of "capitalist contradictions" and the triumph of the proletariat, was gradually weakened by the failure of Communist uprisings in China and in the colonies. The program of the Sixth Congress of the *Comintern* echoed Stalin's conclusion that capitalism had been temporarily "stabilized," and declared that "the victory of socialism is possible in only a few countries, or even only in one individual country." The Third International thus accepted Stalin's decision that, for the time being at least, the Soviet government should concentrate its efforts not on fomenting revolution abroad, but on the task of "building socialism" at home. The Soviet government has meanwhile made every effort to dissociate its foreign policy, directed at establishing peaceful relations with capitalist states whose economic coöperation is needed for the prosecution of the Five-Year Plan, from the openly anti-capitalist program of the *Comintern*.

CHAPTER III

THE GOVERNMENT OF THE
SOVIET UNION

THE predominant position occupied by the Communist party in the Soviet state has occasioned no conflict of authority, since the party is in practice closely identified with the government. The fact, however, that all significant decisions on Soviet policy emanate not from the constitutional organs of the Union, but from the councils of the Communist party, has gradually restricted the functions of the former to ratification and execution of party mandates. Despite this situation, a study of the constitutional structure of the Soviet state is of interest to students of modern politics.[1]

The U.S.S.R. is a federation composed of seven Union republics,[2] in which Michael Kalinin, pres-

[1] Soviet literature on the structure of the federal government consists for the most part of works which merely expound the principal provisions of the Union constitution and make little or no attempt to give a critical analysis. *Cf.* I. N. Ananov, *Ocherki Federalnovo Upravleniya S.S.S.R.* (Sketches of the Federal Government of the U.S.S.R.), Leningrad, State Publishing House, 1925; G. S. Gurvich, *Sovetskoe Gosudarstvennoe Ustroistvo* (The Organization of the Soviet State), Moscow, "Soviet Power," 1930; V. I. Ignatiev, *Sovetskii Stroi* (The Soviet Order), Moscow, State Publishing House, 1928; D. A. Magerovski, *Soyuz S.S.R.* (The U.S.S.R.), Moscow, 1923. For an English work on the subject, *cf.* Walter R. Batsell, *Soviet Rule in Russia* (New York, Macmillan, 1929), which is valuable chiefly for its translations of Soviet laws and constitutions. For articles on current problems of government organization, *cf. Sovetskoe Stroitelstvo* (Soviet Construction), a monthly magazine published by the Central Executive Committee of the U.S.S.R. since 1926, and *Izvestia,* the daily organ of the Central Executive Committee.

[2] For a discussion of the powers exercised respectively by the Union government and by the constituent republics, *cf.* pp. 329–330.

ident of the R.S.F.S.R. and a member of the *Polit-bureau,* performs some of the ceremonial functions usually entrusted to the president of a Western republic, such as the reception of ambassadors. The constitution, however, makes no provision for a president, and entrusts "supreme authority" to the All-Union Congress of Soviets; the latter delegates its legislative powers to a Central Executive Committee which it elects, and its executive powers to a Council of People's Commissars, appointed by the Central Executive Committee.

The administrative system of the Union consists of soviets grouped in a pyramidal formation, with village, town and factory soviets at the base and the All-Union Congress at the apex. The soviet, the only form of organization known to Soviet constitutional law, is a council elected by the "laboring masses" which exercises executive and legislative powers within its jurisdiction, and which meets periodically to examine and ratify the acts and policies of government officials. During intervals between sessions, each soviet is represented by a central executive committee which it elects and, in the more important administrative units, by a smaller body, known as the "presidium."

SOVIET ELECTORAL PROCEDURE

The election of delegates from the lower to the higher soviets or, to use Soviet terminology, the "reëlection of soviets," which is held every two years, is a complicated process which usually takes several months. The whole Union has been redistributed into administrative units which are made to coincide as much as possible with the economic divisions of the country. At the present time vil-

lage, town and factory soviets elect delegates to the
district (*raion*) soviets; the latter send delegates to
the regional (*krai* or *oblast*) congress of soviets, to
which delegates are also elected directly by town
and factory soviets. The regional congress, in turn,
elects delegates both to the congress of the Union
republic in which it is situated and to the All-
Union Congress to which delegates are directly
elected by town and factory soviets.[3]

The class character of the Soviet state is strikingly
illustrated by the Soviet electoral system, which is
marked by three distinctive features: the vote is
granted only to the "laboring" population; voting
takes place on an occupational, rather than a territorial, basis; and the workers enjoy an advantage
over the peasants with respect both to the number
of delegates whom they may elect and the manner
in which they elect them.

According to Soviet political theory, the vote is
not a right, but a social function, and constitutes
the most effective weapon for the protection of the
economic interests of the laboring masses.[4] The
vote is therefore granted to all citizens, irrespective
of sex, religion or nationality, who have reached the
age of eighteen and who either earn their livelihood
by "productive work useful to society" or are en-

---

[3] *Cf.* chart, p. 362. The district (*okrug*), which formerly stood
midway between the *raion* and the *krai*, was abolished in 1930,
when the functions of the *okrug* soviets were transferred in large
part to the *raion* soviets. *Cf.* "Likvidatzia Okrugov" (The
"Liquidation" of *Okrugs*), *Sovetskoe Stroitelstvo*, August 1930,
p. 4; P. Zaitsev, "Likvidatzia Okrugov i Ukreplenie Raionov"
(The "Liquidation" of *Okrugs* and the Strengthening of *Raions*),
ibid., December 1930, p. 35.

[4] S. M. Brodovich, *Sovetskoe Izbiratelnoe Pravo* (Soviet
Electoral Law), Leningrad, State Publishing House, 1925; G. S.
Gurvich, *Istoriya Sovetskoi Constitutzii* (History of the Soviet
Constitution), Moscow, Socialist Academy, 1923, p. 46.

listed in the Soviet armed forces.[5] In addition, foreign workers and peasants residing in the Soviet Union also enjoy the right to vote. Of an estimated total population of 160,000,000, over 84,000,000 were registered as voters in the 1931 elections, and 60,945,000, or 71.8 per cent of the voters, went to the polls.[6]

Disfranchisement, which at present affects some 8,000,000 persons, may be based on political or economic considerations. The political category includes all those directly or indirectly associated with the Tsarist order, notably members of the Romanov dynasty, employees of the former police and gendarmerie, organizers of punitive expeditions, agents of counter-revolutionary governments, such as those of Kolchak and Denikin, officers and employees of the White armies, and finally monks, nuns and clergymen of all religious denominations.[7] The category of persons disfranchised for economic reasons has proved very elastic, and has accurately reflected the government's economic policy at any given time. Broadly speaking, it includes all those who employ hired labor for profit, who live on an un-

[5] *Cf.* Article 64 of the constitution of the R.S.F.S.R.; Batsell, *Soviet Rule in Russia,* cited, p. 80; and corresponding articles in the constitutions of the other Union republics. Persons engaged in domestic pursuits are included in the category of those performing productive work.

[6] *Bulleten Vnutrennei Informatzii* (Bulletin of Internal Information), Press Department of the People's Commissariat of Foreign Affairs, No. 23 (442), May 10, 1931, p. 5.

[7] Article 65 of the constitution of the R.S.F.S.R.; Instruction of the Presidium of the Central Executive Committee of the U.S.S.R. Regarding Eelections to the Soviets, January 16, 1925, *Sobranye Zakonov i Rasporiazhenii Raboche-Krestianskovo Pravitelstva* (Collection of Laws and Regulations of the Workers' and Peasants' Government), 1925, Part I, p. 103; Instruction of the Presidium of the Central Executive Committee of the U.S.S.R., September 28, 1926, *ibid.,* 1926, Part I, No. 66, p. 1209.

earned income such as interest on capital, profits from industrial enterprises or real estate, etc., or who engage in private trade.[8] These general provisions, however, have been altered and amplified from time to time by instructions issued on the eve of elections by the Presidium of the Central Executive Committee of the Union and by corresponding organs of the Union republics.[9] Since 1925 disfranchisement based on economic considerations has been extended to *kulaks* (so-called "rich peasants") and to handicraftsmen employing hired labor. Petty traders and members of free professions engaged in "socially useful" work are exempt from disfranchisement.

The government has been careful to point out that lists of disfranchised persons should be drawn up exclusively by local electoral commissions on the basis of information furnished by local soviets, administrative organs and courts, and not by factory committees, collective farms or other unofficial groups.[10] Despite government regulations, however, local soviets have frequently used their own discretion in according or withholding the franchise, and local officials have on occasion resorted to disfranchisement for the purpose of avenging personal grievances.[11] Disfranchisement, as a rule, is regarded

[8] Article 65 of the constitution of the R.S.F.S.R.

[9] Instructions of the Presidium of the Central Executive Committee of the U.S.S.R., January 16, 1925, and September 28, 1926, cited. It is estimated that 3.2 per cent of the total population in the villages of the R.S.F.S.R. were disfranchised in the 1931 elections.

[10] Instruction of the Presidium of the Central Executive Committee of the U.S.S.R., January 16, 1925, cited; Regulation of the Central Executive Committee of the U.S.S.R. for the Removal of Violations of the Electoral Legislation of the U.S.S.R., March 22, 1930, *Sobranye Zakonov*, cited, 1930. Part I, p. 360.

[11] "Zakon o Lishenii Izbiratelnych Prav i Narushenia Evo na Praktike" (The Law Regarding Disfranchisement and Its Violations in Practice), *Sovetskoe Stroitelstvo*, May 1930, p. 1.

as a form of social ostracism, and is usually accompanied by deprivation of ration cards, medical aid and housing facilities, exclusion of the children of the disfranchised from schools, and even eviction from village or city. To correct this tendency, the government decreed in 1930 that the disfranchised and their families should not be subjected to material hardships, and that children of the disfranchised who have come of age since 1925 should be granted the vote provided they are independently engaged in socially useful labor.[12]

The details of elections, such as time, place and manner of procedure are fixed by electoral commissions appointed in each administrative unit by the latter's executive committee.[13] The electoral commissions are composed of from seven to twenty-one members, depending on the nature of the administrative unit, chosen from the local executive committee, trade and professional unions, the Communist League of Youth, town soviets, peasant organizations, national minorities and the Red Army. The percentage of Communists in the electoral commissions ranged in 1931 from 32.1 for village commissions to 70.1 for regional commissions.[14]

Voting takes place on an occupational rather than a territorial basis, electoral assemblies being held in factories, offices, trade union headquarters, collective farms and other production units. An exception to this general rule is made only for "un-

[12] Regulations of the Central Executive Committee of the U.S.S.R. for the Removal of Violations of Electoral Legislation of the U.S.S.R., March 22, 1930, cited.

[13] Instruction of the Presidium of the Central Executive Committee of the U.S.S.R. Regarding Elections to the Soviets, September 28, 1926, cited.

[14] P. Zaitsev, "Predvaritelnye Itogi Perevyborov Sovetov" (Preliminary Results of Reëlections of the Soviets), *Sovetskoe Stroitelstvo*, cited, March 1931, p. 108.

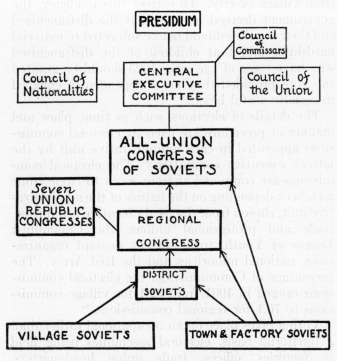

PRESIDIUM

Council of Commissars

Council of Nationalities — **CENTRAL EXECUTIVE COMMITTEE** — Council of the Union

ALL-UNION CONGRESS OF SOVIETS

Seven UNION REPUBLIC CONGRESSES

REGIONAL CONGRESS

DISTRICT SOVIETS

VILLAGE SOVIETS

TOWN & FACTORY SOVIETS

THE SOVIET ELECTORAL SYSTEM

organized" citizens, such as housewives and handicraftsmen, who vote territorially by districts. The
advantage of this system, from the point of view
of the Soviet government, lies in the fact that
the voters do not disperse after the elections, but remain in close contact with each other, and are thus
in a better position to exercise continuous control
over their delegates, and to recall them if necessary.
In 1930 the percentage of recalls ranged from 8.3
in some regions of Central Russia to 65.8 in the
North Caucasus. The chief ground given for recall
was lack of political activity on the part of the
delegates.[15]

Elections must always be held in the presence of
the electoral commission, which records the votes
cast. Candidates may be nominated either before
elections or at the electoral meeting itself by party
and professional organizations as well as by individual citizens, but never by the electoral commission. Opposition groups and even factions of the
party regarded as inimical to the "party line" are
given no opportunity to present their views to the
voters. Elections are usually open, the vote being
taken by a show of hands; candidates receiving a
majority of votes are declared elected.

In every election, be it to the village or factory
soviet or to the All-Union Congress, the workers
enjoy two distinct advantages over the peasants:
towns and factory soviets are entitled to one representative for every 25,000 voters, while village
soviets can elect only one representative for every
125,000 of population; and the town and factory

---

[15] *Calendar-Ezhegodnik Communista na 1931 God* (Calendar
of the Communist for 1931), Moscow, "The Moscow Worker,"
1931, p. 225.

soviets, composed predominantly of workers, elect delegates directly to the All-Union Congress, while delegates elected by the village soviets must pass through two intermediate stages—district and regional congresses—before reaching the All-Union Congress. This difference in the voting rights of workers and peasants is justified on the ground that, during the transition period from capitalism to communism, the class-conscious and politically educated workers must assume leadership over the backward peasant masses. It is argued that when the peasants have reached the economic and cultural level of the workers, the existing differences between the voting powers of the two groups will gradually disappear.[16] This argument is illustrated by the marked disproportion which exists at present between the percentage of Communists elected to village and town soviets; in the 1931 elections it was estimated that only 20 per cent of the membership of village soviets in the R.S.F.S.R. consisted of Communists and *Comsomols,* as compared with over 50 per cent in town soviets.[17] The percentage of Communists increases perceptibly in the higher organs of the system of soviets; 75.2 per cent of the delegates to the Sixth All-Union Congress held in 1931 were members of the Communist party and the *Comsomol.* The predominance of workers in the soviets was also reflected in the composition of the Sixth All-Union Congress, of which 54.7 per cent were industrial workers, 25.9 peasants, and 19.4 employees and intellectuals.

[16] S. M. Brodovich, *Sovetskoe Izbiratelnoe Pravo,* cited; F. A. Shuiski, *Partiya i Sovety* (The Party and the Soviets), Moscow, State Publishing House, 1927, pp. 47–48.

[17] P. Zaitsev, "Predvaritelnye Itogi Perevyborov Sovetov," cited, p. 112.

Despite the fact that non-Communists are elected to the soviets, the latter are regarded primarily as organs for the fulfilment of the "ideals, program and orders" of the Communist party.[18] In the opinion of Soviet writers, the soviet is an institution in which workers and peasants are united with the vanguard of the proletariat—the Communist party —under the leadership of the latter.[19] Soviet spokesmen, however, deny the contention of Western critics that the soviets constitute a dictatorship not of the proletariat, but of the Communist party. They argue that the soviets, through which the laboring masses are for the first time in history admitted to active participation in the government, represent the highest form of "proletarian democracy." [20] Elections to the soviets are consequently viewed not as a sham procedure whose results are practically predetermined, but as "the most important school for the political education of the laboring masses." [21] Government and party organs make every effort to acquaint the masses with the rudiments of "political grammar"—the Soviet constitution, the Communist party program and the Five-Year Plan. All available agencies—schools, clubs, trade unions, the press, the radio, the theatre, the movies—are enlisted in the gigantic task of training a population, large numbers of which are still illiterate, to exercise the func-

[18] Cf. Izvestia, December 7, 1930. The plenum of the Central Committee of the Communist party declared in December 1930 that the soviets should become channels for the "party line," and should be irreconcilably hostile to both Right and Left "opportunism." Ibid., January 16, 1931.

[19] Ibid., December 7, 1930; Shuiski, Partiya i Sovety, cited, p. 53.

[20] Shuiski, Partiya i Sovety, cited, p. 54.

[21] Resolution of the Third Congress of Soviets of the U.S.S.R. Regarding Improvement of the Work of the Soviets, May 20, 1925, Sobranye Zakonov, cited, 1925, Part I, p. 544.

tion of voting.[22] The elections themselves are utilized to focus the attention of the masses on problems of immediate importance, whether defects in transportation or the progress of collectivization: while Soviet achievements are extolled, no attempt is made to disguise existing difficulties. In short, the voters are constantly urged to take an active part in the work of a state whose policies, however, are ultimately controlled not by the elected soviets, but by the self-perpetuating inner group which rules the Communist party.

ALL-UNION CONGRESS OF SOVIETS

The All-Union Congress, which usually numbers about two thousand delegates, approximately seventy-five per cent of whom are Communists, is too unwieldy to exercise real power, and consequently meets only once in two years to receive reports by government officials on such subjects as foreign and domestic policy, the progress of the Five-Year Plan in various branches of national economy and the status of the Red Army, to ratify the acts of the government, and to elect a Central Executive Committee.[23]

In intervals between sessions the All-Union Con-

[22] For a detailed study of Soviet methods of political education, cf. Samuel N. Harper, *Civic Training in Soviet Russia* (Chicago, University of Chicago Press, 1929) ; *idem., Making Bolsheviks* (Chicago, University of Chicago Press, 1931).

[23] The All-Union Congress has met six times since the establishment of the Union—in 1922, when the only item on its agenda was the ratification of the treaty of union, in 1924, 1925, 1927, 1929 and 1931. The congresses of the Union republics generally meet once a year. For the work of the All-Union Congress of Soviets, cf. the stenographic reports of the six congresses held to date, published by the Central Executive Committee under the title *Syezd Sovetov S.S.S.R.* (The Congress of Soviets of the U.S.S.R.)

gress is represented by its Central Executive Committee (TSIK), which usually meets three times a year, for a week or so at a time, and which exercises legislative powers.[24] The Central Executive Committee consists of two chambers: the Council of the Union, composed of 414 members elected by the All-Union Congress from representatives of the Union republics in proportion to population, and the Council of Nationalities, composed of five delegates from each of the autonomous republics and one from each of the autonomous regions of the Union. In both of these bodies the R.S.F.S.R. enjoys a marked preponderance by reason of its large population and of the number of its component republics and regions. The Central Executive Committee elects seven chairmen, one for each of the Union republics,[25] who serve in rotation, and a Presidium of twenty-seven members which must include the presidiums of the Council of the Union and the Council of Nationalities. The Presidium acts on behalf of the TSIK when the latter is not in session.

While the Council of Nationalities is charged with the special task of protecting the interests of the various national groups in the Union, the two chambers enjoy equal powers with respect to legislation. Projects of law are generally first presented by the Council of People's Commissars, individual com-

---

[24] For the provisions governing the organization and powers of the TSIK, *cf.* Chapter IV of the Union constitution and the standing orders of the TSIK, November 12, 1923, *Sbornik Postanovlenii i Rasporiazhenii,* cited, 1923, Part I, No. 21, p. 331. For an English text of the standing orders, *cf.* Batsell, *Soviet Rule in Russia,* cited, p. 527. The TSIK publishes separate stenographic reports of each of its sessions, *e.g., Pervaya Sessia Tzentralnovo Ispolnitelnovo Comiteta Pyatovo Sozyva* (First Session of the Fifth Central Executive Committee), Moscow, 1929.

[25] Michael Kalinin, President of the R.S.F.S.R., occupies the position of senior chairman.

missariats and other government institutions to the Presidium, which after preliminary study submits them to the two chambers of the Central Executive Committee at a joint session. Debates on proposed legislation usually take place at separate sessions of the two chambers. A bill is considered passed when it receives a majority of the votes of those present in each chamber.

COUNCIL OF PEOPLE'S COMMISSARS

While the legislative functions of the Central Executive Committee are in large part performed by the Presidium, its executive powers are exercised by the All-Union Council of People's Commissars (*Sovnarkom*) which it appoints, and which corresponds to the cabinet of Western states.[26] According to Soviet law the people's commissars, whose position is similar to that of Western cabinet ministers, are appointed by and responsible to the Central Executive Committee of the Union. In practice, however, the Communist party exercises a decisive influence over appointments to the Council of People's Commissars. In 1930 when Rykov, who had succeeded Lenin as president of the Council—a position analogous to that of premier in parliamentary governments—was censured by the party for his support of the Right Opposition, he was forced to resign his office in favor of Vyacheslav Molotov, a close adherent of Stalin, who continues

[26] For the provisions governing the organization and functions of the Council of People's Commissars, *cf.* Chapter VI of the Union constitution and the decree of November 12, 1923, establishing the Council. *Sbornik Postanovlenii i Rasporiazhenii Raboche-Krestianskovo Pravitelstva S.S.S.R.* (Collection of Decrees and Regulations of the Workers' and Peasants' Government of the U.S.S.R.), 1923, No. 21, p. 340.

to occupy that post.[27] The Council of People's Commissars is charged with the execution of all measures necessary for the general administration of the Union, preliminary examination of all projects of law submitted to the Presidium and the Central Executive Committee, particularly those concerning the introduction of new or the increase of already existing taxes, and the preparation of the All-Union budget.

The Council of People's Commissars consists of two types of people's commissariats: All-Union commissariats which are common to the whole Union, and unified commissariats, which are duplicated in every Union republic.[28] The All-Union commissariats at present include foreign affairs, war and navy, internal supply, foreign trade,[29] transportation, waterways,[30] posts and telegraphs, and agriculture,[31] while the unified commissariats in-

[27] A few months later, when the party's attack on the "Right heresy" had somewhat abated, Rykov was permitted to return to the Council of People's Commissars as Commissar of Posts and Telegraphs.

[28] Decree on the General Act Organizing the People's Commissariats of the U.S.S.R., *Sbornik Postanovlenii i Rasporiazhenii,* cited, 1923, No. 21, p. 341; Batsell, *Soviet Rule in Russia,* cited, p. 599.

[29] The commissariats of foreign and domestic trade have undergone several transformations since the establishment of the Union. The decree of November 12, 1923, provided for an All-Union commissariat of foreign trade and a unified commissariat of internal trade, which was to take the place of the former commissariat of food. These two commissariats were combined in 1925 into a unified commissariat of foreign and domestic trade. In 1930, however, when the distribution of goods on the domestic market became particularly pressing, this commissariat was divided into the present commissariats of supply and foreign trade.

[30] In 1930, when transportation proved inadequate for the needs of an expanding industry and agriculture, the former All-Union commissariat of communications was divided into two commissariats—transportation (railways and roads) and waterways.

[31] The Commissariat of Agriculture was established in 1929, when the Soviet government launched its drive for collectiviza-

clude the commissariats of heavy and light industry, lumber, finance, workmen's and peasants' inspection, and the central statistical administration.[32] The administration of justice, health and social welfare, which lies within the jurisdiction of the Union republics, is entrusted exclusively to Union republican commissariats.[33]

Each of the All-Union commissariats maintains close contacts with the several Union republics through a representative named either by the Union commissariat or by the central executive committee of each republic. This representative, who usually acts in an advisory capacity, is responsible not only to the All-Union Council of People's Commissars,

tion. Until that time agriculture had been within the competence of the several republics.

[32] In August 1933 the Commissariat of Labor, which had hitherto functioned as a unified commissariat, was merged with the Soviet trade unions. The Council of People's Commissars is at present composed as follows: President, V. M. Molotov; Foreign Affairs, M. M. Litvinov; War and Navy, K. E. Voroshilov; Internal Supply, A. I. Mikoyan; Foreign Trade, A. P. Rosengolz; Transportation, A. A. Andreyev; Waterways, N. M. Yanson; Posts and Telegraphs, A. I. Rykov; Agriculture, Y. A. Yakovlev; Heavy Industry, G. K. Ordjonikidze; Light Industry, I. E. Liubimov; Finance, G. F. Grinko; Workmen's and Peasants' Inspection, Y. E. Rudzutak; Lumber, S. S. Lobov; Chairman of State Planning Commission, V. V. Kuibyshev. It is now planned to split up the Commissariat for Heavy Industry into five or six smaller commissariats dealing with specific branches of industry, such as the electrical and chemical industries, non-ferrous metals, ferrous metals, construction and machinery building. Ordjonikidze, now Commissar for Heavy Industry, may be put in charge of transportation.

[33] In 1930 the Union government abolished the Union republican commissariats of internal affairs on the ground that the functions of Western ministries of the interior are performed in the Soviet state by the Supreme Economic Council (since then divided into three commissariats—heavy and light industry, and lumber) and by the Commissariat of Agriculture, "laboratories of Soviet internal policy," and by organs of the Communist party. Cf. V. Vassiliev, "Likvidatzia Narodnych Commissariatov Vnutrennych Diel" (The "Liquidation" of People's Commissariats of Internal Affairs), Sovetskoe Stroitelstvo, January 1931, p. 25.

but also to the government of the republic to which
he is accredited. Each of the Union republics, in
addition, maintains a permanent representative
in Moscow, who may participate in the work of
the All-Union Council of People's Commissars
whenever the interests of his government are at
stake.[34]

Unlike the All-Union commissariats, the unified
commissariats perform their functions in the Union
republics through corresponding commissariats appointed and dismissed solely by the central executive
committee of each republic. The republican commissariats, however, must execute the directions of
the unified commissariats, which supervise their
work and may suspend or repeal their decrees.[35] The
central executive committee of each Union republic, for its part, may suspend the application of decrees issued by unified commissariats when these
conflict with the Union constitution or laws, or with
republican legislation.

COUNCIL OF LABOR AND DEFENSE

It would be impossible, within the scope of this
book, to examine the organization and functions
of each Soviet commissariat in detail. Particular interest, however, attaches to those departments and
commissions of the Council of People's Commissars
which are concerned with the application of planned

[34] Ananov, *Ocherki Federalnovo Ustroistva S.S.S.R.,* cited,
p. 45 *et seq.*

[35] An exception is made for decrees of republican commissariats based on orders issued by the republican council of
people's commissars; the only action which the unified commissariat may take with respect to such decrees is to register a
protest against them with the All-Union Council of People's
Commissars.

economy and with protection of the Soviet order—
notably the Council of Labor and Defense, the State
Planning Commission, the Commissariat of Workers' and Peasants' Inspection and the State Political
Administration. The Council of Labor and Defense
(STO) which, while not a commissariat, is attached
to the Council of People's Commissars, occupies a
pivotal position in the Soviet system, and may be
regarded as the general staff of the economic as well
as the armed forces of the Union.[36] Its principal
function is to formulate the economic and financial
plans of the Union, to alter these plans in accordance
with existing economic and political conditions, and
to exercise immediate supervision over the performance by the various commissariats of economic policies and measures concerning defense.[37] The importance of the STO may be measured by the fact
that Stalin, who had hitherto occupied no post in
the government, became a member of the STO
in 1930.

The State Planning Commission

The planning functions of the STO are performed
by a special organ, the State Planning Commission
(*Gosplan*), which coördinates the plans of the several republics as well as all enterprises and undertakings in the Union, drafts "a common Union
perspective plan" in collaboration with a whole network of regional and local planning bodies, and su-

[36] The organization and functions of the Council of Labor and
Defense are defined in a decree of August 21, 1923; *Sbornik
Postanovlenii i Rasporiazhenii*, cited, 1923, No. 13, p. 216. An
English text of this decree is found in Batsell, *Soviet Rule in
Russia*, cited, p. 620.

[37] Arkhippov, *Zakon v Sovetskom Gosudarstve* (Law in the
Soviet State), cited, p. 106.

pervises the execution of the plan.[38] The possibility
of establishing a system of "planned economy" which
alone, in Lenin's opinion, would permit the transformation of Russia from a backward agricultural
country into a modern industrial and socialist state,
received serious consideration after 1920, when a
plan for the electrification of the country was first
elaborated. The *Gosplan*, charged with the examination and correlation of data on this subject, prepared a preliminary draft for a Five-Year Plan intended to cover the period 1927–1932. This draft,
amended and corrected, served as the basis for the
first Five-Year Plan, inaugurated on October 1,
1928.[39] The plan contained detailed programs for
the development of every branch of national econ-

[38] The organization and functions of the State Planning Com-
mission are defined in a decree of August 21, 1923; U.S.S.R.,
Sbornik Postanovlenii i Rasporiazhenii, cited, 1923, No. 13. An
English text of this decree is found in Batsell, *Soviet Rule in
Russia*, cited, p. 618.

[39] The date on which the Five-Year Plan was scheduled to
terminate was originally set as September 30, 1933; this date,
however, was shifted in 1930 to December 31, 1933, when the
fiscal year was changed to coincide with the calendar year, and
then to December 31, 1932, when the slogan "The Five-Year Plan
in Four Years" was introduced. For the text of the Five-Year
Plan, *cf.* U.S.S.R., *Piatiletnii Plan Narodno-Khozyastvennovo
Stroitelstva S.S.S.R.* (The Five-Year Plan of National Economic
Construction of the U.S.S.R.), 3 volumes, Moscow, "Planned
Economy," 1929. For a summary of the Five-Year Plan in
English, *cf. The Soviet Union Looks Ahead* (New York, Live-
right, 1929). The economic aspects of the Five-Year Plan, which
lie outside the scope of this book, have been analyzed in a number
of works, the most valuable of which are W. H. Chamberlin,
The Soviet Planned Economic Order (Boston, World Peace Foun-
dation, 1931); Michael Farbman, *Piatiletka: Russia's Five-Year
Plan* (New York, The New Republic, 1931); G. F. Grinko, *The
Five Year Plan of the Soviet Union* (New York, International
Publishers, 1930); and Calvin B. Hoover, *The Economic Life of
Soviet Russia* (New York, Macmillan, 1931). For an official
account of the results accomplished under the Five-Year Plan,
cf. Summary of the Fulfilment of the First Five-Year Plan (Mos-
cow, State Planning Commission of the U.S.S.R., 1933).

omy—industry, agriculture, finance, transportation, etc.—and for simultaneous development in all fields of social activity, notably education. The figures originally set by the plan, which include maximum and minimum "variants," are checked annually by "control figures," prepared on the basis of actual results achieved during the past year, and these "control figures" in turn serve as a basis for altering the estimates of the plan for the following year. The first Five-Year Plan was regarded as but a prologue to a vast program of economic development to be elaborated in successive Five-Year Plans, the second of which was approved in its main points by the Seventeenth Conference of the Communist party in January 1932 and is now in operation.

In addition to the organs specifically charged with the administration of "planned economy," the commissariats of the Union and of the constituent republics, as well as subordinate government institutions, perform important planning functions in their respective fields, subject to the control of the *Gosplan* and the STO. The administration and regulation of state industries, with the notable exception of industries engaged in the production of foodstuffs, controlled by the Commissariat for Internal Supply, were entrusted at first to the Supreme Economic Council, which was duplicated by economic councils in the Union republics, and was responsible to the Council for Labor and Defense. On January 5, 1932, however, the Supreme Economic Council was broken up into three unified commissariats—heavy industry, light industry and lumber.[40] Each of these commissariats will now plan and supervise the work of the plants, trusts and industrial combinations

[40] *Izvestia,* January 5, 1932.

within its field, will regulate the distribution of government credits amòng them, and will assist the State Planning Commission with the preparation of annual "control" figures. Similarly the Commissariat of Foreign Trade, which applies the Soviet government's foreign trade monopoly, annually draws up a plan of exports and imports in conformity with the country's economic condition.[41]

Financial Planning

Financial planning is entrusted to the Commissariat of Finance which, after consultation with other Union commissariats and with representatives of the Council of Labor and Defense, the State Planning Commission and the Union republics, annually prepares a "unified state budget"[42] which, like Western budgets, contains estimates of revenue and expenditures. The Union budget for 1934, submitted to the Seventeenth Congress of the Communist party by the Commissar of Finance on January 1, 1934, estimated revenues at 48,700,000,000 rubles, and expenditures at 47,200,000,000 rubles.[43]

Soviet revenue is derived from two principal sources—taxation, and the income of various state enterprises and undertakings. The most profitable

[41] For a detailed analysis of the work of the Commissariat of Foreign Trade, cf. Vera M. Dean, "Foreign Trade Policy of the Soviet Government," F. P. A. *Information Service*, Volume VI, No. 20, December 10, 1930.

[42] S. A. Kotlyarevski, *Budget S.S.S.R.* (The Budget of the U.S.S.R.), Leningrad, State Publishing House, 1925; *Idem., Budgetnoe Pravo R.S.F.S.R. i S.S.S.R.* (The Budget Law of the R.S.F.S.R. and the U.S.S.R.), Moscow, State Publishing House, 1924; Chamberlin, *The Soviet Planned Economic Order*, cited, p. 96.

[43] *Cf.* report made by Grinko, Commissar of Finance, to the Seventeenth Congress, *Izvestia*, January 3, 1934. The gold ruble at par is quoted at 51 cents.

Soviet taxes are the business turnover tax, the agricultural tax, and customs duties. In addition, the Soviet government levies trade and industry, general income and excess profits taxes, as well as a special tax for cultural needs. The principal items in the non-taxation category are the income from transportation and the administration of posts and telegraphs, revenue derived from state industries, state credit institutions, internal trade—which is almost entirely controlled by the state—and state loans.

In 1934 over 70 per cent of the Soviet budget was to be expended on the financing of national economy —industry (entirely controlled by the state), state and collective farms, transportation, posts and telegraphs, and enterprises conducted by the Commissariat of Internal Supply. Of the balance, 6.4 per cent was to be expended on education and social welfare, 6.1 per cent on administration and national defense, and 7.7 per cent was to be contributed by the Union government to local budgets,[44] which bear the principal expense of health, social welfare and education administration.

The Soviet budget thus serves as an agency for collecting revenue from taxes and from profitable

[44] Grants from the Union budget (which includes the budgets of the seven Union republics) to "local budgets" are intended to cover the annual deficit hitherto experienced by each of the Union republics. An attempt to avoid the recurrence of these deficits—and thus relieve the Union budget—was made by the law of December 22, 1931, which assigned to republican and local budgets a certain percentage of the business turnover tax on republican and local enterprises, as well as a certain percentage of the business turnover tax on All-Union enterprises and on those All-Union undertakings which exploit the natural resources of the respective republics and regions, notably gold, oil and cotton. Cf. report of G. F. Grinko, People's Commissar of Finance, to the Central Executive Committee of the Union, *Izvestia,* December 30, 1931.

state enterprises, such as light industry, and for redistributing capital among state undertakings which are most in need of financial assistance, notably heavy industry and transportation. The financing of Soviet industry, trade and agriculture is effected through four main banks, all operated by the state, of which the State Bank established in 1921 is the most important. The State Bank issues banknotes (*chervontzi*), regulates currency circulation, and provides over eighty per cent of the short-term credits extended in the Soviet Union.[45] Long-term credits are granted to industry by the Long-Term Credit Bank for Industry and Electrification and to agricultural enterprises by the State Bank, while foreign trade is financed by the Bank for Foreign Trade, and housing projects by the Central Municipal and Housing Bank.

COMMISSARIAT OF WORKERS' AND PEASANTS' INSPECTION

The vastness and multiplicity of the tasks which the state would be called on to perform under socialism, and the consequent development of a stifling bureaucracy, have frequently been regarded as an insuperable obstacle to the establishment of an efficient socialist state. The extent to which the Soviet government is aware of this danger may be judged by the virulence of the "self-criticism" which is constantly directed against red tape and routine performance of administrative duties. The extirpation of bureaucracy which, if unchecked, might seriously jeopardize the country's economic life, is regarded as so important that a special organ, the

[45] A. A. Santalov and Louis Segal, *Soviet Union Year Book, 1930* (London, Allen and Unwin, 1931), p. 423.

Commissariat of Workers' and Peasants' Inspection (RKI), has been charged with the task of investigating the administration of all government institutions, of offering constructive criticism for improvement of the state apparatus, and of adjusting the latter to the needs of socialist construction.[46] The RKI is empowered to rationalize the technique of administration, to draft plans for changes in the structure of state organs and to coördinate their work, to examine and analyze Union and republican budgets, as well as all plans of production, to request information from government institutions and officials on matters under investigation, and to assist them in the selection and training of personnel. Finally, the RKI conducts periodic "cleansings" of the state apparatus, in the course of which the work of all government institutions is minutely checked, and employees who have been found inefficient may be summarily dismissed, exiled or even shot.[47] Under the program of reforms proposed by Kaganovich, the RKI would be replaced by a Soviet Control Committee elected by the Communist Party Congress.

THE OGPU

In its unremitting struggle against all administrative abuses, whether bureaucracy, negligence or counter-revolutionary "wrecking" and sabotage, the Soviet government is further assisted by the State

[46] The organization and functions of the Commissariat of Workers' and Peasants' Inspection are defined in a decree of November 12, 1923; *Sbornik Postanovlenii i Rasporiazhenii,* 1923, cited, No. 24, p. 386. For an English text of this decree, *cf.* Batsell, *Soviet Rule in Russia,* cited, p. 611.

[47] For details of the "cleansing" procedure, *cf.* Kudryashev, "Predvaritelnye Itogi Chistki Sovetskovo Apparata v S.S.S.R." (Preliminary Results of the "Cleansing" of the Soviet Apparatus in the U.S.S.R.), *Sovetskoe Stroitelstvo,* May-June 1931, p. 1.

Political Administrations (GPU) which were established in each of the Union republics following the abolition of the famous revolutionary tribunal, the Extraordinary Commission (*Cheka*) in 1922, and by the Unified Political Administration of the Union (OGPU), organized in 1923.[48] The OGPU, which is attached to the Union ⸳Council of People's Commissars, is an extensive system of secret police, somewhat similar to the "Third Division" of the Tsarist chancellery, devoted to the suppression of political unrest, and is charged with the task of consolidating "the revolutionary efforts of the republics in their struggle against political and economic counterrevolution, espionage and banditism," and of protecting the frontiers of the Union.[49] Special military units, whose number is determined by the STO and which now total 45,000, are placed at the disposal of the OGPU, which may, without consulting the regular police or the courts, arrest, imprison, exile or sentence to death any person suspected of counter-revolutionary tendencies. The activities of the OGPU, whose president is appointed by the Union Presidium, are nevertheless subject to supervision by the Prosecutor of the Supreme Court of the Union, who may participate in the prosecution of persons accused by the OGPU.[50]

[48] The organization and functions of the OGPU are defined in a decree of November 15, 1923, *Sbornik Postanovlenii i Rasporiazhenii* (1923), cited, No. 22. For the English text of this decree, *cf.* Batsell, *Soviet Rule in Russia,* cited, p. 609.

[49] The special frontier units of the OGPU must combat all attempts to introduce arms or literature illegally into the country, or to cross the frontiers for the purpose of committing counter-revolutionary crimes. *Cf.* the decree of the Presidium of the Union Central Executive Committee, June 15, 1927, *Sobranye Zakonov* (1927), cited, Part I, p. 1219.

[50] *Cf.* Law Regarding the Supreme Court of the U.S.S.R. and the Prosecutor of the Supreme Court of the U.S.S.R., July 24,

"Counter-revolutionary," as distinguished from ordinary, crimes are defined as acts which seek to weaken, undermine or overthrow the Soviet government, to endanger the external security of the Union or to injure the economic and political order established by the proletarian revolution.[51] Such crimes are held to include armed révolt; seizure of power at the centre or in the provinces for the purpose of detaching territory from the Union or of violating Soviet treaties with foreign states; the maintenance of relations with foreign governments or their agents with a view to obtaining assistance for the overthrow of the Soviet government; the "wrecking" of industrial trade and credit enterprises in the interests of former bourgeois owners or of capitalist states; propaganda or agitation advocating the overthrow of the Soviet government or directly inciting to counter-revolutionary crimes, especially when it seeks to arouse religious or national prejudices; and failure to report any of the above crimes. The punishment prescribed in such cases ranges from various terms of imprisonment, the maximum being ten years, to permanent exile from the Union with confiscation of property, or shooting—the "highest measure of social defense."

The work of the OGPU is shrouded in the greatest secrecy; arrests are usually made by night, and practically no information regarding the subse-

1929, *Sobranye Zakonov* (1929), cited, Part I, p. 1,000. For the functions of the Union prosecutor, *cf.* p. 386.

No official statistics have been published on the number of OGPU executions during the last few years. The first president of the OGPU was Felix Dzerzhinsky, former head of the *Cheka*, who was succeeded in 1925 by Vyacheslav Menzhinsky. The latter died in May 1934.

[51] *Cf.* Law Regarding State Crimes, Crimes against the Administration and Counter-Revolutionary Crimes Especially Dangerous for the U.S.S.R., February 25, 1927, *Sobranye Zakonov* (1927), cited, Part I, p. 283.

quent fate of the arrested persons appears in the Soviet press. Occasionally, however, when so-called "counter-revolutionaries" are brought before the ordinary courts, reference is briefly made in the act of accusation to preliminary investigations conducted by the OGPU. Such was the case in three spectacular public trials—the Shakta trial in 1928, when a number of engineers and mechanics, including three Germans, were accused of sabotage in the Donetz coal mines; the Ramzin trial in 1930, when eight engineers were accused of plotting to "wreck" various industries and to overthrow the Soviet government with the aid of their former bourgeois employers, then living abroad in exile, and of capitalist states, notably France; [52] and the Metropolitan-Vickers case in 1933, when a number of technicians, including six British engineers, were tried on charges of espionage, bribery and "wrecking" of the Soviet electrical industry.[53] These trials would indicate that, following the inauguration of the Five-Year Plan, when the economic activities of the Soviet state not only merged with its political activities but came to overshadow them in the public mind, and when the government had more to fear from

[52] Cf. Le Procès des Industriels de Moscou, 25 Novembre–8 Décembre 1930, Sténographie Intégrale des Débats du Procès des Industriels de Moscou (Paris, Librairie Valois, 1931). The act of accusation in the Ramzin trial stated: "In the course of the past two years the GPU has discovered sabotage organizations in various branches of industry, one after the other. After the Shakta sabotage group, a sabotage organization was discovered in the People's Commissariat of Transportation. After sabotage in transportation came the discovery of sabotage organizations in the war and textile industries, in naval construction, economic construction, chemical products, the gold and petroleum industries, etc." Ibid., p. 1.

[53] For the official verbatim report of the trial, cf. The Case of N. P. Vivitsky et al. Charged with Wrecking Activities at Power Stations in the Soviet Union (Moscow, State Publishing House, 1933, 3 vols.).

economic failure than from political opposition, the OGPU gradually shifted its surveillance from "counter-revolutionary" movements such as "Trotzkyism," which it had worked to eradicate in 1927, to engineers and technical experts, particularly those formerly associated with the old régime. This surveillance, as indicated above, proved a serious obstacle to the development of Soviet industry. The position of the technical intelligentsia, however, was considerably improved in the summer of 1931, when Stalin declared that it would be "stupid and senseless" to regard "practically every engineer of the old school" as a "potential criminal or 'wrecker.'" [54] In March 1934 the Soviet government decided to abolish the OGPU and entrust its functions to a Commissariat of Internal Affairs organized along civil rather than semi-military lines.

THE SOVIET JUDICIARY

The regular courts, which deal with ordinary crimes, such as murder, and with civil actions, take jurisdiction over "counter-revolutionary" crimes only when these are referred to them by the Prosecutor. There being no system of federal courts,[55] justice is administered through the courts of the several Union republics. The Soviet judiciary is not an independent organ of the government, but an administrative department charged with the defense of the social order established by the proletarian revolution against attacks by individuals or classes hostile to it.[56] In the early days of Soviet rule the

[54] *Cf.* Stalin's speech on "New Economic Problems," *The Soviet Union Review,* July-August 1931, p. 152.

[55] *Cf.* p. 385.

[56] Basic Principles of the Judicial Organization of the U.S.S.R., 1924, *Sobranye Zakonov* (1924), cited, Part I, p. 366.

judiciary was regarded as primarily an instrument of class justice. This conception, however, was somewhat modified after the introduction of the New Economic Policy in 1921, which tolerated the existence of the "petty bourgeoisie"—*kulaks* and private traders. While the courts continue to be guided by class policy in the administration of justice, they seek to protect all citizens, irrespective of social origin, against offenses of an anti-Soviet character, even when committed by workers or peasants.

The organization of the judiciary is uniform throughout the Union, and consists of a people's court, a regional court, and a Supreme Court in each Union republic.[57] Variations from this system to meet the cultural, administrative or economic needs of certain regions, may be made only with the consent of the Union Central Executive Committee— a provision which has been criticized as tending toward undue centralization.[58] The Soviet judicial system is based on two main principles—that the courts must be simple and easily accessible to the population, and that they must be so organized as to permit the performance of judicial functions exclusively by persons elected by the soviets from the laboring masses.[59] An early revolutionary decree provided for the "democratic election" of judges— presumably direct election by the population.[60] At

[57] In the autonomous republics the Supreme Court is usually replaced by a court described as "principal" or "highest."

[58] N. V. Krylenko, *Sud i Pravo v S.S.S.R.* (Law and the Courts in the U.S.S.R.), Moscow, State Publishing House, 1927, p. 30.

[59] *Ibid.*, p. 39.

[60] Decree No. 1 Regarding the Courts, November 24, 1917. N. V. Krylenko, *Sudoustroistvo R.S.F.S.R.* (The Judicial Organization of the R.S.F.S.R.), Moscow, Juridical Publications of the People's Commissariat of Justice, 1924, p. 209. Krylenko described this decree as "a vestige of the liberal terminology of pre-revolutionary days." *Idem., Sud i Pravo v S.S.S.R.*, cited.

the present time, however, judges of the people's
and regional courts are appointed by the executive
committees of the regional congresses,[61] to which
they are responsible and by which they may be recalled, while the judges of the Supreme Court in
each Union republic are appointed by the republican executive committee. Candidates for the
bench must have the right to vote, must have
served either in the judiciary[62] or in workers' and
peasants' professional or party organizations and,
in the case of regional and Supreme Court judges,
must have served as judges in the people's
courts.

The people's court, which is the basic unit of the
judicial system, consists of a judge and two co-
judges (or "judge jurors") who have equal powers
with the judge in the administration of justice. The
co-judges, each of whom serves not more than six
consecutive days in one year, are chosen from a
panel prepared by a special committee from lists
of persons elected for that purpose by village, factory and other soviets. No special training or experience is required for the office of co-judge. Trial
by jury, which had never been widely used in Tsarist
Russia, is unknown in the Soviet Union. The jurisdiction of the people's courts, which serve as trial
courts, is being constantly broadened, with the re-

[61] Judges in people's courts may in some instances be appointed by town soviets. *Cf.* Judah Zelitch, *Soviet Administration of Criminal Law* (Philadelphia, University of Pennsylvania
Press, 1931), p. 54.

[62] This provision has been criticized by Krylenko, who argues
that a judge requires no qualification other than experience in
political or social work in workers' and peasants', professional or
party organizations. He demanded that the work of the courts
be simplified, so that every citizen possessing an average political
and cultural education could grasp the questions in litigation
without difficulty. (Krylenko, *Sud i Pravo v S.S.S.R.*, cited, p. 47.)

sult that they now handle over seventy per cent of
the total cases.

The regional courts are usually composed of a
president, two deputy presidents, permanent judges
whose number is in each case determined by law,
and co-judges whose selection is subject to the approval of the regional executive committee. They
serve as courts of cassation and supervision for cases
first tried in the people's courts, and have original
jurisdiction over counter-revolutionary crimes, offenses against the administration, crimes committed
by officials in the exercise of their duties, economic
offenses (such as malfeasance or misfeasance in office), and ordinary crimes against life, health, liberty
and property.[63]

The organization of the Supreme Court in each
of the Union republics is determined by republican
legislation. The Supreme Court serves as a court of
cassation for cases referred to it from regional courts,
and has original jurisdiction over cases of exceptional importance referred to it by the republican
central executive committee, the prosecutor of the
republic or the president of the GPU, as well as
over cases involving offenses in office committed by
members of the republican government.

SUPREME COURT OF THE UNION

The Soviet Union has no federal judiciary as distinguished from the three types of courts found in
the Union republics. The Union constitution, however, provides for a Supreme Court of the Union
which, like other Soviet courts, is not an independent institution, but is "attached" to the Union

[63] *Cf.* Zelitch, *Soviet Administration of Criminal Law,* cited,
pp. 68–71.

Central Executive Committee.[64] The Supreme Court examines cases involving offenses committed in office by members of the Union government; deals with conflicts between the constituent republics, and may appeal against them to the Union Central Executive Committee on the ground that they contradict the general legislation of the Union or affect the interests of other republics; finally, at the request of the Central Executive Committee, it renders opinions regarding the constitutional validity of acts and decrees of organs of Union and republican government. These opinions, however, have the force, not of a decision, but of expert legal advice, and may or may not be approved by the Central Executive Committee.[65]

The Supreme Court consists of a president, a deputy president and thirty judges, all appointed by the Union Presidium, and is divided into three chambers—civil, criminal and military. That the Supreme Court is charged with the protection not only of the interests of the Union, but of those of the Union republics as well, is indicated by the fact that the presidents of the supreme courts of the seven republics participate in the plenary sessions of the court.

In addition to the regular courts, the Soviet Union has several courts and commissions which deal with special questions. Thus property disputes between organs of the government are examined by arbitral commissions attached to the Council for Labor and

[64] The organization and functions of the Supreme Court are defined in Chapter VII of the Union constitution, and in the Law Regarding the Supreme Court of the U.S.S.R. and the Prosecutor of the Supreme Court of the U.S.S.R., July 24, 1929, cited, which superseded the earlier law of July 14, 1924.

[65] Cf. Zelitch, Soviet Administration of Criminal Law, cited, p. 100.

Defense, the economic councils of the republics and the regional soviets. Disputes concerning land organization are referred to land commissions, while infractions of the labor code are dealt with by special chambers of the people's courts. Cases of juvenile delinquency are examined by commissions on the affairs of minors, which are composed of representatives of the commissariats of justice, health and education in each of the Union republics. Finally, military crimes and serious breaches of military discipline come within the jurisdiction of military tribunals, whose decisions are subject to review by the military chamber of the Supreme Court of the Union.

The administration of law is supervised by the Prosecutor (*Procurator*) of the Supreme Court of the Union and by republican, regional and local prosecutors who, in addition to their courtroom duties, are authorized to inquire into the "legality of the acts of all government organs, economic institutions, public and private organizations and of private persons," including the OGPU.[66] The Prosecutor of the Supreme Court of the Union, who is appointed by the Union Presidium and is responsible to it alone, also occupies the office of People's Commissar, or deputy commissar, of Justice. Republican prosecutors are appointed by the central executive committees of the republics and, in turn, name regional and local prosecutors. The Soviet prosecutor enjoys powers equal to those of the courts, and occupies a subordinate position only during trials, when he appears as one of the parties in both civil and criminal cases.

As there are no private lawyers, the defense of

[66] Basic Principles of the Judicial Organization of the U.S.S.R., 1924, cited, Section 63.

accused persons is entrusted to a "college of advocates" which functions under the direct supervision of the courts,[67] and must render legal aid to the population, either for a stipulated remuneration, or without charge when the court rules that the defendants are unable to pay. The "college of advocates," which is a semi-autonomous organization, has been criticized on the ground that it is inconsistent with the spirit of Soviet law, and that legal advice should be furnished to workers not by specialists, but by trade and professional organizations.[68]

Soviet law, as has already been noted, draws a sharp distinction between "counter-revolutionary" crimes, which are regarded as socially dangerous, and ordinary crimes against life and property.[69] The avowed purpose of Soviet criminal legislation is not revenge or punishment, but the prevention of crime and the re-training of criminals for normal life. As a result, the penalty for ordinary crimes is much lighter than for "counter-revolutionary" ones. Thus death sentences, which are frequent in cases of administrative or economic mismanagement, embezzlement of government funds and other acts considered as crimes against the state, are seldom pronounced in ordinary murder cases. Punishment usually takes the form of forced labor for not more than one year or imprisonment for a maximum of ten years, and deprivation of civic rights for a period not exceeding five years. The latter penalty carried with it disfranchisement and expulsion from trade and pro-

---

[67] *Ibid.*, Section 11.
[68] Krylenko, *Sud i Pravo v S.S.S.R.*, cited, p. 122.
[69] Fundamental Principles of the Criminal Legislation of the U.S.S.R. and of the Union Republics, October 31, 1924, *Sobranye Zakonov* (1924), cited, Part I, p. 372.

fessional unions, whose members enjoy important privileges, including ration cards and the right of admission to coöperative stores.

The courts are instructed to differentiate between various crimes on the basis of motivation and of the social origin of the criminal. Thus severe punishment must be meted out when the crime has been committed for the purpose of restoring the "bourgeois" government or, if not aimed directly against the Soviet state or the working class, is potentially harmful to them; when the crime is motivated by greed or accompanied by unusual cruelty; and when the criminal was or is connected with the "exploiting" classes. Conversely, milder punishment is prescribed when the crime has been committed either in self-defense or for the protection of the Soviet government; when it has been dictated by hunger, want, or strong emotion, or has occurred as a result of ignorance; and when the criminal is either a worker or a peasant.[70] The Soviet government believes that, in the case of all crimes except those classified as counter-revolutionary, the offender should be reformed and re-trained for normal life rather than punished, and Soviet penal institutions are regarded by experts as models of human treatment.[71]

THE RED ARMY

While the OGPU and the ordinary courts are charged with the protection of internal order, the external defense of the Soviet Union is entrusted to the Red Army of Workers and Peasants (RKKA)

[70] *Ibid.*
[71] For a discussion of Soviet prisons, *cf.* Elias Tobenkin, *Stalin's Ladder* (New York, Minton, Balch, 1933).

organized in February 1918.[72] During the period of civil war and intervention, when the Soviet government had to repulse attacks on several fronts, the Red Army numbered nearly five million men. The danger over, the government faced the task of demobilizing this army, organized almost overnight by Leon Trotzky, then People's Commissar of War, and releasing men for productive work, at the same time assuring the country's adequate defense. At the Ninth Congress of the Communist Party in 1920 Trotzky declared that the regular army should be limited in numbers. So limited an army, however, was not sufficient, in his opinion, for the defense of the Soviet Union's far-flung frontiers. He therefore proposed to establish, in addition to the regular army, a territorial militia which would have the advantage that its members would remain in contact with production in fields and factories. The units of this militia should correspond to the country's administrative divisions, and should be actively supported by trade and professional unions. Under this system, every member of the population capable of bearing arms would eventually be included in a military unit and would receive some form of military training.[73] Trotzky's thesis was supported by his successor, Michael Frunze, who stated in 1925

[72] For the history and organization of the Red Army, cf. A. Geronimus, *Partiya i Krasnaya Armiya* (The Party and the Red Army), Moscow, State Publishing House, 1928; I. Petukhov, *Partiinaya Organizatsiya i Partiinaya Rabota v RKKA* (Party Organization and Party Work in the Red Army of Workers and Peasants), Moscow, State Publishing House, Division of Military Literature, 1928; B. Tal, *Istoriya Krasnoi Armii* (The History of the Red Army), Moscow, State Military Publications, 1924.

[73] Russian Communist Party, *Deviaty Syezd Rossiiskoi Communisticheskoi Partyi* (Ninth Congress of the Russian Communist Party), March 29–April 4, 1920, Stenographic Report, Moscow, State Publishing House, 1920, p. 353 *et seq.*

that "the surest guarantee of peace is not only a pacific policy, but a strong Red Army," and that the Soviet Union needed a system of defense which, in time of war, would bring to the battlefield not only professional soldiers, but trained masses of workers and peasants as well.[74]

The complete realization of Trotzky's military scheme has so far been prevented by the country's cultural backwardness and by financial considerations. At the present time the Red Army is recruited on the basis of compulsory service for all men between the ages of nineteen and forty.[75] Every year some 1,200,000 men become eligible for service, of whom some 300,000 are rejected as physically unfit. Of the remaining number about 450,000 are accepted for a two-year term of active service, about half going into the regular army of 562,000, which includes land, sea and air forces, while half are taken into the territorial militia.[76] Persons enlisted in the militia continue their work in office, field or factory, but receive military training in their respective administrative districts and participate in annual manœuvres. In addition, voluntary courses in rifle practice, the use of gas masks and the operation of tanks and military lorries are organized for men who have failed to gain admittance to the army or

[74] Union of Soviet Socialist Republics, *Tretii Syezd Sovetov S.S.S.R.* (Third Congress of Soviets of the U.S.S.R.), Twelfth Session, May 19, 1925, Stenographic Report, Moscow, Publications of the Central Executive Committee of the U.S.S.R., 1925, p. 488.

[75] Law Regarding Compulsory Military Service, September 16, 1925. *Sobranye Zakonov* (1925), cited, Part I, p. 850 *et seq.*

[76] W. H. Chamberlin, *Soviet Russia* (Boston, Little, Brown, Revised Edition, 1931), p. 127; *Calendar-Ezhegodnik Communista,* cited, p. 358; N. P. Vishnyakov and F. I. Arkhipov, *Ustroistvo Vooruzhennych Sil S.S.S.R.* (The Organization of the Armed Forces of the U.S.S.R.), Moscow, The Military Messenger, 1926.

to the militia, as well as for women and even children. These courses are sponsored primarily by two civilian organizations—*Avtodor*,[77] which is concerned with the development of transportation and the training of automobile drivers, and *Osoviachim*,[78] an organization of over 10,000,000 workers, Young Communists, students and women,[79] which seeks to increase the country's preparedness for air and chemical warfare.

While military service is compulsory for all citizens, the armed defense of the country is regarded as a privilege of the proletariat: as a result, the Red Army consists predominantly of workers and peasants. Persons disfranchised for political or other reasons are assigned to rear guard units and, in addition, must pay a special military tax.[80] In 1934 peasants constituted 42.5 per cent of the army, while factory workers formed 45.8 and office employees 11.7 per cent. Nearly half of the army are Communists, 129,000 being members of the party and 130,-000 members of the *Comsomol*. The commanding

[77] The full name of this organization is *Obschestvo Sodeistviya Razvitiyu Avtomobilisma i Uluchsheniyu Dorog* (Society for the Development of Automobilism and the Improvement of Roads).

[78] The full name of this organization is *Obschestvo Druzei Oborony i Aviazionno-Khimicheskovo Stroitelstva S.S.S.R.* (Society of Friends of the Defense and Aërial-Chemical Construction of the U.S.S.R.).

[79] S. Kamenev, "Na Strazhe Sozialisticheskovo Stroitelstva" (Protection of Socialist Construction), *Sovetskoe Stroitelstvo*, cited, No. 3, 1931, p. 19.

[80] This tax goes into a fund for the assistance of invalids of the civil war and of the families of men called to active service. Citizens excused from military service on religious grounds may be used in time of peace for fighting epidemics or forest fires, while in time of war they may be organized into special units. Amendment to the Law Regarding Compulsory Military Service, February 8, 1927, *Sobranye Zakonov* (1927), cited, Part I, p. 223.

personnel, which is recruited partly from soldiers who have received special training and partly from graduates of military schools, is also predominantly of working-class origin, and some seventy per cent are Communists.[81] While discipline is strictly enforced, officers enjoy no special privileges and their relations with the soldiers are unusually democratic in character.

The armed forces of the Soviet Union are controlled by the People's Commissar for Defense through the Revolutionary War Council, of which he is president and the Commander-in-Chief a member. This council has immediate supervision not only over the military staffs, but also over the Political Section (PUR), which directs education and propaganda in the army. By means of various courses, clubs, permanent and itinerant libraries and wall-newspapers the PUR, with the coöperation of Red Army party cells, supplies the rudiments of literacy and "political grammar" to soldiers many of whom, especially peasants, come into the army illiterate. The Red Army thus serves as an important training-ground for Communism.[82]

Critics of the Soviet government find a marked divergence between the existence of a powerful military machine in the Soviet Union and M. Litvinov's periodic demands in Geneva for complete and universal disarmament. Soviet spokesmen, however, assert that the Soviet Union, which appropriated about $850,000,000 for armaments in 1934, has an

---

[81] *Calendar-Ezhegodnik Communista, 1931,* cited, p. 490. Tsarist officers constituted only 10.6 per cent of the Red Army in 1930, and 6.7 per cent of the higher commanding personnel.

[82] For a detailed study of the methods employed by the PUR, *cf.* Harper, *Civic Training in Soviet Russia,* cited.

army smaller than the combined armies of its Western neighbors, that it spends less on armaments per capita than any one of the states along its Western border,[83] and that its total military expenditures constitute only 3.5 per cent of the country's budget. It might be argued, however, that the Soviet government, in its calculations of comparative strength appears to leave its militia out of account, and that budgetary comparison is misleading, since the Soviet budget includes industry, agriculture and other branches of national economy which in capitalist countries are owned by private interests.

The Soviet government, nevertheless, declares that it urgently desires peace and that the Red Army is designed, not for wars of national aggression, but for the defense of the first workers' republic against capitalist attack and, eventually, for the defense of the world proletariat. There can be little doubt that today, and for the immediate future, war would be directly contrary to Soviet interests, since it might seriously jeopardize the progress of the Five-Year Plan, and that Stalin was sincere when he said at the Sixteenth Congress of the Communist party in 1930: "Our policy is a policy of peace . . . We do not want a foot of alien soil, but we shall not surrender an inch of ours." To say that the Soviet Union has developed a sudden affection for capitalist states or lost interest in world revolution would be misleading. The Soviet government, however, is

---

[83] This contention is not entirely supported by the League of Nations' compilation of per capita expenditure on land, naval and air forces, based for the most part on information furnished by the various governments, which are as follows: U.S.S.R., $3.58; Poland, $3.07; Rumania, $3.43; Lithuania, $0.002; Latvia, $3.99; Estonia, $4.41; Finland, $4.59. *Cf.* William T. Stone, "The Burden of Armaments," *Foreign Policy Reports,* Vol. VII, No. 20, December 9, 1931, p. 377.

at present more absorbed in creating within the boundaries of the U.S.S.R. a socialist state which may serve as inspiration to workers throughout the world than in spreading the gospel of communism abroad.

SPAIN UNDER THE REPUBLIC

CHAPTER I

PRIMO DE RIVERA DICTATORSHIP

SPAIN has undergone two important governmental changes since the World War: the first on September 13, 1923, when General Primo de Rivera overthrew the Constitution of 1876 and established a dictatorship; the second on April 14, 1931, when the Republic was declared.

The dictatorship of Primo de Rivera was the product of social, economic and political conditions common to many European nations after the World War. These conditions had upset the balance of power between the old political parties, breaking them into factions which fought for the spoils of office without regard to the welfare of the people. The result was an almost complete breakdown of responsibility in government, and a notorious slackening of public morality. This period coincided with a military campaign in Morocco, the inept conduct of which led to the disastrous battle of Annual in 1921, in which the Spanish lost between twelve and fourteen thousand men. Responsibility for this disaster was placed at the door of the government, which was already unpopular, and to some extent at the door of the King. The attempt to investigate the Morocco venture was frustrated by the coup d'état of 1923, and it has been generally believed—although proof is lacking—that one of the motives for Primo de Rivera's coup was to save the King from being implicated in the course of an investigation.

Other reasons for the establishment of a dictatorship at that particular time were not lacking. The post-war depression had struck Spain, depriving the country of markets built up during the war, and throwing thousands of workers out of employment. The situation was particularly acute in Catalonia, where the Anarcho-Syndicalists were strong, and where a Separatist movement had kept the region in a state of chaos for several years. Primo de Rivera declared that the objects of his dictatorship were purification of politics, termination of the Morocco war, and restoration of social stability.[1]

Primo de Rivera's rule was in many respects a period of progress and prosperity for Spain, although this prosperity, like that of other countries, could not withstand the world depression of recent years. The war in Morocco was brought to a successful close. Considerable industrial development occurred between 1923 and 1930 and the government sought to encourage industry by building up the railroads and roads, providing a better system of communication, and organizing a National Economic Council to coördinate economic development. The financial condition of the country was such as to permit inauguration of a public works program sufficient

[1] *Cf.* Agnes Waddell, "Spain under the Dictatorship," Foreign Policy Association, *Information Service,* September 4, 1929; Gabriel Mauro Gamazo, *Bosquejo Histórico de la Dictadura* (5th edition, Madrid, Javier Morata, 1930), gives a critical view of Primo de Rivera; Enrique Díaz Retg, *España Bajo el Nuevo Régimen* (Madrid, Ediciones Mercurio, 1928), is an estimate of the régime from the "official" viewpoint.

to employ surplus workers, thus temporarily stemming the rise of revolutionary labor.

During the first five years of the dictatorship, 1923–1928, Primo de Rivera undoubtedly had the support of the majority of the people. A number of events, however, served to diminish his popularity after that date. Among these not the least important was the prolongation of his dictatorship, which had originally been planned to last only three months. Another reason was a campaign for restoration of the Constitution, fostered chiefly by the old politicians who wished to get back into office, which served to create popular feeling against the dictator. The repressive measures employed against government opponents, especially the newspapers and students, added to Primo de Rivera's unpopularity. The army, too, had been severely disciplined, with the result that the government lost its united support. Early in 1930 the growing unpopularity of the dictator, together with his failing health, precipitated his resignation.

Alfonso XIII then entrusted the government to General Dámaso Berenguer, a second dictator, whose rule proved to be unfortunate for the Monarchy. Primo de Rivera had been *simpático,* attracting great numbers of followers because of his personal qualities; Berenguer proved to be neither a good ruler nor a good politician. His one year in power merely succeeded in arousing public sentiment not only against dictators, but against the throne. He had been intimately connected with the King for a number of years, was partly responsible for the Annual disaster, and his appointment was ascribed to Alfonso's desire to continue a personal form of government. Anti-dictatorship sentiment became anti-Monarchist in character, and led to a revolt in December 1930 which, although unsuccessful, stimulated further revolutionary activity. Berenguer's belated attempts to return to constitutional methods were balked by the refusal of the Left forces to participate in elections, and he was forced to give way to Admiral Aznar early in 1931. Aznar proved even less capable than Berenguer; as a result anti-Monarchical sentiment reached fever heat, and the downfall of monarchy became inevitable.

Alfonso XIII fled Spain on April 14, 1931, leaving a new republic behind him.[2] Spain's First Republic had been ended by a military coup in 1874 after ten and a half months of ineffectual existence.[3] Would the Second Republic meet a similar fate? During the First Republic, Spain had been ruled in succession by four Presidents, none of whom had sufficient strength either in the Cortes or in the country to bring order out of the chaos left by the Monarchy. Would the Second Republic produce men of greater ability? The first Republic lacked organized parties strong enough to maintain it. Would the Second Republic develop such parties?

The First Republic had been a product of Liberalism, the Second Republic of Socialism combined with Liberalism. The prominence of the Socialists in Spain's second essay at republicanism served to raise a number of other questions. Would the Socialists succeed in dominating the new régime and use it to transform Spain into a socialist state?

[2] William E. Linglebach, "The Spanish Revolution," *Current History,* June 1931.
[3] Pio Zabala y Lera, *Historia de España, 1808–1923* (2 vols., Barcelona, Sucesores de Juan Gili, 1930) II, pp. 23–24; Joseph A. Brandt, *Toward the New Spain* (Chicago, the University of Chicago Press, 1933), pp. 173–353.

Would the Republic succumb in the end to reactionary forces, or would Spain, like Russia, carry through its revolution even at the cost of dictatorship? The program of the First Republic was entirely political in character. It sought to construct a new Spain without fundamentally modifying existing economic conditions. The presence of the Socialists in the Second Republic committed it to economic reforms. Were the Socialists strong enough to impose their program, or would they be placed in a position of responsibility while lacking adequate authority? These and many other questions confronted the new Republic.

The fall of Alfonso XIII and the establishment of the Republic were precipitated by the decisive victory of Republicans and Socialists in the municipal elections held throughout Spain on April 12, 1931.[4] This victory was brought about by a coalition of anti-Monarchical groups, some of which had been in

---

[4] For the electoral results, *cf. Anuario Estadístico de España* (Madrid, Instituto de Geografía, 1931), p. 482. In the whole of Spain 80,472 municipal councillors were elected by 5,440,103 voters, of whom 1,104,159, or about 20 per cent, lived in provincial capitals. This 20 per cent elected only 1,729 councillors, or about 2 per cent of the total. Of these 1,729 councillors the anti-Monarchists gained 1,065. If the cities had been allotted a number proportionate to their population, they would have named some 16,000 councillors. For example: Barcelona had one councillor for every 5,350 voters, Madrid one for every 4,620, while Soria, a small town in the conservative section of Spain, could boast of a councillor for every 150 voters, and Avila and Teruel, also small towns, had a councillor for every 165 voters. The number of councillors elected, therefore, did not represent the relative voting strength of Monarchists and anti-Monarchists. In all Spain 34,368 Republicans, 4,813 Socialists, 19,035 Monarchists, 67 Communists, 15,198 representatives of local parties, and 6,991 unclassified candidates were elected. All those not Republicans, Socialists or Communists were considered Monarchists. The Monarchists had, on this basis, 51.5 per cent of the total number of the councillors to 48.5 for the anti-Monarchists. The anti-Monarchists carried 46 of the 50 provincial capitals, however, and showed great strength in the large cities.

existence since the fall of the First Republic, while others were of recent origin.

When the returns of April 12, 1931, showed a decided republican victory in the principal cities and towns, the King was faced with the choice of yielding or maintaining himself by force.[5] General Berenguer, who was Minister of War in the Aznar cabinet, and General Sanjurjo, Commander of the Civil Guard, refused to repress the people. Failing to obtain the necessary support, the King left Madrid on the night of April 14, 1931. A Provisional Government, with Niceto Alcalá-Zamora as President, had already been formed.[6]

THE CONSTITUTIONAL CORTES

For three months after the establishment of the Republic, the Provisional Government ruled alone without the aid of a Cortes. In some cases the work of the Provisional Government was practically definitive, but all actions taken in the first three months had later to be ratified by the Cortes, and the election of this legislative body was one of the first concerns of the new government. Before the elections to the Cortes, scheduled for June 28, 1931, the government took a new electoral census, lowered the voting age from 25 to 23, and fixed the representation at one deputy for every 50,000 of population, making the total number of deputies 470 and giving the urban centers more equitable representation.[7]

[5] Comte de Romanones, "La Republique en Espagne," *Revue des Deux Mondes* (Paris), July 15, 1931.

[6] The final scenes are given in what is probably a fairly accurate account by Julián Cortes Cavanillas, *La Caida de Alfonso XIII* (Madrid, Librería de San Martín, 1933), p. 207 *et seq*.

[7] In the last Cortes of the Monarchy, which had 404 deputies, the rural districts were favored. Under the new apportionment, Barcelona gained 12 and Madrid 13 representatives, and other

Practically the only issue presented to the people was approval or disapproval of the Revolution. The sharp differences which were to develop later had not yet come into the open, and the Republicans and Socialists presented a coalition ticket. The opposition consisted of a few remnants of the old political parties. The Monarchists presented no ticket, but the Agrarian and Basque-Navarre parties represented the forces of the old régime. The Socialist-Republican coalition won a decisive victory.[8] The opposition elected about 60 deputies drawn from the Agrarians, the Basque-Navarre party, and independents of known Right leanings. There was also a small group on the Left which later turned Communist. The new Cortes assembled on July 14, 1931.[9]

CHAPTER II

BUILDING A NEW SPAIN

By the beginning of 1934 accomplishments of the Spanish Republic were considerable, when the difficulties and opposition which it faced are taken into consideration. The Cortes framed one of the

urban centers made gains while some of the country districts either remained stationary or lost. For the pre-Republic figures, cf. *España* (Madrid, Espasa-Calpe, 1925), pp. 524–27; for Republican figures, cf. *Ley Electoral*, published in the *Biblioteca Oficial Legislativa*, Vol. XXVI, by Editorial Reus (Madrid, 1920 and 1933).

[8] The Socialists elected 116 deputies; the Radicals 90; the Radical Socialists 60; the Progressives (Right Republican of Alcalá-Zamora and Miguel Maura) 22; the Republican Action 30; the Federals 17; the Galician Left 16; and the Catalan Left 43. *Luz* (Madrid), March 3, 1932; *Anuario,* cited, 1931, p. 487. These figures include the deputies chosen in subsequent supplementary elections.

[9] *El Sol* (Madrid), and other Spanish papers printed the proceedings of the Cortes.

most progressive of modern constitutions. The army was reorganized, two-thirds of its officers retired, its technical equipment improved and much of its political significance removed. Church and State were separated, the Jesuits dissolved and their property expropriated, the property of the Church nationalized, the religious orders submitted to a law of associations, and forbidden to engage in commerce or industry, or to teach. Civil marriage and divorce were made legal.

In the field of social legislation the Republic made notable achievements. A complete new system of laws was designed to give the worker full protection of labor and wages. Workers were guaranteed rights of collective bargaining, protected by the *Jurados mixtos* and the Labor Delegates, and given the benefits of social insurance. The Labor Department was reorganized in such a way that it afforded a real protection to the worker. The Agrarian Reform Law, which legalized redistribution of land, was well in operation by the autumn of 1933. The Catalan question, for centuries a source of trouble, was handled in a way that made a definite solution seem possible by distributing administrative powers between the state and the region. A tremendous stride toward revolutionizing the schools was made by the establishment of more than nine thousand new schools, the reorganization of the normal schools and the general increase in the pay of teachers. For the first time in the history of Spain thousands of poor children were placed in the classroom. Finally, the Republic began the building of important public works such as irrigation projects, hydroelectric plants, highways, electrified railways, port facilities, and houses for the poor.

THE CONSTITUTION

Spain's new political structure as outlined by the Constitution [1] consisted of a single-chamber Cortes elected for four years, a President elected for six years, a Supreme Court and a Tribunal of Constitutional Guarantees. The President was empowered to appoint a Premier who, with his Cabinet, was responsible for the program of the government, as in England and France. The Constitution broke abruptly with Spain's past, declaring that "Spain is a democratic republic of workers of all classes." Reversing the policy followed for centuries, it declared that "the Spanish State has no official religion," and established freedom of worship,[2] right of divorce, civil marriage and lay education. Property was subject to expropriation for social uses, and the state might intervene in the direction and control of industry, or nationalize public utilities. It was declared that "Spain renounces war as an instrument of national policy," and provided that the President might wage war and make peace "subject to the conditions prescribed in the Covenant of the League of Nations."

Spain became a federative, although not necessarily a federal, republic by Article 8, providing that "regions constituting autonomous governments" may be established and frame a charter which "the Spanish State shall recognize . . . and uphold . . .

[1] For English text, cf. *Current History*, June 1932.
[2] Article 27 of the Constitution provides: "Freedom of conscience and the right to profess and practice freely any religion are guaranteed in Spanish territory, provided public morals are safeguarded. . . . All denominations may observe their rites privately. Public celebration of the rites of a sect in each case must be authorized by the Government." *Current History*, June 1932, p. 377.

as an integral part of the national law." This allowed such regions as Catalonia, Galicia and the Basque provinces to organize governments competent to handle local affairs, and set up standards for determining which powers should be held by the central government and which by the regions. Such regions were not considered to be sovereign states voluntarily surrendering their prerogatives to the central government. Article 18 provided that "all powers not explicitly granted in the charter of an autonomous region shall be considered as reserved to the Spanish State."

Among the most revolutionary provisions of the Constitution were those relating to the Church. In addition to the provisions mentioned above, the Constitution stated that "all' religious denominations shall be considered as associations subject to special laws," withdrew the state subsidy hitherto granted the Church and empowered the Cortes to dissolve religious orders dangerous to the state. The Constitution also limited their rights of commerce, industry and teaching, and the Cortes might confiscate their property.

Conflict over the status of the Church caused the first break in the revolutionary coalition. The Socialists had called for the "ultimate destruction of the Church," and had demanded a provision in the Constitution stating that "all religious orders shall be expelled and their property seized." [3] Alcalá-Zamora and Maura were opposed to such drastic action and favored a moderate policy. As finally adopted, the Constitution chose a middle course, calling for dissolution of the Jesuits, but leaving the status of the other orders to decision by the

[3] *El Sol* and *New York Times,* October 14, 15, 1931.

Cortes. Alcalá-Zamora and Maura, however, resigned in protest against the anti-clerical articles and a new government was formed by Manuel Azaña on October 14, 1931.

Other important Articles of the Constitution extended the vote to all citizens 23 years of age or over, guaranteed freedom of speech and the press, and provided against arbitrary arrest. The right to expropriate property with compensation and "the socialization of property . . . under the same conditions" left the way open to nationalization of wealth, but was in reality a conservative measure which did not satisfy the Socialists. The statement that "work in its diverse forms is a social obligation and shall enjoy the protection of the law" and the provisions for social insurance indicated Socialist influence.

ARMY REORGANIZATION

For more than a century Spain had been at the mercy of an army which was more a political than a military instrument. The King's debt to the army was great, and every attempt to correct abuses which had crept into its organization was halted by the danger of offending it. Primo de Rivera's mistake in antagonizing a portion of the army, as has already been pointed out, was one of the principal causes for the success of the Revolution.

Not only did Republican Spain owe little to the army, but the army as organized and officered in 1931 was a distinct threat to the Republic. If the Monarchist officers, of whom there were many, should seize control of the army, a quick restoration of the Bourbons might be possible. Manuel Azaña, Minister of War, decided that the army must be immediately taken out of politics and made into a weapon for national defense. "In the reform of the army," he said, "the object has been a very simple one, though non-existent up to this time: it has been nothing other than to endow the Republic with a military policy." [4] One of his first moves was to repeal the Law of Jurisdictions which gave the army the right to try all who criticized it.[5] All officers were required to pledge allegiance to the Republic or resign, and to rid the army of surplus officers Azaña decreed that those who wished might retire on full pay.[6] Azaña suppressed the eight or ten captains-general, and supplanted the Supreme War and Naval Council with a court for trying military and naval cases only. He subsequently decreed that any retired officer convicted of taking part in politics should lose his pension. Largely as a result of these measures during the first two and a half years of the Republic's life, the army exerted little if any pressure on the government.

Azaña was also determined to equip the Spanish army for future conflicts. The declaration in the Constitution that "Spain renounces war as an instrument of national policy" and makes a declaration of war "subject to the conditions prescribed in the Covenant of the League of Nations" was generally hailed as a great step in internationalism, and justly so. But war, and not peace, was implied in this article of the Constitution. It was a declaration that Spain would not remain neutral in any future conflict in which the League might take part.

[4] Manuel Azaña, *Una Politica* (Madrid, Espasa-Calpe, 1932), pp. 141–172.
[5] *New York Times*, April 18, 1931.
[6] *The Statesman's Yearbook, 1933; Anuario Estadistico, 1931*, p. 490; *Extracto de organización militar de España*, July 1, 1933.

AGRARIAN REFORM

Spain's most important problem remained the establishment of a prosperous agriculture. Although a notable increase had taken place in industry and the towns had assumed greater importance, some 75 per cent of the people still depended directly on agriculture for a living. In the past Spain had not cultivated all of its soil nor the best of it. About 60 per cent was left uncultivated, and only 27 per cent was cropped each year.[7] This situation had arisen "because access could not be had to much of the good land" and the result had been that "the agricultural classes have had to cultivate other, bad land that should be used for forest." [8] It may be said, in general, that in the southern and western part of Spain land was held in enormous estates, only partly cultivated, while northern, northwestern, and to some extent parts of eastern Spain suffered from excessive division of the land into small farms. The great estates were cultivated largely by landless farm workers who had been completely at the mercy of the landlords, while the regions where small farms abounded were cultivated by renters, share croppers and leaseholders who were frequently dispossessed on any convenient pretense. Even where they owned their land and might not be dispossessed, their farms were usually too small to produce a crop sufficient for the needs of a family.

This situation created a problem which the Monarchy was unable to solve, and on the solution of which the future of the Republic depended. The

[7] Pascual Carrion, *La Reforma Agraria* (Madrid, Editorial Pueyo, 1931), p. 13ff.
[8] *Ibid.*

economic status of farm workers was extremely low and their social condition even worse. Few if any schools were available, and in some provinces illiteracy in rural sections reached 85 per cent. The peasants lived in small villages and hamlets reached in many cases neither by railroad, highway nor telephone. Their cultural life was practically non-existent, and their political hopes were stifled by systematic falsification of electoral results.

The explanation of why this system prevailed and why Spain had done so little to alleviate it must be sought in its origin. Before the nineteenth century Spain was still almost completely feudal in its agriculture. The land belonged to the great military orders, the Church, the nobility and the municipalities. But in practically every case the peasants held rights in the municipal common, in the church lands or in the land belonging to the nobility; and the privilege of grazing sheep, cows or burros on certain public lands was established by custom and law.

This system was radically altered in the past century. Beginning in 1811 and extending on through to 1888 a series of disentailment and mortmain laws were passed.[9] According to Costa these laws took from the "needy" of Spain and gave to the "legislators" five important interests in the land: the right of pasturage, the ecclesiatical tithe, a part of usufruct on the inheritances of the Church, the village lands, and the municipal commons. The passage of these laws meant for the capitalists, he says, "the acquisition of more than half of the Peninsula for the tenth of its value." These laws threw thousands

---

[9] Joaquín Çosta, *La Tierra y la Cuestión Social* (Vol. IV. of the *Biblioteca Económica, Obras Completas* of Costa. Madrid, Biblioteca Costa, 1915).

of peasants off the land, or reduced them to the status of rural proletariat.

The old feudal estate and feudal practices continued to exist side by side with the new domains. Many towns, villages, and individuals paid dues just as they did in the Middle Ages. Most of the good land of Spain was still owned by a few people, either under old title, or through title acquired during the nineteenth century.[10] In some cases this ownership consisted of hundreds or even thousands of small farms. For example, Cáceres Province had twelve owners with 19,000 acres each. "Forty proprietors, the majority resident in Madrid, [had] greater wealth in the province of Salamanca than 100,000 inhabitants of 150 towns."

Moreover, the landlords of Spain, through their economic power, were able to control political life, despite the existence of universal suffrage. Francisco Cambó, political leader and Catalan industrialist, has described the system adopted. He says:

"Everybody was given the right to vote; but, as there were very few citizens prepared to exercise this right—and as the great majority of these few figured in the parties opposed to the régime—there was organized, systematically, the falsification of the suffrage by the creation of *caciquismo*. A contractor of the rudimentary and non-existent public opinion was situated in each province, with branches and agencies in every town and village. He supplied the votes which the citizens did not cast, and made way with those cast by rebellious citizens; it was his

[10] For a discussion of Spain's land problem, *cf.* Salvador de Madariaga, *Spain* (New York, Scribner, 1930); Pascual Carrion, *Los Latifundios de España* (Madrid, Francisco Beltran, 1932), entire; Pazos y Garcia, *op. cit.*

job to assure the triumph of the candidates named by the government. In exchange, the contractor of public opinion was the representative of the government in his district, of just any government; the magistrates and judges were at his command and it was he in reality who administered justice; the treasury official and the district attorneys were subject to his authority and it was he, in reality, who decided the amount of the taxes, and who should pay them; the governor of the province and the mayors were subject to his will . . . and even if the bishop and the parish priests were not, a large number of the canons were, since he had it in his power to name them." [11]

While some technical and social progress took place before 1931, agrarian conditions were still deplorable. The need of reform was urgent, and the Cortes framed the Agrarian Reform Law with a double aim in view: to distribute the soil more equitably and to endow it with the necessary technical assistance, such as irrigation projects, for scientific cultivation; and to build in Spain a new social and political order through improvement of the condition of the rural population.

Owing to opposition from vested interests, the agrarian law was not passed until September 1932. A year was allowed for preliminary study, including a census of the workers, thus delaying actual application of the law until September 1933. The law created an Institute of Agrarian Reform and endowed it with fifty million pesetas a year.[12] Fourteen provinces where the large estates were numerous were

[11] Quoted from Cortes Cavanillas, *op. cit.*, pp. 14–15.
[12] For the Agrarian Reform Law and the Decree, *cf. Gaceta de Madrid*, September 21, 23, 25, and November 5, 1932.

the first to come under the law, but large estates wherever located could be expropriated. No compensation was allowed for feudal estates, but other lands were to be paid for by capitalizing the value shown on the tax records at the rate of 5 per cent for farm incomes up to 15,000 pesetas. The rate then rose to 20 per cent for incomes of 200,000 pesetas and over. The expropriated lands were to be distributed to individual farmers or to associations of farm workers for collective farming, and vacant lands formerly embraced in the large estates were to be colonized and towns built on them. The law provided that "once in possession of the land, the communities will decide by majority vote whether the land is to be worked individually or collectively, and if individually, will proceed to divide and distribute it, taking into account the nature of the land, the capability of the rural families and other factors that will contribute to the maintenance of the economic equality of the members." The land so distributed belonged to the state and the occupant might be dispossessed for abuse of the property, but the Institute was obligated to give compensation for improvements made by the occupant. The Institute also encouraged the formation of coöperative societies for purchasing food, farm machinery and other necessities, and for securing credit.

"All feudal contributions whether in money or in kind [were] abolished without right of indemnification," and a great many charges known as *foros* and *subforos* levied against the land heretofore were subject to revision, as well as the special obligation known as the *rabassa morta* collected in Catalonia. The basic reform was supplemented by a great many auxiliary laws intended to correct any weaknesses it might show in practice. The establishment of irrigation systems, the construction of new roads, agricultural schools and experimental farms were a part of the general scheme of building a new agrarian system.

REGIONAL PROBLEMS

One of the serious problems which the Provisional Government had to face from the first was that of separatism. Four hundred years' effort toward unification had not deprived Catalonia, Galicia and the Basque provinces of their desire to regain the autonomous rights they had once enjoyed. The Monarchy had failed to settle this question, and the First Republic had been torn apart by inability to reconcile the claims of the various regions. Catalonia had been converted from mild, conservative regionalism to violent separatism by the policy of the dictatorship, and would not coöperate with the revolutionaries until promised a satisfactory settlement of its demands. When the revolution came in April 1931, Catalonia established the Catalan Republic. Colonel Maciá announced that Catalonia would be one of the states of the "Federated Spanish Republic." He was persuaded to retreat from this position by President Alcalá-Zamora, on the promise that the Cortes would consider a Catalonian Statute. prepared in Catalonia and approved by a plebiscite. This statute was drafted by a Catalan Assembly known as the Generality,[13] ratified overwhelmingly by the people and presented by Colonel Maciá to the Spanish Cortes on August 14, 1931.[14] Discussion

[13] For full text, cf. El Sol, July 14, 1931.
[14] Ibid., August 14, 1931.

of the Constitution was in progress at the time, and President Alcalá-Zamora suggested that it should take precedence over the Statute, a suggestion which was adopted. The Catalans manifested much impatience over this delay, but the Statute did not come up for discussion until May 1932, and was not finally approved until September 1932.[15]

Catalonia was defined in the Statute as an "autonomous region within the Spanish State."[16] The principal contention of the Catalans, however—that Catalonia was to be considered an independent region delegating certain of its prerogatives to the Spanish state—was denied. The powers granted Catalonia over finances, police, justice, education and social services were extensive, but both in the Constitution and in the Statute the rights of Catalonia were enumerated, and it was declared that the state reserved those not specifically granted. The Statute did not meet the demands of all Catalans. A rather numerous Left Wing demands much greater freedom, and as late as August 1933 *La Falc,* an organization forming a part of Maciá's following, declared: "the Republic has not completely satisfied our desires nor the Statute our national aspirations."[17]

The Basque provinces were not so successful as Catalonia in pressing their demands. Their first efforts to frame a Statute met with failure because of internal dissensions, and only in November 1933 was their Statute approved by a plebiscite, while it did not reach the Cortes until January 1934.[18]

[15] *La Prensa* (New York), December 30, 1931, January 11, March 4, September 26, 1932.
[16] *Gaceta,* September 21, 1932.
[17] *El. Sol,* August 21, 1933.
[18] *La Prensa* (New York), November 7, 1933.

CHURCH AND STATE

That the relations of the State and the Church would be altered under the Republic was evident from the beginning. The only question was how the change would be brought about, and to what extent the Church would be deprived of the privileges it had enjoyed for centuries under the Monarchy. Until 1857 education had been practically the exclusive right of the Church, and a law promoting popular state education passed in that year became a dead letter because of Church opposition. In 1931 half of the children who were in school were being educated by the Church, while both state and municipal schools were under its supervision. Hospital work, nursing, charity and many other functions were still the prerogatives of the Church, and their general deficiency could largely be attributed to the inability of the Church to meet the needs of the nation, and its consistent opposition to further state intervention in these fields. The reputed wealth of the Church had also fanned popular animosity. The Church was tax exempt and received compensation from the state for lands it had lost in the nineteenth century. Its wealth had identified the Church with the capitalist system precisely at a time when both Socialism and Anarcho-Syndicalism were gaining ground. Thus the Church had incurred the enmity of Liberals and Republicans, who considered it an obstacle to education, and of the laboring classes, which objected to its great wealth. Long-standing animosity toward the Church dating from the nineteenth century [19] flared up again in a series

[19] Zabala (*Historia de España,* cited, I, p. 314) says that the people attacked the monasteries in 1834 killing "one hundred religious."

of riots which began on May 11, 1931. Dozens of churches and monasteries were burned or destroyed, and the total property damage amounted to some five million dollars.

The anti-clerical attitude of the Republic soon became apparent. Even the most conservative members of the Provisional Government favored separation of Church and State. Provincial governors were ordered to absent themselves from church services, and negotiations were opened with the Vatican. President Alcalá-Zamora announced late in May, however, that "the Government will not adopt any definite policy toward the Church before a duly elected Cortes can work out the delicate problem of separation of Church and State." [20] It has already been noted that the Constitution provided for such a separation and empowered the government to supplement the Constitution by laws governing religious orders, church property, marriage and divorce. The Cortes had been given a clear mandate to dissolve the Jesuits, a step considered essential because of the growth of the religious orders during the twentieth century.[21] In January 1932 the Cortes dissolved the

---

[20] *New York Times*, May 30, 1931.

[21] Increase in number of clergy in Spain 1900–1930:

Year	Monks	Nuns	Total	Total per 10,000 Population
1900	12,142	42,596	54,738	29.42
1910	13,539	46,357	59,896	30.02
1923	17,210	54,605	71,815	33.16
1930	20,642	60,758	81,400	34.54

Anuario, 1931, p. 664.

Number of communities of religious orders in 1930 and to what dedicated:

	Teaching	Charity	Contemplation	Other	Total
Monks ..	514	35	147	326	1.022
Nuns ...	1,432	1,128	863	463	3,886

Anuario, 1931, p. 667.

Jesuit order and seized its property. At the same time the cemeteries were secularized and religious burial prohibited unless provided for in the will of the deceased. The appropriation formerly given to the Church by the state was cut by one-third in the 1932 budget, and ceased entirely after November 1933.[22] A law permitting divorce was passed in February 1932, giving the civil courts jurisdiction over such cases. Divorce was allowed by mutual consent after two years of marriage, but where divorce was granted for cause the guilty party might not marry until one year after the final decree.[23] In June 1932 a law provided that "from the date of the publication of the present law only one form of marriage is recognized—civil marriage." [24] Another decree provided that "the ecclesiastical corps of the army is dissolved." [25]

These measures provoked bitter opposition to the Cabinet and the Republic. By midsummer 1932 the Catholics were strongly united in the *Acción Católica,* a non-political body for the defense of the Church, and the *Acción Popular,* a political party intended to unite all supporters of the Church. The measures adopted against the Church aroused the sympathy of some of the republican parties for the views of *Acción Católica.* Miguel Maura with his Conservative party carried on a campaign against the Azaña government, and Alejandro Lerroux, although still professing anti-clericalism, objected to the manner in which the anti-clerical legislation had been applied. These forces were not strong enough to stop the attack on the Church, however, and in December

[22] *Cf.* p. 438.
[23] *Gaceta,* May 12, 1932.
[24] *Ibid.,* July 4, 1932.
[25] *Lu* (Paris), July 22, 1932.

1932 a law restricting the religious orders was presented to the Cortes. Owing to the bitter opposition and the obstructionist tactics of its opponents, it was not finally approved until June 1933, and when approved provoked a crisis in the government. The law [26] confiscated the property of the orders, estimated with other church property at $500,000,-000.[27] It also enforced the "prohibition of the practice of industry, commerce or teaching" as provided in Article 26 of the Constitution. According to its terms, all primary teaching was to be taken out of the hands of the orders by December 31, 1933, and all other instruction by October 1933.[28] This last provision led to the publication of a pastoral [29] by the bishops of Spain in which attendance of state schools was strictly forbidden, and the families of the faithful were ordered to send their children to Catholic schools.[30] The religious orders also sought to evade the law by the organization of corporations for teaching, and one of Spain's most prominent intellectuals complained of the "increasing prosperity of the extinguished Company of Jesus which, under

[26] For full text of the law, cf. La Informacion (New York), June 7, 1933.

[27] Ibid., May 19, 1933, and New York Times, June 6, 1933, give this estimate.

[28] The Republic has created 9,620 schools, and 665 kindergartens. It has raised the pay of about 85.5 per cent of its teachers, and in two years approximately 481,000 students were placed in school. The total amount of money dedicated to education by the state increased from 209,861,049 pesetas in 1931 to 310,798,204 pesetas in 1933. For the important work done in education by the Republic, cf. Rodolfo Llopis, La Revolución en la Escuela (Madrid, M. Aguilar, 1933); and Boletín de Educación (Ministerio de Instrucción Pública, Enero-Marzo, 1933), pp. 174ff.

[29] For a copy of the Pope's encyclical condemning this law and of the bishop's pastoral, cf. En Estas Horas de Tribulación, a pamphlet published by the Asociación de propagandistas Católicos de Campostela (Santiago), 1933.

[30] New York Times, June 4, 1933.

a different title, multiplies the number of its schools and prepares itself to enjoy a splendid, though subterranean, existence." [31]

THE REVOLUTION IN THE SCHOOLS

Spain made considerable progress in education between 1874 and 1931; but educational conditions were highly unsatisfactory. Most of the progress came after 1902, when the educational reform of that year placed a far greater portion of the burden of education on the state. Previously the Church played a far more important part in education than the state. Despite the progress made, however, some 45 per cent of the people were still unable to read and write in 1931. The Church schools catered principally to the classes able to pay school fees, and only the very poor went to the primary schools maintained by the state and the municipalities. These were frequently inferior, inadequately housed, and poorly equipped. The teaching staff was deficient in training, and the pay too small to attract the best talent. The Church schools were not required to maintain a high standard for teachers, and too many of their teachers were more zealous than capable. Though Spain had some very excellent schools, both Church and state, there were not enough of them to educate the entire nation. It was estimated in 1931 that some 27,000 schools would be needed to supply the needs of the children not enrolled in any school.

The Republic has attacked this problem with considerable vigor. From 1931 to 1933 some 9,620

[31] Américo Castro, "La cuestión religiosa en España," *El Sol*, August 12, 1933.

schools were created, more than the Monarchy had established in the previous seventeen years. Formerly most schools were one-teacher units; the Republic established 2,619 classes in grade schools. Some 665 kindergartens were established throughout Spain and in the province of Madrid alone some 514 new schools were founded, while Barcelona established 592. At the same time the Republic has raised the pay of some 86.5 per cent of its teachers and licensed many new instructors.[32] Supplying new teachers was not so difficult as it was supposed to be. The failure of the state to provide a sufficient number of primary schools in the past had left a great number of high school and college graduates without a career. The increase in the number of monks and nuns in teaching during this century also tended to prevent many graduates from finding positions. Spain has some 15,000 teachers with the necessary titles for teaching and ready to begin when schools are available.[33]

Not only in the creation of schools did the Republic carry on its educational program, it was necessary also to give the teachers better training. To accomplish this, *cursillos*, or short courses, were organized for the new and old teachers. Approximately 20,000 prospective teachers were enrolled in the courses designed to prepare them for examinations as teachers, and 20,000 teachers already in service took advantage of these courses to prepare them-

[32] *Boletin de Educacion*, Ministerio de Instruccion Publica, Enero-Marzo, 1933, pp. 174ff. Pay for teachers was increased from 2,000 up to 3,000 pesetas in the lower grades. Total teacher pay rose from 116 million to 169 million pesetas between 1931 and 1933. Some 31,775 teachers out of 36,680 received a higher salary than they had under the Monarchy.

[33] Rodolfo Llopis, *La Revolucion en la Escuela*. Madrid, M. Aguilar, 1933, p. 244.

selves for advancement. Some 18,500 in 1931 and 22,000 in 1933 made application for courses preparatory to the examinations for teachers. The Normal Schools, 54 in number, were placed on a higher standard and a School of Pedagogy created in the University of Madrid. To bring the whole nation in line with the program, the corps of supervisors was reorganized and some 165 new members added, dropping the ratio of teachers to each inspector from 173 in 1931 to 131 in 1933.

Outside the schools another form of education was carried on. Many of the rural districts of Spain lacked any contact with the cultural world, and, to reach these, traveling schools, museums, dramas, and cinemas were instituted. These "schools" traveled from town to town, organizing and giving classic Spanish dramas, showing cinemas to children and grown-ups who had never seen them before, carrying copies of the finest sculpture and painting of Spain, and seeking to implant in the people a desire for learning. Music was carried to them by means of gramophones and radios. Libraries to the number of 1,487 were established. Around the Normal Schools and other institutions of learning numbers of "residencias" or homes for the students were built. The total amount of money dedicated to education by the state increased from 209,861,049 pesetas in 1931 to 310,798,204 pesetas in 1933.[34]

The credit for the Educational Reform must go principally to Marcelino Domingo, first Minister of Education, and to Fernando de los Rios, the one-time Columbia University professor, who succeeded him in that place. Both men had traveled and

[34] *Presupuestos Generales del Estado,* Ministerio de Hacienda, 1931 and 1933.

studied educational systems abroad, and were prepared for the work they assumed.

THE REPUBLIC AND LABOR

Organized labor played a leading part in establishing the Republic, and expected to be rewarded for its services. The Socialists especially were under obligation to the workers for their support, and the inability of the Socialists to carry out all their promises greatly contributed to the unpopularity they incurred in 1933. The labor legislation of the Republic,[35] however, constituted a great improvement and may be attributed mainly to Largo Caballero, Socialist Minister of Labor, and Indalecio Prieto, Socialist Minister of Public Works.

A law of Labor Contracts [36] gave the laborer an effective collective bargaining instrument. National employment offices were provided and all private offices closed.[37] The law of *Términos Municipales,*[38] called by Largo Caballero [39] "the most revolutionary of the Republic because it safeguards the political rights of the working class, subjugated before to the economic tyranny of the *cacique*," [40] was particularly effective. It created a classified register of workers in

---

[35] Spain has ratified some thirty conventions recommended by the International Labor Office, twenty-two of them since the establishment of the Republic. In most cases the appropriate legislation has been enacted, but this work was slowed up by the crisis in the government beginning in the spring of 1933. For these conventions, *cf. Los convenios Internacionales de trabajo y su ratificación por España* (Madrid, Ministerio de Trabajo, 1932).

[36] *Labor realizada desde la proclamación de la República hasta el 8 de septiembre de 1932* (Ministerio de Trabajo, 1932), pp. 59 ff.

[37] *Ibid.,* pp. 71ff.

[38] *Ibid.,* pp. 27.

[39] *El Sol,* October 3, 1933.

[40] A political boss.

each municipality [41] and forbade the importation of workers from other municipalities until all local residents of any given occupation were employed. Its object was to prevent the importation of workers in order to lower wages or, as was customary under the Monarchy, to turn an election to the advantage of the *cacique*. None of the legislation of the Republic was more bitterly attacked, and the propertied classes cited it in every petition and at every congress as an assault on their rights.

Republican contributions to labor also include a National Unemployment Fund [42] and a Law of Labor Associations.[43] Coöperatives of consumers, laborers, merchants and farmers were established, but such coöperatives could not transact business except with their own members, and the Ministry of Labor was empowered to audit their accounts.[44] A new eight-hour-day law raised the pay for overtime from 20 to 25 per cent of the regular wage and empowered the Minister of Labor to cut the day to six hours or even less in mines and other exhausting occupations.[45] The accident compensation law was modified to supplant the single payment for injuries by a series of payments ranging from 9 to 75 per cent of the usual wage, according to character of the accident, and guarantee the payments to the laborer by a national fund.[46] Agricultural laborers were also protected by accident in-

[41] The Spanish municipality embraces all of the country to the next municipal boundary, thereby including farming as well as urban territory.
[42] *Gaceta,* May 27, October 2, 1931.
[43] *Labor Realizada,* pp. 85ff.
[44] *Ibid.,* pp. 95ff.
[45] *Gaceta,* July 2, 4, 1931.
[46] *Ibid.,* October 12, 1932, and February 2, 7, 1933.

surance.[47] An Act of May 26, 1931, which modified an older law, made maternity insurance obligatory for employers and allowed a rest period before and after childbirth.[48]

Obviously, whatever benefits labor was to obtain from the Republic would depend on the machinery established to supervise labor legislation.[49] With this in mind, Largo Caballero centralized the Ministry and charged the Minister with final responsibility for law enforcement. The first responsibility for enforcement of labor legislation, however, was placed on the Labor Delegates [50] (*Delegado de Trabajo*) of each province, who were invested with full authority, including the authority over labor formerly exercised by the provincial governors. No labor association could function until its charter was approved by the Delegate, and he might impose fines or suspend such associations. The most important function of the Delegate was to act as the administrative officer for the Minister in each province and to impose penalties for infraction of the labor laws.[51]

Labor disputes and strikes were directly in the hands of the *Jurados mixtos*,[52] juries composed of six representatives of both workers and employers. This idea was not new, but an innovation introduced in Spain made such juries a powerful weapon for the protection of labor. This innovation came in the selection of the president. If the twelve men agreed unanimously, they could choose the presi-

[47] *Ibid.*, June 13, August 30, 1931.
[48] *Los Convenios*, p. 23; *Gaceta*, September 9, 1931.
[49] *Labor Realizada, passim.*
[50] *Gaceta*, May 15, 1932.
[51] *Gaceta*, June 24, 1932.
[52] *Ibid.*, November 28, 1931.

dent; in case they disagreed, this power was exercised by the Minister of Labor. Since the Minister was a Socialist and himself a worker, for more than two and a half years the juries had presidents who sympathized with the worker's point of view. This situation brought a united protest from merchants, industrialists and landlords. In a number of cases heavy fines were imposed on employers for failure to obey the decisions of the juries, and in Madrid the entire directorate of the Merchants' Committee was arrested late in June 1933, and the *Círculo de la Unión Mercantil*, an organization corresponding somewhat to a Chamber of Commerce, was closed. This action naturally caused a protest of the propertied classes, and throughout the summer there was intense activity looking to the union of all merchants, manufacturers and landlords against the labor policy of the Republic. A *Junta Central,* or Central Committee, was formed in July, and among its strongest resolutions were those against the Minister of Labor himself and against the Labor Delegates and the *Jurados mixtos.*[53] No small share of the responsibility for the almost complete paralysis of the legislation of the Republic during the summer of 1933 and the subsequent fall of the Azaña Ministry rests on this Central Committee and its representatives in the Cortes.

One aspect of the labor situation was handled in a way which brought strong criticism of the Republic from friend and foe alike. A considerable unemployment problem faced the new government from its first day. Many of the unemployed were

[53] *El Sol,* July 1, 15, 19, 20, 21, 31, and *Luz,* September 6, 1933, and also other dates give a picture of this controversy from the owners' point of view; *El Socialista* (Madrid) may be consulted for the workers' side of the question.

concentrated in a few of the large cities, and their discontent had played an important part in the establishment of the Republic. To check this discontent, the government launched a public works program which many considered ill-advised and badly planned. Madrid began an extensive project designed to connect the three railways stations by an underground tunnel and endow the city with a complete underground system of transportation. Road-building, electrification of the railroads, irrigation projects, and many other much needed improvements were also started. These cannot be criticized on the ground that they were not beneficial, but the cost was enormous and the projects frequently seemed designed more to give jobs than to construct needed public works. Whether the Socialists were entirely responsible for this public works program, costing more than 860,000,000 pesetas in 1933, the fact that Indalecio Prieto, a Socialist, was Minister of Public Works caused the blame to fall on them.

ECONOMIC AND FINANCIAL CONDITIONS

Enormous sums of money were necessary for the work of the Republic at a time when Spain was feeling the effects of the world depression. When the Republic was established, hundreds of landlords immediately declared that they would not cultivate their lands. This crisis was largely overcome by a decree forcing cultivation, but the Republic did not entirely escape the effects of systematic sabotage by the landlords.

Another economic difficulty concerned the flight of capital. For several months after April 1931, the nobles and rich bourgeoisie of Spain systematically exported their capital. The peseta, which at its lowest was worth 10.34 cents in 1930, sank to below 8 cents under the Republic. The Monarchy, moreover, had bequeathed to the Republic an enormous public debt, amounting to more than 21,000,000,000 pesetas,[54] and a chronic budgetary deficit, together with an unfavorable trade balance. Moreover, the world price of Spain's chief products—olive oil, wine, cork, oranges, flax, and iron and copper ores—declined almost continuously from 1931 to 1933.

Spanish exports fell from 2,299,700,000 pesetas in 1930 to 990,300,000 in 1931 and to 742,300,000 pesetas in 1932.[55] Through the first eight months of 1933 this decline continued, exports falling from 664,014,000 pesetas for the January-August period in 1931 to 434,568,000 pesetas for 1933.[56] There was a slight increase in the volume of goods shipped in this period, but the lower prices kept the net return to Spain far below that of former years. Internal conditions reflected this loss of foreign trade. Industrialists and farmers alike alleged that they could not keep up employment and wages in the face of falling prices. Attempts to cut wages were made at a time when the worker expected to receive better pay, and when the reorganized Labor Department was backing the workers in their demands. Hundreds of strikes and labor disputes further threw the economic system out of joint.

In spite of the depression, the budgetary appropriations of the Republic steadily rose. Total ex-

[54] *El Sol,* April 1, 1932.
[55] These figures are taken from *Resumen Mensual . . . del Comercio exterior de España,* published by the *Ministerio de Hacienda,* and from the *World Almanac,* 1931–1933. The two sources do not agree in all cases but are approximately the same.
[56] *El Sol,* October 11, 1933.

penditures for 1930 were 4,012,500,000 pesetas, leaving a deficit of 158,240,000 pesetas that year. The deficits for 1931 and 1932 were 508,830,000 pesetas and 711,730,000 pesetas,[57] respectively, while the expenses for 1933 were 4,427,281,490—leaving a deficit of 484,663,244 pesetas.[58] To meet this deficit the Republic had to increase the public debt inherited from the Monarchy. This was done by the flotation of bonds totalling 1,385,000,000 pesetas to October 1933.[59]

CHAPTER III

THE SWING TO THE RIGHT

THE Republic accomplished its reforms only by overcoming great difficulties. From the beginning it was forced to meet bitter opposition from both the Left and the Right. Three forces slowed up the republican program: the Anarcho-Syndicalist *Confederación Nacional del Trabajo,* which directed the labor opposition; the reactionary group; and the Cabinet which, being a coalition, was constantly forced into compromises in order to maintain a semblance of unity.

ANARCHO-SYNDICALIST AND COMMUNIST REVOLTS

Spain became a republic at a time when depressed economic conditions were causing a renewal of strike activity. Before the establishment of the Republic, strikes were fostered by the Socialists, Anarcho-

[57] *El Financiero* (Madrid), June 6, 1933.
[58] *El Sol,* January 16, 1934.
[59] *Ibid.,* August 23, 1933; *La Prensa* (New York), October 23, 1933.

Syndicalists and Communists, but when the Socialists became a part of the governing coalition most of their efforts were expended in securing a peaceful settlement of labor troubles through the Socialist Minister of Labor. Both Anarcho-Syndicalists and Communists, however, increased their agitation, and on four occasions attempted the overthrow of the Republic by revolution.

Serious strike activities began in June 1931, and the first determined effort at revolution was made by the Anarcho-Syndicalists, probably aided by the Communists, in July 1931.[1] A seven-day battle was fought in Sevilla from July 18 to 25, with over a dozen persons killed and a hundred or more wounded. This movement failed, but strike activities were not ended. Martial law was frequently declared, and by October 1931 Prime Minister Azaña found it necessary to resort to a law known as the Defense of the Republic granting the government exceptional powers.[2] Arbitrary arrests and holding of prisoners without charge became common. Some nine thousand political prisoners were in jail by the summer of 1933, when this law was supplanted by another, called the "Law of Public Order," [3] giving the government the right to suspend constitutional guarantees and arrest people considered dangerous to the state.

Such drastic action was considered necessary to meet continued opposition, but did not succeed in ending strikes and Left opposition. A second revolt began in January 1932, and was crushed after hard fighting, while a third serious effort of the Left

[1] *El Sol,* July 15 to 26, 1931.
[2] *Ibid.,* October 15 to 21, 1931.
[3] *Gaceta,* July 30, 1933.

occurred in January 1933, and cost the lives of some fifty workers and soldiers. A fourth revolt occurred December 8, 1933. The government's policy of strike-breaking provoked a decided reaction among the workers. The fact that the Socialists were represented in the government gave strike-breaking the appearance of war between the Socialists and Anarcho-Syndicalists.[4]

OPPOSITION FROM THE RIGHT

The Monarchists and other conservative groups were demoralized in the early days of the Republic, but began to reorganize without delay. Their weakness in the Cortes, where they had only 60 out of 470 deputies, prevented any really effectual opposition to the republican program during the first year and, frightened by the socialist legislation of the Cortes, they attempted a revolution in August 1932. The movement failed completely, and the Right groups after that time depended on political action to regain their lost privileges.

Political opposition proved more effective than armed revolt. The formation of the *Acción Católica* for the defense of the Church, and of the *Acción Popular* for political action, has already been noted. The organization of the *Confederación Española de Derechas Autónomas* brought the Right forces into still closer alignment. Originally the Right was represented only by the Agrarian and Basque-Navarre parties. In 1931 and 1932, however, many regional parties were organized for the defense of the conservative interests, and the C.E.D.A. came

[4] *Cf. El Sol* or other Spanish papers of corresponding date for these revolts. The four major ones have been reported in New York papers, and all of them in *La Prensa* (New York).

into existence in February 1933 to give them strength.[5] The C.E.D.A. proposed to revise the Constitution, repeal the anti-clerical laws, abolish the Agrarian Reform and put an end to the preponderant influence labor had exercised since April 1931. In many of these aims the C.E.D.A. was ably seconded by the Central Committee of the merchants, industrialists and landlords.[6] In addition to the Right forces included in the C.E.D.A., Spain had a Fascist movement directed by José Primo de Rivera, son of the former dictator. The Fascists, openly opposed to the Republic, declared that they would rule in Spain even if they had to gain power by armed revolution. They were not as yet numerically strong, but the experience of Italy and Germany indicated that only a short length of time was necessary for the development of a powerful Fascist movement.

POLITICAL REALIGNMENTS IN 1933

One of the most important forces working for reaction was the split in the coalition cabinet. The divergent elements composing the cabinet had been able to unite only because all agreed on one minimum demand—overthrow of the King. Once these elements were in power their differences on political, economic and religious matters came into the open. Only fear of reaction or further revolution kept the inevitable split from occurring sooner than it did. President Alcalá-Zamora and Miguel Maura represented the conservative point of view, their revo-

---

[5] The Carlists, who have been active since 1833, are followers of Don Carlos, brother of Ferdinand VII, who pretended to the throne against Isabel II.

[6] *Cf.* p. 425.

lutionary aims going little further than overthrow of the King and establishment of a democratic republic. Both were Catholic, both represented the land-owning classes, and both had recently been converted to Republicanism. The return to constitutional government satisfied their principal revolutionary demands. Their conflict with the Provisional Government over the Church issue has been noted.

Slightly to the Left at the beginning stood Alejandro Lerroux and Martínez Barrio of the Radical Republican party. Lerroux had for years been the outstanding opponent of the Monarchy and the Church. With the King gone and the Church divested of many of its privileges, he became a fighter without opponents. For a time he coöperated with the government, but in December 1931 his conservative economic ideas caused him to refuse to coöperate with the Socialists, and his stand in favor of centralism as opposed to federalism in government ranged him against the Catalans. He withdrew from the coalition at that time and joined the opposition. The remaining members of the coalition— the Republican Action, Socialists, Catalans, Galicians and Radical Socialists—managed to hold together until 1933, but their ideas were widely divergent and the program of the Republic was seriously held up by constant disagreement and compromise. Azaña was able to keep the Republican-Socialist alliance together only because he could drive the Republicans to accept measures of a more socialistic character than they wanted, and could presuade the Socialists to accept less than they had originally demanded. But neither side was satisfied. The Republicans resented the laws presented by the Socialists, while the latter, closely pressed by Anarcho-Syndicalists and Communists and unable to fulfill their promises to the workers, became alarmed at the prospect of losing their followers and began to talk of revolt and dictatorship. In other words, the character of the political struggle had changed radically by midsummer 1933. The main question was no longer Monarchy or Republic, but whether the Republic was to be bourgeois or socialist in character.

That a political crisis was approaching was evident after April 1933, when elections were held in about one-third of the municipalities. According to Spanish law, unopposed candidates were allowed to take office at the time of the elections of 1931 without the formality of a vote. The April 1933 elections were held to fill these places with new and duly elected officials, and the government parties won less than one-third of the municipal councillors, causing the opposition parties, both Republican and those of the extreme Right, to call on the Azaña cabinet to resign.[7] This reverse at the polls was

[7] It is probably correct to interpret the elections as an anti-government vote, but not necessarily as anti-Republican. The elections were held where 29,804 municipal councillors were seated in accordance with Article 29 of the law in 1931. In 1931 there were 13,940 Republicans, 887 Socialists, 6,065 Monarchists, 10 Communists, 6,043 representing local parties and 2,859 unclassified candidates so seated. This shows that about 50 per cent were either Republicans, Socialists or Communists, all anti-Monarchical, while the other 50 per cent was considered at the time to be Monarchical. Complete returns are not yet available for April 23, 1933. The newspaper *C.E.D.A.* of May 20, 1933, shows that the government parties won 4,356 places, the anti-government Republicans 4,108, and the Right 6,481. This gives the Right 43.36 per cent of the total. *El Sol* (Madrid) gave the vote as 5,048 for the government, 4,206 for the anti-government republicans, and 4,954 for the Right, according to *Current History,* July 1933. Complete returns on this basis would give the Right only 43 per cent of the vote in the districts in which it had 50 per cent in 1931.

followed by a cabinet crisis early in June 1933.
President Alcalá-Zamora forced the Azaña Ministry to resign, but Azaña was returned to office when all efforts to form a cabinet without
him and the Socialists failed. His new cabinet was
never strong. During the summer its weakness became more and more evident, and by August the
program of legislation was almost completely paralyzed by the break-up of the Republican-Socialist
coalition.

Azaña, who had been accustomed to apply the
cloture rule to force his measures through, now
found this procedure impossible, and was obliged
to compromise not only with the opposition Republicans but with the Agrarians, avowed enemies of
the régime. The explanation of this situation lies in
the division of his supporters. The Federal party
was split, and discontented with the Azaña program; the Catalan Left was absorbed in regional affairs; the Galician Left was disgruntled over the
slowness with which the regional aspirations of
Galicia were granted, and was opposed to the Azaña
Ministry because of a projected treaty with Uruguay
which injured its cattle interests; the Radical-
Socialist party was engaged in an internal struggle
for leadership which soon split it into a pro-Socialist
wing headed by Marcelino Domingo, and an anti-
Socialist wing under the leadership of Gordón Ordás.

The eventual fall of the Ministry was inevitable,
but it was hastened by a second set of elections.
The Constitution provides that the Tribunal of Constitutional Guarantees shall have, in addition to
other members, one judge from each of fifteen regions elected by the municipal councillors. The elections held on September 3, 1933, resulted in a sec-

ond defeat of the government.[8] This development caused the resignation of Azaña and the formation of a ministry under Lerroux on September 13. The Republican parties which had refused to coöperate with Lerroux against the Socialists in June now accepted places in his ministry. Lerroux did not survive the first vote of confidence on October 3, however, and President Alcalá-Zamora entrusted the formation of a coalition of Republicans, excluding the Socialists, to Martínez Barrio of the Radical party. The President granted this ministry a dissolution of the Cortes and set general elections for November 19, 1933, with a supplementary election to be held on December 3 in districts where no candidate received the 40 per cent of the total vote required by law.

The significance of this general election was evident. Spanish voters, including 6,000,000 women who were to vote for the first time, were to have the first real opportunity to express their opinion of the Republic. At the time of the election of the Constituent Cortes in 1931 the economic principles of the various parties were so vague that the voters did not know for what program they were voting. This uncertainty had cleared up by 1933, and four chief alternatives were before the people: [9] the extreme Right represented by the C.E.D.A., organized by Gil Robles; the Right Center represented by Lerroux and Maura; the Republican Left with Azaña

[8] The government elected only five of the fifteen judges elected by the regions. *Cf. El. Sol*, September 5, and *La Nacion* (Madrid), September 5, 1933. *La Nacion* gives incomplete returns showing 12,910 pro-government votes against 34,193 anti-government votes. The Radical party (Lerroux) elected four judges, and the extreme Right, six.

[9] *La Prensa*, November 13, 1933; and *El Sol*, November 17, 1933.

as the outstanding figure; and the Socialists. In general, all of the Right parties were grouped around the C.E.D.A., while the Left were badly divided. The C.E.D.A., for example, allied itself with the Fascist organization, and with the *Lliga Regionalista,* the conservative Catalan party headed by Francisco Cambó; the Radical party of Lerroux, the Radical-Socialists of Gordón Ordás and the Conservative party of Miguel Maura went on the ballot together. The conservative, almost reactionary, character of this alliance is demonstrated by the adhesion of Melquiades Alvarez of the Liberal Democratic party, a former Minister of Alfonso XIII, and of Santiago Alba, another former Minister, both of whom joined Lerroux on the ground that he gave the best hope for a "united anti-Marxist party." The conservative character of the Radical party was also demonstrated by its alliance in certain electoral districts with the C.E.D.A., an alliance aimed at the Socialists. Azaña allied his Republican Action with the Indepedent Radical-Socialists of Marcelino Domingo, and with the Galician and Catalan Left. The Socialists went on the ballot alone, except for very limited coöperation with some of the Left parties in a few provincial districts.

The Right and Right Center parties won a sweeping victory.[10] The alignment in the newly elected Cortes was almost the exact reverse of that in the former Cortes. Where the Right had been able to

[10] *La Prensa* (New York), December 5, 6, 1933.

    Right — 207 deputies composed of:

Acción Popular	62
Agrarios	86
Basque Nationalist	14
Monarchists	43
Independents	2

elect barely 60 deputies in 1931, the Left elected
less than a hundred in 1933. Some reaction had been
expected and predicted before the election, but that
the Right would win so completely was a surprise
even to the leaders of the Right parties. Approximately two-thirds of the deputies were members of
the C.E.D.A., whose principles were those of the
Monarchy, or of the group centered around Lerroux,
whose program was distinctly conservative.

The Republican parties of the Left, including the
Republican Action with Azaña at its head, the Independent Radical Socialists under the lead of Gordón
Ordás, and the Federals, were practically exter-
minated, dropping from a membership of well over
a hundred to a mere handful. Considerable disorder occurred during the elections and charges of
unfair tactics were numerous. Botella Asensi, Minister of Justice in the Martínez Barrio cabinet, resigned as a protest against the policy of the Prime
Minister and alleged that Lerroux had an under-

The Center — 167 deputies composed of:

Radicals	104
Conservatives	18
Lliga Regionalista	25
Liberal Democrats	9
Progressives	3
Independents	8

Left — 99 deputies composed of:

Esquerra (Catalan Left)	19
Orga (Galician Left)	6
Radical Socialists	1
Independent Radical Socialists	4
Republican Action	5
Catalan Socialists	3
Socialists	58
Federalists	2
Communists	1

These figures may be changed slightly when all disputed seats
are allotted, but such changes as may occur will not alter the
significance of the election.

standing with the extreme Right. This charge was given plausibility by Lerroux's action in withdrawing his candidate from the supplementary election held in Madrid on December 3, leaving the field to the extreme Right and the Socialists. The latter, who lost half of their representatives, also protested against irregularities in the elections, and Largo Caballero threatened that any attempt by the Right to take possession of the government and destroy the work done by the Republic would be met with armed revolution and a dictatorship along Communist lines.

The new Cortes met on December 7, 1933, and immediately became the battle ground for Right and Left, the former demanding the repeal of many of the essential reforms of the Republic. The formation of a government was entrusted to Alejandro Lerroux of the Right Center, but he depended for his majority on the votes of the Right parties, especially the Agrarians led by Martínez de Velasco and the Popular Action led by José María Gil Robles. This dependence forced him to present measures for abolition of the law of *Términos Municipales,* and modification of the character and functions of *Jurados mixtos.* The cabinet also proposed to appropriate some 30 millions of pesetas annually for the rural clergy and to send Pita Romero, Minister of Foreign Affairs, to Rome to study the terms for a new concordat.

These measures aroused the apprehensions of both the moderate and the extreme Left, who saw the entire revolutionary program threatened. The Anarcho-Syndicalists seized the opportunity to revolt, and while they were defeated the seriousness of the fighting—in which more than a hundred were killed and several hundred wounded—indicated that they had lost none of their aggressiveness. The republican Left, under the lead of Azaña, continued to advocate democratic methods, while the Socialists remained badly divided on the question of tactics.[11] Julián Besteiro and Fernando de los Ríos advocated evolutionary socialism. Indalecio Prieto attempted to revive the Republican-Socialist Conjunction, while Largo Caballero called for a dictatorship of the proletariat. The Right matched the Left in threats of dictatorship. José Primo de Rivera began a vigorous campaign of Fascist propaganda calling for destruction of the democratic régime, and Gil Robles prophesied that "sooner or later power will be given to the Right so that they may save Spain from a semi-Soviet dictatorship of the extreme Left." On January 1, Largo Caballero directed a shaft at Primo de Rivera, declaring: "We Socialists will join with the Communists and Anarchists if the Fascists attempt to establish a dictatorship in Spain."[12]

The belligerency of both sides was increased by the realization that the November 1933 elections had not been so complete a victory for the Right as at first supposed. The Socialists and the Left could point out that, while they had scarcely one-fifth of the deputies in the Cortes, their popular vote amounted to about half the total.[13] Another indication of the strength of the Left was offered by the municipal elections held in Catalonia on January 14, 1934, in which the Catalan Left decisively defeated the conservative parties. The violence attending this

[11] *El Sol*, December 8–17, 1933.
[12] *La Prensa*, January 2, 1934.
[13] *Journal des Nations,* January 31, 1934.

election indicated the increasingly bitter feeling between the parties, and as the Right realized their
increasing weakness they showed more tendency to
let force settle the issue.[14]

Meanwhile the struggle within the Socialist party
came to a head with the resignation of the Executive Committee of the General Workers' Union,
which had been dominated by Besteiro, and the election of a pro-Largo Caballero committee which believed in revolution.[15] Prieto seemed converted to
this point of view also, and on February 4 declared
that the time had come for the Socialists to study
the program to be followed "when they had seized
power." [16] The Right parties seemed determined to
force the Left into revolt before the projected
"united front" of radical labor parties could be
formed. This was done by repeal of the measures
passed while the Left was in office and by the constant attempt of Gil Robles to force the labor leaders into statements that would make them subject
to prosecution.

Thus, three years after the establishment of the
Republic in Spain, the Left was placed in a position
similar to that of the British Labor party or the
Socialists and Communists in Germany. The fundamental issue between Socialists and Communists in
Spain, as elsewhere, was whether socialization
could be accomplished by peaceful means or whether
violent revolution was a necesssity.

[14] El Sol, January 16, 17, 1934. Colonel Francisco Macia, the
leader of the Catalan Left party, died on December 25, 1933.
[15] La Prensa, January 29–31, 1934.
[16] Ibid., February 5, 1934.

INDEX

441